Made in the USA
Lexington, KY
02 December 2014

Women and Welfare

Theory and Practice in the United States and Europe

Edited and with an Introduction by
Nancy J. Hirschmann
Ulrike Liebert

Rutgers University Press
New Brunswick, New Jersey, and London

Library of Congress Cataloging-in-Publication Data

Women and welfare : theory and practice in the United States and Europe / edited
and with an introduction by Nancy J. Hirschmann and Ulrike Liebert.
    p. cm.
    Includes bibliographical references and index.
    ISBN 0–8135–2881–X (alk. paper) — ISBN 0–8135–2882–8 (pbk. : alk. paper)
    1. Public Welfare—United States—Congresses. 2. Public Welfare—Europe—
Congresses. 3. Welfare state—Cross-cultural studies—Congresses. 4. Poor
women—United States—Congresses. 5. Poor women—Europe—Congresses.
6. Feminist theory—United States—Congresses. 7. Feminist theory—Europe—
Congresses. I. Hirschmann, Nancy J. II. Liebert, Ulrike.

HV91.W58 2001
362.83'8'0973—dc21

                                     00–039039

British Cataloging-in-Publication data for this book is available from the British
Library

Manufactured in the United States of America

To our mothers Audrey E. Hirschmann and Ursula Liebert, valuing their care and labor for our welfare.

Contents

Nancy J. Hirschmann and Ulrike Liebert

Preface

This volume originated at a conference at Cornell University in October 1997 that brought together feminist theorists and empirically oriented Americanists and comparativists interested in examining current welfare politics from a gender perspective. With welfare reform under way throughout the industrialized West, we thought it appropriate to include a diversity of approaches and methodologies, as well as of disciplinary foci. We also hoped that the conference would provide an opportunity for participants to rethink various aspects of their research in ways that would reflect the questions raised by scholars working out of different methodological perspectives and thinking about different sets of substantive issues. We believe that assumption has borne fruit. This gathering of feminist scholars, writing on and thinking about welfare politics and the welfare state, became an occasion for stimulating reflections and provocative discussions. Since the conference, the essays in this volume have been revised and partly or wholly rewritten, in light of these exchanges of ideas and perspectives. (Not all papers presented are included here, and one single-author contributor, as well as several coauthors, did not attend the conference.) The sometimes difficult, sometimes heated dialogues between feminist theorists and empirical analysts, as well as the interactions between Americanists and comparativists, resulted nevertheless in a more unified perspective. Indeed, it was the interdependence of the findings of these diverse subfields of feminist scholarship that made theoretical reasoning and empirical analysis, as well as American and comparative perspectives, equal partners. The synergy of the conference exchanges produced a more integrated, collective vision of the future of a feminist, woman-friendly welfare state.

Accordingly, we would like to thank all conference participants for their collaboration and contribution toward this effort. Additionally, thanks to Cynthia

Daniels, the editor of the Women and Politics Series at Rutgers, and to the director of Rutgers University Press, Marlie Wasserman, for their interest, support, and assistance, not to mention patience. Thanks also to Kathleen Paparchontis for her excellent editing. We also wish to thank the German Academic Exchange Service (DAAD) as the major contributor to the initial conference, as well as the following departments and programs at Cornell University: the Institute for European Studies, the Department of Government, the Women's Studies Program, the Mario Einaudi Center for International Studies, the German Cultural Studies Program, the Society for the Humanities, and the University Lectures Committee. Thanks to particular individuals include first and foremost Mary Fainsod Katzenstein, who was an original coorganizer of the conference; Tammy Gardner for her administrative assistance; and April Brinkman, Sydney Van Atta, and Matthew Hirsch for their research and technical assistance.

Women and Welfare

Introduction

Nancy J. Hirschmann and Ulrike Liebert

Engendering Welfare, Degendering Care

Theoretical and Comparative Perspectives on the United States and Europe

Many believe the welfare state to be one of the great achievements of Western democracy in the twentieth century. For the first time, a collective commitment to improving individual life chances and social well-being was institutionalized, and yet, at the beginning of a new century, state-guaranteed social welfare appears to have passed its time. The social welfare state everywhere has come under increasing internal and external pressure, raising serious doubts whether it will survive. Economists, political scientists, journalists, policy analysts, and feminist scholars from all disciplines are debating in all Western democracies issues of welfare state retrenchment, realignment, resilience, and change. Conservatives who more than two decades ago began questioning whether the welfare state deserves to be preserved at all, are now being joined not only by liberal economists but also by many feminists—although for quite different reasons.

In the United States, a new federalism—cutbacks in funding at the federal level, in combination with efforts to turn over federal funds, not to mention the establishment and supervision of welfare policies and programs, to the states— has resulted in what some have seen as a retrenchment of the welfare state. Not only central government expenditure decreases, but policies such as restricting the increase of payments for additional children (called family caps), the introduction of two-year maximums and five-year lifetime limits for receipt of welfare payments, as well as obligations to perform work outside the home to obtain benefits, are all cited as evidence not only that "welfare as we know it" is coming to an end, but that the welfare state of the twentieth century is meeting its demise. At the same time, many of these very same programs, particularly workfare, can

1

also be taken as evidence not of retrenchment but of realignment; that is, rather than disappearing, the welfare state is taking new forms and adopting new tasks. Such realignment is not necessarily benign, of course. Gone are surprise bedroom checks to ensure that no man is living with a welfare mother, perhaps. But forcing women to work for minimum wages in dead-end jobs or to perform community service for less than the minimum wage, and sometimes even at the cost of interrupting efforts toward education, seems to demonstrate that the punitive, anti-women ethos of the welfare state is alive and well, and as powerfully patriarchal as ever.

In Europe, by contrast, it was the renewed push toward supranational governance, and especially toward an Economic and Monetary Union (EMU) introduced by the Maastricht Treaty of the European Union that, since 1992, has urged member states to cut back on their costly public sectors. To qualify for EMU and to meet the convergence criteria with their caps on domestic budget deficits and debts, governments, in one form or another, took measures to restructure public services and infrastructures, turn public functions over to private agencies; slim healthcare and pension systems; or cut back on public childcare, old-age care facilities, or parental allowances. Many of these public sector realignments and retrenchments of social welfare policies have put particular strains on women and seem to have feminized the social costs of welfare state reforms due to European integration.

It is hardly surprising that feminists should debate the crises and the future of the social welfare state, and the complex issues of global justice they raise, as well as possibilities for feminist reform in the European Union and in the United States. Given their critiques of new patriarchal forms and of the feminization of the social costs of welfare reforms, feminists would not necessarily side with the defendants of the preexisting welfare regimes, either. Paradoxically, various feminist critiques of the welfare state question retrenchment and realignment as critically as they excoriate the welfare state itself. Indeed, current welfare state transformations cannot be adequately addressed without considering feminist analyses of the modern patriarchal welfare regimes. In the first place, it has been women's movements that effectively contributed to the politicization, delegitimation, erosion, and transformation of those traditional gender orders that had constituted the very foundations of traditional welfare regimes with their particular mixes of states, markets, and families as providers of welfare (see Gordon 1990b, 1994; O'Connor, Orloff, and Shaver 1999). Second, as a consequence of these appreciable changes in gender roles in combination with socioeconomic developments, women of different classes and races, working women, and in particular working mothers in Western democracies are confronting the welfare state with a variety of new needs, expectations, and demands that differ considerably from those of the women in the early stage of welfare state development. Third, women's organizations and political representatives have become agents in welfare politics and are playing an increasingly more effective role in shaping public policy.

All three changes—the new position of women in the social division of labor, women's new demands on welfare state policies, and the weight that women's representatives have gained in welfare politics—are crucial for understanding the dilemmas of the welfare state and for assessing alternative routes for the transformation of the welfare state that has been under way for the past decade. The present chapters cut across and develop particular aspects of these changes, ranging from a rethinking of the care work that occurs in the so-called private sphere of the home, to women's direct official impact on welfare policy and legislation outcomes, to reconfiguring the central themes and goals found in welfare policies. These feminist analyses highlight important aspects of the dynamics that underlie the crises, changes, and outcomes of social welfare politics. Coming from a broad array of interdisciplinary approaches—ranging from the traditional social sciences, most prominently political science with its subfields of American politics and comparative politics, as well as sociology, to feminist theory, including theoretical analyses of the work that women engage in on behalf of the family as well as the critical questioning of whether the welfare state should be preserved at all—these feminist approaches have generated a comprehensive research agenda with a variety of challenging questions: Can the welfare state be redesigned so that it will gain in legitimacy and appear worth perpetuating in this century? How can the idea of a woman friendly or a gender-just welfare state be theoretically developed? Is the state an appropriate framework from which to launch a feminist welfare regime, or would it simply reinscribe the patriarchal power relations that feminists wish to escape? What, vis-à-vis the state, are the shortcomings and the potential of the market and the private sector from the perspective of a gender just model of welfare regime? And is such a model viable at all, if we consider the new external pressures of regional integration and global interdependencies?

Some of these questions may be in tension with others without, however, obscuring the fact that the notion of the welfare state remains central to them all. Indeed, the question whether the welfare state can be reinvented along feminist lines—and if so, how—is the fundamental question with which the various contributors to this volume are concerned. Their perspectives are informed by various disciplines—including political theory and philosophy, American politics, comparative politics, economics, law, city and regional planning, international development, and cultural studies—and by comparative analyses drawing on the United States, Europe, and Australia. In spite of this diversity, the common thread is taking issue with current political strategies and analyses of welfare state retrenchment that are supposed to be gender neutral and the question whether the welfare state necessarily reproduces gender inequalities and hierarchies, or whether—and to what extent—it can be instrumental in transforming them. A particular aim of this book is to try to join both dimensions of feminist scholarship: feminist theory and empirical, comparative gender analyses of social welfare politics.

Social Welfare: Theory and Practice

Because scholarship on social welfare—whether feminist or not—primarily tends to be empirical and policy oriented, the question of what political theory and philosophy might have to contribute is a legitimate one. Seeking to overcome the divide between theory and empirical research is nothing alien to feminist scholarship; on the contrary, the need to link theory and practice is a commonplace assumption among feminists. Yet, with only a few notable exceptions of feminist comparative research projects on issues related to social welfare politics (Lewis 1993, 1998; Sainsbury 1994a, 1996, 1999b), the controversial issues that a small (though growing) group of feminist theorists have raised about the welfare state have rarely stimulated systematic empirical or comparative research on gender issues. This volume is a collaborative effort to at least narrow this gap. Frameworks and categories developed in the first part by feminist theorists and philosophers will be taken up, discussed, and tested by Americanists and comparativists. Discussions of controversial issues in feminist theory, in turn, will draw on empirical results of case studies and crossnational assessments of the various welfare regimes, using these either for generating general theoretical propositions or for identifying gaps in our empirical knowledge.

Theory contributes to empirical welfare scholarship in a number of ways. In the first place, theory sets out and defines the normative assumptions that go into particular empirical analyses: What standards of legitimacy do particular studies use? And what standards do the dominant discourses and regimes that feminists critique use? What epistemological issues impede the effectiveness of feminist criticisms of public policy? What are the ethical implications of various policy recommendations put forth by mainstream policymakers as well as the alternatives advocated by feminists?

Second, theory helps feminists gain critical purchase on the very meaning of the term feminist: Who are the women envisioned as the target population of particular studies? Do differences among women in terms of race, ethnicity, or national origin influence how feminists approach the question of welfare policy and the welfare state? Similarly, how do these categories, as well as that of class, intersect with gender? For instance, if poor women, or mothers, or widows receive social or welfare benefits by definition, the question of desert has class as well as race implications. Specifically, middle-class white widows who are forced onto welfare because of the premature death (and poor financial planning) of their husbands implicitly are identified as the model of the deserving welfare recipient. The model of the undeserving recipient is equally stereotyped: in the United States, as an African American woman who not only has grown up on welfare, but ensures her continuation in the system by having babies for the sole purpose of increasing her welfare check; and in European Union member states, as a lazy compatriot, an extra-EU political asylum seeker, or a resident from EU-neighbor countries freeriding on more generous domestic welfare benefits. Economic opportunities, or lack thereof, afforded by welfare make EU citizenship a relevant issue; therefore, these opportunities are influenced by nationality. In the United States, workfare makes class a relevant issue, influenced by race as racism still functions in the marketplace.

Finally, theory helps foster a discourse analysis not only of the welfare debates in Western democratic legislatures and societies, but also of feminist and other leftist solutions because these are no less prone to racial, national, and other biases. Given the power of right-wing rhetoric in the welfare debates in the United States and Europe, understanding how language and meaning translate into concrete political outcomes is a vital element of a feminist analysis of welfare politics. From the Reagan-era disparagement of "welfare queens" who are too lazy to work (clearly something only someone who had never raised a child could claim) to the somewhat more subtle, and less obviously racist, claims of the debate about the Personal Responsibility and Work Opportunity Reconciliation Act (PRWORA; approved in July 1996)—that welfare benefits create a cycle of dependency that can only be cured by a tough love that forces single mothers off welfare and into work—an antistate as much as antiwelfare hysteria increasingly has captured the public imagination. This mindset has made the feminist job of supporting the case of women not only an uphill battle but also virtually a no-win situation. Should feminists defend a maternalist welfare regime with its state-guaranteed entitlements for women as wives, as mothers or, more recently, even as working mothers—and accept the risk of reinscribing women in their traditional roles as primary caretakers? Or should we take on the workfare challenge by advocating a universal breadwinner model with better jobs and wages for working mothers—and accept the parallel risk of creating crosspressures that only upper-middle-class (and usually white) women can buy their way out of (Fraser 1994)? Have further alternatives emerged in welfare policy debates elsewhere? The ability to completely recast the debate, to focus on ideas such as the work involved in taking care of children or other dependents or on the need to end poverty, depends vitally on understanding the ways that the dominant discourse cossets the feminist, not to mention nonfeminist, imagination. Thus, theory stimulates empirical analyses of welfare politics in important ways.

In turn, crossnational comparative analyses of welfare reform and retrenchment politics are instrumental in advancing feminist theory. In the first place, these comparisons help prevent the cultural bias sometimes found in U.S. or European feminist theories by fostering more imaginative visions of a postpatriarchal welfare state or visions of a feminist welfare society. Empirical and comparative studies of the United States and Europe provide evidence on the many possible innovations and variations of welfare reform policies and their gender-related outcomes.

Second, feminist comparative analyses follow a variety of methodologies, making use of structural quantitative or culturalist qualitative comparisons as well as comparatively designed, in-depth case studies of single countries. The methodological variety of such studies provides theory with basic material for articulating the normative assumptions at work in policy discourses. They help theorists realize that any practical solution will have to be complex, multilayered, and contextual.

Finally, empirical studies provide theory with grounding for its visions. That is, feminist theory is often marginalized in the social sciences because it is seen as normative, and therefore not practical or useful. By integrating theory with empirical analysis we hope this volume can overcome this objection; empirical studies provide important reality checks on normative theorizing, helping feminists negotiate the delicate balance between conceiving the possible and realizing the achievable, sketching alternative feminist scenarios that are grounded in the facts as well as in the consequences that can be expected from particular courses of action. It is our hope and belief that linking theory and empirical analysis will provide new perspectives in designing comparative research in theoretically more sophisticated directions, and using the results of comparative studies, in turn, will further advance a feminist theory that reflects the lived realities of women's experience. Thus, we expect to turn those issues that have remained most controversial in feminist welfare state theory into empirical research questions that, in part, will be addressed in this volume and, in part, might stimulate future research. Indeed, the interdependence of these various chapters make theory and practice, as well as American and European politics, equal partners in this collective endeavor.

Deconstructing the Welfare State: Theoretical Issues of the Gender Welfare Regime

In any feminist consideration of public policy, normative issues are usually in play. Feminists, sensitive to gender and race oppression that is almost always inherent in supposedly neutral standards in mainstream social policy, have recognized the importance of basic normative and political evaluations of such neutrality. Because women, and among them single mothers, are the main recipients of social assistance programs such as the former AFDC, this awareness is particularly relevant, even crucial, to feminist analyses of social welfare policy.

Accordingly, the opening chapters of this volume are concerned with the theoretical and normative dimensions of a feminist approach to welfare discourse and policy. The theoretical arguments contained in these chapters provide a general framework for the subsequent more empirically and policy-oriented sections of the book. They raise important questions about concepts that policymakers and empirical social scientists routinely call into play: the state, justice, rights, equitable or fair distribution, and of course, the buzzword of recent welfare debates in the United States, responsibility.

How do the chapters in part 1 accomplish this? A key strategy is to introduce and explain concepts that policymakers do not expressly draw upon, but which nevertheless underwrite and support public policy; issues such as care, dependency, citizenship, rights, and freedom. A feminist analysis reveals these concepts to be of vital importance to understanding women's relationship to the state and public policy and, perhaps more important, to changing that relationship to empower women through greater justice.

Of these, the theme highlighted most centrally in all four chapters is the issue of care, although the authors may define care somewhat differently and take varied views of its value and role. For Martha Fineman and Eva Kittay, care is inextricably tied to dependency: the issue of care for dependents, and particularly of how care makes the caretaker dependent as well, is central to their analyses of dependency as welfare discourse articulates women's relationship to the state. Fineman argues that there are two kinds of dependency. One is inevitable dependency, a biological fact of human existence; for instance, we are born helpless, and without caretaking by some other(s), we will die. Some of us will become sick and will require care by others to get well; some of us will grow old and feeble, and the availability of care will determine how long we live, and in what conditions. Given the inevitability of dependency for all of us, Fineman points out the hypocrisy of a welfare policy that denigrates, stigmatizes, and punishes dependency. The assumption of independence on which such policies are based is not only counterfactual, but delusional—tied to a need to deny connection and relatedness which is at its base patriarchal.

Moreover, Fineman shows that care produces vulnerability even as it responds to it; that is, the provision of care generates a secondary or derivative dependency for the caretaker. Thus, a new mother caring for a young child may be less able to fend for herself and may, in turn, need a certain level of care herself. Because the needs generated by inevitable dependency are met predominantly by women's unpaid (or poorly paid) labor, we deny its importance to our lives, we ignore how dependent our entire society—indeed, any human society—is on those who provide care. This denial makes the myth of the independent individual possible, and potent. But Fineman's identification of these two kinds of dependency provides the framework for recognizing the importance of care work and for reformulating public visions of dependency in ways that can empower those who perform that work, usually women.

This need to dispel the myth of the independent individual motivates Eva Kittay's chapter. She pushes Fineman's arguments about the inevitability of dependency further by theorizing a notion of dependencies as nested, as existing within other dependency relationships that are not only multiple, intersecting, and overlapping, but also involve a dynamic and interactive vision of relationship. Though dependency can be a one-way relationship, it often is not, and those who are dependent in one sense or at one time may provide care to others in other senses or at other times. Dependency, thus, is often a matter of degree, not the either/or that welfare policy assumes.

This argument leads to a rethinking of dependency and of care, or how dependency is responded to. Recognizing, like Fineman, the vulnerability that care work creates for the caregiver, Kittay proposes a notion she calls *doulia*, which involves prescriptions for taking care of caretakers; of recognizing the work contained in caregiving activities, and of the need for resources that caregiving creates in terms of time, money, and emotional sustenance. Doulia derives from the ancient notion of the *doula*, or one who cares for the caregiver. For instance, a new mother, who is typically exhausted emotionally and physically during at least the first weeks or months of her infant's life, may not have the time or resources to care properly for herself: a doula would not care for the new infant, but rather would provide care to the new mother. Doulia thus entails the recognition that not only is care work *work*, but it also is demanding work that is socially so important it deserves material resources and institutional recognition.

On this model, a feminist revisioning of the welfare state would involve the state's filling the role of doula; that is, it would be seen as a provider of care and resources for the caregiver, to support him or her, without taking over the care itself. Given the role of the state under current welfare policy, permeated with rigid surveillance, distrust, and punitive policies, the notion of doulia and of viewing the state as a doula, or an institution to serve caregivers, could significantly change how welfare is conceptualized and enacted. It would also radically change the relationship of careworkers (largely women) to the state, Kittay argues, for it opens the way to viewing dependency work as a foundation for social citizenship.

The notion of citizenship is central to Joan Tronto's chapter which, in important ways, develops basic principles and provides details of what Kittay's practice of doulia might involve within an institutional context. Indeed, Tronto explicitly calls for a new vision of the welfare state as a caring state, as one that fosters and facilitates the provision of care for its citizens and recognizes people who provide care as engaged in activities of citizenship. By focusing on the work that single mothers and other caretakers perform, and how important this work is to the state—and, in fact, to the privileges that middle-class taxpayers receive as a matter of course from that state—Tronto, like Kittay, suggests that care can be justified as an important foundation for citizenship. Tronto's argument also echoes Fineman's point that almost all of us who live in Western industrial nations receive subsidies from our governments ranging from old-age pensions to home mortgage deductions that do not result in our being labeled pariahs. Rather, such subsidies are part of the collective enterprise of any democratic project. In that sense, viewing care as a public, and not just a private activity, allows us to re-envision the state as a provider of care.

Tronto's chapter also provides a transition to the traditional concerns of politics and political theory with her discussion of equality and democracy, and moves us closer to what a public policy of care, and one that recognizes both inevitable and derivative dependency, might entail. By highlighting the citizenship implications of caring labor, Tronto facilitates a rethinking of the state altogether—its justification and its purpose. If we are citizens by virtue of the care that we give and receive, then rights to care as well as rights not to care—to opt out of caring when one does a disproportionate amount of it—are essential to discussions about how care is to be allocated as a resource and performed as an obligation. Tronto thus brings into the feminist discussion of welfare and care the normative dimensions of more overtly political and policy-related concerns, as she engages directly with a feminist redefinition of a woman-friendly welfare state.

But given the patriarchal legacy of states in the Western world, if not universally, is it wise for feminists to be invoking the state as a solution to welfare? Certainly, it is difficult to envision welfare without the state; most feminists shudder at the prospect of hinging social welfare payments on private charity as some social conservatives advocate. At the same time, by institutionalizing care through a feminist welfare state, feminists may be downplaying the dangers of allowing the state an active role in women's lives. Such a state seems to run contrary to many feminist concerns about the freedom and autonomy to control and direct our own lives. Furthermore, a focus on women's dependency and caregiving work runs the danger of reinscribing women's roles as caretakers, of reducing women's identity to the very role that has historically hindered their access to political power and hampered their efforts toward equality. The question, then, is how to deal with care in ways that avoid such patriarchal reinscription and at the same time recognize it as socially important.

Such notions are at the heart of Nancy Hirschmann's chapter, which examines a pervasive political concept, freedom, from the perspective of women on welfare. She inquires into the fit between the dominant understandings of freedom found in political theory and the experiences of women on welfare. She argues for a rethinking of freedom in relation to welfare in ways that capture and interweave both the standard concepts of mainstream thinking, such as rights, and women's experiences of care that are central to welfare provision. In the process, however, the meanings of such terms are transformed. Thus, for instance, Hirschmann argues for a more complicated and multifaceted understanding of freedom that takes into account the ways in which policies and attitudes of sexism and racism not only prevent women from attaining what they want but also shape women's wants. Although a caring state might seem counterproductive to freedom, Hirschmann points out that the fear that a caring state would be too interventionist ignores the fact that current welfare policies, for all their talk of independence, already intervene highly in women's lives, and indeed construct women's very subjectivity.

Thus, following the call for institutionalized rights suggested in the first three chapters, Hirschmann argues that care and rights, which are generally seen as opposed to one another, need to be seen as interdependent and, indeed, that a feminist rethinking of rights through care is vital to a successful effort to claim welfare rights. Like Tronto, Hirschmann emphasizes that a political concept of care incorporates key qualities that are essential to public welfare policy—such as universality and impartiality—at the same time that it deploys key insights feminists have offered about the need for contextuality and specificity. And like Fineman and Kittay, Hirschmann also suggests how complicated the relationship between care and social inequalities are: those who need care are, by virtue of their needs, in a vulnerable and hence inferior position; and those who do the care work hold an inferior position because they need to be cared for in turn, but are not. As all four chapters reveal, if welfare policy regimes are about inequality, they are also centrally about care: they are supposed to provide the resources to enable certain people to care for those in need. While the patriarchal welfare state guarantees the impoverishment of women, infantilizes them, and makes them subservient to and dependent on the state as punishment for not being subservient to and dependent on individual men, a postpatriarchal welfare regime built on a caring state can be expected to be different. As Gilligan and Wiggins (1984) argue, care can attenuate inequality; that is, the provision of care can provide disadvantaged or unequal individuals with resources that make them more equal.

Similarly, the issue of social or welfare rights has been part of leftward advocacy of welfare since the turn of the century and has posed a particular problem for feminists. If rights are powerful tools, then feminists should not be too quick to give them up; but if they are built upon assumptions of women's inferiority, then they have to be restructured from the bottom up. This paradox has generally resulted in feminists dividing along dichotomous lines between those who wish to save and use rights, but not redefine them; and those who believe that such redefinition entails their rejection, and good riddance. Just as Fineman and Kittay seek to redefine care and dependency in ways that neither preserve the status quo of women's inferiority nor dismiss care as unimportant, Tronto and Hirschmann seek to redefine rights in ways that do not entail their rejection, but rather changes the foundations of what rights are and what they are based on.

Welfare Reform in the United States

The theory chapters in part 2 provide a normative foundation for the critical examination of the more empirical dimensions of welfare reform policy, as the book turns to comparative assessments of welfare retrenchment and re-alignment in the United States and Europe. Given the comparable bitterness, but also the substantial differences in debates over welfare reform in the United States and in Europe, it may not be surprising that this volume deals with both areas in two separate sections (although comparative perspectives are included in both sections). In the United States, the so called Personal Responsibility and Work Opportunity Reconciliation Act (PRWORA) was the result of many months of political wrangling between liberals and conservatives in a political climate that was generally hostile to welfare, defined in the U.S. context primarily as Aid to Families with Dependent Children, or AFDC. The PRWORA basically denation-alized welfare as a program by replacing AFDC with Temporary Assistance to Needy Families (TANF), which turned funding over to states in the form of block grants, along with a great deal of discretion and latitude to construct welfare pro-grams and policies, decide how payments would be made, and under what con-ditions. States decide eligibility criteria, benefit levels, specific work requirements, and, indeed, whether to provide support at all. For all its failings, AFDC did pro-vide a kind of entitlement to poor parents raising children (see Mink 1995, 1998), but under TANF, welfare has become much harder to obtain and much further away from the right advocated by the chapters in part 1, not to mention by wel-fare activists since the turn of the twentieth century (Bussiere 1997; Sarvasy 1989; Skocpol 1992).

The chapters included in this section all document and detail the specifics of these policies and their impact on poor single mothers. The authors present an accounting of how the bill passed through Congress as well as the impact of its resulting policies on women's lives. But compared with the attention to care and dependency in the theory section, the analyses of the U.S. welfare reform focus on different aspects of welfare retrenchment. Rather than attending primarily to the kinds of work welfare payments are supposed to compensate—namely care work, and predominantly care of children—we see a focus on other types of work: specifically the work women representatives did to keep welfare reform from be-ing as punitive as conservatives originally envisioned it; the work that women on welfare have to do in order to receive benefits, namely market labor; and the work that nonrecipients—once again, usually women—need to perform to make welfare work for those who actually receive it.

Susan J. Carroll and Kathleen Casey explore the first category of representative's work by detailing the efforts of Republican women in the U.S. House and Senate to curb some key aspects of the welfare reform bill that were seen to hit women particularly hard. Granted that feminists can agree that the PRWORA was not a woman friendly, much less feminist friendly, piece of legislation, Carroll and Casey show how much worse it could have been, indeed would have been, but for the actions of these women in Congress. Furthermore, given that Republicans were behind the most severe cutbacks in welfare funding, as well as behind the new federalist impulse that involved block grants to states that were then to develop new ways to structure welfare, Carroll and Casey's research makes a strong case for the argument that women make a difference in setting policy and, in particular, that they made a difference in the welfare reform bill. Indeed, without wishing to downplay the antifeminist flavor of the bill, one could say that the picture Carroll and Casey paint echoes, if only faintly, Kittay's concept of doulia, in that it was women legislators, sensitive perhaps to the needs and vulnerabilities that dependency work produces, who took on the job of looking out for those who perform that work.

Ann Orloff, Heidi Hartmann, and Hsiao-ye Yi emphasize a different aspect of women's work, namely women's participation in the labor force and its relation to welfare payments and reform. Though both recognize the double burdens that the demands of caring for children and participating in the labor force place on women and urge a policy that takes such burdens into account, at the same time Orloff, Hartmann, and Yi believe that women's participation in wage labor is the only way out of poverty. The key, both chapters note, is the conditions under which this is expected of women: are there supports in place, such as childcare and healthcare, to enable women to accept jobs? Do these jobs that women can obtain pay well enough to actually make a difference in their economic well-being, in their economic independence? Or do they simply keep women at the same level of poverty while making life even more difficult for them by demanding the double day of care work and wage labor? Are there training programs available if women's low-grade skills keep them from better jobs? Do welfare programs encourage education, necessary to women's ability to get and keep better jobs? Though these kinds of questions were raised in some of the theory chapters, they are attended to much more explicitly here.

Ann Orloff's analysis explores how and why the United States has eliminated the entitlement of poor mothers to receive state subsidy for caregiving as a full-time activity. Her findings present an important reality check for feminist theorizing about the issue of a woman-friendly welfare state because she situates welfare reform in the context of broader gender patterns characterizing the U.S.

policy regime. Welfare reform in the United States, she argues, was neither "simply a reflection of social and political powerlessness of women, the poor, and people of color," nor was it a "straightforward adaptation to the realities of mothers' employment." Though power resources and organized interests did count, she claims, it was predominantly the neoliberal legacy of the U.S. policy regime, with its market-supporting and -enhancing character, on one hand, and the articulation of gender equality projects with women's labor market participation, and particularly the high degree of gender sameness in the institutionalized expectations about men's and women's employment, on the other hand, that helped create the context within which the fundamental policy shift through the PRWORA became possible. In this new context, she emphasizes the Earned Income Tax Credit, the importance of which has been strengthened as a way to lift people out of poverty. Though in its current form it does not go far enough, it does at least appear to indicate that, contrary to pessimistic predictions of many on the left, paid work, and even work that does not pay all that well, is a better source for the capacity to form an autonomous household than previous transfer payments by the state for full-time caregiving. Orloff's conclusion that such programs need to be expanded to make wage work a realistic and viable option as a real road out of poverty, especially for single mothers with dependent children, presents a challenge to feminist theory and comparative analysis: to redesign a woman-friendly social welfare regime such that women may choose to depend less on the state and instead rely more on markets.

In response to the work responsibility dimension of welfare reform, Hartmann and Yi argue that women on welfare have already exhibited such responsibility, although in discontinuous ways. That is, women on welfare do work, and have always worked; however, what has prevented such work from lifting women out of poverty, and off welfare, is employment volatility—the frequency with which women are forced to leave employment due to the lack of economic and social supports, such as healthcare and childcare, that would enable them to maintain steady employment. Hartmann and Yi's research suggests that work requirements are redundant because most women already work, and insulting because they imply that women seek to avoid labor, when in fact what women seek to avoid is poverty. It is in that struggle where PRWORA, for all its rhetoric of independence, fails women, as Hartmann and Yi detail. Women do not need to be told to work, they need programmatic supports to enable them to work. Rather than work requirements, women need work flexibility. Rather than an obligation to work, Hartmann and Yi thus suggest, feminists should be thinking in terms of a right to work and all that such a right would entail: training, transportation, good wages, healthcare, childcare, and safe and decent housing.

However, given that these expansions to existing programs are not in place, how are women to get by in the meantime? Lisa Dodson demonstrates a third kind of work that women perform within the existing parameters of welfare reform, work that enables welfare recipients to meet the often impossible demands of caring for children as single parents and participating in wage labor. Through her interviews of women on welfare, as well as other women who interact with the women affected directly by the PRWORA, and particularly by mandatory workfare, Dodson develops a different approach to policy analysis. Her interpretation is informed by the critical awareness of power that is fostered by the experiences of the women actually affected in their lives by what Congress and state legislatures have decreed. Dodson's interviewees reveal lives that have become impossible, as women are torn by the conflicting and mutually contradictory demands made on them as single parents who must work for the privilege of remaining in dire poverty. What appears most lacking from governmental welfare policy, Dodson's interviewees point out, is the wisdom that women learn "at my mother's table," the pragmatic demand to respond to others in need, to do what needs to be done regardless of what the rules say, to survive. In a sense, then, these chapters move from the most upbeat and optimistic assessments of women's relation to welfare reform, to the most pessimistic and disheartening picture of what life on these reforms is really like.

Realigning Welfare States in the European Context: Empirical Assessments

Dodson's analysis especially highlights the hardships that the PRWORA and particular state welfare policies have brought down on women in the U.S. context. The other foregoing chapters present powerful insights into the processes and effects of welfare retrenchment in the United States as well. If looked at from abroad, indeed, the U.S. situation seems hopelessly distressing and the situation in Europe arguably less severe. European welfare states in the 1990s appeared to have been relatively resilient with less dramatic cutbacks, thanks to the popular legitimacy of welfare programs and to well-organized groups of welfare state clients and public sector employees defending the status quo (Pierson 1996; compare Clayton and Pontusson 1998). Social welfare states in Europe have adopted a variety of caring functions for children, the elderly, and disabled persons, and they seem to display a more women friendly quality than in the United States (Hernes 1987; compare Lewis 1993; Sainsbury 1994a). But the comparative analysis of gender relations and welfare states reveals powerful variations among the different systems of social welfare provision throughout Western Europe, especially during the 1990s, as entitlements and/or public sectors were cut back and welfare states underwent processes of retrenchment, restructuring, or realignment (Ruggie 1996; Sainsbury 1996).

For almost three decades, European welfare states have been said to be in crisis. Although to variable degrees, all of them suffer from older strains arising from their domestic economies and societies, such as economic stagnation, demographic changes, women's increasing demands for jobs, and the persistence of structural unemployment, combined with more recent pressures proceeding from the international environment, challenges due to global competition and, in particular, to the politics of European integration. In this context, new issues have entered the feminist welfare debate: Under the constraints that governance in the European Union entails, does a gender-just welfare state have a future in the European Union? Is it conceivable that the multilevel system of governance in the European Union presents a more appropriate framework from which to launch a vision of a postnational feminist welfare regime that better meets women's needs and goals? Or is this vision doomed to die because of a general trend of the more generous European welfare states toward the liberal and less generous welfare state of the United States?

Europe provides a unique laboratory for studying these worlds of gender-neutral, gender-discriminating, or gender-reinforcing social welfare institutions: the patterns of how gender welfare is politically constructed and institutionalized, how welfare subjects are gendered, and what gender-differentiated outcomes they have. Recently, European integration has provided an opportunity to study how national welfare systems cope quite differently with global change and European integration. Compared with the United States, the European Union is advancing feminist scholarship on welfare state transformation in the context of global changes. From the perspective of gender relations, new social inequalities and a high level of social exclusion are seen as likely consequences of the globalization of trade and production. The restratification of societies and the restructuring of feminized labor forces, however, vary, depending on the competitiveness of countries, the adoption of programs to re- or deregulate markets, the flexibility of labor markets, the privatization of public services, and the legitimation of discourses on international competitiveness (Jenson 1996). In the United States, strengthening the role of the states at the expense of the federal government occurs in the context of a debate that ostensibly emphasizes neoliberal values such as individual responsibility, work ethics, and a minimal state while at the same time enforcing traditional values about women's proper roles. In the European Union, by contrast, a common public discourse on the social dimension of the European Union is emerging on the supranational level as well. However, national welfare reform debates continue to differ substantially, although in a context in which political dynamics strengthen supranational governance at the expense of the fifteen member state governments. These domestic debates are embedded in quite different institutional settings and normative premises of social welfare provision that range from the social democratic Scandinavian to the liberal Anglo-American regime type, and include a variety of Continental and Southern European conservative regimes. They are built on a range of gender regimes that differ in the relative strength of their patriarchial orders—in whether they have institutionalized a strong, medium, or moderate breadwinner model (Ostner and Lewis 1995) and whether they are predominantly private or public. Despite the diversity of these gendered national welfare regimes, twelve member governments of the European Union have agreed on the strict fiscal discipline of the European monetary union. Having committed themselves to a common set of convergence criteria as defined by the 1992 Maastricht Treaty, it is nevertheless open whether one single type of monetary union will be conducive to one single type of European welfare regime.

All four chapters in part 3 are concerned with the issue of a woman-friendly welfare state and how this idea can be used as a critical standard so that the most salient dimensions of social welfare regime variation in Europe and the United States will become visible. Yet, the comparative approaches that Joyce Mushaben, Marcia Meyers, Janet Gornick, Katherin Ross, Susan Christopherson, and Ulrike Liebert have adopted differ substantially.

Joyce Mushaben addresses the paradigm shift that occurred in U.S. welfare policy in 1996 from a comparative angle, contrasting it with recent changes in the German Sozialstaat that appear to be geared toward reinforcing "arcane notions of gender dependency and women's worthiness as mothers or homemakers, first." Mushaben's configurative thick description of the United States and Germany—including East-West disparities—highlights similarities and differences in the gender politics of welfare reform in the two countries. With her gender politics approach and her "most different systems comparison," she specifically focuses the substantially different ways in which gender roles are being de- and reconstructed in both systems. These gender-based differences in welfare policies are all the more surprising, given that some of the pressures and the crises afflicting the two cases appear similar—for instance, the political-economic dynamics, with the problem of mounting national debt, or the unprecedented impact of demographic changes—and given that welfare policy makers share a set of common goals, such as cost containment, the fostering of individual responsibility, and the reduction of labor costs to employers. In her conclusion, Mushaben argues that gender stigmatization is alive in both countries, although the modes and degrees vary tremendously: while U.S. policymakers abandoned the "cult of true womanhood," sacrificing the value of motherly childcare for the sake of a false independence, relying on paid work, German policies have revalued women's maternal roles, though at the price of their economic dependence.

Marcia Meyers, Janet Gornick, and Katherin Ross, in their analysis of "gendered welfare state variation" in thirteen industrialized countries, argue that there is a systematic relationship between family poverty and welfare state provisions, namely public income transfers to families with children and employment supports. Their assessment of the United States, Canada, Australia, and ten European countries is based on a statistical analysis of a microdata set of the Luxembourg Income Study. Among the countries included in their comparison, they find cases in which rates of female employment are similarly high, but where the numbers of poor two-parent families with at least one child under age six vary enormously: most widely between the United States, with nearly one out of five families, on the one hand, and Sweden, with fewer than one in thirty families being poor, on the other. Their account of differences in the degree to which welfare regimes succeed in reducing family poverty emphasizes contrasting state philosophies and practices especially with regard to public support for families and corrections of the labor markets. The coauthors conclude that a woman-friendly welfare state may well be one that is parent-friendly by supporting the efforts of both men and women in combining private caregiving and wage work without undue—and gender-biased—sacrifices to either family well-being or employment opportunities.

Offering somewhat of a mirror image to Kittay, Fineman, and Tronto's concern with care, Susan Christopherson discusses a crossnational analysis of the restructuring of care work performed by public sector-professional childcare and elderly care. In her analysis of changes in the public-private mix of care provision in the Organization for Economic Cooperation and Development (OECD) countries, Christopherson finds important interactions between these public sector reforms and gendered labor markets. Driven by cost reduction calculations, welfare reformers take advantage of women's historically marginal labor market position. Gendered wage differentials between the public and private sector present an incentive structure to policymakers. In Christopherson's view, the repercussions from retrenchment policies harm women. Female caregivers in the family, as well as in the public or private sector, constitute a relatively invisible, weakly organized labor force, so it appears politically acceptable to shift the costs of socially necessary care to them—women both in families and as workers. Thus, Christopherson argues, the decentralization, refamilization and privatization of care most often result in barriers to women's career mobility, and class differences among a few highly skilled professionals and an expanding group of low-skilled, low-waged workers can only increase. However, against this background of her rather skeptical assessment of overall crossnational trends, she also suggests in her overview of restructuring strategies and their differential influences on the workforce that social policymakers in Scandinavian welfare regimes perform relatively better by adopting woman-friendly standards for restructuring the public care sector.

In the concluding chapter, "Degendering Care and Engendering Freedom: Social Welfare in the European Union," Ulrike Liebert addresses the issue of a gender sensitive welfare regime from three related angles: as a normative standard; as a topic of empirical, crossnational research; and as a controversial issue of European integration. In the first section, she discusses how the controversial vision and idea of a woman-friendly social welfare regime can be better clarified. By drawing on Nancy Hirschmann's concern for women's (positive) freedom on one hand, and on Joan Tronto's notion of care as a basis for social citizenship on the other, she seeks to combine both norms for engendering the triangle model of the welfare regime. This revision aims at turning the analytical model that mainstream research has constructed for capturing different configurations of state, market, and household (family) into a normative standard for assessing the gender sensitivity of social welfare regimes that is complex enough to comprise distinct dimensions.

In the second part of her essay, Liebert illustrates this model empirically. By drawing on recent feminist contributions to crossnational social welfare research, she highlights substantial variations within Europe and between Europe and the United States, with respect to policies and institutions enhancing women's freedom, and with respect to the recognition of care. In the third part, Liebert discusses various propositions about the viability of the model of a gender-sensitive welfare state under the constraints and in the context of the new opportunities deriving from the processes of European governance. The question whether a gender-just welfare state can be redesigned in the context of EMU (Economic and Monetary Union) in a way that care will be degendered, and freedom will be engendered, is discussed in this framework. After all, the European Union offers the new framework of a regulatory transnational regime, with new sets of opportunities as well as new types of constraints for transforming national gender orders inscribed into welfare states. Feminist EU-analysts are still divided on the significance and implications of these changes. But, it is arguably the case that any model of a gender-just welfare regime in Europe must take into account the new mode of governance in the multilevel system of the European Union.

Liebert's chapter thus brings the volume full circle, as empirical political analysis provides the grounding for pulling theoretical claims into the real world of women's lived experiences in and through welfare states. Ending far from where we began, however, these chapters will hopefully leave the reader with a sense of the complexity of welfare as a social problem that affects women strongly. Feminist de- and reconstructions of welfare theory, gendered reconfigurations of a model of welfare provision based on states, markets and households, and comparative gender studies all converge in dismantling the racist, sexist, and class biases of modern democratic welfare states, and attempt to discern what new directions more inclusive welfare policies must take if they are to address the needs of today's citizens. The complexities involved in this endeavor have, as we have said, inspired us to gather these works with their diverse methodologies and arguments. But it also makes the goal we set out, of interaction and crossfertilization similarly, perhaps correlatively, complex, and perhaps even impossible to achieve in a single volume. To the degree that we have failed to fully realize the vision with which we started, we hope at the least to have pointed to ways for future research and collaboration among feminists engaged in comparative and theoretical research in the United States and Europe.

Part 1

Deconstructing the Welfare State

Theoretical Issues

One

Martha Albertson Fineman

Dependencies

In both political and public arenas, the debate over welfare reform continues to rage. Some participants in this debate assume that welfare reform can and should do away with public financial support for those who rely on welfare subsidies for themselves and their families. This debate has targeted single mothers as paradigms of welfare gone wrong. The single mother is viewed as a burden on the taxpayer and, as a political construct, as pathologically dependent upon the dole. The assertion is that single mothers have relied on public support to such an extent and for such an extended period of time that it has had a considerable negative effect on their personalities and their potential for productive lives in society.

These characterizations of welfare mothers rest upon a certain set of assumptions. One assumption is that dependency is an avoidable condition, the consequence of self-indulgence, weakness of will, and laziness. Independence, in contrast, is associated with productivity and strong moral character. Another assumption is that certain types of societal transfers (subsidies) are earned, and the recipients are therefore entitled to receive them; other subsidies are charitable concessions to those too irresponsible to provide for themselves.

In this chapter, after discussing the contemporary discourse in our society concerning dependence versus independence, I discuss how only certain individuals are cast as dependent because of the specific type of subsidy they receive. It is the nature, not the fact, of subsidy distinguishes the independent from the dependent. I argue that all individuals in the United States, including those who consider themselves independent, receive some form of subsidization; subsidy takes many forms. Although it can consist of direct grants, favored treatment of some individuals or groups by political bodies, such as tax assistance or relief, is also a type of subsidy. Another form of subsidy is provided to some by the labor of others, as in the realm of the family where men and children derive significant benefits from their consumption of women's unpaid caretaking labor.

Though certain kinds of dependency and their related subsidies can stem from societal circumstances, dependency and subsidy as social phenomena are inevitable and universal. Those who have been young (all of us) and many of us who will become elderly, disabled, or ill were, or will be, dependent on others for our care. Further, this dependency reaches beyond the individual level—all of society relies on the subsidy of caretakers in performing an essential and valuable function without which society could not reproduce itself.

The final section of this chapter examines two solutions that have been successfully argued as responsive to the perceived dependency problems with and of single mothers: (a) the encouragement of the traditional nuclear family and (b) the efforts to force single mothers into the paid labor force. I maintain that these solutions are inadequate and doomed to fail because they rely on unrealistic assumptions about the nature of dependency and the possibility (as well as the desirability) of living an independent life. Romantic visions of the family and simplistic applications of an outmoded work ethic in the absence of other reforms will not begin to solve the problems in today's society—this is the real crisis of dependency.

Dependency Discourse

In revisionist and regressive policy discussions, such as the debates over the welfare system, the dependence has been used to indicate pathological behavior. This pejorative is contrasted with independence—a state of grace attained by individuals who take personal responsibility for themselves and who meet their family obligations.

There are a series of related negative associations attached to dependency. Dependence is decadent—its byproducts are laziness and degeneration, poverty and crime. It is a way of life, transmitted to the young, generating cycles of dependency. Dependency justifies, even compels, negative judgments. As a result, both political parties enthusiastically endorse punitive measures to spur dependents toward independence. Even charitable efforts are cast as potentially harmful because, as popularly imagined, they perpetuate dependence and the receiving party, a person whose character arguably has already been warped by dependency, will misuse the generosity. Harsh disciplinary measures are considered warranted because they alone can turn individual failure into self-sufficiency.

Positive cultural images are associated with the ideal of the independent person—one who adheres to a rigorous work ethic, is upstanding, and law abiding.

The positive lesson for youth to learn from an independent adult is that, with hard work, individual merit is rewarded. Material success is equated with both personal worth and individual merit. Through attaining self-sufficiency, one earns one's place in society, and the material goods one receives are deserved. An independent person makes his or her own way and does not ask for handouts or rely on charity. Independence is, in fact, the reward for living an unsubsidized existence.

In the first instance, these descriptions of dependency and independency are built around the abstract concept of the individual. This focus influences the way we think about dependence. Structural and ideological contexts are rendered invisible, and the individual is assumed to operate free from constraints. This individual is a free agent, in charge of his or her actions and responsible for his or her circumstances. The individual is also the recipient of corresponding rewards or punishments, just deserts, meted out within a meritocracy that provides equal access and opportunity for all.

Furthermore, although individual success is measured largely in material and economic terms, there is no real appreciation for advantages provided by unequal distributions of wealth or other social goods in society. Conceptually, the individual stands alone—the only relevant unit of social policy; his or her position in the social and economic hierarchy is essentially unaffected by existing allocations of societal privileges and benefits or by burdens imposed by racism, sexism, or ideologies of family responsibility and cultural norms. The individual has no relevant history, nor is he or she located in the context of the greater society—nothing is considered that might distort the assignment of blame or praise for his or her personal achievements.

In this discourse, individuals do build families, however. And, these families take on the characteristics of the individuals who build them. Thus, good individuals belong to families, which are perceived as independent, autonomous, and self-sufficient. Families labeled as deviant—broken families or other pathological groupings, such as single-mother-headed units may become dependent. They are potential failures because they are incomplete and not self-contained (Fineman 1995). The pathological families and the dependent individuals who live within them produce social problems and drain society resources. People in these social categories are discouraged from reproducing themselves either biologically or culturally.

This rhetoric has been uncritically incorporated into policy discussions. I want to complicate, and thus contest, the dominant dependency discourse. Once we begin to examine the nature of dependency, we see that social policy built on distorted and simplistic notions of the individual are inadequate to address the very real problems facing our society today.

Dependencies and Subsidies

Governmental Subsidies

The receipt of a subsidy is evidenced by some direct financial assistance from the government. A subsidy is often used to indicate that one is dependent. The fact of subsidy, however, is not remarkable; subsidies are common. Therefore, the place to begin a challenge to existing social policy is with the observation that in the United States we all are dependent on public subsidy. We all live subsidized lives, whether the subsidy we receive comes from the government in the form of direct assistance (such as food stamps, assistance checks, and certain payments to businesses) or through indirect assistance programs (those that typically benefit wage-earning individuals and certain families and businesses).

One important question to consider is why we stigmatize some subsidies, but not others. Stigma seems related to how we perceive the process and product of subsidy. If subsidization produces (or promises to produce) something we perceive to be of social value (such as jobs or a common good like medical research), it likely will not be viewed as a subsidy at all, but will appear more like an investment. If a subsidy is viewed as earned (such as Social Security payments), it is considered as part of an insurance system. Investment and earned subsidies are not only socially acceptable, they are to be encouraged by policy. In contrast, other subsidies (particularly those that go to the poor such as welfare benefits) are highly stigmatized—they are considered neither generative nor earned and deserved and lead to dependence.

When we consider the variety of government expenditures (subsidies) that benefit families, we find significant difference in public attitudes. Some subsidies, such as welfare, are highly visible. Others, like those designed to assist wage-earning families, are ignored in the debates. But, wage-earning families do receive significant governmental subsidy through the tax system. Various provisions in the tax code allow a percentage of wages or compensation to go untaxed. For example, some employers provide health insurance benefits and spending accounts that shield money for payment of medical and childcare expenses from taxation. By not taxing these forms of employee compensation, the government assists some families and consequentially loses potential general revenues.

Deductions and tax credits are another form of selective subsidy delivered through the tax system. Home mortgage interest, for example, can be deducted from gross income, and some childcare expenses may qualify to earn tax credits. The revenue the federal government forgoes as a result of these subsidies must be made up by either taxing other forms of compensation or by cutting spending through curtailing government assistance programs, many of which benefit other families.

The point is that whether tax money is first collected and then distributed to favored families and individuals or is never collected from them at all, tax policy provides for only some families in society. The tax system in this regard has been labeled a spending program as well as a revenue raising one. The logic behind that characterization is the realization that any departure from a normative tax system through things such as income exclusion, deductions, deferrals, or credits conceptually functions the same as a tax expenditure. The Canadian government recognizes this analysis of the tax system and has incorporated it into its tax policymaking process. As a result, the debates about whether the tax system is an appropriate tool by which to deliver subsidies for social and economic activity has been vigorous (Young 1997).

Subsidization through Unpaid Family Labor

As important as governmental subsidy is, another, more significant subsidy needs to be explained. Because money need not actually change hands for a subsidy to exist, subsidization occurs within families. This subsidy consists of the time and energy expended by some individuals who take care of others, often at the expense of the caretaker's full market participation and job development. This labor subsidy needs to be made visible and explicitly interwoven into public discussion about dependency.

Far from being recognized or compensated, caretaking work is taken for granted. Labor overwhelmingly supplied by women working as mothers, wives, and daughters is not considered when calculating the gross national product. The recipients of this type of subsidy are not taxed on the value they receive, and they do not consider themselves dependent as a result of their acceptance of another's time and effort. Yet, this labor is of substantial benefit to the children, the husbands or lovers, the elderly and ill parents, and others who appropriate it within families. This labor is also essential to the functioning of businesses and of governments—to society at large. Family labor produces workers and consumers, students and service providers, future voters and taxpayers. All of us benefit directly and indirectly from the reproduction of our society that occurs in the home. Further, this labor, hidden within families, has implications on an ideological level. The uncompensated work of caretakers allows us to indulge in myths of independence and autonomy. It relieves the rest of us from our collective responsibility for the dependency inherent in this process of social reproduction.

Family labor as subsidy is invisible primarily because we do not understand dependency. Both governmental subsidies in the form of tax benefits and women's unpaid labor in assuming caretaking roles should cast serious doubt on the assumptions underlying dependency discourse. Nearly all individuals, not just those receiving welfare transfers, benefit from governmental support. And, individuals who are economically self-sufficient frequently rely on the unpaid labor of women within the family.

Universal reliance on some forms of subsidy should not be misunderstood or distorted within the confines of the current dependency debate. The scope and nature of subsidy support the conclusion that dependency is not something that we can ever eradicate: all governmental subsidies could cease, and men could finally take up equal responsibility for domestic and childcare tasks, but dependency would not go away. As discussed below, some forms of dependency are inevitable, and these must be considered, factored into policy discussions in nonpejorative ways.

Inevitable Dependency

My own analysis has been that marriage has historically served as the natural repository for dependencies. The family is the institution to which children, the elderly, and the ill are referred—it is the way that the state has effectively privatized dependencies that otherwise might become the responsibility of the collective unit or state. In considering this assertion, it is necessary to look at dependency as a complex human phenomenon, assuming many forms, not reducible to one simplistic category. Thus, some dependency is inevitable. Far from being a pathological condition associated with human failure, dependency is an inevitable part of the human condition. It is universal, a shared experience. All of us were dependent as children, and many of us will become dependent as we age, become ill, or are disabled. In this regard, I view inevitable dependency as a biological category.

To make a claim for social resources, dependency must be rooted in inevitability and universality. These characteristics of inevitable dependency support the assertion of collective responsibility—as an essential and inherent human characteristic, it must be addressed through social response. Until fairly recently, inevitable dependency in the United States and all other industrialized democracies was the object of progressive social welfare policies (Tragardh 1990). Inevitable dependents constituted the deserving poor, epitomized by innocent children entitled to protection by the state through collective resources dedicated to their education and welfare.

There is another important dimension to an understanding of dependency, however. Here I distinguish inevitable dependency from something that I label derivative dependency. If dependency in its biological manifestations is universal and inevitable, then we all need caretakers to provide for us during certain parts of our lives. The simple (entirely obvious even if typically overlooked) realization is that caretakers of inevitable dependents are themselves dependent on economic and institutional resources in order to provide that care. Therefore, this type of dependency is derivative. Derivative dependency is neither inevitable nor universal. Many members of our society manage to escape direct caretaking of others.

In U.S. society, derivative dependency, while not universal or inevitable, is gendered. Caretakers, within as well as without the family, are typically women (Estin 1993). Women are socially assigned their caretaking roles as wives, mothers, and daughters within families. The social assignment of dependency is even more pronounced (and less challenged) when it comes to care for the elderly or ill. Daughters (or daughters-in-law) are those to whom elderly parents look for expected accommodations (Nelson and Nelson 1992, 747). Women are also overwhelmingly found in caretaking positions as the hired help, receiving low wages and, typically, no social security or other benefits (Niemi 1994, 13). Women are the societal caretakers within the uncompensated sphere of the private family (Estin 1993, 776; Siegel 1994, 1,214; Davis 1996, 16–17). Through the family, society segregates and hides the reality of dependency work—assigning the responsibility for social reproduction to the mother and homemaker. The economic or market role performed by the head of the household complements her specialized role.

Of course, it need not always be women who do dependency work. Who fills the needs of others and how they should do so is socially produced and defined. Still, history, tradition, and cultural myths about the family inform and affect our actions and reinforce the assumption that dependency work is women's work.

There are other issues. Society may have assigned the responsibility for dependency, but under what conditions should those so assigned be expected to fulfill their caretaking roles? How will the value be determined for the product of these roles? In considering these questions, it is essential to remember that caretaking requires the sacrifice of individual autonomy and entails compromises that negatively affect economic and market possibilities. If we recognize dependency as inevitable and, therefore, of societal concern, how can we value caretakers and reward caretaking?

By designating dependency to the private sphere, we have foregone the opportunity to develop a theory of collective responsibility for children and other dependents. But, the family is failing. As the increase in childhood poverty and growing social injustice and instability indicates, we can no longer assume that families alone will handle inevitable dependency. The fact that society considers dependency a private matter and does not compensate caretakers is an injustice that has had negative and indefensible consequences for many women and children. We need to raise the question: why is dependency not a matter of collective responsibility and concern—the basis for a claim to societal resources on the part of caretakers?

This question and a search for provisions for justly sharing our collective responsibility for the dependent and weak should have been the basis for reconsideration of our family policies. Unfortunately (and unrealistically) the solutions that politicians have most recently offered in the welfare debates for inevitable and derivative dependency were marriage and maternal work. Marriage was perceived as a solution in the sense that it was thought to ensure male economic responsibility for wives and children. If women refuse or are unable to marry, male economic responsibility can be established through paternity proceedings and child support orders. Further, if this did not work, the default was work. If a person is unemployable, attendance at short-term training programs and participation in job searches is mandated for continued assistance. Public works positions are provided for those unable to find a job in the private market. Politicians plead with private employers to hire current welfare recipients. They impose time limits on aid with faith that jobs are there for willing workers.

Proposed Political Solutions to Problems of Dependency

Resorting to either marriage or market work as solutions to poverty and a way out of dependency illustrates how myth has overtaken reality in contemporary policy debates. While in some instances welfare reforms have decreased the number of people on welfare, they are doing little to actually improve the position of those living in poverty (*As Welfare Rolls Drop* 1998). Former welfare recipients and the working poor are forced to seek assistance from charitable institutions to obtain food and shelter (Revkin 1999).

Marriage and Other Forms of Establishing Male Economic Responsibility

While empirical information refutes the general applicability of the traditional ideal of a male who, as head of the household, provides economically for his wife and children, legal attachment of men to women and children is considered to be the panacea for many social ills. In light of the stunning scope of child poverty, marriage is seriously suggested by some to be the appropriate social policy of first resort.

Despite the rhetorical promulgation of the institution of marriage as the solution to dependency, empirical indications are that the institution in its traditional form is a rarity. Traditional marriage was a life-long commitment to an institution with well-defined, complementary gendered roles. Husbands fulfilled their role by meeting their economic obligations and providing discipline and control over their wives and children. Wives provided services to the husband, including childcare and homemaking.

The most telling statistic indicating the decline of the traditional family is the divorce rate. The Bureau of the Census estimates "that half of all marriages entered into since 1970 could end in divorce, with the majority of the parties remarrying" (Lugaila 1992, 8). Corresponding to resort to divorce are statistics that indicate that traditional marriage and family are no longer central to contemporary lives. Many individuals are marrying at older ages. Further, increasingly, both within and without marriage, couples are foregoing having children; procreation is no longer a mandate within marriage.

Feminist criticism of marriage has certainly contributed to a sense of disillusion with the institution. Adherence to the belief that marriage should be a lifelong commitment is shaken when the potential violence in traditional marriage is revealed. Domestic abuse is increasingly recognized as a widespread problem transcending race and class lines. A 1984 National Crime Survey found that "women were victims of family violence at a rate three times that of men, and that of all spousal violence crimes, ninety-one percent were victimizations of women by their husbands or ex-husbands"(Thomas and Beasley 1995, 1,128). These figures indicate the nature and extent of private violence and call into question the wisdom of policies designed to persuade or coerce women to stay with male partners.

Furthermore, even among the many people who do marry, the expectations for the institution have changed significantly. These altered aspirations are reflected in laws that reject the traditional characterization of the family as a hierarchical, role-differentiated institution in which the legal identities and abilities of husband and wife are merged under notions of marital unity.

The legal rejection of the traditional model marriage in which the male role was as the head of household and the female was as his helpmate, clearly subservient to her husband and children's needs, seems irreversible. Problems with the traditional ideal arose when new, egalitarian, expectations for marriage displaced old notions. Today, both partners in a marriage are considered equals in law. Both are likely to think they are entitled to pursue market rewards. Both are expected to share domestic tasks. Gone from our formal official discourse is the hierarchical organization of the common law marriage described so graphically by Blackstone (1799) under the doctrines of "unity" and "merger" (459–470).

We now speak of a marital partnership and presume marriage to be an egalitarian relationship. Further, under the dictates of equal protection analysis, wives are considered equally responsible for the financial obligations of an economically dependent spouse and/or children. These legal changes reflect real and irreversible ideological changes in our expectations for and about marriage. This is particularly true for women.

One potential dilemma resulting from women's altered expectations about market work is that the family is potentially left without a caretaker. In response, some women limit the number of, or completely forgo having, children. Others who can afford to, hire someone to care for the children. This solution comes with its own set of problems for professional moms as evidenced by Zoe Baird and Kimba Woods (Friedman 1993; Marcus 1993).

Further, there is an important debate about whether hiring childcare providers is a feminist solution given that these domestic workers are often underpaid and do not receive benefits. Equality for middle-class and professional women may hang on their ability to treat other women as less than equals and exploit their labor in much the same way men have traditionally exploited women's domestic labor. In either case, it is the labor of women that is uncompensated or under-compensated.

Regardless of the actions women take and the concomitant problems that may result, the traditional model of the homemaker confining her time and energy to the demands of her role within the family is rejected by young women who are unwilling to sacrifice personal career and market advancement for full-time, uncompensated caretaking.

In addition, even if traditional marriage was something to which a couple aspired, marriage in contemporary society fails to adequately address dependency. Given a variety of market realities, the breadwinner/housewife model is no longer viable for most families. Families need more than one paycheck to support themselves at a comfortable level and not fall behind. This is true for the middle class and particularly true for the working poor.

Primary reliance on men and marriage as the way to resolve the dependency needs of children and their caretakers also ignores the abundance of unemployed and poor men who can hardly provide for themselves, let alone assume responsibility for women and children. Even among the middle class, there has been a real loss in wages and opportunities. Men who have experienced work-force downsizing over the past few years are effectively denied the ability to provide for their families. As well-paying jobs disappear, many men find themselves on a downwardly mobile career path in jobs without benefits and security. Middle-class victims of the global market and economic readjustment increasingly cannot be counted on to provide sufficient amounts of child support to lift children out of poverty, regardless of whether they are married to the childrens' mothers.

As the foregoing indicates, relying on men to support children is problematic. Although many men wish to provide for their children but cannot because of dire economic straits, many other men do not consider themselves economically responsible for their children, in particular after divorce or when they father children outside marriage. Increasingly, men are not living within the family unit. Never-married motherhood seems to be becoming a viable option for women of all races and social classes. Recent census figures show an increase in never-married motherhood. A survey of unmarried women aged eighteen to forty-four showed an increase in never-married motherhood from 15 percent in 1982 to 24 percent in 1992. The rate of births by unmarried women with at least one year of college education increased from 5.5 percent to 11.3 percent. For women in professional or managerial positions, it rose from 3.1 percent to 8.3 percent (Barchu 1993).

A significant and emerging social reality is the family composed of a single mother, whether divorced or never married, and her children. This changing demographic has been labeled as a problem that can be resolved only by tying the absent male to the family unit through paternity proceedings and establishing his economic responsibility through child support orders.

Difficulties surround the idea of child support as the solution to poverty. First, despite years of stiffening the collection process and federal assistance for state efforts, collection of child support remains a serious problem. Federal reforms to enforce child support obligations are hindered by the failure of many states to enforce child support obligations (Family Welfare Reform Act 1987, 134–143). Moreover, delays in instituting wage withholding and approval of federal funding have contributed to a low rate of payment collection under the reforms (162–172).

Second, even in states with improved collection records, the costs of enforcement are substantial and administrative costs eat into the benefits realized. Finally, and of particular interest in view of the assertions that child support will alleviate child poverty, is the fact that, even if awarded and collected, the average amount of child support received is very low. The most recent census figures provide that in 1985, the average child support received was only $2,200 (U.S. Bureau of the Census 1985, 2). This amount represented a decrease in real terms. How far do such amounts go toward eliminating poverty even when successfully ordered and collected? For nonmarital children, the situation is even bleaker. Paternity proceedings, which attempt to force paternal responsibility for children born outside marriage, frequently compromise women's privacy but, nevertheless, are far from universally successful in establishing any type of bond between father and child.

Maternal Work

Perhaps, because statistics reveal that the traditional family model cannot be the solution in a world where families often need two working adults and where many women refuse to adopt traditional family roles, imposing a norm of maternal market work is considered by some proponents of welfare reform to be appropriate social policy. Maternal work has, in fact, been strongly proposed as a solution to welfare mothers' dependency.

It is in this context that the dependency discourse is most pernicious. And, unfortunately, it is necessary, in view of the current political rhetoric, to assert the basic fact that mothering *is* work. If motherhood in general entails work, poor motherhood entails even more work, and poor motherhood, while receiving public assistance, is one of the most burdensome types of mothering. Poor women dependent on public assistance and/or charity must deal with bureaucrats and bureaucracies (Simon 1983, 1,198). To meet day-to-day needs, these women and their children endure hardships and confront obstacles that the process and its personnel place in their way. Further, these mothers often must raise their children in horrendous conditions. Single-mother families are disproportionately found in poor neighborhoods, essentially abandoned by police and increasingly deprived of social welfare programs. Motherhood in these neighborhoods means daily encounters with potential violence. One should not wonder that some poor mothers fail at raising their children to become productive, tax-paying citizens—the real wonder is that so many succeed in mothering under such adverse conditions.

The second fundamental point in the maternal work debate is the assumption that jobs are waiting for current welfare recipients. This assumption is essential to the logic underlying welfare reform proposals and is central to much criticism of welfare recipients. Very little empirical study has been done, but indications are that there is some trouble with this assumption (Newman 1999).

The Newman study (1999) found that low paying jobs are in short supply in the inner city, with approximately fourteen people applying for every one job that opens. Furthermore, it appears that the oversupply of job seekers is pushing up the credentials that applicants must have to secure a job. This shift in qualifications in the job pool may explain why 73 percent of those who applied, and were rejected, for fast food work had not found work of any kind a year later.

Newman (1999) also points out that the change in the demographics of low-paid workers means that it is now older workers, those in their twenties, who are more likely to be high-school graduates and have a greater chance at success. The average AFDC recipient is far less qualified in terms of education and recent job experience than those who were successful in the study

In addition, it seems that single parenthood is an independent negative indicator for employability. This is true partly because employers seem to prefer applicants who are commuting from distant neighborhoods, a situation that makes childcare arrangements and costs associated with commuting more burdensome. The preference for applicants with recent job experience also works to the disadvantage of many single parents (Newman 1999).

The logic of workfare rests on the premise that the problems of the poor are the product of their own choices and individual weakness and failures—not as structural or produced by societal forces. Therefore, it is a simple moral equation we have constructed with which to judge the poor: if work is the solution for poverty, and that solution is within individual control, then if an individual does not work, he or she is morally culpable; thus, any punishment and deprivation he or she receives is justified. If we assume job opportunities exist, then women who do not work are lazy and shiftless, and society is justified in restricting or eliminating their assistance as we heap upon them scorn and hatred.

This discourse fails to take empirical realities into account. We have experienced large-scale economic dislocations over the past decade and are just beginning to feel the fallout from the transformation to a global economy. These market trends exacerbate existing historic unequal conditions that have already disadvantaged many working-class and poor women. This argument applies to poor men's employment prospects as well. This situation further diminishes the possibility that marriage is a viable solution for the poverty of women and children. Poor men are the most likely partners for poor women. The economic factors that negatively affect female work opportunities also affect their potential partners as a group.

Significantly, many researchers indicate that a typical welfare recipient does not lack the will to work. Instead, individual incentive is sapped by the problems faced in finding a permanent job that pays enough both to provide for a family and deal with childcare responsibilities that remain even after finding a job (Handler 1995, 85).

Ironically, well-considered work-based welfare reform programs that try to address this reality can wind up costing states more than cash grant programs do. Given the rhetoric of budgetary austerity and taxpayer relief that initiated welfare reform, it seems politically difficult for states to now allocate more money to those they have previously vilified. Wisconsin is confronting this dilemma. In 1996, the state spent about $9,700 for each family on welfare. This year, after implementing a work-based program, it will spend about $15,700, a 62 percent increase (DeParle 1997, 33–34).

Real Reform

Clearly, the solutions for welfare and dependency—urging a traditional family model on the one hand, or maternal work on the other—are insufficient or unrealistic methods of resolving the problems. What would real welfare reform look like? First, we should confront the misperceptions and myths that obscure the problem. We should insist our politicians recognize and address the fact that motherhood is work. As important societal work, it should be compensated. Most industrial democracies accomplish this through a universal governmental transfer in the form of a child allowance or through a basic income guarantee (Rainwater and Smeeding 1995, 14–22).

It is important that caretaking benefits be universal—given to all caretakers. Bearing the burden of dependency in a society should be considered work deserving of public compensation, regardless of other sources of caretaker wealth. The universal nature of such programs underscores the inappropriateness of partitioning certain children and other dependents and their caretakers into stigmatized, need-based programs where they become easy targets for criticism (Fineman 1997, 15–16). Any problem that an unwarranted accumulation of resources by a wealthy caretaker generates could be addressed through a progressive tax system.

In addition, we must insist that social policies be based on the realization that the needs of inevitable dependents do not disappear if the caretaker is engaged in market work. It is essential to remember when considering maternal work as a solution for poverty that the demands of mothering do not disappear when women enter the work market. There are still caretaking tasks to be done. Furthermore, as things are currently arranged, market work is often incompatible with caretaking work. This realization naturally suggests an additional direction for reform.

We need to think about significant structural changes in market institutions that would allow the reconciliation of motherhood with market work. These could be the product of governmental regulation or accomplished through a system of incentives (subsidies). The point is that it should not be left to the individual employer's goodwill. It must be mandated as important public policy. To further this objective, it would be helpful to reframe the current workfare discussion so that issues associated with work do not exclusively focus on poor welfare mothers, thereby isolating them from other women. The point should be made that all women (and men too if they are caretakers) have problems if they try to combine market work and motherhood.

Once a more inclusive perspective is gained, it is clear that the real issue is not whether there is an obligation for women to work, but whether there is a right to work that is going to be protected and supported by social policies. This stance presents the family and work issue from the caretaker's perspective. It should not be the anonymous, disembodied taxpayer of the welfare debates who drives the rhetoric, but the mother seeking to combine work and caretaking in a way that will not sacrifice the demands of either. Such an emphasis would not only mean seriously attempting to create jobs and training programs for poor unemployed women and men, but also regulating the wage structure, and standardizing health, pension, and other benefits.

Assuming there is a right to work also means making necessary changes in the workplace. Services such as daycare and provisions for paid family leave would be provided. Employers will be required to pay family wages to working caretakers. On a structural as well as an ideological level, we need reforms that counter the pervasive assumption that the American worker is an unencumbered individual, free to participate in an inflexible nine-to-five schedule, without concern for ill children, school vacations, or other caretaking glitches, because some woman is taking care of all of that at home, for free (Drakich 1989, 83–87; Briscoe 1992; Quindlen 1992, A21; Xinhau News Agency 1992).

Adopting the suggestions about the reorientation of the workplace to accommodate caretaking would mean that women could realistically be both economic actors and mothers. The question might arise as women are enabled to perform in both spheres, what will be the role for men? Perhaps, a true reevaluation of fatherhood, of masculinity, one that is neither hierarchical nor patriarchal, will occur. Such a reevaluation will be painful, even threatening, because revisioning gender equality challenges the dominant roles men have historically occupied in the traditional family. This may explain why we continue to resort to myth rather than to substantive change.

It is time to reconfirm the fact that can no longer ignore the injustice perpetuated when family policy in this country is fashioned and formulated on myths and symbols that are no longer empirically valid, nor ideologically desirable. Policies that rely on the traditional nuclear family as the means to escape poverty and provide for inevitable and derivative dependents foster the assumption that the maintenance of intimacy—everything from contraception to responsibility for the day-to-day care of children—is primarily a private task. Challenging this idea must be the basis of real welfare reform. Only when a persuasive theory of collective responsibility is articulated can we begin to build humane welfare policies.

Summary

True welfare reform would not be bogged down in simplistic notions about dependency, stigmatizing certain individuals as pathological. True reform would embrace the notion that everyone in society—both those welfare recipients who are currently labeled dependent and the members of other, more fortunate classes who receive their subsidies through the tax system or social security—is the recipient of governmental support in some form. Further, rather than being considered an unfortunate or disreputable state, dependency would be recognized for what it is: an inevitable result of the human condition. To this end, those who care for dependents, who perform the essential and indispensable societal task of nurture and care, would not be dismissed as dependent, but compensated and respected for the valuable labor they provide.

Two

Eva Feder Kittay

From Welfare to a Public Ethic of Care

Welfare Reform is a Feminist Issue

Workfare, the work first core of welfare reform, is hailed by its supporters on the Right as promoting personal responsibility, instilling family values, and providing a cure for welfare dependency. For those on the Left who oppose it, workfare is thought to be an inadequate response to the poverty welfare is meant to alleviate, especially when jobs are not available or, when available, do not pay enough to pull workers out of poverty. Yet, both positions, in different ways, assume a conception of the citizen based upon a male model of the independent wage earner. Both see the person currently using welfare as someone who can only be incorporated as a full citizen by eventually fulfilling the role of the independent wage earner. Neither questions the conception of social cooperation that presumes, but does not credit, women's unpaid labor as caretaker (Piven 1985; Pateman 1989a; Young, 1995; Abramovitz 1996; Mink 1998; Fineman, this volume).

Defenders of the welfare state tend to see welfare as a response to inequalities generated by capitalism and need-based welfare as a response to poverty—poverty de-gendered.[1] Yet TANF (Temporary Assistance to Needy Families), like its predecessor, Aid to Families with Dependent Children, mostly affects women and their children. Feminists, whether critics or proponents of the welfare state, have long seen welfare as a woman's issue—as patriarchal control over the lives of poor women (Johnnie Tillmon referred to welfare as "The Man"[2]), but also as an essential safety net for all women.[3] Commenting on welfare reform, Kate Millet remarked, "The Man walked out—he quit."[4] But poverty remains, and it is poverty with a woman's face.

In reading the literature by men, and some women, one comes to wonder, why when women are poor, do theorists fail to ask if there are not particular causes of women's poverty?[5] The presumption is that when it comes to getting jobs, gender inequity is nonexistent—that the joblessness of these women is independent of the gender-related vulnerabilities they face at home, in the family, and in the economic sphere. There is no talk of gendered wage inequity, of the gendering of familial caretaking responsibilities, of gendered susceptibility to spousal abuse, and sexual abuse in the workplace. Why are the conditions faced by women, especially those caring for dependents, not highlighted in these discussions?

Inattention to gender issues should be of special concern to feminists, and not only for the obvious reason that feminists must always be alert to analyses where gender is ignored. Women's increased impoverishment has, paradoxically, coincided with their increased presence in the workforce and their expanded opportunities for equality.[6] It is arguable that feminist gains for some women aggravate the condition for others, especially those who benefit least by strides toward equality of opportunity and reproductive rights legislation. Expanding job opportunities for women (as well as declining wages) have encouraged the expectation that even women with children will be employed. But as Linda Gordon points out, "The fact that most mothers today are employed . . . nurtures resentment against other mothers supported (if only you could call it 'support') by AFDC" (1995, 92). As systematic, formal barriers to social goods are removed, injustices that remain become less visible, and those who are unable to take advantage of opportunities are blamed for their own distress.[7] Equality of opportunity can be a double-edged sword.

With respect to reproductive rights, progressive legislation benefits poor women least, as they often lack the educational and financial means for getting contraception and abortions. But they are held accountable for each pregnancy and birth as if they had the same access to both contraception and abortion (as well as satisfying and well-paying jobs) as middle-class women. Even women who support feminist organizations will say of poor women, "Why do they have children if they can't afford them."[8]

If it is indeed the case that the very demise of legal barriers to women's economic and political participation and women's increased control over reproduction through contraception and abortion rights are responsible for this presumption of gender equality, then feminists have a special responsibility to concern themselves with welfare reform efforts. Naomi Zack (1995), in another context warns, "You must dismount a tiger with great care." The efforts of some women to dismount the tiger of patriarchy may well have left less well-situated women in mortal danger. In particular, it has facilitated analyses that ignore the concerns of women who have turned to welfare to support their families.

Feminists have a special responsibility to concern themselves with welfare and the current welfare reform; we ignore these to our peril. Welfare reform is first a challenge to the reproductive rights of women. Herein is the significance of resurrecting illegitimacy—an ugly idea steeped in sexual inequality.[9] Despite some pious calls for ending violence against women in the home, the constriction of aid to solo mothers deeply affects women's exit options in abusive relationships. As some current studies indicate, more than half of the women who make use of public assistance are coming out of situations of domestic violence.[10] Mandated workfare makes a mockery of feminist demands for fulfilling and well-paying nonfamilial labor. To be compelled to leave your child in a stranger's care or with no care at all and to accept whatever work is offered is another form of subordination, not liberation. And it devalues the traditional work women have done.

Welfare reform's challenge to feminism and its aspirations to improve the lives of women of all races and in all their variety can be seen in even a brief consideration of the legislation. The policies used to justify the abandonment of women in need reveal an agenda by the Right that is something other than ending poverty. It is also not intended as a way of ending the dependency of the woman it targets. This agenda aims rather to end her dependency on the state and to encourage a dependency on a wage-producing man.[11] The first welfare legislation passed by the House of the 104th Congress, HR. 4, "The Personal Responsibility Act," was slated as a bill "[t]o restore the American family, reduce illegitimacy, control welfare spending and reduce welfare dependence" (1995: Title 1).

If restoration of the American family has an innocent ring to those not influenced by feminist criticisms of the family, a closer look at the act proves more troubling. Not only sexism, but racism too forms a subtext. The very first part of the bill is "Title 1–Reducing Illegitimacy." It begins:

It is the sense of the Congress that:

1. Marriage is the foundation of a successful society.
2. Marriage is an essential social institution which promotes the interests of children and society as large.
3. The negative consequences of an out-of-wedlock birth on child, the mother, and society are well documented as follows: . . . (H.R. 4, 1995: Title 1)

A full deconstruction of the language of the act is in order. Title 1 lists questionable statistics on illegitimacy and its putative ill effects, which are, curiously, disaggregated by race. What begins as a discussion on illegitimacy becomes one about single-parent mothers and teen-age mothers—falsely implying that single-parent mothers, as a rule, were mostly or mostly started out as out-of-wedlock mothers and also falsely implying that most women who give birth while still in their teens are not married to the fathers of their children.

The language betrays an ideology in which both solo motherhood and female teenage sexuality are deviant female behaviors that need to be controlled by appropriately punitive social policy.[12] In the few places where any blame is attached to men, the men are represented as deviant, and specifically as young black men engaged in crime. For example: "(O) the likelihood that a young black man will engage in criminal activities doubles if he is raised without a father and triples if he lives in a neighborhood with a high concentration of single-parent families" (H.R. 4, 1995: Title 1).

One must wonder why crime of young black men, born to and raised by black single women, is noted in particular. Because neighborhoods with high concentrations of single-parent families are also very poor neighborhoods, the criminal activity could just as well be attributed to poverty. But instead, the act links crime to single parenthood as it couples (O) above with (P): "(P) the greater the incidence of single-parent families in a neighborhood, the higher the incidence of violent crime and burglary" (H.R. 4, 1995: Title 1).

The document concludes: "(4) in light of this demonstration of the crisis in our Nation, the reduction of out-of-wedlock births is an important government interest and the policy contained in provisions of this title address the crisis" (H.R. 4,1995: Title 1).

The language signals racism coupled with sexism directed at single mothers: criminality is racialized, as is single motherhood. This crisis rhetoric evokes a fearful mythology: the matriarchical black family as imperiling the United States with its disorderly progeny, and as a dreaded replacement of the traditional (white) heterosexual marriage.[13] With such an ideology dominant in the minds of the architects of welfare reform, it is perhaps not surprising to find Lawrence Townsend, Riverside, California's welfare reform director, make a remark in which misogyny is starkly revealed and racism is only somewhat veiled: "Every time I see a bag lady on the street, I wonder, 'Was that an AFDC mother who hit the menopause wall—who can no longer reproduce and get money to support herself?'" (quoted in Williams 1995, 6). While some conservatives worry now that workfare might, in fact, not redirect women's dependency from the state to men (e. g., Horn and Bush 1997), workfare programs for women with dependent children are in full force throughout the land.

As welfare is a feminist issue, feminists must use this moment to understand how, as the slogan of a feminist advocacy group, the Women's Committee of One Hundred, declares, "A war against poor women is a war against all women." This moment, however, should also be seized as an opportunity to reconsider the basis of welfare. We need to muster the political will to shape and support welfare policies that can serve women raising families without stigmatizing those in need.

That is, we need to ask how we can fashion policy that does not insist that all women must fit the Procrustean bed of the male wage worker, that recognizes the demise of the family wage, and that recognizes the dependency of those for whom mothers care without reducing the mothers themselves to dependency and control. Another way of putting this is to ask whether we can conceive of social welfare policy that will sustain the concept of social citizenship for women.[14] As feminists have argued, social recognition and support of the caring labor done by women is a requisite for women's social citizenship—that is, their full measure of equality and freedom (Fineman 1995, this volume; Fraser 1997; Hirschmann, this volume; Mink 1995; Orloff 1993a, this volume; Sevenhuijsen 1996; Young 1995). [15]

Traditional Justifications for Welfare

The contemporary Right/Left debate reflects a number of different understandings of the basis of the welfare state by both those who endorse it and those who oppose it. Reviewing these in light of the feminist questions that welfare reform poses will help us formulate and justify welfare policy conducive to the equality and flourishing of women and their families.

The welfare state—and especially those policies directed at the poor—aim to eliminate poverty as well as to protect its citizens against failures of the market. In a money economy, there are three obvious solutions to eliminating poverty: provide money, needed goods and services; or the means to earn money lawfully, that is, an adequately paying job. Of course, matters are never so simple. Questions arise. What constitutes a need for goods or services? How much money and how much access to goods and services will alleviate poverty?

The call for a guaranteed income has a venerable history.[16] It is, however, not a solution often adopted. Within a market economy, the satisfaction of needs, the creation of needs, and the negotiation of what constitutes need is tied to one's participation in a relation of reciprocity between the production of wealth and its consumption. To participate in such a reciprocal relation involves social co-operation, a requisite for citizenship in contemporary Western society.[17] This participation is marked primarily by labor that is compensated through wages or salaries. Paid labor defines independent. To stand outside these reciprocal arrangements reduces one to the status of dependent, someone dependent on an individual, a charity, or the state.[18]

But as even the earliest proponents of a market economy saw, a market economy, in and of itself, will not guarantee that all who can and want to work will be adequately employed. The dynamism of a capitalist economy produces great wealth, and great poverty. Such poverty is morally unacceptable in the midst of wealth and leads to political instability. Attempts to redress inequity encounter what Donald Moon (1988) has called "Hegel's dilemma," a dilemma articulated but never resolved by the philosopher in his *Philosophy of Right*. For while the redistribution of wealth can mitigate poverty, such redistribution (through cash transfers or the provision of goods and services in kind) may, on the one hand, undermine a citizen's sense of participation in community and so undermine the citizen's sense of self-worth. If, on the other hand, the state steps in to create jobs, such action interferes with the autonomous functioning of the market, and thereby disrupts the machine that generates wealth.

The creation of the welfare state is nonetheless a compromise between capitalism and democracy. This is true at least where democracy is understood to be incompatible with economic disparities great enough to destabilize a free society or to render the idea of equal political participation empty. Some welfare programs have been developed to skirt the offense to self-respect.[19] Populist policies, such as progressive taxation or free public education, have redistribution in the service of community and equality as their goal. Social insurance policies also avoid undermining self-respect by considering benefits to be "earned entitlements" intended to "protect citizens against the predictable risks of modern life" (Marmor, Mashaw, and Harvey 1990, 27).[20]

In contrast, two other visions of welfare, residualism and behaviorism, are solely aimed at the impoverished. Residualism establishes a safety net—a floor beneath which individuals must not fall. Behaviorism attempts to alter the behavior of the poor.[21] While populist and social insurance policies avoid one horn of Hegel's dilemma, residualist and behaviorist policies do not spare their recipients a goring. The scar marks its bearer as possessing the character flaw of dependence.[22]

Welfare debates today are most often between residualists on the Left and behaviorists on the Right.[23] The Right, emphasizing the evils of dependency on state support, has pushed us to the current legislation of workfare (or should we call it unfair work). The Left does not question the debilitating effects of dependency nor does it dispute the premise that a job is preferable to a handout (see, e.g., Solow 1998). It favors policies of job creation for persons who are employable but not employed. [24]

Supporters and foes alike nonetheless recognize that not everyone in a society is able to perform waged work, even if jobs are limitless. Individuals may lack the capacities required for employment and may instead have: ill health, disabling conditions not corrected for in the work environment, disabling conditions for any form of employment, or inadequate education or training and no means by which to alleviate these. Nor does any society expect *everyone* to work. Within most industrial societies, we exempt, even prohibit, children from working and do not presume that those over a certain age will continue to work.

Aid to Dependent Children, the forerunner of AFDC, was aimed precisely at those women who were presumed to be justifiably not engaged in wage labor, that is white women (Jim Crow laws prevented black women from qualifying)[25] with children who fit the traditional role of wife, but who had been widowed or abandoned.[26] While previous social policies attempted to distinguish between deserving and undeserving poor women, the removal of obstacles to women's employment has opened the door to characterizing all unemployed poor women as undeserving. In the process, many of the distinctive characteristics of women's poverty, and in particular the responsibilities women tend to carry in caring for and maintaining dependents, has been ignored.

The Maternalist Justification of Welfare

As we have noted, at the inception of U.S. social policy, the poverty of women was thought to be distinctive, and policies to serve these women were addressed to their particular situation.[27] The story of how a welfare program initiated by women for women became the despised program we now call simply welfare is a fascinating, if depressing, story.[28] At best, it is a story of progressive maternalism, which gained power through the efforts of well-educated upper- and upper-middle-class women before women had gained the vote. At worst, it is a story about how these same women, mostly white, used the social benefits conferred on them to Americanize (and thus erase native ethnic identities of) Eastern and Southern European women, even at the cost of preventing those benefits from being extended to black women and non-European immigrants.

The progressive maternalists, adopting a philosophy of social housekeeping, were maternalists in that they wanted to bring women's values into the public sphere.[29] But, as the city's housekeepers, the eyes of the well-meaning reformers were primarily directed at the end result—the child. They bypassed the mother as a citizen in her own right.

The maternalists' feminist vision resonates with certain feminist visions today, especially those associated with the feminist morality of care.[30] Although there are doubtless many significant differences between the historical case and feminists today, the historical example alerts us to some of the dangers lurking in the otherwise worthwhile project of bringing women's value of care, of concern for children, and so forth to the public arena. For how, and in what spirit, we try to import these values makes all the difference.

Dependency Revisited

The question before us today is whether, and how, we can envision a welfare that addresses women's lives and provides them a basis for social citizenship. To argue for the conditions of women's citizenship, we need to shift our attention on dependency away from the social/political/economic/moral registers that Fraser and Gordon (1994b) explicate. For there is another use of the term that gets lost but which we can retrieve in the acronym AFDC, Aid to Families with *Dependent* Children. Human development, disease, disability, and decline result in inevitable dependencies (see also Fineman [1995; this volume]). The relationships in which these dependents are cared for I call dependency relations. Dependency relations, as I conceive them, have as their core, a dependent (or charge) and a dependency worker (one who cares for the charge). Dependency relations require support from additional sources to be sustainable. I call this support the provider (Kittay 1995, 1996, 1999).

Dependency relationships, which are all too easily eclipsed when society is understood as an association of independent equals, constitute the fount of all social organization (Baier, 1987; Held 1987; Pateman 1989a; Fineman, 1995; Kittay, 1996, 1999).[31] The bonds of political association among equals, however binding they may be, are not as powerful as those created by caring relationships. These intimate ties allow individuals at different stages of life to withstand the forces that act upon them (Kittay 1996, 1999). As Virginia Held (1987) has argued, the intimate bonds of dependents and their caretakers make civic order and civic friendship possible (see also Schwarzenbach 1986). In the solo mother and her children, we find the distillation of these founding social relations.

The Derived Dependency of Dependency Workers

The welfare dependency which so exercises the critics of welfare is not the dependency of the children, but that of their mothers. Yet, these two dependencies are linked. Feminist research has established "that in all industrialized Western countries, welfare—tending to children, the elderly, the sick and disabled—is largely provided in private households by women without pay, rather than by states, markets and voluntary nonprofit organizations" (Orloff 1993a, 313). That is, women not only do most of the dependency work, they do it without pay. In more highly developed economies, at least, caregiving is rarely compatible with wage earning. Given the structure of our contemporary industrial life and its economy, it is unreasonable to expect women to simultaneously provide the means to take care of dependents and do the caring (to use a useful distinction in the term caring that Joan Tronto [1993] has introduced). This also means that without additional support, one cannot participate in the reciprocal arrangements of production and consumption, as defined within a market economy.[32] The requirement for support then constitutes a condition of derived dependency for dependency workers, especially those who do unpaid dependency work (see Kittay [1999] and Fineman [this volume]). Even dependency workers who are paid incur vulnerability to derived dependency since this dependency is, in large measure, due to their relation to the dependent and the nature of dependency work. The dependency of the dependency worker is derivative, not inevitable—it is structural, not characterological.

There are three features of dependency work that together are responsible for vulnerability to derived dependency. First, because dependency work involves the charge who is in many ways helpless without the caretaker, there is a moral obligation that transcends the bounds of most jobs. Second, dependency work requires a degree of attachment and commitment to the charge commensurate with the responsiveness to, and anticipation of, needs characteristic of dependency work that is well done. That is, we want caretakers who care. Third, the work of dependency care, is functionally diffuse rather than functionally specific (Darling 1983). A caretaker has to perform not a fixed set of tasks, but whatever acts are appropriate for tending to her charge's general well being.

The urgent needs of the charge, the commitment of the dependency worker to the charges well-being, and the diffuseness of the caretaker's responsibilities cause conscientious caretakers to concentrate their efforts on the well-being of the charge, to put the well-being of the charge above their own interests if necessary, and to not abandon a charge when caring for that person fails to suit their interests. The dependency worker is not only economically vulnerable, but is also less able to make her social and political voice heard, especially when it goes against the provider of the material support that helps sustain her and her charge. Nor do the regulatory models and legal rights that govern citizen-state or citizen-citizen interactions adequately limit the obligations, as well as properly compensate the labor, of dependency workers.[33] For all these reasons, dependency workers are liable to incur a dependency that has a character different from the dependency on the economic and governmental forces to which all workers are subject (see also below).

Patriarchal family structures, whether the nuclear family prevalent in industrial societies or the extended family forms of agrarian societies and peasant communities, are responses to the requirement that dependency relations require support. Nevertheless, as feminist critiques of the patriarchal family have shown, they are neither the only nor the best response. Within these structures, dependency work is assigned by gender, not by skill or disposition, and the dependency of the dependency worker is the condition of her vulnerability to exploitation, abuse, and all the ills against which feminists have fought. In capitalist welfare states, patriarchal state support in the form of welfare has been the response to the solo mother in need.[34] Again, it has been a poor response—better than none, but too little, too stigmatized, and too intrusive. The welfare repeal, also known as reform, is no response at all. The demand that women on welfare work (for wages) fails to value or even recognize the unpaid dependency work of the women using welfare to support themselves and their children, and indeed, the unpaid work of all mothers. In the name of fostering a fictive independence, it refuses to acknowledge the obligation of the social order to attend to the well-being of dependents and of their caretakers, and to the *relation* of caretaker and dependent upon which all other civic unions depend (Kittay 1996)

Political theories (on which social policy depends for its justifications) are intended to capture the conditions for justice. The relationships of dependency and care are viewed as standing outside these public domains. Since the publication of Gilligan's *In a Different Voice*, feminist theorists have pointed to the distinction between principles of justice and principles of care. They have taken political philosophies to task for ignoring the principles of care. Perhaps we should say, along with Susan Okin (1989) and Marilyn Friedman (1987), that the distinction between care and justice should not be overdrawn. Justice is not served if principles of care are not incorporated within the social order; care is not served if it is meted out without reference to principles of justice. Good caring requires a relationship between the one cared for and the one caring. But the one caring must not be treated without justice or caring. Her needs must be met if a just caring is to be possible.

The Citizen and Social Goods

Theories of the just state tend to neglect these considerations. The result is that they fail to include among the social goods those that bear on the needs of dependency workers, dependents, and the relations of dependency. Because of its power and influence, Rawls's theory of justice serves as a good starting point for asking what a theory that incorporates the concerns of dependency would look like and how it would reshape our conception of welfare. Consider the idea of the citizen as the free, independent, and equal to whom rights attach. This is the citizen who enters freely into exchanges with equals with a sense of justice and a conception of his own good. He benefits from social cooperation with equals and partakes of the burdens of such cooperation. Within this conception of society as an association of equals, however, neither interactions with dependents nor the dependencies that result from caring for dependents figure. They vanish from the moral features of citizens, the social goods that are crucial to their citizenship, and the conception of social cooperation.[35]

Consider for a moment Rawls's characterization of free and equal citizens. The moral features of the citizen are those that contribute to political and civic participation with equals. Rawls speaks of citizens as having two moral powers: an ability to form and revise one's conception of one's own good and a sense of justice. These powers give rise to the political and civil rights that are given prime consideration under liberal democracies. If we figure in the exigencies of life in a market economy, we can include the social right to not have all of life's interactions commodified. These two moral capacities call for a set of social goods necessary for their exercise. This set of goods, which Rawls calls primary goods, serves as an index for making comparative assessments of interpersonal well-being.

The list, unaltered through the many revisions of Rawlsian theory, includes:

1. The basic liberties (freedom of thought and liberty of conscience);
2. Freedom of movement and free choice of occupation; against a background of diverse opportunities . . . as well as [the ability] to give effect to a decision to revise and change them;
3. Powers and prerogatives of offices and positions of responsibility;
4. Income and wealth; and finally
5. The social bases of self-respect . . . (Rawls 1980, 526).

Examining this list, one may identify the first as political rights, the second and third as civil rights, and the final two as social rights. Omitted from the list are just the sort of social goods that are critical for women's social citizenship. These are the goods of dependency care and relationships of caring.

That is to say, a conception of a just state must include an understanding of the citizen as having not only two moral powers, but also a third, the capacity for responding to those in need with care.[36] The exercise of this moral power requires additional social goods, namely "(a) the understanding that we will be cared for if we become dependent; (b) the support we require if we have to take on the work of caring for a dependent; and (c) the assurance that if we become dependent, someone will take on the job of caring for those who are dependent upon us" (Kittay 1999, 102). The basic liberties, choice of occupation, the powers and prerogatives of public office, and income and wealth provide us with many of the political and civil rights of citizenship. But if we are not assured that when we are called upon to do the work of caring for a dependent, we will not thereby lose the ability to care for ourselves (and so for our charge as well), we have not yet attained the full powers and capacities necessary to function as free and equal citizens. These, then, are the social goods all citizens, but particularly women, require for social citizenship. We have yet to discuss how these might translate into demands for particular social policies.

A Public Ethics of Care as Justifying Welfare

I have claimed that the ideal of the independent citizen presumes an equality and reciprocity of social relations that is blind to the inherent dependencies in which we all are immersed. To incorporate dependency and the dependency relation into social relations, we need a concept of interdependence that recognizes what is not precisely a relation of reciprocity but a relation that I characterize as nested dependencies (Kittay 1995, 1996) These dependencies link those who need help to those who help, and link the helpers to a set of supports. If we look at women's poverty and the social response to welfare from the vantage point of the dependency relation, and we attempt to reconstruct our understanding of social goods and cooperation from this perspective, we get a different conception of and argument for welfare than those justifying either the safety net (residual) or the social control (behaviorist) model.

If we agree that the care of dependents is basic to any society and that the care should be provided without treating persons unjustly, and that a nonfungible relation between a dependent and a caretaker is the most desirable arrangement,[37] then an ethical justification of welfare, and indeed of the welfare state, is to support dependency relations. The purpose of welfare needs to be at once to care for dependents and to mitigate the costs to dependency workers for their participation in the dependency relation. But to be politically viable, this welfare must not be restricted to the poor but extended to cover dependency work more generally.

As we look for a way to bring a care ethic to the public arena, the contemporary version of social housekeeping, we need both a conception of social goods and a notion of social cooperation that acknowledges dependencies and the need for care and employs the notion of reciprocation appropriate to a situation where one member of the relation is incapable of reciprocating. Such a concept of social cooperation I call *doulia,* adopting a term that derives from the Greek word for a service,[38] and which I have adapted from the name of type of caregiver, the *doula,* who assists the postpartum woman. In a public conception of doulia (service), we acknowledge the social responsibility to care for the caretaker.

Some families within the United States have traditionally availed themselves of a paid care provider, the baby nurse, who displaces the mother by taking over care of the infant. The doula, instead, assists by caring for the mother as the mother attends to the child (Aronow 1993). The newborn's needs and the mother's somewhat depleted physical and emotional energy call for one such as the doula to help.

We are each implicated in a set of dependency relations at some point in our lives, either as the one who needs care, as one called upon to care, or as one responsible for obtaining care for another. We may reciprocate the caring we received by ourselves caring for the same person or by seeing that this person is cared for. But we also may reciprocate by assuring care for still another individual who must depend on us in the way we depended on another. This sort of reciprocity is captured in the colloquial phrase: "What goes round, comes round."[39] This notion of reciprocity and fairness is not dyadic; it involves at least a third party,[40] and even an infinite spiral of relationships that reaches both into our past and looks toward future generations. It calls for a collective, social responsibility for care that extends the notion of service provided by the doula to a public conception of care.

We can articulate a principle of doulia: "Just as we have required care to survive and thrive, so we need to provide conditions that allow others—including those who do the work of caring—to receive the care they need to survive and thrive" (Kittay 1996, 233). We are all some mother's child. We all have been deemed worthy of another's care (see Kittay 1999). The caretaker is herself some mother's child, herself worthy of care. Only when the larger society assumes its obligation to attend to the well being of the caretaker can the caretaker fulfill responsibilities to the dependent without being subject to exploitation, which some have called compulsory altruism (Taylor-Gooby 1991 cited in Orloff 1993a).

A Vision of Welfare Based on Doulia

Robert Goodin (1988) writes that the justification for the welfare state is, ultimately, an ethical one, namely to address the needs of dependents. His argument is that "those who depend on particular others for satisfaction of their basic needs are rendered, by that dependency, susceptible to exploitation by those upon whom they depend. It is the risk of exploitation of such dependencies that justifies public provision—and public provision of a distinctively welfare state form—of those basic needs" (1988: 121). Much can be said for understanding welfare as the protection of the vulnerable. I, however, have argued that the vulnerability in need of protection is not only the dependent who is disadvantaged by age, illness, or disability.[41] A just welfare state needs to counter the vulnerability of the dependency worker as well. The concept of doulia justifies the welfare extended to the solo mother, and this justification can be more broadly implemented. Not only must welfare be extended to impoverished solo mothers, but it should be extended to all dependency workers, on a model that moves away from residualism toward the universalistic models of social insurance and populism.

What sort of welfare policy would be suggested by a principle of doulia? Before pursuing the specifics, a couple of concerns need to be raised. First, who is properly in the position to speak for the policy needs of the dependency worker and the dependent? Second, should we base policies on a dependency relation where the charge is utterly dependent—the model I have largely discussed?

Whose Voice?

Doulia is a principle by which the caregiver is enabled to care for herself as well as her charge. Similarly, the dependency worker's job is to enable the charge to function to the full extent of her capabilities. Therefore, the principle of doulia itself dictates that the provisions of welfare must be determined with the participation of both the dependency worker and the dependent. To the extent that either can speak for themselves, they are the ones to do so. That is, both the dependent and the dependency worker themselves must be involved in what Fraser (1990) has called "the struggle over needs interpretation." The feminist theorist and advocate must be careful not to follow the model of the invasive baby nurse rather than the assisting doula. Nonetheless, because the dependent may not be (fully) capable of political speech and dependency work does partially deprive the dependency worker of political voice, interventions are crucial.

Partial Dependencies

It may seem that the relationship between caregiver and care receiver that I have sketched is unduly asymmetric and so a flawed model upon which to base policy. Frequently, we are in relationships where another is dependent on us, and where we are equally or only somewhat less dependent on the other. Two adults, each of whom is ill or incapacitated, may be reciprocally dependent in this way; for example, two aging spouses; a couple with AIDS; two disabled adults who live together; an aging mother who requires some assistance from a daughter, but who is, nevertheless, capable to baby-sit her daughter's children; and so forth. These relations are at least as, and perhaps more, frequent than the case of the fully capable adult who cares for a fully dependent child or adult. More frequent still are the cases where we provide care for someone who is not fully dependent—the school-aged child; the young teenager; a weakened, but not fully incapacitated, elder parent; a disabled child or adult who can, with only some assistance, function well in ordinary situations of school or work.

I have discussed the more stark case of full dependency because I wish to highlight a particular structure of obligation and reciprocity that pertains to the case of dependency, where the party who is assisted is not in a position to reciprocate. It is clear that a newborn cannot reciprocate—she cannot say "Mom, take a break. I'll cook up a meal for us while you take a nap." The fully dependent individual may or may not be able to reciprocate later in his or her life. The obligation to that fully dependent individual sits nested within the scope of responsibilities of the person to whom she is most vulnerable—whether a parent, an adult child, a friend, a paid dependency worker. But, I have urged, the vulnerabilities created by the care of a fully vulnerable person creates a set of obligations which, in turn, sits nested within the scope of responsibilities of another to whom the dependency worker is most vulnerable. This may be, again, a familial relationship, or it may be institutional relationship. Eventually, the responsibility spills out to the larger social order of which the dependent and dependency worker are a part. The taxpayer pays for social programs that reimburse families and dependents; the citizen obligates the state to assure rights and responsibilities to see that care is adequately provided and compensated. This is the conception that provides a theoretical framework which can receive specification through explicit programs and policies.

In the case of lesser degrees of dependency, this structure of reciprocation and obligation is retained, though modified to the extent that the relationship assumes the character of equal, independent individuals. The greater the dependency of the charge, the more fully does the dependency worker need support and provision reciprocated by the provider. The greater the dependency of the charge, the more embedded is the relationship of dependency in the nested dependency that radiates outward to society at large. The less total the dependency, the more the dependent is capable of reciprocating, the more insulated is the relationship from wider circles of dependency and reciprocation. Where there is inevitable dependence, even when partial, the dependent individual, by definition, will not be able to fully reciprocate. An implication of a public conception of doulia is that what the dependent cannot reciprocate should be supplied through public provision. Another implication is that public provision should be used to enable the dependent individual to realize the full extent of her capabilities and reciprocate to the degree that she is able.

Such ramifications of a public principle of care for partial dependency can be illustrated by two types of cases. First, consider a pair of ailing elderly spouses. One has a crippling arthritis that especially prevents her from functioning well on certain days. The other has developed severely impaired vision, though she can see well enough to be fully capable within her house or a familiar environment, but is unable to maneuver a less predictable environment without assistance. The reader can construct various sorts of reciprocal arrangements that such a couple can work out to allow them to live relatively independently as a team. But there will be situations, perhaps just on certain days, in which one partner will either be severely taxed in attending to the other or both partners will fail to have important needs met. It is at such times that the principle of doulia applies, and it falls to the larger social structure of which the couple is a part to provide assistance and relief.

Another sort of case is illustrated by considering a disabled individual who can function largely independently of assistance, as long as the social and physical environment do not provide undue obstacles. Consider an adult who is paraplegic and who requires the use of a wheelchair for mobility and some assistance in some daily tasks of living. Given a nondiscriminatory social environment, a properly accessible physical environment, and the assistance of a personal attendant, that person is fully capable of being employed and maintaining herself. According to the conception of doulia that I am sketching, at least some, if not the full cost, of what she requires to maintain herself should be supplied through public funds, including the salary of the personal assistant. Invoking the principle of doulia, we can say that such a partially dependent person, one who needs assistance dressing and taking care of important life functions, has both every right to the care and is not directly obligated to reciprocate those services (by full payment for a personal attendant, for example). To the degree she can operate independently, she is obliged to engage in reciprocity of the usual sort (by, for example, paying taxes).[42] A third type of case is presented by the mother of a growing child. As a fully able child grows and matures, she has reciprocal obligations to her caretakers in proportion to maturation. The mother taking care of children under five years old is in a different position of need than one caring for school-aged children and adolescents.[43] To the extent that her children continue to need her care and supervision, even though they may be able to fend for themselves to varying degrees, the mother remains a dependency worker who is still handicapped relative to the unencumbered individual who has no such responsibilities. These added responsibilities continue to make her vulnerable to exploitation and intrusion from employers, as well as unscrupulous or abusive lovers/boyfriends/spouses, and continue to disadvantage her in a competitive workplace. It is here that the principle of doulia would dictate that the mother has a right to a supplemental income predicated on the persisting need her dependents have of her and/or services which allow her to discharge her duties as a dependency worker while she is otherwise employed.

In short, the dependency worker is entitled to support to the degree that dependency work would impede her ability to function in a manner equivalent to fully functioning, unencumbered adults. Anything below this benchmark leaves her open to exploitation.

Dependency Work is Work

With the above considerations in mind, let us discuss what welfare policies may be entailed by the concept of doulia.[44] Central to a revised conception of welfare based on a public ethic of care is the recognition that all dependency work is a social contribution that requires reciprocation, not by the cared for but by a larger social circle in which the dependency relation is embedded. Such goods and reciprocation can be recognized in a number of ways.

As I have already noted, the traditional family, with its breadwinner and caretaker, forms one such embedding nest, at least for the care of young children. Because it does, many conservatives, but also some liberals, have seen the two-parent family as the best solution to welfare dependency.[45] Is it? Let us presume the viability of the traditional family—ignore for the moment the social forces that have hammered away at it and at the questionable justice of its gendered division of labor. Let us imagine a family form and an economy in which one breadwinner can produce income sufficient to support a couple of children, as well as another spouse who does the domestic labor and caring work, and let us suppose that this family is not governed by traditional gender divisions of labor. The dependency worker cares for the dependents; the breadwinner, whom we will also call the private provider supports the dependency relation with resources sufficient to maintain all. This is then a private arrangement that presumably calls upon no additional social supports and so is self-sufficient.[46]

There are at least three problems with this analysis. The first is conceptual, the second is economic, and the third is ethical and a matter of justice. First, it is a mystification to speak of such a structure as self-sufficient. Although dependency work results in the dependency worker's derived dependency, all employment involves some dependency. The provider is dependent on an employer, and still more significantly, dependent on an economy in which her or his skills, services, or products are marketable. The waged worker, that is, is him/herself in nested dependencies—dependent on an employer, who is dependent on a market and on a particular configuration of economic structures and forces (such as interest rates, global competition, and so forth). A private provider does not lend self-sufficiency to the dependence relation, because this self-sufficiency is a conceptual chimera in a capitalist economy. The appropriate contrast between a dependency worker and other workers is not between those who are self-reliant and those who are dependent, but between those whose labor results in some types of vulnerabilities rather than others.[47]

Second, an economically self-reliant provider/caretaker model requires sufficient compensation to support a family. The fact of structural unemployment, as we all know, means that not all providers can find employment, especially employment adequate to support a family. The poverty rates among families with two adults present indicate that having a sole provider is a goal that eludes many families.[48] In most two-parent families the wife has primary responsibility for domestic work and dependency work, but also holds down a job, often part-time, almost always not paying as well as her husband's. The pure provider-caretaker model has been hybridized. The change comes partly from women's aspirations and partly from economic necessity, because the average weekly inflation-adjusted earnings have declined 19 percent between 1973 and 1996 (U. S. Department of Labor, Bureau of Labor Statistics).

Dependency work and provision can be so divided that each of two partners engage in each of the two forms of labor and relationship. But more often, even the hybridized model follows many of the same structural features as the pure model.[49] The hybridized dependency worker continues to assume primary responsibility for dependents and remains largely (though not totally) dependent on the income of the hybridized breadwinner partner. If the marriage falls apart, the financial suffering falls largely to the one who remains largely responsible for dependency work.

Third, as I have suggested earlier, the work of dependency care disadvantages the dependency worker with respect to her (or his) exit options if the relationship with the breadwinner becomes fragile. Orloff has argued that the social right of citizenship for women involves economic independence from men and the capacity to form and sustain autonomous families. Social citizenship for women then means a guarantee of the right to care for her children and other vulnerable dependents without having to be economically dependent on a man. Her vulnerability to the good graces of the private provider means that she has what Sen (1989) terms a disadvantage of bargaining power in relations of cooperative conflict. This handicap is a source of the myriad injustices that pervade the intimate relations of family life, and consequently deprive woman of the social citizenship that the welfare state affords the male worker by "decommodifying" his labor (Orloff 1993a, 319). The consequences of cooperative conflict and economic dependency on an individual man are aggravated by women's subordinate position in the larger society, that is, by the likelihood that she will receive a smaller paycheck, that she is susceptible to sexual intimidation on the job, and so forth. But the injustices of intimate life, particularly when one is responsible for the well-being of a dependent continue (albeit to a lesser degree), even if many of the public injustices are corrected. Furthermore, even if dependency work is not gendered, the disadvantage in cooperative conflicts such as the family would itself be a consequence of dependency work on a private provider model.

Policy Directions

This means that a just reciprocation for dependency work could not presume the so-called private arrangement of the traditional breadwinner-caretaker model—or even the hybridized model—and urges universalizing benefits for dependency work. Just as workers' compensation and unemployment insurance became programs that were universally available to workers, with benefits rationalized and routinized (and extended without stigma), so must compensation for dependency work (Waerness 1987).

I can envision a payment for dependency work, which can be used to compensate a mother for her time caring for her child or allow her to use the money to pay for daycare. Alternatively, it can provide money for a son or daughter to care for an ailing parent or pay someone else to perform the service. The level of reciprocation, furthermore, must allow the dependency worker not only to survive, but also to have the resources to care for the dependent as well as herself. For both herself and her charge, she needs health coverage (as all workers and all dependents should get) and certain in-kind services or goods or monetary equivalent, such as housing.

The conception of doulia respects not only the nature of dependency, but also the caretaker as a worker. Like other workers, they need vacations, exit options, retraining when they are no longer needed at their present employment. And like all work, dependency work must be degendered, in fact, not only in name. This suggests public education programs for dependency work, especially for young boys and men.

Workers, however, usually are accountable to those who pay their wages. One problem with having public support for dependency work is that when the state pays for the labor of caring for one's own children, or one's aging parents, then, arguably, the state can claim the right to oversee the quality of work and the input of the worker. Such intrusion into the private domain runs counter to much liberal thought. Can we justifiably say to the state, "be the 'public' provider, be the one who pays the dependency worker her salary, but then (except, of course, when the dependency worker violates the trust of her charge and begins to be abusive or negligent) stay out of the 'private' dependency relation"? As feminists, we cannot reply that putting the matter this way (either no public support intrusion into family life or no public support and state surveillance of family affairs) may rely too much on an untenable dichotomy of the public and private. For state oversight of personal relations, except to protect against abuse and the perpetuation of sexist oppression, runs counter to most feminist as well as liberal aims.

I believe the understanding of social cooperation inherent in the concept of doulia can resolve our dilemma. Ordinary concepts of reciprocation dictate that if I provide you with a product or a service, you compensate me for the product or the labor I poured into that product or service. Lines of accountability follow the lines of reciprocation. If you do not pay me, I do not receive the benefits for which I labored, and I hold you accountable, and it is my right to do so. If you pay me, but I do not deliver the goods, you do not receive the benefits for which you paid, and you hold me accountable and now, it is your right to do so. There is no third party affected by the transaction; each party is accountable to the other, except the state may have a duty to insure that both parties honor their agreements.

Unlike most standard cases of employment, the labor of the dependency worker is foremost to benefit the dependent, not the provider. A provider other than the beneficiary compensates the labor primarily because the charge cannot. Being a provider, then, is not the same as being a employer, one to whom I, as a worker am responsible. I am primarily accountable to the direct beneficiary of my actions, that is, to my charge. Just as any other worker, I have a right to demand compensation for my labor. Because the dependent, virtually by definition, is not in a position to compensate, the compensation comes from another source, for example, the provider. The right to demand that the work be well done, however, is the right of the dependent. Whether or not it is a provider, the state has the duty to see that the dependent is not neglected or abused. In the case of a party as vulnerable as the charge that obligation is a special trust, one which derives not from a state's role as a provider, but from the state's normal duty to protect its citizenry. Such a duty is not an open ticket to intrude upon intimate or caring relationships or to regulate the life of the dependency worker. The state's responsibility as a public provider is derived from its responsibility to make available to all its citizens the bases for full membership in the community. The duty of the public provider leaves in place all citizens' rights against undue state intrusion.[50]

Adequate public support of dependency work, then, would significantly alter the dependency workers' bargaining position, making both them and their charges better able to respond to abuse within the family and less subject to intrusive state regulation. Even the miserly AFDC program was primarily a boon to women with children escaping abusive relations. A welfare program that universalizes compensation for dependency work (whether or not another able adult was present in the home) would allow women to leave abusive relations without the stigma of current welfare participation.

Within our own society, dependency workers—paid or unpaid—are generally poorer than others. Paid dependency workers, such as child-care workers, are the most poorly paid workers relative to their level of education and skill (Hartman and Pearce 1989). In hospitals and nursing homes, orderlies and aids, those who do most of the hands-on dependency care of patients and clients, are the lowest paid staff. Female-headed households account for the poorest families in the United States. Doulia requires that dependency work that is currently paid work be well paid. It is not enough that women be able to have affordable childcare. We are not adhering to a principle of doulia when we exploit other women who care for our children.

And finally, a concept of doulia would be accepting of any family form in which dependency work is adequately realized. It would not privilege any particular family form, but would honor different arrangements in which dependency needs were met—not only the heterosexual couple with children but also a gay or lesbian couple with an adopted child; an adult child caring for an elderly parent; a gay man tending to his partner with AIDS; a lesbian woman raising her lover's children, and caring for her lover, through a bout of breast cancer; a single-parent household with an adult disabled child; or variously related adults living and raising children together. A concept of doulia only recognizes need grounded in inevitable dependency and vulnerabilities arising from the responsiveness to such needs. This is not to say that specificity of sexualities, race, class, age, ability, and gender are not importantly called into play in the interpretation of need and the best ways to respond. So again, how the need is defined and how it is to be satisfied is something that must be negotiated by those in the dependency relation. A concept of doulia then, also must give voice to those who are caring and being cared for.[51]

Underlying the debate over AFDC has been the question of the visibility and the social responsibility for the dependency work of women. By keeping responsibility private, poor women will stay poor, and those not poor will be impoverished if they try to raise families without male support. As feminist researchers have pointed out, "in all industrialized Western countries, welfare—tending to children, the elderly, the sick and disabled—is largely provided in private households by women without pay, rather than by states, markets, and voluntary non-profit organizations: all Western welfare states depend upon this care" (Orloff 1993a, 313). This means that women share the vulnerability associated with this work. The category of dependency worker, however, is not simply another universal among women. It is a category in which the interests of women of different race or class can be turned against each other. White women benefit from the dependency work of women of color; wealthy women benefit from the dependency work of poorer women, and so forth. Glenn points to the difficulties that await an effort to unite women around issues of care. She writes:

> With the move into the labor force of all races and classes of women, it is tempting to think that we can find unity around the common problems of 'working women.' With that in mind, feminist policy makers have called for expanding services to assist employed mothers in such areas as child care and elderly care. We need to ask, Who is going to do the work? Who will benefit from increased services? The historical record suggests that it will be done by women of color . . . and that it will be middle-class women who will receive the services. (1992, 36)

Applying this scenario to the needs of employed middle-class women and regulations insisting that women on welfare find employment, Glenn (1992) wryly points out that the apparent coincidence of interest comes apart when one recognizes that at current wages, childcare work will not suffice to bring the welfare mother out of poverty, and if wages are raised, the middle-class woman will not be able to afford the less-advantaged women's services. Feminism will come apart unless women think and speak together about forging policies that will benefit both sets of women and will lessen the increasing disparity between them.

The call for a concept of doulia and universal policies is not to smooth over these difficult issues between women with different interests and from different races and classes, nor to reinstate universalism as if none of identity politics, postmodernism, and race critical theories mattered. The call for universal policies is not universalism. Universal policies do not suppose that we are alike in some designated characteristic. They only presume that if anyone has access to a resource that is deemed to be a social good and a requisite for full membership within a community, each should have access to such a resource solely by virtue of their membership within a given community.

As I indicated earlier, universal policies have had their critics. They have been criticized as not sufficiently redistributive and as benefiting most those who need them least. But universal policies that are formed from the perspective of the least well off and formed to serve their needs first are less likely to be deficient in this respect than other universal schemes. A good model is provided by the case of disability. Ramps and modified sidewalks meant to serve the disabled, but available for all to use, have benefited many populations for whom they were not envisioned without diminishing their usefulness to the disabled.

The universal policies advocated on a conception of doulia, derive from the need that women have to function as full citizens in a post-industrial world. Unless dependency work comes to be more equitably distributed and compensated, women will continue to be exploited by paid or familial dependency work. By beginning with the needs of the poorest and most stigmatized, we can find our way to meeting the needs of many more without sacrificing those of the women most defeated and neglected.

Notes

1. Among these writers are some women who do not view welfare as a predominately women's issue. Some of these writers also emphasize race. Examples of the works I have in mind include Jencks (1992); Marmor, et al. (1990); Gutman (1988).
2. Tillmon was a welfare mother and National Welfare Rights Organization leader. She spoke of welfare as "a supersexist marriage" in which we trade in "a" man for "the" man. (1976, 356)
3. Many of these feminist writers see welfare in terms of both gender and race. For some examples of these analyses see Abramovitz (1996); Sassoon (1987); Skocpol (1992); Gordon (1990b, 1994b); Mink (1995).
4. Delivered at the Teach-In on Welfare at SUNY Stony Brook, Stony Brook, N. Y., March 1997.
5. Diana Pearce put this point in this fashion at a panel on women and welfare at Yale University, May 1995. I borrow my formulation from her.
6. According to a report from the Center on Budget and Policy Priorities, *Despite Economic Recovery, Poverty and Income Trends Are Disappointing* (Washington, D.C.: Center on Budget and Policy Priorities, October 1994) in 1993, 37.4 percent of the nation's poor were women over eighteen years of age, 40 percent were children.
7. In fact, the victims of social circumstances frequently blame themselves especially harshly in an environment of equal opportunity rhetoric. See Bartky (1990, 30.)
8. This is a remark I have heard repeatedly from women who consider themselves liberal and feminists. One officer of the NOW Legal and Educational Defense Fund remarked that she had rarely seen so much negative mail and threats to withdraw support as when the organization took up the fight against the family cap provision of state welfare plans. The family cap provision prohibits the use of public assistance for any child born while the mother was receiving welfare. The very availability and legality of contraception and abortion, victories of feminism, make the situation of those women who do not or cannot avail themselves of these reproductive means more precarious still. They now are blamed for their condition not only by conservatives, but by many liberals as well.
9. Few notions are as sexist and unjust: a child is made to suffer for the actions of its parents, and the stigma attaches itself to the woman and the children she has borne outside of marriage, but not to the man who sired these children.
10. A recent study released by the McCormack Institute and the Center for Survey Research

(both at the University of Massachusetts, Boston), found that among a representative sample of the Massachusetts Transitional Aid to Families with Dependent Children (T.A.F.D.C.) caseload, 65 percent would be considered victims of domestic violence by a current or former boyfriend or husband using Massachusetts state law definition of abuse.

11. Although it is also arguable that, especially as legislators have in mind women of color, they are also concerned with the withdrawal of the labor of these women from the low-wage service industries. As Jacqueline Jones (1985) so vividly documents, black women, in contrast to white women, have always been viewed as workers from the time of slavery through Reconstruction and Jim Crow. The impact of this fact on welfare legislation is discussed in Abramovitz (1996) and especially in Mink (1990).

12. It is important to point out that the empirical facts do not support claims that welfare payments to impoverished women with children influenced the incidence of single-parent households, never wed mothers, mothers having additional children while on welfare, or teenage-age pregnancy. See Center on Hunger, Poverty, and Nutrition Policy, 1995.

13. See Orloff (this volume) for a discussion of the relation between ideology and differing welfare state provisions, especially with respect to the issue of race and U. S. policy.

14. For the notion of women's social citizenship see, for example, Piven (1985); Siim (1988); Pateman (1989a); Gordon (1990b); Orloff (1993a, this volume); Skocpol (1992).

15. As economic independence is understood as a good for all citizens, women's right to such a good cannot be questioned. That women should have a right to form and sustain autonomous families does not immediately follow from the types of rights usually presumed for citizens of a liberal democracy or even a social democracy. While such a right seems to me to be exactly what is necessary, the question is whether it can be justified on grounds acceptable to those who also accept the premises of a liberal/social democracy and whether it can serve as a justification for welfare. This argument is not made in Orloff's (1993a) excellent article. Instead, she argues that since social citizenship is understood as desirable, and decommodification is a gendered condition of social citizenship, more apt for men then women, we need to find a condition that corresponds to the lives led mostly by women. This is an argument that can motivate feminists, but one still needs to show that the corresponding condition disadvantages women unfairly—that is, that it amounts to an inequitable distribution of the benefits and burdens of social cooperation between men and women, that this condition benefits the larger social group while simultaneously disadvantaging women. That is the point of the argument in this section of the paper. See also Orloff, this volume.

16. See Van Parijs (1995). Also note the demand of the Welfare Rights Movement of the 1960s for a guaranteed annual income.

17. See Kornbluh (1998), "History of the Welfare Rights Movement . . . " for a discussion of the demand for consumer rights of credit by the women of the National Welfare Rights Organization and their action against Sears Department Stores.

18. For an excellent discussion of how the term independent came to be associated with wage labor and dependent became attached to those who were excluded from wage labor see Fraser and Gordon (1994b). They point to three groups that epitomized a dependent status: paupers, slaves, and women. As they narrate the semantics of dependency, children, the disabled, and the frail elderly do not figure in the primary use of the term.

19. See Marmor et al. (1990) for a discussion of the distinctions between social insurance, residualist, behaviorist, and populist welfare policies.

20. Although redistribution is not the goal of social insurance policies, they too redistribute wealth, since what is received as a benefit by a participant normally exceeds what is paid in by that individual.

21. Although behaviorism makes explicit the view that poverty is the fault of those who are impoverished, residualism as practiced in the United States today, makes such an assumption implicit by the treatment of its beneficiaries.

22. See Fraser and Gordon (1994b) who argue that dependency, which in preindustrial times was seen as a structural social feature, has in industrial society and still more strikingly in postindustrial society come to be seen as a character feature of the poor who rely on public assistance, and poverty itself is viewed as a character flaw.

23. Even as the Left tries to protect residualist programs from being eviscerated, the target of the Right is broader. Many programs such as social security, progressive taxation, and even public education are targets. I want to argue that by restricting a defense of welfare to residualism, especially with respect to welfare's impact on women, supporters of the welfare state may lose the opportunity to respond adequately to both the narrow and the broad attack.

24. That is what is implied in the question "Where are the jobs?" to which the welfare dependents are to turn in their newly forged (and forced) independency. Within this debate, the welfare recipient is gendered male and the self-respect sapping dependency of the unemployed worker—it is his needs that are at issue. Shortly after the passage of the welfare reform bill, the cover of the Sunday *New York Times Magazine* featured an essay by Harvard sociologist William Julius Wilson, author of *When Work Disappears: The World of the New Urban Poor*. The photograph showed a group of black men standing on an urban ghetto block, seemingly unemployed. The problem of work and welfare was pictured as distinctly black, urban, and male.

25. The years preceding the passage of the bill instituting AFDC saw the entrance of large numbers of black women. The black woman in the United States, not being accorded the white woman's privileges and expectations of family life (Jones 1985; Spillers 1987) was for a long time considered employable and so not deserving of welfare benefits. With the emergence of the Civil Rights movement in the 1950s and 1960s and the mobilization of the National Welfare Rights Organization, many black women gained access to public assistance. But Abramovitz points out, that even as late as 1966, "many states refused assistance to black women if their eligibility for AFDC interfered with local labor market demands" (1996, 333).

26. In the words of the 1937 Committee on Economic Security, it was "designed to release from the wage-earning role the person whose natural function is to give her children the physical and affectionate guardianship necessary not only to keep them from falling into social misfortune, but more affirmatively to make them citizens capable of contributing to society" (Cited in Abramovitz [1996, 313]). The 1962 amendments to the Social Security Act allowed fathers who were unemployed to receive aid and permitted states to require work in exchange for benefits (Abramovitz 1996, 333). However, as Abramovitz points out, the debates in Congress concerning workfare suggested that there was "general ambivalence" about having women be forced to find employment rather than care for their children. Efforts to tie welfare and working for benefits were tried repeatedly from 1962 onward, but the full-scale overhaul of the model was only accomplished in August 1996. We need to recognize that the declarations of 1937 and the debates of 1962 are scarcely conceivable today, when nearly half of the women with children of preschool age are in the workforce. See also Mink (1998).

27. When, as in our recent past, the aged constituted the majority of the poor, our nation looked for solutions that were adapted to that population. The solution, arrived at in the 1970s, was not to force every able-bodied elderly person to get a job, but to tag Social Security benefits to inflation and to secure medical benefits for the elderly (Marmor, et al., 1990).

28. Feminist scholars have documented the influence of women in constituting the welfare state in the United States (both as beneficiaries and as social workers and administrators of the welfare system) and in drafting the policy that was to become AFDC (Fraser, 1990; Nelson, 1990; Sapiro, 1990; Gordon, 1994b).

29. Along with establishing a Children's Bureau within the executive branch of government, the Sheppard-Towner Act, and Mother's Pensions, they were also responsible for legislation which monitored mothers' sexuality, reviewed the women's housekeeping standards, and intervened in feeding and rearing habits and customs retained from the Old World. They were also responsible for labor legislation, which protected women from some of the abuses of employers but also reduced the earning capabilities of low-income women—the income of the very mothers they were meant to help. Because the benefits provided by Mother's Pensions were kept very low, it was difficult for the families to survive without women's (and children's) supplemental wage labor, labor made less accessible to them by the protective labor laws. Gwendolyn Mink writes: "The fruits of maternalist social policy research were policies designed to improve motherhood through cultural reform. The beneficiary of these policies was the child, the conduit her mother, the social goal the fully Americanized child" (1995, 27).

30. It also resonates with efforts to question the fixity of the public-private divide. Both facets emerge in the suggestive use of Daniel Bell's term, the public household, (Bell 1976) by feminist theorist Michele Moody-Adams (1997). She points to social policy "that seeks to use public power and the vast resources of the public household to legislate against certain behavior rather than to provide positive social support that might help prevent the behavior in the first place" (12). Although she argues that such "reactive" policies are inimical to the viability of truly liberal democratic institutions, I propose elsewhere (Kittay 1996) that the principles of liberalism, as articulated by John Rawls, for example, are not adequate grounds for what both Moody-Adams and I agree are the more positive policies implied by the notion of the public household. Developing a basis for arguing for positive policies such as socially responsible family policy is the purpose of what follows. For a helpful way of conceiving care in the public domain that is not maternalistic in this negative sense, see Tronto (1993) and in this volume.

31. See Greene (1976) for a discussion of the importance that independence and manhood had in the minds of the signers of the Declaration of Independence and in the U.S. Constitution when they considered who was created equal. Also see Young (1995) and Kittay (1996).

32. Note that I am discussing the support needed to do the actual work of dependency care. But one can have responsibilities for the care of dependents that result in having to do dependency work because one has another sort of support, namely childcare, eldercare, flexible work hours, paid family leave, and so forth.

33. See Handler (1987) who shows the inadequacy of these models for dependents and dependency workers alike. He discusses these models with respect to medical care, special education for the mentally retarded, and care for the elderly. Handler takes a communitarian approach to meeting needs of dependents.

34. See Adams and Winston (1980, 88–99) for a comparative study of welfare and family assistance in the different economic systems of the United States, Sweden, and China.

35. See MacIntyre (1999) for an argument that virtue theory can incorporate the importance of caring for dependents and that it needs to do so.

36. For an argument that this moral capacity is not reducible or included within Rawls's other two moral powers, see Kittay (1996, 237). Also see Schwarzenbach (1986).

37. The dependency relation is necessary because the ethical obligation to tend to and be responsive to someone who is significantly dependent is best discharged when that responsibility is held by a relatively small group of persons. When many persons are all held equally responsible at any given time, the dispersed responsibility is generally accompanied by a diffused attention. The needs of the dependent are more easily missed, as everyone can easily assume that another is watching and responding (See Goodin 1985). Furthermore, much good dependency work depends on the ongoing nature of a relationship, which means that dependency workers are not fungible workers. These points are more fully elaborated and argued for in Kittay (1999).

38. I wish to thank Elfie Raymond for helping me search for a term with the resonance necessary to capture the concept articulated here.

39. The importance of this ethic within the African-American community is documented in Stack (1974).

40. Thanks to Anita Silvers for this formulation.

41. In Schmidtz and Goodin (1997), a later work, Goodin takes these matters into account. His is a superb defense of the notion of collective responsibility against those who maintain the primacy of personal responsibility.

42. It should also be noted that over one-third of the AFDC population (34.5%) consisted of women who either cared for a disabled child (8.4%), a disabled adult (7.0%), or had a disability severe enough to limit their employability (19.1%) (Adler 1993).

43. One indication of this is revealed in an IWPR study of time use over a two-year period of single mothers who were receiving AFDC. The major import of their study was that most of the time was spent either engaged in wage work, looking for jobs, or studying as well as caring for children. However, they also found that 40 percent of the time spent on AFDC during the two-year study was spent caring for children under five years of age, compared with 4 percent for children between 6 and 12 years of age (in the summer months). As most of the women studied, even those with the youngest children, packaged work and welfare, this finding does not reflect the hours children spent in childcare (Spalter-Roth 1995).

44. Fraser (1997) has listed a number of criteria by which to evaluate proposals for the welfare state. The criteria are guided by an ideal of gender parity. I invite the reader to consider the proposals put forward here in terms of these criteria.

45. See, for example, Etzione et al. (1998), Galston (1998), and Popenoe (1996).

46. This is close to the vision articulated by the 1996 vice-presidential candidate Jack Kemp in one of the vice-presidential debates. He envisioned an economy that could support a family with one breadwinner and one stay-at-home parent, although he was quick to add that the stay-at-home parent would not have to be the woman! It is interesting to have the ideal of the family wage, a concept fought for by the left in this country, re-emerge as a proposition by the right, at the same time when they are legislating the entrance of women (usually without male support) on welfare, even those raising children as young as two years of age, into the labor force for a minimum wage.

47. Orloff (1993a) points out that one way of characterizing the difference between welfare

programs geared to men and those targeted at women is that the former are meant to shield the citizen against the worst effects of market failures, while the latter are meant to shield against familial failures. In this respect, it is important to see that when the benefits are intended to deal with familial failures, it is the fate of the children rather than the adult women which is most likely to have public sympathy. Women again come to be seen as conduits rather than as persons and citizens in their own right.

48. According to the *Current Population Survey* of March 1994, 9 percent of married couples were poor, while single mothers comprised 46 percent of the poor; of all poor families 12 percent had at least one year-round, full-time worker and 32 percent had at least one member who worked at least thirty weeks during the year. These figures are based on a rate of poverty that all experts agree are set too low.

49. Why this is so is an interesting sociological question. It is also interesting to contemplate the possibilities for gender equity within the family if such an arrangement within the home is coupled with genuine gender equity in the public domain of paid employment and political and social power. In spite of all of women's advances, this remains a utopian vision whose possibility of realization remains in the realm of speculation.

50. Furthermore, where the provider is not privatized and individualized as it is in families, the dependency worker has an option that is available to other workers, and that is to organize. This does not mean that the dependency worker take the option of strikes—walking out on dependents. They have, however, available mobilization strategies used by other politically organized groups. The model of the National Welfare Rights Organization is perhaps useful here.

51. Since this essay was first composed, a group of activists and feminist scholars, of which the author is a member, have put together a proposal intended to change the discourse around welfare, especially in light of the 2002 expiration date for TANF, when it must be reapproved to continue to be law. The document, "An Immodest Proposal: Rewarding Women's Work to End Poverty" is available on the Web site: http://www.welfare2002.org.

Three

*Home is the place where, when you have to go there
They have to take you in.*

—*Robert Frost*

Joan C. Tronto

Who Cares? Public and Private Caring and the Rethinking of Citizenship

As welfare states cut spending on social services, they draw upon some widely held but unstated assumptions about the nature of care and of human nature to buttress their views. Insofar as individuals strive to be independent of others, government largesse causes dependency, which is harmful. Insofar as care is intensely personal, it has been easy for states to slide toward the presumption that care is also intensely private. As existing tropes for good caring continue to presume an autonomous and willful care receiver, the image of bureaucratic or inadequate caring joins the parade of horribles against which neoliberals posit an ideal of free choice.[1]

Neoliberals presume that the free market will always step in to fulfill whatever human needs exist. In reality, though, few people have been paying attention to where the burden of caring work actually falls. To draw the analogy with Marx's argument in "On the Jewish Question": just as the liberal state freed itself from the burdens of religion when it abolished religious qualifications for citizenship, so too the neoliberal state frees itself from the burden of recognizing who now does the various forms of caring work as the state reduces services.

Privatizing care is an insidious way to reduce the state's level of accountability for its citizens' welfare. Citizens have, for the most part, failed to act politically in the face of such policies. Feminists, especially, have been caught in an interesting dilemma. On the one hand, many feminists have tried to stop the onslaught of neoliberal arguments. They have carried out a rearguard action to defend welfare programs that they previously found hopelessly inadequate. On the other hand, feminists have been reluctant to argue for a maternalist understanding of the welfare state and of their role in it (Cruikshank 1994). Because women have been for so long described and confined by the boundaries of the private sphere of care and by maternal and related images of women as selfless care providers, meeting neoliberal arguments with demands for greater support for domestic care seems reactionary at best. As it is presented, then, this dilemma forces feminist thinkers to choose between two unsavory providers for the care that people need in their lives: bureaucracy or family. Failing to accept either of those two choices, neoliberals have blithely assumed that the answer lies in a third way: the free market.

As with most dilemmas, the best way to resist this one is to escape from the bifurcated choices that it seems to present. The neoliberal arguments and the feminist responses to them both presume a model of care that is no longer viable and a model of the citizen that is out of date. In this chapter, I will argue that for citizens in welfare states to fare well, we must recognize that all citizens in the welfare state, men as well as women, rich and powerful individuals as well as poorly paid and disregarded care providers, are profoundly engaged in activities of care. Indeed, I will argue that we need to redefine our conception of citizenship and with it, the boundaries between public and private life, to include caring as a fundamental aspect of human life.[2]

Rethinking Citizenship, Rethinking Families
Citizens

Models of citizenship define the boundaries between public and private life and determine which activities, attitudes, possessions, and so forth are to be considered worthy in any given state.[3] Citizenship shapes our most deeply held values about justice and fairness and guides our view of what good citizens in our society should do. Models of citizenship also include an implicit account of what citizens are like before they come to the public arena. States exclude children and others who have not been thought to have achieved majority from active citizenship. Previously, property ownership or appropriate military weaponry was a condition for citizenship. Such inclusion and exclusion are not only a reflection of norms and values, though; citizenship reflects winners and losers in the political game with the highest stakes: who has a voice that counts when policy is discussed.

Societies conceive of citizens in terms of the contributions that they make to the society. Historically, citizens have been conceived as warriors, as burgher-merchants, as farmers, as artisans (Isin 1997). It is instructive, perhaps, to recall here the Aristotelian model of the citizen as one who participates in public life, but whose actual conditions of life presuppose a separate realm of existence in which economic activity and the work of care go on (see, among others, Stiehm

1984; compare Yak 1993). Thus, the Aristotelian citizen floats his citizenship on previously accomplished work that is beneath the observance of political institutions but nonetheless is essential for his life.

The set of presumptions for citizenship changes with models of citizenship. Whereas property was once conceived as a necessary prerequisite for independence and thus for citizenship, that model of the citizen no longer exists (compare Isin 1997). As many astute observers have noted, the conception of the welfare state that informs postwar life presumes a particular model of citizens (e.g., Pateman 1988b; Culpitt 1992; Bussemaker and Kersbergen 1994; Lister 1997). This discourse on citizenship in welfare states has followed the lead of T. H. Marshall in identifying citizens primarily as workers (see, among others, Marshall 1992 [1950]). What this model fails to see, however, is that workers require care to remain capable of work; this care work is an invisible prerequisite for worker-citizens.

Assumptions about workers abound; for example, there is an assumption that citizens live in a nuclear family characterized by heterosexual marriage for purposes of procreation and intimacy. In this model, the division of household labor consists of a male breadwinner whose productive labor allows him to bring home a paycheck and a female supporter who converts the raw material of paychecks into clean clothes, prepared food, a cozy home, and other forms of care through her reproductive labor (compare Weinbaum and Bridges 1979; Schwarzenbach 1996). These rigid gender roles and the family structure persist intact for most of the adult lifespan; as children mature, they are expected to form their own nuclear family units, thus reproducing the pattern. As Marshall (1992 [1950]) observed, this model presumes that the citizen is a worker.

This separation of public and private life was, at the time and in the framework that Marshall wrote, deeply gendered (at least ideologically; he ignored women's role during war economies). Because men and women are almost equal in number in society, and given the norm of heterosexual marriage, most households consisted of men who worked and women who cared. This model of the household is no longer viable.[4] The second wave of feminism has, as one of its most profound consequences, increased the participation of women in the paid labor force (United Nations Development Programme, 1995). Although the increase has not been as dramatic in all industrialized welfare states, in most the model of citizens as workers with care workers depending upon them is no longer accurate.

Yet, as more women work in the paid labor force, they are caught in a double bind, working a second shift (Hochschild 1989) in which they must do both their caring work and paid work outside the household. Although men are beginning, albeit slowly, to contribute to work within the household, their efforts most often target the best and most worthy jobs, leaving much of the tedious, time-consuming, and organizing tasks to women.

Many welfare programs in the twentieth century can be understood as replacing either the earnings of, or actual person of, the breadwinner male (compare Sarvasy 1992; Ostner 1994; Saraceno 1994). Thus, just as housewives were dependent on husbands, so too recipients of state programs are perceived as dependent on state allocations and, in this way, not fully citizens.

Nevertheless, even in the context of citizen-as-breadwinner, the model of the autonomous household did not work. The need for professional assistance in care has grown dramatically in the latter half of the twentieth century. Strides in healthcare have allowed for a highly technical process of medicalized care. Because families have become more geographically dispersed, wisdom passed from generation to generation about such subjects as childcare has become eviscerated, and various professional caregivers have taken its place.

In the past two decades, these trends have accelerated. Children of working parents require daycare. In societies such as the United States where suburbs have sprouted and spread without adequate systems of public transportation, family caregivers must serve as chauffeurs. The range of caring activities has grown. Care includes not only the direct work of hands-on caring within the nuclear family's household; it also includes the caring work now delegated to the market in the form of hired labor to do household chores, prepare food, clean clothing, and so forth.

Marshall's account of the citizen-worker was drawn deliberately to emphasize the possibility for social cohesion within a society in which workers could expect their work to count as a contribution.[5] Nevertheless, another way of looking at the struggle for citizenship recognition is to view it as the outcome of a political struggle in which the expanded definition of citizenship is a result of a political process in which demands for inclusion are finally recognized. People become citizens when they can make claims that require political recognition.

Families

Where did families fit into this model? As many feminist scholars have noted, this image of a citizen-worker presumed a family that consisted of a breadwinner and his dependent wife and children (see, among others, Bussemaker and Kersbergen 1994). Even as a model, this image of the citizen did not describe every family in the immediate postwar era and it was not considered the ideal among all people in advanced welfare states. Nevertheless, in the past fifty years, this model of family life has become increasingly mythic in most welfare states.

In the first place, families have disintegrated. Divorce rates are high. More children are being born out of wedlock. Fewer people are marrying, and fewer women are having children. People are living longer, to an age of frailty, and the traditional system of care and support provided by the heterosexual, child-raising family unit is no longer sufficient. Fewer than half of American households currently contain children under the age of eighteen. About one fourth of all U.S. households now consist of a single person living alone (see, e.g., Day 1996).

In the second place, the feminist revolution has broken the caste system that kept the majority of middle-class women out of the full-time workforce. When norms kept middle-class married women from working, or at least constrained their employment to roles with work schedules suitable to motherhood, family care was presumed to be automatic. Now, more women work and the United States is among the leaders of industrial countries where increasing numbers of wives and mothers work. The result is that many women now work, and so the automatic assumptions about who provides care can no longer be taken for granted. As women engage in paid labor, they do not necessarily surrender their roles as primary care givers. What does happen, though, is that they no longer have any leisure.

In the third place, the uncontested image of the family as best caregiver has come under serious attack (compare Omolade 1994). Of course, many people in families do their best; many parents sacrifice for children and children for parents, many siblings support one another through youth and adulthood. Nevertheless, there is a dark side to such care as well. The modern nuclear family has turned out to be a realm of great inequality, danger, and unhappiness. Whether we consider data about levels of sexual abuse and physical violence, the number of adults who report that they would rather not be cared for by family members, or the norm of independence and not being a burden that informs the ways of life of many elderly people, many indicators suggest that the relentlessly nuclear family implodes upon itself. It may be that children need other sources of power outside their parents. It may be that the burdens of parenting are just too great. It may be that the vaunted decline in birthrates that comes with modernization is a sign of failure, not success.

Despite any other significance this decline portends, it is clear that it changes the family's caring role fundamentally. To presume that adult children will take care of aging parents, that mothers will take care of children, that spouses will take care of their spouses sent home early from the hospital, creates burdens of care that many people cannot or will not assume. Increasingly, a gap has widened between the ideological construction of home as "haven in the heartless world" and the reality of what it is like for everyone when someone has to return home and be taken in. The small number of relationships involved in most American nuclear families cannot bear the burdens placed upon them by expectations for material and personal satisfaction; by physical needs for food, clothing, and shelter; by the absence of viable forms of social support that range from adequate public transportation to safe public spaces such as neighborhood parks in which children play.[6]

And these burdens are not distributed equally among family members. The data overwhelmingly show that girls, women, daughters, sisters, and wives bear the burdens of caring for children, elder parents, and spouses. In light of these realities, the finding of the British sociologist Janet Finch (1996) is perhaps not so extraordinary: in asking people about their experiences of care, she discovered that no consensus exists about what are the proper levels of caring for other adults in one's family. Clare Ungerson (1997) has observed that relying on family members for care creates tensions for individuals as they try to determine whether to pay for such services. From these observations about families, I draw two conclusions: (a) humans need more care than they want or expect to receive from or give to their families, (b) we are at an interesting historical moment when great change may occur.

In writing about the growth of social movements, Frances Fox Piven and Richard Cloward (following Marx) observed that "[f]or a protest movement to arise out of these traumas of daily life, people have to perceive the deprivation and disorganization they experience as both wrong, and subject to redress" (1977, 12). Political change is only possible if the stresses of contemporary life seem to have an identifiable cause. A political discussion about the changing nature of citizenship brings forth a number of possibilities within which to develop a framework for understanding these existing and coming changes. The current framework presumes that the citizen is a person who works and contributes to society primarily though economic production. Work entitles citizens to certain kinds of state benefits that repay the citizen for his contributions to the state. The reproduction of citizens depends upon the existence of families that can convert workers' pay and state benefits into the care that humans need to survive. The boundary between public and private life is drawn at the entry into the family. The activities of care (except when they are understood simply as another fungible form of work) are beyond the concerns of the state. Yet, as many feminist critics have noted, this model of the citizen-worker is not yet a model that includes everyone as a citizen. People excluded from the paid work force, either because of caste-like exclusions, because the economy is not able to absorb a surplus population, or because of the continuation of traditional ways of life (breadwinner/homemaker models) are not fully citizens. And economic status distinguishes, by this model, between more and less worthy citizens.

Is there a way to conceptualize citizens so that their lives outside of work and engagement in all of the other meaningful activities of daily life might count as part of what it means to be a citizen? I believe so, and offer this modest proposal: let us think of citizens as engaged in a citizenship act when they are engaged in processes of care. This will transform the way that we think about public and private life and change the prospects for progressive politics.

A Modest Proposal: Citizens as Carer
Defining Care

Imagine a world in which care is given its rightful place as a central human activity.[7] Berenice Fisher and I have defined care broadly as

> "a species activity that includes everything that we do to maintain, continue, and repair our 'world' so that we can live in it as well as possible. That world includes our bodies, our selves, and our environment, all of which we seek to interweave in a complex, life-sustaining web" (1990, 40).

This account of care sees care as an activity in which humans engage to the end of living well in the world. While it is not the only activity in which humans engage, care is a large part of our lives, and often activities that are pursued for other ends have caring dimensions within them. Care is not only a physical process of performing chores, though; it is also a way of thinking and a kind of approach that people use (see Ruddick 1990 on how care is a practice).

Many people are disturbed by the breadth of this definition of care and the fact that it refers to activities and attitudes directed at the self, significant others, and distant others (see, e.g., Sevenhuijsen 1998, 23, n. 9). Yet, the point in pulling together all of these seemingly disparate activities, attitudes, and virtues into one conceptual framework is to reveal something else: how thoroughly all of these aspects of human life have been shoved off the central stage and into the background. As Val Plumwood (1993) has noted in her brilliant analysis of the nature of "backgrounding" as one of the elements of dualistic thinking, when some aspect of life has been backgrounded we might take this as a first step toward thinking through the relationship of the backgrounded piece of life to the foregrounded aspects. Plumwood notes that the purpose of dualistic thinking is to diminish an element of life that is essential but inconvenient within the foregrounded framework. So, we might ask, why have thinkers worked so hard to keep care in the background?

Care calls into question precisely what is at heart in the contemporary image of the citizen (and, for that matter, the citizen throughout most of the Western political tradition). If humans need care, then that fact belies the presupposition of the rational, autonomous individual. To acknowledge the existence of care and its central place in human life requires that we also acknowledge the following:

- Humans each have a history in which they have been highly dependent and in which they are all vulnerable to being dependent again.
- Humans have roles, obligations, and senses of attachment to others in the fulfillment of their needs.
- Humans have needs that (from the perspective of this rational, autonomous, individual) interfere with people's abilities to accomplish their "life projects" or ends (compare Rawls 1971 and Walker 1999).

This care perspective, then, sees human nature differently than does our familiar social/political/moral framework. To think in terms of care is not, however, to think romantically: care inevitably involves questions of conflict, inadequate resources, unattainable ends, and disputes over how to achieve care in a pluralistic way (Tronto 1996). Still, the modest proposal that I would like to suggest is that we conceive of citizens as carers, that is, as people engaged in processes of care, both as givers of care and receivers of care. In this way, my modest proposal intends to go further than Trudie Knijn and Monique Kremer's account of inclusive citizenship (1997a). Their account does not unseat the image of worker-citizen but adds that citizens need care and need time to care. I am proposing something more radical, then, a view in which citizens' activities are no longer conceived only in terms of their economic productivity or their military contribution. Instead, citizens make contributions to the state through the caring work that they do. Care work should become a fundamental criterion for determining citizenship.

Some Illustrations

Suppose that workers are forbidden from working more than twenty hours a week at paid labor so that they may attend to their caring responsibilities.[8] Or, imagine that the United States genuinely is a meritocracy which awards positions on the basis of genuine ability. But ability is always relative to an understanding of citizenship. Hence, in the United States today, certain citizens gain extra merit through the performance of special citizenship duties. Extra points on civil service exams are currently awarded for military service; suppose that we so valued care. Then, we might award extra points in college entrance examinations for applicants who had taken care of children, parents, neighbors, spouses, or extra social security payments for childcare workers, or bonus pay for launderers.

Although much of the care work in our society (paid and unpaid) is currently done by women, it is also important to note how much of that work is also reserved for people of lower class status and/or for those in racial groups designated as other than white. To accept this model of merit for care would change radically how we distribute goods and value in our society. And we can take this distinction one point further. As the Norwegian sociologist Kari Waerness (1990b) has noted, not all care is the same: she distinguishes three categories. Some care is necessary care, in which people who receive care are themselves incapable of providing that care for themselves. Some necessary care requires special training, for example, providing medical assistance; other forms of necessary care require little extra training or skill, for example, to help frail elderly people go to the store. Some care is spontaneously necessary (you are out of town, your car breaks down, and someone stops to help). Other care, which Waerness calls personal service, involves care that one could do for oneself, but because it is distasteful, tedious, and so forth, one hires someone else to do it. In a society that valued care, there might be penalties for using too much personal service care, or people might receive greater amounts of merit for engaging in necessary or spontaneous care.

This is a thought experiment, not a public policy pronouncement, but do note how it changes our conceptions of what is valuable and what should receive which kinds of reward in society. In the first place, to notice all of the caring work that supports the autonomous actor belies his or her lack of dependence. Calling attention to all such caring work allows us to see more clearly how policies, markets, and individuals currently place value on various forms of care. We might notice, for example, how the caring work of some is undervalued in order to bolster the economic productivity of others. Within this thought experiment, the child who decides to ignore a sick relative to study will not necessarily end up in a better position than one who helps others. The value of being only self-regarding is undone by this model of citizenship as engagement in activities of care (compare Waerness 1984).

This illustration suggests how much we would have to change our framework. It also suggests that some questions would become central to our political analysis. The following are examples of questions that would become crucial to resolve publicly:

1. In the first instance, care depends upon the way in which a given society defines needs. What caring needs exist is a question asked prior to the questions of who cares for whom. Much contemporary philosophical discourse about distributive justice can probably be understood in terms of this question. Having determined what constitutes needs, distributions are then made based on needs.

2. Another question concerns the shape of power and privilege in a situation of care. I have argued that those with greater power and privilege in society are able to exert their power and to display their privilege by being care demanders.[9]

3. It is essential, in discussing care, to raise the moral problem of otherness. Care receivers and caregivers often perceive one another with suspicion and with a tendency to transform some into others. Differing positions of power and privilege create presumptions about people's differences that can be quickly solidified into categories of otherness. The process of transforming "an other" into "the other" is a complex psychological process, but it is not only or entirely a rational one. Indeed, on a rational, abstract basis, people may deny that they are treating others as other, although they are. As a result, when one person or group transforms some person or group into the

other, they must also structure into their lives an ignorance of the other (see, among others, Mills 1997). Uncovering such ignorance and labeling it as a moral failure rather than simply a lack of knowledge involves guilt and shame. Hence, to delve into questions of otherness inevitably involves looking at the interaction of emotions and reason.

"Interdependence" and Responsibility

My illustrations also make clear that rewarding care would require a change in our views of human nature. With what, however, should this model of the autonomous actor be replaced? Feminist scholars have long advocated a position in which the image of independence associated with the rational autonomous actor is replaced with a model of the interdependent people. In this framework, the fact that people need and give care to others across their lives replaces the narrower construct of a fully developed and capable adult. In this alternative vision, humans exist as children, as old people, as people who are sometimes disabled, and as people who are interwoven into the networks of care to support themselves and these others.

One large part of this paradigm shift, however, is to see care responsibilities as collective responsibilities and not as individual ones. Furthermore, though, such a change can only occur through a political process, not through a social process. While these premises sound much too abstract, in concrete terms they take us back to the crises over family mentioned earlier. For example, children are future citizens, but decisions about whether to have children are made in the most private way. The decision of an upper-middle-class woman to have only one child or perhaps two at the most is very much shaped by her sense of the costs to both herself and her family and her career. She is likely to react with great anger, then, to decisions that others make to have more children. Insofar as we think of children as a responsibility of individual families, then it makes sense to conduct a cost-benefit analysis of how much children cost. On the other hand, we will have to think differently about children if we understand them as citizens toward whom all other citizens have responsibilities. That the process has to be political is necessary to reconstruct the costs of choices that women and men in different work and class settings perceive differently. One solution to such conditions might be to limit the number of work hours for everyone; another solution would be to provide family allowance benefits.[10]

Reconceiving the Welfare State as a Caring State

What would it require to stop thinking of citizens primarily as workers with unacknowledged family roles? It would require that we rethink the nature of care, the nature of households, and the role of citizens. There are several areas where such rethinking must occur.

Institutions

What institutions are the best ones for care? There are at least three mechanisms for care in our culture: bureaucratic or other large-scale institutions (whether public or private), the market, and the family/household (Fisher and Tronto 1990). Were care held in higher public regard, we might have a more systematic political discussion about what institutions are best able to do which kind of caring work. But if we start from the fact that people's needs for care are different and that people have different ideas about the best ways in which their needs can be met, it is probably the case that we would, in a good society, provide citizens with a variety of choices. Within professional institutions of care, we might insist upon greater levels of accountability. Within the market, we might want to create some regulations to prevent exorbitant pricing, and so forth. Though the family is often assumed the proper institution for caring, there are many problems with families as institutions for care.

Institutionalized care is the response to the growth of new needs as care moves from the household (in recent years, organized into families) to other arrangements. Until a few years ago, as many have noted (Tronto 1996; see also Jenson 1997), care was hardly theorized at all. It is important to realize, though, that leaving all of the unmarked, untheorized, undescribed care in the household was part of an intellectual framework that saw the head of the household as the main participant in the outside world (compare Pateman 1988b). As women and workers demanded their inclusion in political life, the process of defamilization was the other side of the same coin. This process accelerated in the last century during the growth of welfare states, and feminist scholars such as Ruth Lister (1995) and Jane Lewis (1997) now argue that it is useful to use defamilization to analyze welfare states from a gendered perspective (see also Knijn and Ungerson 1997b). Yet, I propose that we need to think of defamilization not only as an analytical category, but also as a human process that we can control (compare Marcuse 1971). To rethink defamilization will require that we rethink citizenship fundamentally (Lister 1995). Trudie Knijn and Monica Kremer (1997a) have argued in a recent article in *Social Politics*: solving the dilemmas of defamilization is the logical completion of the long historical arguments made by women for inclusion.

Feminists have not been too eager to embrace "defamilization" as a goal for feminism. Jean Bethke Elshtain (1982) attacked feminists for being against the family and opening a rift within second wave feminism in the United States. This argument soon became a key turning point against the popularity of feminist arguments. If feminists are going to work out a more adequate vision for future family life, then they need to conceptualize defamilization not as a passive social process over which they (and others) have no control. A first step to a more adequate feminist theory of the family requires that feminists think about the value of family care. Before we lament what we have lost, we should ask what it is we are losing. Once we have an answer to that question, we are able to look more closely at the current processes that are at work.

In speaking of family care as a model for human caring, we need to distinguish the myth from the reality. Despite the view of academics that the family has changed throughout history, within the culture of the United States, family appears as a natural phenomenon. Family care is naturalized so that the family appears not to be an institution at all. There is no political discussion of the role of the family when it is natural. The process of naturalization is another way to leave things unnamed and voices silenced (compare Pateman 1988b; Gullette 1997).

Before dismissing this natural family, though, it is useful to ask: what makes family care so desirable? First, family care seems somewhat automatic. In fact, it rests upon clearly understood lines of power and obligation: children and parents, spouses, aunts and uncles, servants know what they owe others. Second, family care is highly particularistic: each family evolves its own ways of doing certain things. Part of the pleasure in being cared for by a family member is that he or she understands your peculiarities, likes and dislikes, and particular needs. Third (at least since the family ceased to be primarily a unit of production, in which one's relation was also that of producers to one another), care in the family has a clear purpose: it is taken to be an expression of love.

Given that the family as an institution seemed to focus so well on people's needs, it is not surprising that there is a great deal of nostalgia for its old forms. Despite these benefits, though, nostalgia for old forms of family care misses an important point: changes in family care are not only about the disappearance of family care but are about the increasing complexity of modern care. Until professional health structures grew, for example, people expected to live and die in their homes. Until antibiotics, death was often caused by fast-moving infections as well as by long-term chronic illness. And until recently, children of the working class were expected not to be educated but to become workers and often at a very early age. The field, mine, or workhouse, served as daycare.

Leaving aside our sentimental views of the family, the challenge we face is: can institutions be similarly arranged so that they provide the same elements of care that the family ideally provided? I will suggest that the same three elements can be present, but not in the same way. The beauty of relationships in the mythic, glorified family past was that they need not be discussed, but rather were taken for granted. In any other institution, aspects of care within the institution need to be worked out consciously. This does not make these elements less achievable, but it does mean that they become more visible. Whether this conscientiousness is a heavy burden, or perhaps the opening-point of biopower's new ethics (compare Foucault 1986), a postmodern care of the self remains an open question. In fact, I would argue that the need to foreground relations and practices of care are likely to raise many important ethical and political questions that are worth our serious attention.

These three elements, then, are (a) a clear account of power in the care relationship and, thus a recognition of the need for a politics of care at every level; (b) a way for care to remain particularistic and pluralistic; and (c) for care to have clear, defined, acceptable purposes. These three elements stand us in good stead in evaluating how institutions meet the caring needs of citizens. These elements also spell out what it would take to think adequately about care as the basis of citizenship.

Rights

If we look at care not from the standpoint of the institutions of care but from the standpoint of the individuals engaged in caring work, the radical potential of this proposal becomes clearer. I am suggesting that we conceive of people engaged in care as citizens on that basis. Such a notion obviously makes citizenship a universal category and requires us to rethink what it might mean to assert a citizenship right.

There are at least two ways in which rights might be an appropriate vocabulary within which to have the discussion of care. In the first place, we might extend our definition of social rights to mean that individuals have a right to receive care. In the second place, we might want to note that in addition to a right to care, we might also want to describe a right not to care. As Janet Finch (1996) has argued, people not only need care, they also need the opportunity not to care. If people feel forced to care, then they are engaged in these processes not by choice but out of some sense of hardly articulated obligation. As Finch points out,

> I have no doubt that some people will see it as a view that undermines the importance of the family but I would argue that it is precisely the opposite. In seeking to remove external pressures on what is given and received within families, I would argue that our fellow-citizens would thereby be given greater freedom to develop, in ways that they themselves have chosen, those relationships that are personally satisfying. (1996, 208)

Therefore, any conception of a right to care must also forgive any particular individuals from any particular obligation to care (compare Hirschmann 1996a). This points to the problem of caregiving subsidies as the proper form for welfare state policies, as Nancy Fraser (1994) has observed (see also Knijn and Kremer 1997a).

The important point to make about rights and care is that it is possible to continue to believe that people have rights to be cared for in some manner. Prejudging that family members should be the first to provide such care constrains their lives and continues to restrict women more than men (compare Fraser 1994). Different people will make different choices about whom they would prefer to provide them with care and in what settings; people will make different choices about what caring work they prefer to do. A society that places sufficient value on care itself will allow many alternatives for such caring while at the same time guaranteeing that some minimal level of care will be provided when and if necessary.

The Value of the Caring State

Every prior account of citizenship established some people as worthy of citizenship but required that others labor to care for, and create the conditions for, that person's citizenship. When we understand how all humans are engaged in caring processes, then to make caring the precondition for citizenship expands our conception of citizens. In the end, the reason to think about citizens as carers is that it allows us to end the exclusionary conceptions of citizenship that have prevailed to the present. This conceptualization turns the neoliberal position on its head. Rather than solving all public dilemmas of welfare provision by transforming them back into private dilemmas, it makes private dilemmas about the adequacy of care into public dilemmas.

I argue that there are a number of advantages, both for conceptual clarity and for political strategy, of adding the metaphor of citizens as carers to our usual ways of perceiving citizens.

Public/Private and the Politics of Needs Interpretation

To make an activity a mark of citizenship is to imply that it is public and not just private. One of the restrictions that has traditionally displaced care from our central human concerns is the view that care is private (compare Tronto 1993, chap. 1; 1996). One criticism of the view presented here, that care is among the activities of a citizen, is that to admit caring into citizenship requires the abolition of the public/private split.[11] This criticism rests upon a false notion about the ways that public and private are now both implicated in the ways that we think about citizenship. Not all citizenship activities are entirely public even if they are not entirely private. The traditional notion of the citizen-soldier presumed that the citizen came prepared for soldierly duties: that may even have included providing one's own weapons, armor, horse, or other implements (and thus also excluded some from participating as citizens, due to this inequality of private resources). And while the citizen-worker makes public contributions through his or her work, the worker usually works for a private company. That some citizenship activities are partly private and partly public may actually accord better with the way in which caring already cuts across public and private life.

In reality, the nature of caring activities has changed substantially in recent decades. Just as economic production was once limited to the household and is no longer, so too in industrialized states the activities of care are no longer limited to the household. This is true whether we describe highly professionalized aspects of care (such as medical care) or fairly nonprofessional forms of care (such as cooking, cleaning, washing laundry, etc.). In thinking about these aspects of life as more public—that is, resolved outside of the household—does not require that there should be state regulation of them though, in fact, state regulation increases as these aspects of life become more regularized and professionalized. Because this process is already ongoing, to recognize and to be able to speak clearly about the nature of these changes gives us an important vantage point from which to engage in these activities. Furthermore, the process of determining needs themselves is always a political process, "the politics of needs interpretation" (Fraser 1989a). As is obvious from the preceding discussions and given the complexity of care, care can only be done well if there are sufficient "rhetorical spaces" (Code 1995) in all of the possibly affected institutions so that an open and honest discussion can proceed.[12] Because all citizens require care and need to be involved in the processes of needs interpretation, we might eventually arrive at a point in which, through the exploration of the infinite varieties of needs, it is possible to argue for universal human dignity or equality out of such concrete differences rather than out of an abstractly held principle.[13]

Questioning the Gender Regime of Welfare States

The other point worth observing is that in changing the nexus between care and household, we open a possibility for changing the automatic associations of care with those who have traditionally been in the household: women, servants, and those who are confined (either because they are too young or too infirm or too old, etc.) to the household. There are many advantages of broadening our perspective of carers to include everyone. In the first case, it allows us to pursue questions of responsibility for care more broadly. In the second case, it allows us to explore the dimensions of power and privilege along care lines more distinctively: who is able to command the care of others and who not? (Waerness 1990b). Perhaps most significant, it allows us to insist that caring is a process involving both caregivers and care receivers. In describing care receivers as citizens as they receive care, rather than as dependents, invalids, wards, we open the possibilities to restore proper forms of human agency and dignity to ourselves as receivers of necessary care. Too often, recipients of care are viewed simply as passive objects of the activities of others. Nevertheless, care receiving is also a kind of activity: one can do it well or badly, engage in other pursuits while one receives care, show gratitude or not, and so forth. All humans engage in care receiving, whether they acknowledge it or not. In a society in which accomplishment is stressed, care receiving is usually placed in the background, if not even feared and despised. To look closely at such activity and to endow it with its own accounts of practices and virtues adds to our knowledge of what it means to live a fully human life.

Additional Advantages for Feminist Politics

From another perspective, thinking of citizenship as caring work has important implications for feminist politics. As Sibyl Schwarzenbach (1996) has argued in her account of civic friendship, to make a realm of life that has largely been women's and make it part of the activity of the commonweal is to provide a deeper way to value women's lives. Another advantage of thinking from the standpoint of citizens as carers, is that it eliminates a common mistake in contemporary understandings of feminist argument. Once we recognize all citizens as engaged in caring, then the issues of care cease to be misinterpreted as elements of cultural feminism: a simple glorification of the traditional female or feminine.

But most important, thinking of caring activities as part of our citizenship activities also opens the ground for redescribing what feminist politics have accomplished, what feminist politics have not accomplished, and where the conflicts among feminists have been and persist. This point would require another chapter of its own, but let me just provide one or two examples: to some extent, one of the great accomplishments of the women's movement has been to free women from almost caste-like restrictions about professions: and many of the professions that were widely open to women were primarily caring professions.[14] This has meant a shift in the ways that many caring professions are staffed: some of these changes are for the good, others are not so good. Another example: as more women have begun to work outside the household, new conflicts arise among women (and often along class and/or race lines) about the provision for childcare and its cost, quality, and so forth. Raising these discussions to public attention will result in their more adequate resolution.

A Disadvantage? Reconceptualizing Public and Private

There is an obvious disadvantage to thinking of care as part of citizenship. To some extent, there is a great advantage in being able to think of care as private rather than as a kind of public activity.[15] The danger in making care too much a part of the public realm and discourse is that it opens it up to the possibility of being overly controlled, in a Foucauldian way, by the processes of professionalization, bureaucratization, and so forth. There is a danger that instead of making more public decisions and matters that are now private, such ways of thinking of care as private will instead come to dominate public life.[16]

While it is possible to blame feminist privatized ways of thinking for such intrusions of private matters into public life, to do so ignores the fact that such processes of control are underway and would not stop or disappear if feminists no longer tried to understand them. On the contrary, the best way to change undesirable social processes is to highlight how they work and to bring political pressure to transform them into directions that are more desirable. In this case, to reopen the public discussion about what is public and what is private, what we owe to others in our society and what we do not would create the possibilities for basic political change.

Rethinking the Welfare State

Part of the great accomplishment of the neoliberal state has been to make us accept the thinking that to be a citizen is to be a consumer of state goods. No less a commentator on the nature of citizenship in the social welfare state than T. H. Marshall made this point when he tried to suggest that the welfare state must wean citizens from social rights and convert them to a concern with civil rights instead. T. H. Marshall[17] described the model of seeing citizens as holders of social rights (i.e., as people who make claims on the state by asserting a right to social welfare benefits) as ultimately disempowering:

> As for social rights—the rights to welfare in the broadest sense of the term—they are not designed for the exercise of power at all. They reflect, as I pointed out many years ago, the strong individualist element in mass society, but it refers to individuals as consumers, not as actors. There is little that consumers can do except imitate Oliver Twist and "ask for more," and the influence politicians can exert over the public by promising to give it is generally greater than the influence of citizens—or those who care about these things—can exercise over politicians by demanding it. (1981, 141)

Yet, we may well ask, what civil rights are of interest to citizens in Marshall's state? On the one hand, we might think of the civil rights of democratic participation, both within the political order and within the economic arena of union or other worker-involved policy. Interestingly enough, these activities have also been squeezed into the disempowering pose of the consumer. (This is true whether we are describing the transformation of political campaigns into advertising campaigns or the kind of soft tyrannies in companies that call minimum wage workers associates and manage them to keep them satisfied.) As long as we conceive of the state as an institution that provides for people's needs, then we are left thinking of the state as the actor in social and political life and as citizens as passive recipients of the state's largesse. The neoliberal critique of the state's ability to perform caring tasks has flowed from this framework. To view the state as supporting people's activities of care, however, restores people as the actors who engage in care. Once this conception of the citizen changes, much else can change as well.

Allowing the political order to recognize the key dimensions of human life that are part of the ethic of care provides an opportunity for genuinely inclusive citizenship. Humans are not only soldiers or workers—they are also children and sick people, people who are vulnerable and facing death. Only a political order that allows all people to have a role is genuinely inclusive. The neoliberal thinking prevalent today continues to ignore the reality of people's lives. As long as those who are in power are relatively unaffected by the dilemmas of everyday life, they are unlikely to change. It is time for those of us who care about caring to transform our private virtue into a public demand.

Notes

1. See Michael Ignatieff (1985), whose concern that the needs of strangers will demand that we distort the state into trying to be compassionate, thus ruining both the state and genuine compassion.
2. Several important scholars have addressed the need for a feminist redefinition of citizenship, and I have benefited greatly from their work. See, among others, Sarvasy (1992); Vogel (1994); Knijn and Kremer (1997); Lister (1997); Sevenhuijsen (1998).
3. There is a huge and burgeoning literature on this topic of citizenship. See, among others, Vogel (1994); the new journal *Citizenship Studies* (1997–); Turner (1997); Lister (1997).
4. For a parallel argument that sees the problem in a related way (not in terms of household structure but in terms of an existing gender regime), see Fraser (1994).
5. Interestingly enough, Marshall (1992) set some conditions for the adequate functioning of citizen-workers: he suggested that there had to be a uniform culture for citizens.
6. It is in light of these devaluations of the household that I read Arlie Hochschild's discovery (1997) that people are beginning to find relief in their workplaces that perhaps used to be reserved for the household.
7. There is much literature by feminists on the ethic of care. Significant thinkers from whose work I have learned a great deal, see, among others, Finch and Groves (1983); Waerness (1984). Ruddick (1990); Ungerson (1990); Sarvasy (1992); Held (1993, 1995); Manschot and Verkerk (1994); Bubeck (1995); Hekman (1995); Sevenhuijsen (1998). See also Jaggar (1995) for a review essay on care in ethical theory.
8. Several thinkers have made such a proposal: see Folbre (1994); Hochschild (1997). In France, to solve problems of unemployment, a maximum cap on hours worked has been created; whether and what effect this thirty-five hours of work a week rule will have on caring is not yet clear.
9. See Tronto (1993), chapters 4 and 6. See also, among others, Colen (1985); Gregson and Lowe (1994).
10. As this example suggests, to talk about care is to demolish the notion that all women share identical or common interests.
11. For example, Plato's arrangement of the Guardians' families in the *Republic* is surely a form of making caring into a public activity: this is not my intention.
12. Which is not so easily accomplished: cf. Bickford 1996.

13. It will require a much longer essay to make this epistemological argument; I draw inspiration for this assertion of the argument from Code (1995) and Walker (1997).
14. I deliberately have used the term *professions* rather than *occupations* here. Note the class advantage that is conveyed.
15. Compare Patricia Boling's (1996) useful assessment of the nature of privacy .
16. This argument was made most powerfully by Mary Dietz (1985) when she argued that maternal thinking is by its nature privatized and outside of the scope of decisions that are properly political. I have several responses to Dietz's argument. In the first place, Dietz assumes that someone engaged in maternal thinking is incapable of making discerning judgments that distinguish between different levels and types of care. I believe that the much richer account of care that I have presented here answers this objection. In the second place, while I share profoundly Dietz's commitment to public reason, surely in the past dozen years we have seen the kind of public commitment that she would endorse almost entirely disappear from public life in the United States. It might be seen as somewhat disingenuous for me to suggest, but does the current drawing of the boundary between public and private life really protect public-minded thinking?
17. Sheila Blackburn (1995) has made the suggestion that feminist critics of the welfare state need to be more attentive to the logic and arguments of the Beveridge Report; I have not done so here but her warning is well taken.

Four

Nancy J. Hirschmann

A Question of Freedom,
A Question of Rights?
Women and Welfare

As the Personal Responsibility Act has taken hold on the concrete realities of women's lives—realities that the more empirical chapters in this volume document—it has become apparent that a classic political theory concept, namely freedom, is something that needs to be thought about.[1] This might seem a surprising statement, even esoteric (which some might snidely say is in keeping with political theory's role in political science), but on closer examination, the question of freedom has lain at the heart of the debates over welfare reform in recent years, particularly in the United States. In both Europe and the United States, welfare can, at least in theory, be seen as a series of programs developed as a resource to empower citizens, to enable them to liberate themselves from certain restrictive conditions such as poverty, unemployment, old age, poor health. In women's case in particular, welfare payments such as AFDC in the United States and maternal benefits in Europe can be seen to provide a certain degree of financial independence from individual men, particularly under scenarios of destitution after widowhood or abandonment, or the need to escape abusive marriages.[2]

Yet, scholars such as Linda Gordon (1994) and Mimi Abramowitz (1988), not to mention those in the present volume, all reveal that this liberation was always at least ambivalent, if not an outright failure, entailing many more constraints and restrictions than powers and freedoms.[3] In practice, welfare often seems more about institutionalizing social control over women than liberating them from economic destitution or empowering them to be economically independent. Feminists agree that "being on welfare" (in U.S. parlance) involves strict and intrusive scrutiny by the state over women's sexuality and mothering, as well as their participation in wage labor. Moreover, the small dollar amounts given to welfare mothers, as well as the form it frequently takes—subsidized rent in often substandard housing, food stamps rather than cash, having to work in low-grade, unskilled labor—often makes welfare extremely punitive, restricting women's options and freedom of action in many ways. Such inequities might seem to have more to do with "justice" than "freedom"; but as John Rawls (1971) perhaps unintentionally showed us, principles of freedom are central to questions of justice (Hirschmann 1992, ch. 2). And indeed, what seems "unjust" to feminists about welfare is precisely the way in which it arbitrarily restricts some people, particularly single mothers, while allowing others who receive much larger subsidies, such as corporations, a great deal of freedom.

The relevance of freedom to welfare goes beyond the immediate restrictive effects on women, however. As many of the chapters in this volume at least implicitly, if not explicitly suggest, feminists need to redefine the *framework* within which welfare discussions take place. As Ann Orloff maintains, feminists cannot "simply look at what the welfare state does for or to women. . . . Rather, gender must be incorporated into the core concepts of research on the welfare state" (1993, 306). Freedom is one such core concept, and feminist attempts to reconstruct the welfare state in more woman-friendly terms need to consider it. In this chapter, I am concerned primarily with U.S. welfare reform, because despite the view offered by this volume that welfare retrenchments are occurring throughout the modern industrialized states, no other welfare state (with the possible exception of Great Britain) has displayed the kind of elaborate ideological debates that have taken place in the United States over the past decade.[4] The relationship between this discourse, the policies that have emerged from it, and the ways in which these policies are enacted in practice, raise important questions relevant to women's freedom. In particular, the dominant discourse over welfare reform in the United States, by capturing a particular strand of freedom theory, has forced feminists into a reactive stance that not only ignores key dimensions of women's construction by and through the welfare state but also cuts off fruitful avenues for constructing an effective political strategy. The Right has particularly appropriated the internal dimensions of liberty, namely desire, will, and identity, leaving feminists to focus on the external factors, namely restraints and resources, and this bifurcation has had some negative effects. Looking at welfare through a more complex understanding of freedom can help feminists understand what is happening in welfare reform and retrenchment, and reformulate the welfare state in women-friendly ways that enhance women's freedom.

Freedom Theory and Welfare Discourse

The relationship between welfare and freedom is complicated both by the amazing ambiguity displayed in popular Western usage of the term *freedom*, and by how freedom is deployed by state actors in the welfare debates. Indeed, the political theory literature on freedom is extremely varied, ranging from a neo-Hobbesian descriptivist account of behavior to the most value-laden prescriptive account of actions.[5] But most formulations of freedom still divide along the lines offered by Isaiah Berlin (1971) of negative and positive liberty.[6] According to Berlin, what defines negative liberty is an absence of external constraints on action; if I wanted to leave the house but my husband blocked my way or broke my leg to prevent me, he would be restricting my freedom. Berlin's general notion that restraints come from outside the self, that they are "other," is an important tenet of negative liberty; other people's direct (or, in some cases, indirect) participation in "frustrating my wishes" (Berlin 1971, 123) is the relevant criterion in determining restraint. Furthermore, these desires that I must be able to pursue unimpeded if I am to be free, are seen as coming from me and from me alone. Desires may be reactions to external stimuli (smelling newly baked cookies makes me want one), but the important fact is that I can identify a desire as *mine*, regardless of why I have it (whether I am a sugar addict or simply hungry is immaterial). Negative liberty draws clear-cut lines between inner and outer, self and other, subject and object: desires come from within, restraints from without; desires are formed by subjects, by selves, they are thwarted by objects, by others.

Positive liberty challenges this dichotomy in three ways. First, it concerns itself with the positive provision of the conditions necessary to take advantage of negative liberties, such as providing wheelchair access to buildings or scholarships for education. The definition of barriers as external impediments is too narrow; for instance, freedom to education is rather hollow if you cannot get into the building or afford tuition. Taking a more contextual and communal notion of the self, positive liberty views individual conditions such as disability, as well as social conditions such as poverty, as barriers to freedom that can be overcome by positive action, or the provision of conditions the individual cannot accomplish on her own.

Second, positive liberty focuses on what might be called internal barriers: fears, addictions, compulsions, which are at odds with my true self. It therefore involves qualitative evaluation about our desires, which can be higher or lower, significant or trivial, genuine or false; it is not enough to experience an absence of external restraints because the immediate desires I have may frustrate my will. For instance, while trying to quit smoking or to combat an eating disorder, an argument with my department chair initiates a craving for a cigarette or an entire bag of Oreo cookies. Positive liberty says that if I were to give into these cravings, I would be not just weak willed but *unfree* because I am violating my true desire, on which I have reflected at length.

This understanding of desire, however, also involves the strong possibility that others may know my true will better than I, particularly when I am in the grip of these self-destructive desires: as you snatch the cigarette or Oreo from my lips, you are preserving my true self from false desires and enhancing my liberty. Often called the second guessing problem, because others claim to know what you want better than you do yourself, it is the most troubling aspect of positive liberty: determination of the will by others, and specifically by the state. The classic instance is Rousseau's general will; because laws embody the true will, he says, then by forcing me to obey the law, the state is only "forcing me to be free," that is to follow my true will whether I know it or not (1973, 177). This is the nightmare that Berlin particularly fought against, with good reason. But what Berlin and other negative liberty advocates seriously underplay is the idea of an individual having conflicting desires and a divided will. That is clearly the sentiment behind the claim that the compulsive binger or addicted smoker is unfree: I really want to quit smoking, but the stress is pushing me to cheat. Similarly, perhaps my husband broke my leg because he was trying to keep me from meeting my cocaine supplier; I've been struggling for months to kick my addiction but she called me at a particularly vulnerable point. In these cases, I want two mutually exclusive things—to smoke or binge or take drugs, and to quit—and most people would probably have to agree that quitting would be a better choice, a choice that would be more consistent with my continued freedom, and hence the choice I really prefer to make. So it is at least an open question whether the person who prevents me from doing these things impedes my liberty or enhances it.

Positive liberty's notion of a divided will leads to the third way in which it expands on negative liberty, and that is the notion of subjectivity: how is it that I have the desires I have, why do I make the choices I do? By holding that some choices are better or more liberating than others, positive liberty seeks to interrogate desire and the process of choosing. Whereas for negative liberty, choice is simply the ability to act on whatever desires I have, for positive liberty choice is a complex process of negotiation and relationship between what we commonly call internal and external factors; between will, desire, and preferences on the one hand, and forces that not only inhibit or enable the realization of such desires, but also contribute to or influence the formation of these desires on the other. In other words, positive liberty is concerned with the social construction of the choosing subject. The idea of social construction is that human beings and their world are in no sense given or natural, but the product of historical configurations of relationships. Who we are, what we want, our beliefs and values, our way of defining the world, are all shaped by the particular constellation of personal and institutional social relationships that constitute our individual and collective histories. Such contexts are what make meaning possible; and meaning makes reality.

Social construction is important to a feminist approach to freedom. Because if, as feminists have long argued, patriarchy—or the privileging and power of men as a group over women as a group—significantly characterizes the contexts in which we live, then male domination and privilege are and have been an important part of that construction; its laws, customs, rules, and norms have been imposed specifically on women by virtue of sex to restrict their opportunities, choices, actions, and behaviors. Certainly, patriarchy is not the overarching force that it was when coverture prevailed and women were legally prohibited from rights and privileges that at least Western women take for granted today, such as suffrage or education. But masculine gender privilege still exists in less overt forms in most Western societies, where the notion of welfare is applicable, and shapes many women's experiences in powerful ways. For instance, if we want to say that women are not naturally assertive in pursuing their desires, we could also say that that is because patriarchy has eroded women's confidence by allowing violence against them, by discriminating against them in pay and promotion, and ignoring them when they speak. Such a context constructs the inner self, identity, and subjectivity of women such that the internal barriers many women often experience—fear, anxiety, lack of confidence, diminished self conceptions and abilities—as well as the apparently self-defeating preferences some women express—such as loyalty to an abusive mate—can be seen to a significant degree as a result of a patriarchal construction of social relations and gendered identity (see Hirschmann 1995).

Indeed, the notion of social construction reveals that the dichotomy between internal and external implied by Berlin's counterposition of two concepts of liberty—positive and negative, equal and opposite—is itself problematic. For instance, in a society that pays women a bare subsistence subsidy for raising children, that requires them to reveal the most intimate aspects of their personal and sexual lives, and that demands that they enter the labor force even at the cost of foregoing education, that considers them cheats if they try to rise above subsistence poverty by working on the side, the self conceptions of recipients are likely to be affected, manifested by shame, powerlessness, victimization, anger, or some combination of these. But to blame welfare mothers for these self conceptions—as the dominant welfare discourse tends to do—ignores the generative source of such feelings, which are arguably reasonable responses to unreasonable situations. These factors are not just internal, but become constitutive of what women not only are allowed to do, but to be as well: how women think and conceive of ourselves, what we can and should desire, what our preferences are, our epistemology and language. Of course, this applies to men as well; the power relations of race, gender, and class, which set the parameters for what we can say and think, the alternative possibilities we can envision and, hence, what we *can* desire and how we *can* think of ourselves as choosing subjects shape both women and men's understanding of reality and the self. Because patriarchy generally privileges most men as a class over most women, however, men as a social and historical group are the primary creators and enforcers of these rules and, moreover, the rules themselves allow men more power, choice, and freedom than they do women. Welfare is an excellent example: though welfare reform impacts poor people of both genders, it is women, and particularly single mothers, who were the overt targets of reform and who, as the major recipients of AFDC, are by far affected the most by its transformation into workfare and TANF.

The example of welfare suggests that social construction is not merely a local phenomenon. That is, the social construction of welfare subjects is not the product of recent welfare discourse in and of itself, acting in a social vacuum. Rather specific local phenomena such as welfare policies develop within a larger context of gender, race, and class; broader, but no less socially constructed categories that have slowly grown, changed, and evolved for decades, even centuries, in response to changing local phenomena. In this sense, the immediate experiences of welfare participants are filtered through the light of these larger experiences and categories of meaning.

Freedom Theory and Conservative Discourse

The location of social construction's power in the interaction of local phenomena with broader social and linguistic categories is particularly apparent when we consider the debates over welfare reform that took place in the United States in the mid-1990s. Conservatives have repeatedly hammered home the argument that welfare is a dependency, an unhealthy state from which recipients should want to free themselves (see Fineman, this volume). Certainly, contemporary antipathy toward welfare, and the birth of the Republican reform movement, had its basis in the image of the Welfare Queen, which arose well before the mid-1990s; indeed it dates back to Lyndon Johnson, through Richard Nixon, and culminating in the language of race and class antagonism that the Reagan administration favored. The Welfare Queen, who is usually black and sits at home watching television while the welfare checks come pouring in, having baby after baby as a way to fill her coffers, is shiftless and lazy, but clever enough to manipulate the system and rip off taxpayers, indeed feeling an indignant sense of entitlement to being supported in her laziness by the tax dollars of hard-working (white) Americans (Painter 1992, 201–202; Albiston and Nielsen 1995). This vision has persisted, with both male and female members of Congress calling women on welfare "wolves" and "alligators" (Bussiere 1997, 167; Seccombe 1999, 11) and many, including the Clinton administration, talking in terms of a "culture of welfare" (Health and Human Services 1995).

By the 1990s debates, the image of the Welfare Queen began to intermingle with a contrasting, but no better and certainly no less stereotypical, image of the pathological dependent; maybe not everyone on welfare was evilly defrauding the government—they were merely victims of their reliance on the system. Dependency robs them of rationality so they cannot even see the mess they are in, cannot see that welfare is precisely what is keeping them down. Indeed, politicians have likened welfare to drugs, and the language of addiction has been an important subtext, if not overt theme, in antiwelfare rhetoric. This supposed pathological dependency has left welfare recipients clueless in terms of the fundamentals of living an independent life. Lacking skills, even the most rudimentary ones such as how to get up on time and how to dress for work, they are unable to obtain even the most basic minimum-wage job, let alone to keep one should they get it. Indeed, they even lack the desire to work, not only out of a sense of entitlement to other people's money—a sense that, like the drug addict's, is completely irrational and cannot be argued with—but also due to simple ignorance about how the working world operates and low self-esteem that prevents them from even trying. And they certainly do not know how to raise their children, thus deepening the outrage of subsidizing them for that purpose (see, e.g., Fineman 1991; Williams 1992). Thus, welfare is like a drug, which makes its victims unable to cope with life at its most basic and prevents them from seeing that they are addicted and from taking action to break the habit. (Indeed, in keeping with the narcotic theme, perhaps one could argue that the latter image of helpless incompetent could have emerged out of the former queen image, just as the street-smart drug dealer who sells to support his habit becomes taken over by his addiction, turning from evil manipulator to hapless victim.)

Many feminists have rebutted these stereotypical images, showing that they are based on racist as well as sexist misconceptions and pointing out that many recipients are white;[7] that most recipients generally do not stay on welfare for more than two years, and often for less time; that many already work for wages to supplement benefits or cycle between welfare and work; and that welfare is often seen as a last resort in response to a crisis situation such as divorce, a child's serious illness (because the low-wage jobs women often hold do not provide health insurance), or escape from an abusive partner (Pavetti 1992; Spalter-Roth and Hartman 1994; Hartman and Yi, this volume). Feminists have also challenged the assumption that the middle class and wealthy are independent of state support though they may receive Social Security, Medicare, and income tax deductions for home ownership, their children, or even businesses (Fraser and Gordon 1994b; Albiston and Nielsen 1995; Fineman, this volume). But these arguments have had very limited influence on the political debates and public imagination. Instead, reforms have taken a form that some of its defenders, particularly Newt Gingrich, have likened to tough love. Getting people off welfare is in their own best interest, it is in the interest of their liberty and self-respect, and the only way to do that is to force them off: family caps, workfare, and time limits will all, to borrow from Rousseau's infamous phrase, force them to be free.

Indeed, these measures resonate deeply with positive liberty, particularly its second-guessing, the notion that others can know your true will and best interests better than you do that raises the hackles of liberals and feminist alike. Perhaps in reaction to this, feminists have tended to move into the negative liberty camp. We devote most of our time and attention to the important task of pointing out how reforms take choices away from women; choices in reproductive freedom (Norplant, family caps), in pursuit of education and employment opportunities (having to stop education to take unskilled jobs),[8] in developing long-term life plans (since "work first" programs require a recipient to take any job, she is effectively prevented from trying to develop a rational career plan that offers financial remuneration and opportunities for advancement), in marrying (under so-called bridefare, married mothers may care for their children full-time, but unmarried welfare recipients must work, in an overt effort to encourage women to get and stay married [Mink 1998]) and, indeed, simply in *living* without being punished for being poor (not only the two-year limits but the push, in the meantime, to get women off welfare as quickly as possible, no matter how). Mink's labeling of the Personal Responsibility and Work Reconciliation Act (PRWORA) as "a moral straightjacket, conceived and enacted to . . . intensify the disciplinary function of social policies affecting poor women" (1998, 66) clearly articulates the notion that reforms seriously undermine women's freedom and autonomy.

Feminist efforts to reveal the punitive and restrictive character of these reforms is vital work and, obviously, must continue. Nevertheless, they reflect a primarily reactive, defensive strategy, which means that the Right still dictates the terms of the discourse. The fact that many (though not all) feminists seem to have taken a largely negative liberty perspective, focusing on the harms to women that reforms bring about, poses a challenge to feminists concerned with welfare because it has cut off important parts of the spectrum of freedom theory and pushed us into positions that may not be strategically best for women.

The concern is that underneath these important feminist arguments may lie a basically individualist impulse: women's entitlement to welfare payments is often cast as an individual right without attention to the larger issues of why it is that women are the ones who care for children. Inadequate attention is paid to how women on welfare make choices, how their choices and desires come into existence, what it is that women on welfare want, how they formulate those desires, and how they would like to see those desires fulfilled and realized (see White 1993): in short how the subjectivity of women on welfare, their identities as choosing subjects, are constructed. After all, it is not just the case that we happen to have a mean-spirited, racist, sexist legislature in office and that all feminists have to do is vote them out to fix welfare: these legislators may be all those things (but see Carroll and Casey, this volume), but they also are the expression of a social context of racism, classism, and sexism that pervade the very fundamentals of the reality that we live. At the same time, of course, they are not just innocently responding to a predetermined identity. Social construction differentiates, and yet sees the connections, between the individual sexist actions of particular individuals—the local or micro forces—and the larger, macro social structures that make those actions possible. Thus, social construction is not just a false patina over a contrary truth; in the end it will at least partially materialize its own ideology and become the truth.

Hence the so-called hard core, long-term welfare recipients, which many feminists tend to ignore and the Right tends to exaggerate, may in fact be a product of welfare as conservatives claim, neither an independent existence to which welfare is an innocent response nor a complete figment of the right-wing imagination. The Pennsylvania Department of Public Welfare, for instance, documents that of the 25,800 welfare recipients statewide who were the first to face the two-year cut-off deadline in March 1999, 70 percent had been on welfare for three years or longer, and 40 percent had received assistance for more than seven years (PDPW 1999b; Yant 1999). These numbers, reported in the Philadelphia *Inquirer*, are disturbing. But looking more deeply at these statistics reveals that the recipients included in these figures do in fact cycle on and off as feminists have argued.[9] This creates fodder for an ideological dichotomy. The Right (and welfare bureaucrats) focus on the seven years, such that a recipient who goes on welfare for two years because her husband left her after the birth of her third child, then gets a job for a year, then goes back on welfare for another nine months because she was laid off, finds another job for ten months, has to quit because it does not pay well enough to enable her to afford childcare, is on welfare for thirteen months, gets another job but has to quit eleven months later because of a child's medical crisis when her low-paying job provides no health coverage is represented as someone who is on welfare for seven uninterrupted years because of personal failings. A more accurate picture of her life is not one of dependence, but of entrapment: she has tried, and succeeded, in getting off welfare several times, but the structural factors of poverty compounded by gender, (race?), and motherhood always force her back. And indeed, she has tried to use welfare to maintain her independence and failed not through her own fault but through welfare's structural perpetuation of poverty. The question then becomes not how do we change her psychology, but how do we change the structural factors—such as poor pay, no national healthcare, and inadequate affordable childcare—that make it so difficult for her to work.

Thus, the focus on "seven years" distorts the reality of the welfare experience and constructs the welfare subject as pathologically dependent. The feminist temptation to focus on the cycling and the working, however, is also somewhat reductive of the problem. Feminists are rightly angry with the Republican sleight-of-hand that takes the image of the hard-core dependent as the template for describing all welfare participants. Feminists have been forced to rebut that image and have achieved some success. Often, though, feminists end up rejecting it altogether, and that is a mistake; it risks romanticizing welfare recipients as completely capable but downtrodden, victims of the patriarchal machine. Women are on welfare for many different reasons and under many different circumstances, and feminists have to address those differences. This requires us to attend to internal as well as external factors. Although shifting attention from long-term recipients to those who already combine welfare with wage work and who are in the system only temporarily may be an effective strategy for countering right-wing stereotypes, at the same time it tends to push aside those women who have had the most difficult time with welfare and in getting off it. Kathryn Edin (1991), for instance, argues that the longer recipients are on welfare, the more difficult it becomes to escape it (see also White 1993). By framing the problem in terms of responding to the conservative discourse, creating counternarratives to its story of pathological dependence, and concentrating our efforts there, we become captured by its terms and end up ignoring or forgetting the rest of the picture.

Thus, rather than reject the Right out of hand, a better strategy might be to concede that conservatives may be correct that welfare is the problem, that it creates a cycle of dependency, but to reject the reasons it gives for this cycle: that is, it is not the subsidy itself that produces dependency, but the lack of anything else—such as education, training in high-tech skills, or childcare, as well as the dehumanizing conditions under which the subsidy is granted, particularly the small amounts, as well as the intrusive state regulation—that traps women in poverty. Feminists have at least implicitly made these arguments before; but their full engagement also requires recognizing the psychological effects of welfare policy and the construction of the welfare subject. For instance, Lisa Dodson's interviews of women on welfare repeatedly reveal a psychic toll taken by endless waiting, unhelpful and even exploitative caseworkers who refuse to provide advice or guidance, the contempt that many in social services barely hide for their "clients," leading one women to say that welfare "is supposed to make you feel helpless, make you feel you are trash" (Dodson 1998, 116). Those conditions—"the little erosions that wear you down into someone you don't want to be" (115)—have helped construct the welfare subject (see also Dodson, this volume).

Hence, other feminist scholars have documented a lack of self-esteem and confidence, depression, and erasure of identity among women who are on welfare (Rogers-Dillon 1995; Elliott 1996; Dodson 1998, 126–128). Women report feeling "like dirt," "so ashamed I could die," "intimidated," "like a stone" (i.e., emotionless), "a dummy." (Edin 1991; see also Walker 1996). Faced daily with the humiliation of state surveillance, and particularly of male caseworkers, drug counselors, or public housing building managers who engage in sexual harassment or even blackmail (Dodson 1998, 130–134); the dehumanization of grinding poverty because assistance is so minimal; the contradictory messages that "good" mothers stay home and care for their children, but that single mothers on public assistance who do this are lazy cheats; being reviled by almost everyone not on public assistance, ranging from the grocery store clerk who takes your food stamps to the supposedly objective media that launches attacks that are based on misstatement of fact (DeParle, 1994; Flanders 1996); the foreshortening of your vision of the possible brought about by lack of education and social isolation: all have profound effects on the construction of selfhood and subjectivity. The fact that the Right has taken this truth and perverted it into a rationale for hatred and persecution should not keep us from understanding the power of the welfare state in constructing women as dependent welfare subjects.

The Construction of Welfare Subjects

This construction happens on several interactive but distinct levels. The first involves the materialization of reality as mentioned before; the ways in which discourse creates the material reality it describes. For instance, by using the belief that welfare is riddled with fraudulent cheats to keep payments punitively small, welfare policy, in fact, forces recipients to cheat; or by relying on racist assumptions about recipients to develop "work first" policies that fail to acknowledge racial differences in employment patterns and opportunities, welfare policy in fact increases the proportion of blacks to whites on welfare. In this, social construction is both a false representation of truth and materializes its claims into truth.

Kathryn Edin's interviews of women on welfare in Chicago illustrate the materialization of the cheating trope in welfare discourse. By demonstrating that the cost of rent, food, and other living expenses fall considerably short of public assistance allowances—even accounting for food stamps and subsidized housing—Edin demonstrates the necessity for many women on welfare not to report money received from relatives, to work under a false Social Security identity, to fence stolen goods, or sell drugs or sex. As one woman Edin interviewed said, "Public Aid is an agency that I believe can teach a person how to lie. If you tell them the truth, you won't get any help. But if you go down there and tell them a lie, you get help." As another put it, "Public Aid forces you into deceit and dishonesty, things you normally would not think of doing." It is not that these women see themselves as cheats per se, but that welfare policy forces them to act in ways that fulfill the stereotype. Edin points out that such cases represented choices "between being good mothers and good citizens. In every case, concern for their children's welfare [that is, trying to obtain sufficient income to care for them through illegal means] outweighed moral qualms" about "cheating" (1999, 269–270).

That these women do not necessarily see themselves as cheating indicates that this social construction may operate more directly on the material level; that is, it forces them to act in ways that can objectively be defined as cheating, even if subjectively experienced as struggling to be a good mother. But such acts, and their characterization in public discourse, inevitably have some effect on the internal subjective identity of participants, even if they are not determinative. These effects involve the second sense of social construction, which pertains to the construction of identity and subjectivity. In Edin's study, indeed, the feelings of shame, low self-worth, and depression that many of her respondents expressed would seem to contradict the interviewees' stated assertions that such behavior is simply a way for them to provide for their children, to be good and strong mothers in the face of adversity. Edin documents feelings of shame and low self-worth not as reasons for going on welfare, but as the result of being on welfare and having to engage in survival behaviors in which these women would not otherwise engage. In this picture, the production of welfare subjects operates on a deeper level; the empirical reality that these women live influences the self-conceptions of even the most self-consciously resistant subjects.

The construction of identity, however, operates on a third level of social construction, for welfare discourse and policies are mapped onto larger, deeper, and even more hidden discourses of race, class, and gender that have already done substantial amounts of work in the construction of subjectivity. Such constructions not only make it difficult for welfare participants, so directly subject to state power on a daily basis, to resist, they also make the general feminist effort to battle welfare reform extremely complicated. For instance, why have feminists not been successful in getting the public to see the hypocrisy of Republican family values that chastise white middle-class women as selfish for working while chastising poor and particularly Black women as lazy for not working? One obvious answer is that such contradictory discourses play off double standards so commonly accepted that most people do not even see them as such. The fact that many middle-class working women—even married women—would not even *be* middle class and able to stay off public assistance if they did not work is completely elided as class becomes the acceptable focus for racist sexism. And particularly in the context of mothering, it seems our capacity to accommodate contradictory claims is endless; as psychoanalysts from Freud to Chodorow have demonstrated, mothers never seem to be "good-enough" (Chodorow 1978, 33) and the mother-bashing of both poor, nonworking mothers and upper-middle-class working mothers that predominantly white male politicians perpetuate (e.g., see Casey and Carroll, this volume) demonstrates the generalized ambivalence that

Westerners feel towards the mother. Because guilt is the easily exploitable but constant companion to mothers of all races and classes in the West, women themselves are constructed in ways that ensure that resistance will be overwhelmed. Hence, middle-class mothers express ambivalence about working although they enjoy their jobs, just as welfare mothers critique fellow recipients for their dependency and laziness (Seccombe 1999). This is not to say that such feelings are false consciousness; rather, it is to point out that the reason it is *women* who are expected, and put in the position, to feel ambivalent is at least in part a construction of the gendered social relations of childrearing (Hirschmann 1992).

At an even more complicated level, of course, this kind of feminist critique continues to risk the error of romanticizing welfare recipients and ignores another powerful scenario in the social construction of the welfare subject, particularly for women of color—namely that getting pregnant and going on welfare may be a form of resistance. [10] Anger against white capitalism, in which you perceive yourself as having no chance to rise above the bottom rung of the economic ladder; against a democracy in which you perceive yourself as disenfranchised because of the color of your skin; against even a feminist movement in which all the women are white and middle class, and unresponsive to your situation: any or all of these may well breed a cynical—even if justifiable—view that you will be poor no matter what you do, that there is no way out. Indeed, Catanzarite and Ortiz (1995) suggest that the measures that welfare reform encourages—particularly marriage and labor-market participation—benefit white women much more than women of color, who seem to be more soundly locked into poverty regardless of what they do.[11] In such a scenario, going on welfare could be a kind of protest action, one that suggests a certain degree of rational calculation borne of efforts at resistance, of taking advantage of and hence exploiting the system that has been built on an exploitation of you.

In this scenario, poverty and racism, rather than welfare per se, may be the primary constructing forces, but these forces obviously dovetail with welfare and gender in powerful and debilitating ways. For such resistance reinscribes these women in the very system of power they may aim to destabilize through their actions: going on welfare as an act of resistance does not do anything to change a young woman's status as poor and powerless. Indeed, it would seem to make her more subject to the regulatory power of the capitalist state; if welfare reform has made nothing else clear, it is the complete vulnerability of women on welfare to state power, regardless of the circumstances that led them to it in the first place. Is it possible for such behavior to actually destabilize the racist/capitalist/patriarchal system? Does it not simply guarantee the further invisibility of such women in the minimum-wage economy? Indeed, has their resistance simply been scripted by the structure of racist and patriarchal power that has their continued powerlessness in its sights?

Freedom, Care, and Welfare Rights

The relevance of such questions to freedom may be subtle, but it is unquestionable from both a negative and positive liberty perspective. Within negative liberty, attention to social construction allows us to expand the notion of restraint or barrier by highlighting the ways in which welfare has been structured to inhibit women's liberty by presenting externally imposed limitations and blocks to the pursuit of things that they may not only want to do, but perceive as important to their development, growth, and even survival. It also demonstrates that the construction of welfare is fed by, and in turn feeds into, understandings of gender and race that are culturally and historically specific, though they are often claimed to be natural, inevitable, or given. Social construction reveals that the fact that women are the predominant participants in welfare programs is not due to personal failings on the part of individual women to get and keep a job or a man, but rather to the more basic fact that it is predominantly women who care for children and other dependents (Kittay and Fineman, this volume); that women may cheat not because they are immoral or pathological, but because public assistance does not pay enough to allow them to provide this care; that women on public assistance do not have wage-paying jobs not because of laziness but because of the inadequacy of—or inability to purchase on their own because of the low wages they are likely to earn—the childcare and healthcare they need because they are also mothers. It further points out that women's responsibility for care is hardly a fact of nature but of socially constructed social relations of production and reproduction, relations that can and must be changed if women are to be able to pursue a full range of human options. It allows us to see that welfare is a social construct that plays off larger constructions of gender (women should be mothers, they should be dependent on individual men), race (black women are lazy and dishonest, you have to keep an eye on them and make them earn their living), and class (white middle-class women should be fulltime mothers; the poor are poor because they are lazy and, therefore, have only themselves to blame). The recognition of these as social constructions lets us see that they are not natural or essential, but human-made products of racist, sexist, and classist social policy that interfere with women's freedom to lead their lives as they wish.

From a positive liberty perspective, social construction's relevance goes even more deeply, to the formation of the desiring subject. The provision of enabling resources such as education, childcare, healthcare, housing, and transportation would allow women to pursue the goals of economic well-being, familial and professional self-development, satisfaction, and security. The removal of welfare's stigma by pointing out that welfare's entrapment is a result of structural limitations, rather than participants' personal failings, aids in the removal of certain internal barriers such as low self-worth, fear, anxiety, and anger. More than that, social construction engages us in a reconsideration of the choosing subject of welfare, of the individuals, predominantly women, who end up in the socially vulnerable role of caregiver. By challenging the inevitability and naturalness of women's role as rearer of children, caregiver for the sick and elderly, and private-sphere care provider for men, social construction allows us to call into question the fundamental assumptions about the sexual division of labor on which welfare policies are based.

Social construction thus allows us to see that women's caregiving roles sit at the heart of welfare debates for both models of liberty, whether overtly or implicitly. The centrality of care work to a feminist reconfiguration of the welfare state goes back to its earliest days; the fact that women have always performed this care work has underlined the fact of feminist involvement in welfare reform. For instance, Wendy Sarvasy (1992) argues that early welfare feminists viewed gender as a socially constructed product of, and foundation for, power; by acknowledging the ways in which gender differences had been constructed through these power inequalities, then not only gender, but citizenship, rights, and welfare could be rethought. Sarvasy argues that early feminists believed that focusing on the caregiving work that women typically engaged in was essential to such a rethinking, for it located the particularity of women's experiences within a dialogue of universal access. The goal of securing citizenship for women involved a rethinking of rights such that both particularity and universality, both gender neutrality and recognition of actual gender inequalities, both mothering and paid labor, could all be combined in a single vision. Through their social constructivist lens, feminists formulated "a new notion of the citizen-mother as a professional providing a socially supported activity within the context of full political rights" (Sarvasy 1992, 346) that recognized women's maternal roles without reducing them to those roles, and without falling into the trap of republican citizenship that eliminated women from the public sphere and ensured their dependence on men.

It is significant for my own argument about freedom that Sarvasy gives central importance to the notion of rights in her analysis. Granted, rights are not an exact equivalent to freedom, but they are extremely close and interdependent; the point of rights is precisely to protect liberties, rights are tools to exercise the power of the state in the protection of those liberties. Indeed, rights are the only cognate of freedom to which feminists have paid explicit attention in relation to welfare, and hence provide a useful window onto the tacit model of liberty that underwrites feminist approaches to welfare. The notion of welfare rights for poor mothers is a theme that continually repeats in the history of welfare, and one that has considerable currency today among feminists who have sought to make AFDC/TANF more like other welfare payments such as Social Security, workers' compensation, and unemployment, which, for all of their problems, are still considered entitlements, or rights (Fraser and Gordon 1992; Bussiere

1997; Mink 1998). Moreover, rights are seen as a tool of freedom, both negative—by arguing for greater independence in the form of more money and less surveillance over women's lifestyles—and positive—by demanding more resources such as childcare, training for well-paying jobs, better employment opportunities, and transportation to areas offering these opportunities.

In a contemporary echo of the picture Sarvasy paints, Elizabeth Bussiere (1997) argues that freedom was central to the battle of the National Welfare Rights Organization (NWRO) in the 1960s and 1970s to establish welfare rights in the United States; and that this effort failed because of dedication on the part of the Court to a predominantly negative liberty view of procedural rights, when a positive liberty view of substantive rights, particularly to a minimum standard of living, was really at the heart of the struggle for welfare rights. Though Bussiere leaves out of her understanding of positive liberty the important dimensions of internal barriers and social construction I have articulated here, her observation about the negative liberty focus of both lawyers and courts is instructive. She reveals that although the progressive goals of establishing rights to subsistence income motivated the NWRO and Legal Services lawyers, the strategy they took was patently conservative, construing legal questions as narrowly as possible, trying to move the courts only inches at a time, dealing with individuals rather than groups or social categories, and failing to attend to cultural contexts. For instance, in a Supreme Court case involving one-year residence requirements before being eligible for welfare, the NWRO lawyers argued that such requirements violated a constitutional right of individuals to travel freely between the states—an argument that the Court found persuasive (see *Shapiro v. Thompson*, 394 U.S. 618 [1969])—rather than making a case for subsistence rights based on national citizenship (Bussiere 1997, ch. 7). In practice such an approach—in contradiction to the proclaimed goals of the NWRO—conceived of welfare recipients not as a collective group, but rather as a coincidental collection of individuals who could be protected only through gaining rights that each could use individually and separately. Obviously, since the lawyers prevailed, we must conclude that this was a logical legal strategy, and indeed it has been invoked in more recent cases in California and Pennsylvania (e.g., *Saenz v. Roe*, 119 S. Ct. 1518 [1969]; *Maldonado v. Houston*, No. 97–1893 [3d Circuit Sept 9, 1998] Clearinghouse No. 52168). But Bussiere suggests that is also why the larger goal of establishing welfare rights failed; they needed to state the right to subsistence, particularly for single mothers as a collective group. The lawyers may have won the battle, but they lost the war.

Moreover, she suggests, this strategy with its overtly negative liberty focus was at least implicitly a function of the socially constructed gender- and race-based division of labor. Bussiere notes that women who made up membership of the NWRO—98 percent poor African American mothers—wanted the white male lawyers responsible for plotting the litigation strategy to utilize "maternalist" arguments in articulating the grounds for welfare rights. While the leaders/ lawyers kept to a belief that the only way to obtain welfare rights was to make single mothers' plight part of a larger movement for a welfare state, Bussiere argues, welfare mothers believed that the interests of poor and working men would supersede their own interests and preferences in such a strategy. They sought recognition for the specific work they did in caring for children, and for the special problems and difficulties they faced in performing this labor, whether they did it full-time and exclusively, or whether they combined mothering with wage labor (Bussiere 1997, ch. 7).

This construction of rights through care might seem counterintuitive given that, at least since Carol Gilligan's 1982 book *In a Different Voice*, the relationship between care and rights has been seen as antagonistic, if not antithetical. Gilligan postulated two different models of moral development: a rights model that defines morality in terms of rules, abstract principles, and a hierarchy of rights-as-trumps; and a care model that defines morality in terms of responsibility and responding to need, and that is based on face-to-face conversation, interpersonal dynamics, relationship, and context. Because of the association of these models with males and females, respectively, Gilligan's argument has led many feminists to challenge the notion of rights as masculinist.[12] Within the context of welfare, however, it becomes apparent that care is a necessary precondition of rights, that what is "wrong" with rights is its rejection of care. Given the history of racist and sexist exclusion that feminists have long attributed to the notion and practice of rights (Pateman 1988; Hirschmann 1999), what is needed to make a conception of rights truly equitable and accessible to all are the fundamentals of the care model. Rather than opposing care to rights, a conception of rights can be developed *within* a care approach, which is what I believe both Sarvasy and Bussiere's analysis of welfare activism at least implicitly suggest.

Such a conception is beyond the present chapter, which is focused more explicitly on freedom (but see Hirschmann 1999). But consider, for instance, the most common criticism lodged against the care model: it cannot serve as a general moral theory because the importance of relationship would result in favoritism, whereas rights are impartial. A careful consideration of the care model reveals that it does not reject such central rights values as universality and neutrality, but rather requires their reconfiguration. In Gilligan's treatment of the "Heinz dilemma" (Heinz's wife is fatally ill, but he cannot afford the medicine that will help her; should Heinz steal the drug?), the girl "Amy" never suggests that Heinz should steal the drug because it is his *wife*—someone close to him, whose death would affect him personally—who is sick. Such reasoning would display the favoritism of which critics complain; it is not, however, the reasoning which Amy displays (indeed, Amy says that he should not steal it at all, a fact most such critics ignore). Rather, Amy tries to consider the needs of everyone involved; everyone is equally entitled to a prima facie consideration of care. It is only when details reveal greater or lesser need or ability that determinations of specific and appropriate expressions of care can be made. After all, we never know *why* the druggist will not give Heinz the drug; for instance, perhaps his child is also sick, and he needs the money for her operation. Or perhaps he is facing imminent bankruptcy because of the large chain drugstore that has recently opened in town, and letting Heinz have the drug for free will seal his fate.

By sitting down and talking the problem out as Amy prescribes, such details would presumably be articulated; and from such details can emerge a solution that is fair to everyone (e.g., installment payments; or perhaps the pharmacist can help Heinz confront his HMO which has denied payment of experimental drugs. Of course, such solutions do not address the questions of why Heinz's health insurance will not pay for the drug, or why Heinz might not even have insurance, both of which importantly conjoin issues of care and entitlement). Such a communicative approach to the dilemma represents a different notion of impartiality, one that is worked out through more knowledge rather than less, through concrete particularity rather than general abstraction; but it is impartiality nonetheless. Care may require particularity—the need to know concrete details in order to assess the needs of a particular person in a particular situation—but particularity is not the same thing as partiality. If everyone is equally deserving of care—if care is a foundation for rights—then favoritism does not follow (see also Tronto, this volume).

What is particularly noteworthy about revisioning rights through care is how much it contrasts with the dominant approach to rights as a conflictual claim against others found in negative liberty and classical liberal discourse. Stemming back at least to the state-of-nature contractarians, rights were conceived as civil—and for some, such as Locke, also natural—grantings of power that applied to individuals exclusively. Individuals were conceived as separate and distinct from all others, with relationships possible only by chosen agreement (or in Hobbes's case, sometimes by force, which in his view amounted to the same thing). Within the negative liberty view of rights, a right is a "trump," to borrow from Ronald Dworkin (1977), a claim that puts an end to disputes over distribution of resources or conflicting interests, a kind of weapon that individuals can use to beat back the claims of competing individuals. Moreover, the individuals at the heart of this negative liberty vision of rights were for the most part propertied white men, as decades of feminist critique of liberal theory compels us to recognize: its initial institutional application only to propertied white men; its definitions of key concepts like property and equality in ways that not only left out white women and people of color but also depended on their subservience and classified them as forms of property; its conceptualization of individualism that ignored the importance of the relationship and connectedness that women's lives ensured (Pateman 1988; Hirschmann 1992).

Using rights as weapons for the disempowered may seem the correct strategy to take in a time of welfare retrenchment. Ironically, though, it is precisely this negative liberty view of rights as antagonistic claims that has enabled conservative Republicans to scale back such entitlement programs as AFDC, food stamps, WIC, and Medicaid, as well as to provide tax cuts to the wealthy. By emphasizing the conflictual character of rights—which pits the providers (taxpayers) against the receivers (especially welfare mothers and children)—the claims of welfare rights can be denied because within this conflictual framework, it is the powerful who decide whether a right exists and whether to honor it. Furthermore, by viewing responsibility as something that recipients must exercise (because their poverty is evidence that they are irresponsible) but that the privileged need not (because they already are responsible, by working and paying taxes), again imparting a conflictual and individualist character to the debate, this conservative move is greatly facilitated. A kind of class warfare is engaged that reinforces the lines of economic privilege and power, which in turn facilitates the perpetuation of the public discourse of taxpayers as responsible citizens and welfare recipients as either cheating or pathological.

This claim about the negative liberty focus of welfare rights might seem to contradict the positive liberty themes I attribute to the conservative discourse of dependency. But of course, my point above was not that the right-wing appropriation of positive liberty themes proved the inherent conservatism of positive liberty but rather that feminists need to reclaim its progressive potential. Indeed, the two claims strongly cohere, because the overt positive liberty orientation of current welfare discourse is founded on and feeds into the worst elements of negative liberty, particularly abstract individualism, where welfare mothers must "just do it" and pull themselves up by their own bootstraps (a particular feature of "work first" provisions), combined with the patriarchal erasure of women's humanity that feminist theorists have traced for decades. It may be for this reason that programs such as workfare—where, in the supposed interest of making welfare recipients independent, of liberating them from the cycle of welfare, of empowering them to become contributing, responsible, taxpaying citizens, recipients are forced to take low-wage, dead-end jobs that provide little if any training in skills such as computer programming, welding and construction, or office management, which could lead to economic independence (Mink 1998)—do not actually fulfill the criteria of positive liberty; can anyone honestly believe that my true will is to perform mindless minimum wage labor rather than pursue a college degree which would enable me to obtain a much higher-paying and intellectually stimulating job (Dodson 1998; Halper 2000)? Welfare discourse takes the most conservative elements of both models of liberty, smuggling the libertarian individualism of negative liberty into an overt positive liberty framework: the second-guessing of positive liberty informs its dominant discourse of defining the character of the welfare subject or recipient, while the abstract individualism of negative liberty underpins its rejection of welfare rights.

This recognition, I believe, is what leads the feminist reconception of rights to embrace elements of positive liberty, as Sarvasy and Bussiere both implicitly illustrated; a conception of rights that does not merely make trumping claims on the state, but rather one that involves recognition of the socially constructed sexual division of labor, and specifically how this construction creates women who are forced to choose caretaking roles and yet are desirous of fulfilling their ascribed caretaking duties under maximally conducive conditions such as economic stability. Moreover, the melding of care and rights is significant in its implications for freedom because it is founded on a recognition of the social construction of motherhood and of women's social roles as caretakers: it is because women care for children, men, the sick, and elderly that "welfare" in the form of public assistance has had to develop in response to the tacit recognition of the centrality of that work to the democratic state. But because women are socially constructed as noncitizens by virtue of this very labor (Tronto, this volume), welfare policy has developed in the ambivalent way it has, simultaneously forced to recognize women as entitled to support by virtue of that labor, but never providing sufficient support to fully respect that entitlement or that labor.

At the same time, it is crucial to note that the vision Sarvasy articulates was never realized in practice; the foundation of positive responsibility and the importance of care work to welfare rights was subverted by racist and classist reconstructions of motherhood in the early part of the twentieth century, as Mink (1995) argues, and it was denied outright by the NWRO lawyers, as Bussiere (1997) documents. Though Sarvasy is careful to argue that early activists sought a feminist welfare state, not a maternalist one, the trope of maternalism was impossible to displace; and maternalism has historically embraced a white middle-class model of mothering that takes the patriarchal nuclear family as a natural given simply substituting the state for the father/husband when he is absent. Because of the larger sexist context of male power, whenever feminists talk about care, the shadow of essentialism hangs over us; and talking about the care work women do as the foundation for welfare rights risks reinscribing women in the very same social roles and stereotypes that have fostered and permitted their disempowerment vis-à-vis the welfare state. In this light, the reconstruction of welfare rights in terms of care runs the risk of further restricting women's freedom, rather than enhancing it.

Social construction can help prevent this reconfiguration of rights through care from falling into a racist, essentialist maternalsim. First, it reminds us that if women are in fact more caring than men are, to a large degree, that is because they have always been required to perform caring labor. Second, it points out that that fact does not negate or delegitimize care as a moral category. That is, by attending to the historical and political context of care, social construction forces us to negotiate the contemporary empirical realities of care work—that women currently do most of it and hence we need to respond to the needs of their particular experiences—and the future vision of deontological gender neutrality—that is, developing policies that encourage men to partake in it by ensuring that rights accrue to care work regardless of who does it. By raising the question of why it has been women who have always expressed care and been responsible for caregiving labor—and thereby raising questions of how to change that so that it is not women's exclusive responsibility but rather one that falls on men and women alike—such an approach can broaden care beyond gender while acknowledging its gendered foundations.

Welfare rights based on women's caring labor would, then, degender care: as one might glibly, if not cynically argue, if the state recognized care work as important and paid it a decent wage, more men might be willing to do it. More significant, it uses women's historical responsibility for caring labor not as a rationale for their continuing to do it, but rather as a basis for understanding its dynamics and how those dynamics fit into, shape, and are shaped by the larger political and social context of inequality between men and women, between rich and poor, between whites and people of color. By refusing the naturalization of care, we can gain a clearer insight into the sex/gender, class, and race dynamics that construct care work as a practice. Such insight can lead to the institution of welfare policies that more directly address actual, rather than assumed needs, of actual care workers, rather than of abstract stereotypes (Kittay, this volume).

Constructing Freedom

Thus, the social construction dimension of positive liberty gives a more radical potential to the reconfiguring of welfare rights through care. In many ways, welfare is the perfect issue for this reconfiguring of rights and freedom, by containing all of the supposedly contradictory elements of the two camps at once: individual integrity, and caring for family; claims and demands on the state, and responsibility to and for others; autonomy, and a rethinking of the self through relationship. A focus on caretaking will make welfare more woman friendly and free, at least by providing mothers with greater resources and a wider range of choices in how that care is exercised. A consideration of women's freedom demands that women have as wide a range of choices open to them as possible, whether they desire to give care full time—in which case larger stipends are needed—or to combine care work with wage labor or to work full time—in which case women need better pay and opportunities, better protection from sexual and racial discrimination and harassment, in addition to good quality childcare and transportation.

Of course, the phrase "as possible" is key; once we move from the abstract principled claim that we need to honor, respect, and value care to the actual practices and policies of doing so, issues of cost come to the fore. As positive liberty shows us, freedom can never be about abstract choice, but must be located within contexts of community and relationships that define one's choices. Paying individual caretakers to care for one or two children full time in an isolated nuclear family is extremely inefficient and costly, leading Orloff et al. to suggest that it is unrealistic to question whether "women's caregiving claims . . . will survive at all" and to argue that welfare must be market driven (O'Connor, Orloff, and Shaver 1999, 144, 148).[13] Accordingly, I agree with Orloff's (this volume) conclusion that provision of care-related supports must be developed in conjunction with work-related supports.

This is more than a matter of efficiency, however; it is also a matter of freedom. By this, of course, I do not mean the conservative positive liberty maneuver that requires women to participate in wage labor under the guise of forcing them to be free. Rather, I mean that choice also requires a restructuring of other social institutions like the family, so that such choices about distributing and structuring care work and wage labor are not simply excuses for keeping these burdens on women. Making options available such as shared parenting with a partner in a traditional family structure or living in a nontraditional family structure, both of which would likely entail men's taking a greater share of responsibility for care work, will increase women's positive and negative liberty by not only providing a greater array of choices to women, but also by reconstructing what it means to be the woman and mother who makes these choices. Whereas negative liberty shows us the ways in which welfare limits women, how it robs them of choice and power, a positive liberty focus can reveal how the conditions of sexism and racism within which mothering takes place produce welfare subjects. Part of the feminist project to develop a more woman-friendly welfare state, therefore, involves reclaiming positive liberty discourse from the Right and deploying it to our own ends. Positive liberty, by pointing our attention to the social construction of the individual subject, as well as to the need to understand individuals' desires and abilities in social contexts that enable or restrain those desires and abilities, also requires that we rethink the fundamental conceptual vocabulary that engulfs welfare debates and discussions. In that strategy lies a powerful potential for the liberation of welfare.

Notes

1. This chapter was written in part during an NEH fellowship at the Institute for Advance Study in Princeton, New Jersey. Thanks to the institute, the NEH, and to Cornell University for leave time, research facilities, and financial support. Earlier versions of this

paper were presented at the 1998 annual meeting of the American Political Science Association; the Institute for Advanced Study; and The Walt Whitman Center, Rutgers University. Particular thanks to Susan Brison, Elizabeth Bussiere, Evelyn Huber, Mary Katzenstein, Eva Kittay, Ulrike Liebert, John Stephens, and Michael Walzer for their helpful comments. Thanks also to Rosey Ernst, whose independent study on welfare and race made important bibliographic contributions to this essay.

2. As Mimi Abramowitz notes, ADC was "designed to release [mothers . . .] from the wage-earning role" so as to enable them to care for their children and "to make them citizens capable of contributing to society" (1988, 315); see also Piven (1996); O'Connor, Orloff, and Shaver (1999), e.g., p. 148.

3. This is arguably truer in the United States and "liberal" welfare regimes than the social democratic or even conservative-corporatist welfare regimes of northern Europe, which tend to provide more generous benefits to mothers and others; see Huber and Stephens (1999).

4. For instance, British Prime Minister Tony Blair has denounced a "workless class" bred by state welfare policies in terms similar to the U.S. discourse of a "culture of dependency," six months before the British Parliament voted to cut funding for unemployed single mothers in need of assistance and to begin means testing for benefits for the sick and disabled. See Lyall (1997) and Hoge (1998). Thanks to April Brinkman for pointing these articles out to me. Other discourses, such as that of the Christian Democrats in Germany, a country which provides far more generous welfare benefits on the overt conservative premise of keeping women in the home raising children, provides a different, but no less fruitful avenue for analysis in the relationship between welfare discourse and freedom. See chapters in this volume by Mushaben and Liebert.

5. See Flathman (1987) for an excellent survey of the range of definitions of freedom.

6. The several paragraphs here discussing Berlin are adapted from, and are considered at greater length in, Hirschmann (1996b, 48–51).

7. According to Mink (1998), "in 1994, adult recipients in AFDC families were 37.4 percent white, 36.4 percent Black, 19.9 percent Latina, 2.9 percent Asian, and 1.3 percent Native American" (120), which means that there are more women of color on welfare than white women. However, the numbers of white and African American women are roughly equal (Flanders, Jackson, and Shadoan 1996, 34; Seccombe 1999, 15); and given the diversity of ethnic groups that make up nonwhite recipients, the stereotype of African Americans as the "typical" welfare recipient is still false.

8. Although in Illinois pursuing education is considered equivalent to working for purposes of continuing to receive welfare, this is the exception, not the rule. In Pennsylvania, for instance, "vocational education, general education, and education in English-as-a-second language or job skills training"—but not college or graduate education—can be used to meet the work requirement for a maximum of twelve months; after that period, "the recipient who wishes to continue education or training will be required to participate in another work-related activity in addition to the education or training" (Penn. Dept. of Public Welfare 1999a, 20). For accounts of welfare's resistance to recipients' pursuit of education, see Dujon (1996), O'Neill (1999), and Halper (2000).

9. This fact is mentioned neither in the report nor in the Philadelphia *Inquirer* article; rather it was revealed in response to my specific question about this in a telephone conversation with Information Specialist Susan M. Aspey of the Pennsylvania Department of Public Welfare. However, she had no knowledge of more detailed figures that

would break down precisely what percentage of the seven years the average recipient actually received benefits. This suggests that the discourse of welfare dependency is not simply an ideologically driven conservative discourse but a supposedly neutral bureaucratic one that constructs the welfare subject in this way.

10. Thanks to Liz Bussiere for some stimulating email exchanges on this topic.

11. Indeed, they find that though white women not in the labor force are eleven times more likely to live in poverty than whites who worked full time, women of color were only five times as likely to live in poverty as their employed counterparts, thus signifying that "white women's work effort had a greater impact on reducing the risk of poverty than was true for African American and Latina women." Similarly, marriage made twice the difference for white women than women of color; single white women had poverty rates eight times that of married white women, but for single minority women, the increase was (only) four times as much (Catanzarite and Ortiz 1995, 132–33). Certainly, these figures could be taken to show that employment and marriage can help some women escape poverty, but at the same time the fact that women of color have a very high chance of remaining poor whether they work or marry also feeds into the scenario that I am describing in the text and reveals welfare reform's solutions as at best simplistic and racially biased.

12. Including, some might argue, myself. In Hirschmann (1992), I use the work of Gilligan as well as object relations theorists such as Nancy Chodorow (1978) to develop an argument that social contract theory is "structurally sexist" (Hirschmann 1992, 10), and that feminist values of caring and connection derived from such psychological research pointed toward a redefinition of the concept of obligation. In the process, I critiqued standard rights discourse as similarly masculinist. Some will undoubtedly read this chapter as a retraction of my earlier work, but that would be to misinterpret both my book and the present chapter. My critique of rights in *Rethinking Obligation* was a critique of the classic liberal vision, but did not preclude the feminist rethinking of rights that I am engaged in here. Both here and in *Rethinking Obligation,* I argue that women's historical experiences of care need to inform—not to replace—public discourses and political theories, and that doing so should lead the way to reconfigurations of central liberal conceptions, such as obligation and rights. Just as obligation, which is seen in liberalism as a product of individualistic choice, had to be rethought through notions of connection, relationship, and positive responsibility, so do rights, which are seen in liberalism as similarly individualistic and importantly related to choice and consent, need to be rethought in terms of care, connection, and positive responsibility. See Hirschmann (1999) for a fuller explication of my views on how such a reconfigured conception of rights should be developed.

13. Indeed, even in Sweden, which is often cited as *the* model of a woman-friendly welfare state, and which allows fifteen months of caretaker leave for either parent, such benefits are market driven: the right is not to be compensated for care work per se, but to a job in the market economy, a right that in turn entails not being penalized for the work interruptions that having and caring for a baby brings about. Furthermore, benefits are linked to wages; specifically, benefits total 80 percent of the caretaker's working wage, with much lower amounts going to caretakers not in the labor force. Thanks to John Stephens for pointing this out.

Part 2

Welfare Reform in the United States

Five

Kathleen J. Casey and Susan J. Carroll

Welfare Reform in the 104th Congress

Institutional Position and the Role of Women

On August 22, 1996, President Bill Clinton signed into law the Personal Responsibility and Work Opportunity Reconciliation Act of 1996 (HR 3734) (PRA). The signing of this bill represented a fulfillment of Clinton's promise during the 1992 presidential campaign to "end welfare as we know it" (*Congressional Quarterly* Sept. 21, 1996, 2,696). This landmark welfare reform legislation ended the federal guarantee of cash assistance to low-income families that had been in place for six decades, replacing direct federal assistance with a program of block grants to the states. Through this legislation, Congress essentially gave the states authority to create their own welfare programs as long as they met certain federal requirements, including the requirements that welfare recipients find employment within two years of receiving benefits and that adult recipients receive a maximum of five years of aid during their lifetimes (*Congressional Quarterly* Sept. 21, 1996, 2,696–2,705; Women's Policy Inc. 1997, 78–88).

In this chapter, we examine the efforts by women members to influence the provisions and the fate of welfare reform in the 104th Congress. The media devoted little attention to any actions that women members of Congress undertook which may have helped shape or influence welfare reform legislation. Except for a couple of well-publicized incidents involving women members, most observers who closely followed progress of the welfare reform bill through Congress know little about the role women played. One incident occurred during the first session of the 104th when Barbara Cubin, a very conservative Republican Congresswoman from Wyoming who was first elected in 1994 under the banner of the Republicans' Contract with America, spoke during debate on the floor of the House. Cubin was widely quoted as saying:

The Federal Government introduced wolves into the State of Wyoming, and they put them in pens, and they brought elk and venison to them every day. . . . The Federal Government provided everything that the wolves need for their existence. But guess what? They opened the gates and let the wolves out, and now the wolves won't go. Just like any animal in the species, any mammal, when you take away their freedom and their dignity and their ability, they can't provide for themselves, and that is what the Democrats' proposal does on welfare. (Pear 1995)

The second aspect of women's involvement that attracted attention because it angered many feminists was the high level of support among women senators of both parties for The Personal Responsibility Act (HR 4), the welfare reform bill considered in the first session of the 104th Congress, which was ultimately vetoed by President Clinton. Six of the seven women U.S. Senators, including Democrats Barbara Mikulski, Patty Murray, Dianne Feinstein, and Barbara Boxer, voted in favor of the bill on September 19, 1995. The only woman Senator to oppose HR 4 was Carol Moseley Braun. These two well-publicized features of women's involvement with welfare reform—Cubin's comments on the floor of the House and women senators' votes in favor of HR 4—paint a disturbing picture for feminists who believe that welfare reform is harmful to women and that the presence of larger numbers of women in public office will make a difference in women's lives.

We argue, however, that a quite different and more complicated picture of women's involvement emerges if one looks beyond the headlines. We find that several women members of Congress influenced the provisions of welfare reform legislation in the 104th Congress in both the first and second sessions. Overall, women members had their strongest impact on provisions relating to childcare, child protection, and child support, and throughout this chapter, we highlight women's efforts in these areas.

Their institutional position as members of the minority party in a highly charged, partisan environment, constrained the possibilities for Democratic women, and men, to influence welfare reform legislation. Because Democratic women were not involved in drafting the legislation and were locked out of backroom negotiations, they worked where they had a voice—on the floor and on relevant committees. Many Democratic women in the House positioned themselves against the terms of welfare reform as forwarded by House Republicans and spoke in opposition to legislation on the House floor. In general, however, it was not the women who spoke on the floor, but rather those who served on the committees charged with considering welfare reform, who had the greatest opportunity to influence the legislation. With limited success, these Democratic congresswomen chipped away at the provisions they found most unacceptable, such as block granting programs for child welfare and childcare and worked to strengthen child support enforcement.

Like their counterparts in the House, Democratic women in the Senate were in the minority party, a situation that restricted their potential to influence welfare reform legislation. Nevertheless, Democratic women senators were active and visible in the welfare reform debate. They tried, mostly failing but a few times succeeding, to shape welfare reform legislation in ways they viewed as more fair and more equitable.[1]

However, the key female players in the welfare reform saga in the 104th Congress were not Democrats, but Republicans. Because their party controlled both houses of Congress, Republican women members were much better positioned than their Democratic counterparts to influence welfare reform and, for this reason, we focus in this chapter on the efforts of Republican women. Among Republican women, those senior members who served on committees with jurisdiction over welfare reform had the greatest influence on welfare reform and, consequently, moderate Republicans, especially Nancy Johnson in the House and Nancy Kassebaum in the Senate, were best positioned institutionally to affect welfare reform. These women used their positions and influence to modify welfare reform legislation in ways they found important. As we demonstrate in this chapter, through their efforts in shaping childcare and child protection provisions, Republican women members of Congress helped to make the overall impact of welfare reform legislation somewhat less harsh on women and children than it otherwise might have been. Republican women also helped expand the scope of the legislation in one important respect, insuring that men as well as women be required to exercise "personal responsibility" in the area of child support.

Rationale for the Study and Research Design

Our analysis is positioned between two relatively distinct bodies of gender-related research, both of which have grown considerably and attracted much scholarly attention in recent years. The first is the literature on gender and the welfare state. In a widely read essay, Linda Gordon (1990a) identified three stages of development evident in the interdisciplinary feminist scholarship about welfare: (a) documentation of the discriminatory nature of welfare programs, (b) development of structural critiques emphasizing the social control functions of welfare policy, and (c) examination of the role of women's activism and their influence in the development of the welfare system. Felicia A. Kornbluh observed that the most recent scholarship, much of it coming after publication of Gordon's essay, is producing an even more complicated, yet sophisticated, understanding of the welfare state politics. She explained:

> Feminist scholars, who began insisting on the significance of gender in social policy under twenty years ago, have come to an increasingly nuanced

understanding of how gender-based power helps create state policies and determine their effects. . . . "Social control" turned out to be a myth, or, at best, a rarely realized ambition of social workers, philanthropists, and welfare administrators. Welfare policies like widows' pensions and A(F)DC contained sexist assumptions about women's primary responsibility for child rearing, but they also offered (and were designed to offer) recipients some degree of economic and personal autonomy—*and* to exclude Black women, some immigrants, and women with lax standards of sexual morality. Future studies of the intersections among gender, race, empire, and sexuality in welfare states only promise to make the picture more complicated. And that is probably all for the best. (1996, 194)

As the essays by Gordon and Kornbluh illustrate, the interdisciplinary literature on gender and the welfare state has contributed to our understanding of how social structures, ideological forces, and extra-institutional activism have influenced the development of the welfare state and its policies. Nevertheless, the lack of attention to what happens *inside* institutions of the state is a weakness of this literature. Scholars who have focused on the historical development of the welfare state in the United States have thoroughly examined the role that activists outside formal state institutions play, especially the activism of organizations such as the National Consumers' League, the General Federation of Women's Clubs, and the Women's Trade Union League (see, e.g., Skocpol 1992; Sklar 1995). They have less often considered the decision-making process within the state itself, especially the role that women who occupy formal positions of authority within the state play.[2] Yet, an understanding of the role played by women within the state is critical to developing more comprehensive analyses and theories regarding women's agency in the construction of welfare policies.

A quite different group of scholars, primarily political scientists, have focused explicitly on the attitudes and actions of women who occupy formal positions within the state, especially elective offices. Unlike the literature on gender and the welfare state, much of which has been historical in both approach and focus, most work on women in public office has been empirical in approach and contemporary in focus. In examining women public officials, scholars have focused largely on two sets of interrelated questions: (a) Why are there so few women public officials? What are the reasons for the numerical underrepresentation of women in office? (b) What difference does the presence of larger numbers of women in office make? Does increased numerical representation of women lead to increased substantive representation?

These scholars of women in public office have demonstrated that women officials in the United States tend to be more liberal and more supportive of feminist policy positions than male public officials of the same party. Moreover, they have shown that women elected officeholders are more likely than their male counterparts to be involved with legislation that advances women's rights as well as legislation on issues associated with women's traditional roles as caregivers in society such as healthcare, the welfare of children and families, and education (e.g., Dodson and Carroll 1991; Thomas 1994).

Nevertheless, the literature on women in public office has not been particularly sensitive to institutional context and the ways that institutional factors both facilitate and constrain the impact that women public officials can have both individually and collectively. Some research has examined the effects of "critical mass" and the presence of women's caucuses or other forms of organizing among women in influencing the impact of women officeholders (Dodson and Carroll 1991; Thomas 1994). And at least one study has assessed the extent to which institutional differences in two state legislatures influenced the effectiveness of women serving in those legislatures (Blair and Stanley, forthcoming). For the most part, however, research on women in public office has been based on surveys and interviews which compare the self-reported attitudes and behaviors of women public officials with those of their male colleagues across a variety of issue areas. Rarely has attention been devoted to questions about how much and in what ways the actions of women public officials are influenced, constrained, or enabled by the institutional context in which they function.

The present chapter adds to both the literature on gender and the state and the literature on women public officials. Our analysis contributes to research on gender and the welfare state by examining women's intra-institutional activism and the extent to which, and ways in which, women members of Congress were involved in the creation of welfare policy. This research is based largely on analysis of documents and interviews with thirty-eight women members of Congress and thirty-three congressional staff members and lobbyists who played key roles, or worked for members who played important roles, on legislation in the issue areas we investigate. Our analysis adds to the literature on women public officials by examining the ways in which institutional factors enabled and constrained the impact women members of Congress were able to have on the Personal Responsibility and Work Opportunity Reconciliation Act of 1996 (HR 3734). It is hoped that this research will begin to bridge the gap between the literature on gender and the welfare state and the literature on women public officials.[3]

The External and Internal Environment of the 104th Congress

Consideration of welfare reform legislation by the 104th Congress took place within a larger context that helped shape and constrain both congressional debate and the fate of the legislation. Changes in the environment both external and internal to Congress are important to understanding the actions of women members of Congress and the impact they had on welfare reform.

The 1994 elections were critical to shaping the composition of the 104th Congress and moving the institution in a much more conservative direction. The media heralded the 1994 elections as the revenge of the "Angry White Male." Men turned out to vote in 1994 at a slightly lower rate than women but, in contrast to women, men voted substantially more Republican in 1994 than they had in either the 1992 or 1990 congressional elections (Burke 1994). In addition, the rate of voter turnout dropped notably from 1990 to 1994 among African American and Latino voters of both genders and among voters with incomes of $10,000 or less. Meanwhile, turnout increased from 1990 to 1994 among white voters and among voters with incomes of $50,000 or more (U.S. Department of Commerce, Bureau of the Census 1995).

These turnout and voting patterns resulted in the election of the most conservative Congress in decades. In the U.S. House, Republicans took control for the first time in forty years, outnumbering Democrats 230 to 204 (with one independent). For the first time since 1986, Republicans gained control of the Senate by a margin of 53 to 47 (*Congressional Quarterly* Jan. 7, 1995). As the *Congressional Quarterly Almanac* observed: "Both chambers were populated by a new cadre of lawmakers more intensely anti-government than any other in contemporary times. A large group of conservative freshmen, especially in the House, displayed remarkable ideological cohesion" (Austin 1996 1–3).

Republican candidates for Congress campaigned in 1994 on a ten-plank platform known as the "Contract with America." The welfare reform plank in this platform promised to convert direct public assistance into block grants to the state, cap welfare spending, require recipients to find work within two years of qualifying for assistance, and impose a five-year lifetime limit on eligibility for welfare benefits (Austin 1997). The Republican majority in the House, under the leadership of Speaker Newt Gingrich, was strongly committed to dismantling the federal welfare system. The Democratic president, Bill Clinton, while disagreeing with Republicans on some of the specifics, had also pledged to end the welfare system during his 1992 campaign for the White House.

Strong public sentiments for welfare reform reinforced Congressional and presidential support:

> Gallup Organization surveys in the mid-1990s strongly suggested the half-century-old consensus on welfare had collapsed. Nearly three-quarters (71 percent) of a December 1972 Gallup sample favored maintaining or increasing existing levels of welfare spending. . . . By 1994, only 48 percent thought welfare spending should remain steady or increase. An overwhelming 90 percent in the 1994 poll believed the welfare system to be in crisis. (Golay 1997, 169)

As Congress debated welfare reform throughout 1995 and 1996, public support for welfare reform increased. A July 1996 Gallup poll showed that welfare was ranked by the public as the fourth most important issue facing the country following crime, the economy, and the budget deficit. In 1996, 71 percent of the public agreed that people who had not found a job after two years should be denied further benefits compared with 58 percent of the public in 1994 (Golay 1997, 160–170).

By spring 1996, welfare reform appeared almost inevitable. Republicans controlled both houses of Congress, and under the leadership of Newt Gingrich, House Republicans were determined to implement all the provisions set forth in their Contract with America. Republican Party unity was exceptionally high, especially on votes on provisions of the Contract (Austin 1996, 1–7). President Clinton's pledge to reform welfare helped reform become a salient public issue with overwhelming support for change. Even for the most liberal members of Congress the question was not whether welfare reform legislation would pass; indeed, it appeared it would. Rather, the question confronting these members was how harsh and how punitive the provisions of that legislation would be.

Welfare Reform in the 104th Congress: The Legislative Process

The Personal Responsibility and Work Opportunity Reconciliation Act of 1996 (HR 3734) dismantled the federal entitlement program known as Aid to Families with Dependent Children (AFDC) and replaced it with a block grant called Temporary Assistance for Needy Families (TANF). However, welfare reform in the 104th Congress cannot be understood by looking only at the debates around HR 3734 that took place during the spring and summer of 1996. Rather, the final bill was also a product of the debates surrounding the passage and subsequent veto of its precursor, HR 4 or the Personal Responsibility Act, introduced in the early days of the first session of the 104th.

HR 4 was itself the culmination of several years of debate during which both Republican and Democratic party task forces reviewed current welfare policy and recommended reforms. Most Democrats were in favor of providing some reform through welfare-to-work programs while maintaining the basic concept of entitlements to assistance. In contrast, for many Republicans, welfare had come to symbolize all that was wrong with "big government." Consequently, the goal for most Republicans was to dismantle welfare programs, especially AFDC, and shift the responsibility of providing assistance from the federal government to the states.

On January 4, 1995, the Republicans' welfare proposal was introduced as HR 4, the Personal Responsibility Act. Three House committees had primary jurisdiction over the bill—the Ways and Means Committee, the Economic and Education Opportunities Committee, and the Agriculture Committee. The Ways and

Means Committee considered most of the important provisions of the welfare reform package such as establishing block grants for cash benefits and child welfare programs, setting work requirements, funding childcare programs, reducing Supplemental Security Insurance, imposing a cap on family size, enforcing time limits for benefits, limiting some social services to legal immigrants, and denying welfare benefits to unwed, teenaged mothers. To appease moderate Republican members of this committee, GOP leaders modified certain provisions by easing the financial penalties on unwed mothers and adding provisions to force noncustodial parents to pay child support.

The Republican majority on the Economic and Educational Opportunities Committee also supported dramatic changes in welfare programs. They voted to fold nine childcare programs into the existing Childcare and Development Block Grant, create the Family and Nutrition Block Grant to provide food and nutrition to pregnant women and young children, replace the existing school breakfast and lunch programs with a block grant, impose a restriction on legal immigrant access to nineteen federal programs, and restrict the access of illegal immigrants to twenty-three programs.

The Agriculture Committee considered a bitterly contested proposal to cut the food stamp program and require recipients to find work. The bill, as it emerged from this committee, proposed to reduce spending by capping food stamp allotments, ending automatic cost of living increases, and denying benefits to legal aliens.

When GOP leaders brought HR 4 to the floor, they were able to maintain solid support for their bill, in large part because they had incorporated some provisions championed by moderates. While some moderate Republicans were still uncomfortable with parts of the legislation, they believed that the Senate would temper the House version of the bill (*Congressional Quarterly* Mar. 23, 1995, 873). Democrats, in an unusual display of partisan unity, uniformly blasted the bill throughout the floor debate, painting the Republicans as heartless for cutting programs for school lunches and nutritional programs for pregnant women and infants. On March 24, after four days of acrimonious floor debate, the House passed the bill by a vote of 234 to 199 with very little Democratic support.

Welfare reform in the Senate was less drastic, although Republican Senators were wedded to the centerpiece of House reform, turning AFDC into a block grant. While the Senate generally accepted the tenets of the House version, senators were less comfortable with the idea of block granting other programs, such as food stamps. Moderate Republicans were able to temper the House version through amendments to the bill drafted in the Senate Agriculture Committee (food stamps), the Finance Committee, and the Labor and Human Resources Committee (childcare).

After a day and a half of floor debate in August 1995, Majority Leader Bob

Dole pulled the measure off the floor when it became clear that seven core moderate Republicans would not support it. However, after several modifications to the bill on and off the floor (including an optional family cap and increased daycare dollars), the Senate passed a revised version of welfare reform by a vote of 87 to 12 on September 19.

The conference report, adopted by the House on December 21 by a vote of 245 to 178 and the Senate on December 22 by a vote of 52 to 47, reconciled differences in the House and Senate bills. Nevertheless, on January 9, 1996, President Clinton dashed any hope of welfare reform in the first session by vetoing HR 4.

In February 1996, the National Governors Association breathed new life into welfare reform with its passage of a proposal to overhaul welfare and Medicaid. The governors' initiative was largely based on HR 4, but it had some important changes making it more palatable to moderate Republicans and the president, namely a $4 billion increase in childcare funding and an optional family cap provision.

On May 22, 1996, Congressional Republicans introduced a revamped proposal to overhaul welfare, which included a highly contentious provision to end the existing entitlement of Medicaid. The new bill retained the centerpieces of HR 4 by imposing work requirements and time limits on welfare benefits, block granting federal monies to the states while giving states wide latitude in spending decisions, sharply reducing social services for legal immigrants, and basically ending welfare's status as an entitlement. The bill differed from HR 4 by incorporating some of the more moderate features of a welfare reform plan that the National Governors Association adopted, including a $4 billion increase in childcare funding and an optional family cap provision.

A major obstacle to this bill was removed in July 1996 when the Republicans dropped the provision to convert Medicaid into a block grant; President Clinton had promised to veto any bill that included this provision. Ultimately, the welfare reform bill with various amendments added by the relevant committees was reported out of the House Budget Committee as HR 3734. Republican leaders left little to chance and limited amendments from the floor by introducing all reforms to welfare as a budget reconciliation bill. House members were only allowed to vote on two amendments—an unsuccessful Democratic substitute and a successful proposal to restrict food stamp eligibility. The House passed HR 3734 on July 18 by a vote of 256 to 170.

The Senate began floor debate on the day the bill passed in the House. The bill became more palatable to moderate Republicans and Democrats with the addition of an amendment assuring Medicaid coverage to nonpregnant women and to children up to age thirteen, the removal of language that would have allowed some states to gain control of food stamp programs through a block grant, and the elimination of the family cap provision. After substituting the text of the Senate bill, S 1956, for HR 3734, the Senate voted passage 74 to 24 on July 23.

The Conference Committee compromised on some key issues that appealed to moderate Republicans and Democrats: the family cap requirement was dropped; a comprehensive system for enforcing child support was adopted; funds for childcare were increased, and states were prohibited from penalizing single parents who proved they could not work because they could not find childcare for children under the age of six; states were allowed to use federal funds to provide vouchers for children whose parents lost benefits; and the block grants for food stamps and child protection programs were eliminated. In addition, the report included some provisions that appealed to both conservative Democrats and Republicans. The final bill denied cash assistance and food stamps to convicted drug felons and allowed states to deny Medicaid coverage to those who were dropped from welfare rolls because they did not meet work requirements.

On July 31, after a meeting with top advisors, President Clinton announced that he would sign the bill if it passed. He expressed continuing concern over the provisions denying aid to legal immigrants and the deep cuts in food stamps. He vowed to overturn both of these provisions in future legislation, but he acknowledged that Congress had made many of the changes he had sought.

On the same day, the House adopted the Conference report by a vote of 328 to 101 in a somewhat anticlimactic debate. House Republicans were almost unanimous in their support, while Democrats split their vote, 98 to 98. The Senate voted on the report the next day and approved it by a vote of 78 to 21. Democrats again split their votes, while Republicans almost unanimously supported the legislation. With President Clinton's signature, the Personal Responsibility and Work Opportunity Reconciliation Act of 1996 became law, effectively ending welfare as we had known it. Table 5.1 summarizes recent welfare provisions.

Efforts and Impact of Republican Women in the House

Given the Republican majority in the House, Republican women were in a better position than Democratic women to influence the specifics of welfare reform legislation. Indeed, for the first time in forty years, the House Republicans were the majority and more women than ever, although still only a few, were in positions of power. Nancy Johnson (R-CT) chaired the House Committee on Standards of Official Conduct (Ethics), and Jan Meyers (R-KN) chaired the Small Business Committee. In addition, Nancy Johnson chaired the Oversight Subcommittee of the Ways and Means Committee. A few women were also included in the inner sanctum of the House Republican leadership. Susan Molinari (R-NY) was Republican Conference Vice-Chair, and Jennifer Dunn (R-WA) was invited to join the "working group" of advisors to newly elected Speaker Newt Gingrich, who later appointed her to his ten-member transition team. According to Nancy

Table 5.1
Comparative Welfare Provisions By Proposal

	HR4 INTRODUCED JANUARY 1995 VETOED JANUARY 1996	*NATIONAL GOVERNORS ASSOCIATION PROPOSAL* FEBRUARY 1996	*HR3734* INTRODUCED MAY 1996 SIGNED AUGUST 1996
Block Grants for Cash Benefits	• Yes, $16.3 billion	• Yes	• TANF block grant replaces AFDC • $16.4 billion through 2001 • Contingency fund
Work Requirements	• Within 2 years	• Left to states to decide	• Within 2 years • Parents with child under 6 can work 20hrs/week • 12 month exemption with child under 1 year • Minimum 20 hours until 2000 thereafter 30 hours
Family Cap	• Yes, required	• Yes, optional to states	• Yes, optional to states
Time Limit for Lifetime Benefits	• 5 years	• Left to states to decide	• 5 years
Restrictions for Legal Immigrants	• Ineligible for food stamps • Ineligible for SSI	• No provisions	• Ineligible for food stamps • Ineligible for SSI
Restrictions for Unwed, Teenage Mothers	• State option to deny benefits until 18 years old	• Optional to states	• $20 million incentives for states who decrease out-of-wedlock births without increasing abortions • Unmarried parents under 18 qualified only if attend high school or alternative educational or training program
Child Support Enforcement	• No provisions	• No provisions	• New procedures to establish paternity and enforce child support orders • Required state registries to track status of all child support orders
Child Protection	• No provisions	• No provisions	• Retained eligibility under AFDC rules • Required states to give preference to adult relative when determining child's placement
Child Care	• Folded into Childcare and Development Block grant • Total $11 billion between 1997 and 2002 • Additional $1 billion annually for discretionary fund	• Called for increasing child care dollars	• Folded into Child Care and Development Block grant • Total $13.85 billion 1997 to 2002 • Additional $1 billion annual discretionary funds through 2001 • States required to spend as much of their state funds as they had on AFDC-related child care during FYs 1994 and 1995. • Required to submit a state plan for funding
Food Stamp Restrictions	• Cut individual allotments • Able-bodied 18-50 year olds without dependents required to work • Food stamps block granted • Double penalties for fraud and abuse	• No provisions	• Reduced individual allotments by 3% • Able-bodied 18-50 year olds without dependents required to work • Pregnant women exempt and those otherwise exempt from work registration

Johnson, the most noteworthy development regarding women members in the 104th Congress was not their increased numbers in the House as a whole, but rather "the increased number of women in power. When the Republicans took over, they didn't shrink from giving women the positions that they earned by seniority."

In the area of welfare reform, the efforts of one Republican woman, in particular, stand out above all others in the House. As a senior member of the Ways and Means Committee, which had jurisdiction over most of the important provisions of the welfare reform bill, Nancy Johnson, by all accounts, carefully picked her battles with her Republican colleagues and, by our count, on welfare reform she won quite a few. In committee and behind the scenes, Nancy Johnson used her seniority and challenged the Republican leadership to move on some key provisions, including child support enforcement. According to one Republican staffer:

> Republicans were very reluctant to accept a lot of things that Nancy [Johnson] . . . and Barbara Kennelly [were] pushing. . . . They were *very* reluctant. Then, it's almost like they heard the drum roll from outside [and realized] they could potentially be perceived to be anti-child support and anti-family. So they had this one incredible meeting which I didn't attend. It was only Republican members. And Nancy came out of there winning like ten out of twelve things that she wanted, or something really phenomenal.

According to those we interviewed, Johnson effectively pushed her colleagues on child support enforcement in this meeting by asking the question, "Do you really want to be this tough on women and children and be seen as not being tough on dead-beat dads?"

In fact, Nancy Johnson and other women members of Congress of both parties deserve considerable credit for the child support enforcement provisions that were included in the final welfare reform legislation. The child support enforcement provisions in the Personal Responsibility and Work Opportunity Reconciliation Act of 1996 (HR 3734) were the same as those included in the Personal Responsibility Act (HR 4). The provisions in the Personal Responsibility Act were drawn from HR 785, legislation introduced by Nancy Johnson on behalf of Congressional Caucus for Women's Issues early in the first session of the 104th Congress. Johnson's bill, HR 785, was originally drafted by the Congressional Caucus for Women's Issues under the leadership of cochairs Patricia Schroeder (D-CO) and Olympia Snowe (R-ME) and introduced during the 103rd Congress.[4]

In addition to her efforts on behalf of child support enforcement, Johnson also worked hard to increase funding for childcare. According to Johnson, the proposal to increase childcare funding was contentious among Republicans. While the Republican women pushed for adding more money to the Childcare and Development Block Grant to fund both women on welfare and those leaving the rolls, some Republican men argued that the drop in the numbers of people on welfare meant that there would be "free money" that states could use for childcare. For Johnson, "that was a legitimate argument, [but] it simply wasn't satisfactory, partly because of the perception [that Republicans don't care about children] and partly because . . . under the Democrats, the 1988 bill failed because we didn't fund day care. . . . So, if we are going to get people into the work force, and have someone else take care of their children, we absolutely had to have [increased funding for childcare]."

The issues of child support enforcement and childcare formed the foundation of what Nancy Johnson characterized as Republican women's commitment to attending to the issue of economic opportunity for women within welfare reform. According to Johnson, she worked closely with Ways and Means Chairman Clay Shaw (R-FL) to "leverage independence" for poor women. While Republican men were sympathetic to the goal of independence, Johnson credited the Republican women on the committee with spearheading the initiatives on childcare and child support, arguing "it just helped having women saying, well, we need more day care."

In addition to championing childcare and child support enforcement, Johnson helped save Medicaid coverage for older children and women. Johnson believed that Medicaid was crucial to helping women find jobs and move off the welfare rolls. She explained:

[D]ay care and healthcare are essential. You cannot ask a mother to work if working means that she leaves her children alone or she can't take them to the doctor when they are sick. That's inhuman and you're forcing her to make a Hobson's choice that responsible parents shouldn't make. You can't stay in the workforce if you can't provide healthcare for your children.

According to one lobbyist for children's health, Johnson is known for her tenacity. This lobbyist:

give[s] her a large share of the credit for dogging at the very end of the process. There was a very serious issue about protecting Medicaid coverage, primarily for mothers. Once you ended AFDC . . . you face[d] the problem of whether the people who would have been eligible for AFDC would be able to get Medicaid because the programs [were] linked. Many of the children would continue to be eligible . . . because [of] a series of legislative changes. . . . But older children [13 and up] and women would have absolutely fallen through the cracks. And it was very much as a result of Nancy Johnson and John Chafee. . . . At the very end they fought and fought until that was straightened out. I have to say they took the lead over Democrats, over the administration. They did it!

While most of Johnson's maneuvering was behind the scenes, she also forwarded amendments in the Ways and Means Committee and on the floor of the House. One of her successful amendments in the first session of the 104th Congress clarified that recipients who were working, looking for a job, or receiving on-the-job training could apply those efforts toward their work requirements. In the second session, Johnson offered two amendments in committee. The one that passed provided that all welfare recipients would be eligible for Medicaid coverage if they did not otherwise have medical coverage. The rejected amendment prohibited states from penalizing any parent who needed childcare for a child ten years old or younger and who could not find work within a specified amount of time. On the floor, Johnson, along with three other Republican women, proposed an amendment to increase the authorization level for childcare block grants by $750 million for the next four years. It passed by a voice vote. The great effort that Johnson put into trying to amend the proposed welfare reform legislation exemplifies what we heard in the interviews about Johnson's tenacity and her commitment to the issues that affect the health and welfare of children.

Jennifer Dunn (R-WA), a second-term member of Congress who along with Johnson served on the Ways and Means Committee, also was active and influential on provisions regarding childcare and child support enforcement. According to Dunn, who identifies herself as a conservative, welfare reform was the issue "where [she] made the biggest difference." Like Johnson, Dunn saw her institutional position as crucial for making the changes she deemed necessary. In fact, she chose the Human Resources Subcommittee in order to help "rewrite welfare." According to Dunn, women could only affect the way Congress thought about policies and women:

> as long as [women] are at the meeting. . . . Now that we [the Republicans] control the majority, that kind of thinking starts much earlier, because we generate the legislation now. So I think that when [women] are in the room, and with the general training that we've begun to do with our male colleagues . . . we've begun to have quite an impact

Republican staff generally agreed that Jennifer Dunn had an impact on the debates on childcare and child support. According to one Republican who staffed a major committee, Dunn was an important player behind the scenes who worked to increase childcare funding in HR 3734 and to educate Republican men on the child support enforcement issue. Dunn viewed the education of her male colleagues as one of her responsibilities and a necessary precondition for change. She explained: "I have been a single mother for twenty years, since my kids were six and eight. So there are issues I understand and can interpret for my male colleagues. I have become a resource they turn to on certain votes."

Indeed, according to the Republican staffer, Jennifer Dunn actually played a greater role behind the scenes than did Nancy Johnson "simply because she was on the [Human Resources] Subcommittee, and Nancy Johnson was not. [Nancy Johnson, as chair of the House Committee] had a lot of distractions and obligations that Jennifer Dunn didn't have."

Even on the floor during the debate on HR 3734, Dunn showed her commitment to increasing childcare funding. Along with Nancy Johnson and two other Republican women, Dunn cosponsored the amendment for additional childcare funding. In Dunn's view, additional funds for childcare were necessary if women were to move off the welfare rolls. On the floor of the House, she explained, "Mr. Speaker, as a single mother who raised two sons, I know how difficult it is for women to go back to work" (Congressional Record 1995).

Nancy Johnson and, to a lesser extent, Jennifer Dunn were the most visible Republican women and the only Republican women who served on any of the three committees that considered welfare reform legislation in the House. Several Republican women, however, were concerned about the depth of the cuts and the breadth of the changes proposed by the original versions of both HR 4 and HR 3734. As one Republican staffer explained:

> I think the bill in the 104th Congress was such a radical change to welfare . . . that the Republican women . . . were really motivated and took on the responsibility to change the bill. . . . Something about a bill that threatened to send women and children off welfare and who knows where, I think really was alarming. And I also think the congresswomen better understood that without childcare, people can't go to work. Nutrition programs, whatever their faults are, work; children need to eat. I think that the Republican women, at some basic level, understood that better than some of their [male] counterparts.

An example is Connie Morella (R-MD), who cosponsored an alternative welfare reform measure entitled the *Castle-Tanner Bipartisan Welfare Reform Act of 1996* and, in her capacity as cochair of the Congressional Caucus for Women's Issues, helped organize bipartisan efforts to temper the final welfare reform bill. For example, under Morella's leadership, the Congressional Caucus on Women's Issues (1995) wrote a letter to the conference committee that considered HR 3734. According to a staff member, the letter advocated "three specific changes in childcare: more money, health and safety standards, and state responsibility," all of which "were ultimately adopted."

Efforts and Impact of Republican Women in the Senate

The Senate is a very different institution than the House. First, there are only 100 senators as opposed to 435 representatives, which allows any single individual to have more influence. Second, while committees are very important and much work on legislation is done in committee, they are less important than in the House. Through debate and amendments on the floor, individual senators can often make an impact even if they are not on the relevant committees, which is seldom the case in the House.

Women members of the Senate from both parties were particularly active in floor debates over welfare reform. For example, of the forty amendments offered on the floor from September 8 to September 19, 1995, when the Senate, during the first session, considered its version of HR 4, ten were sponsored by women. Thus, the women, who constituted only 8 percent of all senators, were disproportionately active in debating the Senate version of HR 4. Because S 1956, the Senate's version of HR 3734 that was passed during the second session, was considered as a budget reconciliation bill, floor debate was limited to twenty hours and only amendments relevant to federal revenues and outlays were allowed. Consequently, women members had few opportunities to propose amendments to this second welfare reform bill.

While there were fewer Republicans than Democrats among the women senators in the 104th Congress, the Republican women were at an advantage by being members of the majority party. Nancy Kassebaum (R-KS) had the most impact of the three Republican women senators largely because she chaired the Senate Labor and Human Resources Committee, which had jurisdiction over parts of welfare reform. In addition, she was the sole woman senator on the conference committee that reconciled differences between House and Senate versions of welfare reform legislation. Her influence was enhanced through her association with a group of moderate Republicans known as the "Mod Squad."

Kassebaum made major contributions to the welfare reform legislation that was enacted into law in two areas that were of strong concern to her and also within the jurisdiction of her committee—childcare and child protection. In May 1995, the Labor and Human Resources Committee under Kassebaum's leadership unanimously approved S 850, a bill which reauthorized the Childcare and Development Block Grant of 1990, preserved most of the federal requirements regarding licensing and health and safety standards, and consolidated three childcare programs into one block grant. Kassebaum later offered this bill as a floor amendment to the Senate version of HR 4, and it was approved by a wide margin. Kassebaum noted, "The primary goal of this bill is to ensure that there is a seamless system of childcare where it counts—at the point where the parent, child, and provider meet" (*Congressional Quarterly* May 27, 1995, 1,507). A Republican staffer who was familiar with the work of Kassebaum and the committee explained:

> One of the things that had bothered Senator Kassebaum for a long time . . . was the fact that you had seven different federal childcare programs, all of which had different rules, different guidelines, different implementation at the state [level] by different agencies in the state.

If a parent on welfare had a child in one childcare program, then lost her job and had to pull the child out of childcare, then found another job and tried to enroll the child with another childcare provider, the child had to start at the bottom of the waiting list. With a seamless system, according to this staffer:

> All of the money . . . runs through the same system, with the same application, with the same requirement, with the same data collection, with the same everything. So, that means that the thing that changes in terms of the child and the parent is the sliding fee scale. If they're working, they're going to have to pay more. If they're not working, they are going to have to pay less. It's not going to cause a change of providers by any way, shape, or form.

In addition to her concern about creating a seamless childcare system, Kassebaum used her position as committee chair and conferee to push for other childcare provisions that she considered important. A staff member who was involved in this effort explained:

> [The Personal Responsibility and Work Opportunity Reconciliation Act of 1996] for the first time, applies minimum state and local licensing and a minimum assurance of federal guidelines in terms of quality to the entitlement money on childcare. We also tripled the amount of money going into childcare. So, those were really crucial, and they were things she fought for very hard. And it was a hard-fought battle, and . . . she has a spine of steel. . . . And the seamless system was something that was critically important to her, as was the licensing, as was the assurance that at least some portion of these funds be spent to insure . . . the quality of childcare, another big issue for her. . . . And we got 'em in part because of this group of 13 [the Mod Squad], and in part because she is just stubborn.

The other issue which Kassebaum, by all reports, cared passionately about was the preservation of child protection programs. The House version of welfare reform legislation would have altered the funding for foster care, adoption assistance, and child abuse prevention and treatment. It would have replaced direct federal assistance for such programs with block grants without restrictions on how the money was spent. In contrast, the Personal Responsibility and Work Opportunity Reconciliation Act that became law made only modest changes to child protection programs, for the most part, retaining their existing structure and funding. Nancy Kassebaum was a major reason why the final legislation did not include the House provisions. Kassebaum's committee had jurisdiction over child protection issues, and the Senate version of the bill did not include the House's provisions to block grant the funding for child protection programs. The House and Senate versions had to be reconciled, and a staff member explained what happened as follows:

A meeting took place between the House leadership, the Senate leadership, a couple of the key players. . . . Nancy Kassebaum and John Chafee were called into the meeting, and for over an hour the eighteen [other people in attendance] tried to convince John Chafee and Nancy Kassebaum to accept the block grant or some version of the block grant. And they said, "No." They said repeatedly, "No." And finally, seeing that you had two very immovable objects, and again remembering that they were tied into this group of 13 [the Mod Squad], that's when it [the block grant] got dropped out.

Olympia Snowe's (R-ME) impact on welfare reform came largely through her participation in an informal group of moderate Republicans, which varied from seven to thirteen in number, who banded together in support of several provisions they cared about and wielded considerable power because their votes were key to insuring passage of a welfare reform bill. As noted above, Nancy Kassebaum also participated in this group, which staff affectionately referred to as the "Mod Squad." One Republican staff member described the origins of the Mod Squad as follows:

We got together originally because we thought we'd been shut out of a lot of the debate. . . . It started off where they [the Republican leadership] would call every Republican staffer down to a room in the Capitol, and they would proceed to go through the bill. And then they would say, "Who's got a problem with this?" . . . Only about nine people were consistently raising their hands saying they had a problem. . . . And we . . . would come back the next time and they hadn't addressed our concerns.

After one particular meeting where the staff members who had "problems" were chastised for failing to go along with the leadership, the dissident staffers began to meet almost daily to discuss their mutual concerns. The Republican staff member further explained:

A lot of it was just very informal. . . . There were very few times that we had all of our bosses write a letter together or anything like that. But we found out what our strength was—the vote. . . . We had enough to tip the vote either way.

Another Republican staff member explained how the Mod Squad worked:

This was not just staff putting things together. The members [of the Senate] had regular meetings to discuss both strategy and the issues, and all of them talked. We had coordinated such that each of us had a specialty. . . . Within those areas . . . [we each did] talking points. . . . Every member, all the thirteen members, used the same talking points. . . . It was very powerful in that you couldn't peel anyone off.

The Mod Squad pushed for a package of eight changes that altered the Senate version of HR 4 in a more moderate direction. According to *Congressional Quarterly*, among other accomplishments, the moderate group was able to:

- overturn a provision that would have denied cash assistance for children born to welfare recipients;
- block conservatives from inserting provisions denying welfare checks to unwed teenage mothers;
- modify the bill to require states to continue at least 80 percent of their welfare funding over five years; and
- add $3 billion over five years for childcare for welfare recipients and modify the bill so that recipients with children age 5 or under who are unable to get childcare are not penalized for not working (Sept. 16, 1995, 2,805).

Because the leadership needed their votes to pass welfare reform and because they stuck together, the Mod Squad was very successful in getting the changes they wanted.

As part of the Mod Squad, Snowe's major influence was informal and often behind the scenes. One Republican staff member noted, "Senator Snowe was very involved. She really energized a lot of the moderates." Another Republican staffer observed, "Snowe is . . . meticulous. . . . She is somebody that when she talks, people listen." While Snowe's influence during the first session of the 104th was largely through her participation in the Mod Squad, in the second session she played a more formal role as well. During Senate deliberations on the final welfare bill, she proposed an amendment that she cosponsored with a Democrat, Christopher Dodd. The amendment, which was approved by a voice vote, required that states increase by one percentage point the amount of the Childcare and Development Block Grant that must be spent on improving the availability and quality of childcare (Clemmitt, Primmer, and Simms 1997, 87).

Kay Bailey Hutchison (R-TX), the most conservative of the three Republican women senators, was the least involved with welfare reform. She was not on a committee with jurisdiction over any aspect of the legislation. Nevertheless, Hutchison led an ultimately unsuccessful effort to change the proposed formula for distributing federal funds to states. In 1995, she organized thirty senators from southern and western states to sign a letter urging that states should receive a share of funds based on the number of poor children living inside their borders. The formula included in the bill proposed that states would receive funds in proportion to the federal funding they had received in the past for AFDC and related programs. Bob Graham (D-FL) put forward Hutchison's proposal as an amendment in the Senate Finance Committee; the amendment, however, was defeated (*Congressional Quarterly* June 24, 1995; *Congressional Quarterly Almanac* 1996). Hutchison's home state of Texas would have benefited significantly from the change in formula she and her colleagues proposed.

Discussion and Summary

Women in Congress were by no means united in their views on how to reform welfare in the 104th Congress. Even among Republicans, they spanned the ideological spectrum in their attitudes toward welfare reform, ranging from the very conservative perspective of Barbara Cubin to the far more progressive views of Connie Morella. Nevertheless, the overall impact of the involvement of women seems to have been to temper or moderate some of the harsher effects of the proposed legislation, and in the case of child support enforcement, to expand the legislation in a way that many feminists would find desirable.

On the surface, these statements seem paradoxical. How could women have exerted a predominantly moderating influence when, in fact, they shared no common point of view on welfare reform? The explanation is that institutional factors made a few Republican women important players while relegating most other women, including the very conservative freshman class and almost all the Democrats, to the sidelines. In particular, the importance of seniority and institutional position combined to make the influence of moderate Republican women particularly strongly felt.

Republicans controlled both houses, and in a highly partisan environment such as that which characterized the 104th Congress, few Democrats were able to directly influence welfare reform legislation though many Democratic women tried mightily to do so. The freshmen women in the House, certainly the most conservative cohort of women elected to Congress in recent history, had no institutional basis for exercising influence. They could do little more than speak on the floor during debate. The women best positioned to influence welfare reform legislation were the more senior Republican women, most of whom were moderates.

This analysis has pointed to three areas in the welfare reform legislation that the 104th Congress considered where Republican women clearly had their strongest impact: childcare, child support, and child protection. Funding for childcare was increased and childcare programs were consolidated into a "seamless system" because of the efforts of women members such as Nancy Johnson and Nancy Kassebaum. Similarly, provisions were included in welfare reform legislation providing for federal regulation of licensing and insuring quality control largely because of the efforts of these women.

The child support provisions included in the final bill were drafted by the Congressional Caucus for Women's Issues and introduced and advocated for by women members, both Republicans and Democrats. Republican women members worked to insure that the welfare reform legislation was not just aimed at welfare mothers, but also at dead-beat dads. And they pushed for effective enforcement of these measures.

Child protection programs remained in place with their existing funding and structure largely because women cared about protecting these programs. Nancy Kassebaum, reinforced by her ties to the Mod Squad, played a critical role in removing from the final legislation potentially harmful provisions that would have converted funding for child protection programs to a block grant with little federal control.

The two women who were perhaps able to have the greatest influence on welfare reform legislation were two moderate Republicans, Nancy Johnson in the House and Nancy Kassebaum in the Senate. These are not the two congresswomen whose names are most closely associated with feminism. Yet, these women clearly cared passionately about issues such as availability of quality childcare, child support enforcement, and the preservation of child protection services. Both fought tenaciously, often against their party leadership, to make welfare reform legislation stronger and more equitable in these areas.

The efforts of Jennifer Dunn, ideologically more conservative and with closer ties to the Republican House leadership than her colleague Nancy Johnson, also were critical in increasing childcare funding and securing approval for child support enforcement provisions. Other moderate Republican women such as Olympia Snowe and Connie Morella played important roles.

Some feminist advocates who were strongly opposed to the Personal Responsibility and Work Opportunity Reconciliation Act of 1996, including a few we interviewed for this study, dismiss the efforts and accomplishments of Republican women members of Congress on welfare reform as ineffective or insufficient. Clearly, Republican women of the 104th Congress, like their male colleagues, believed that welfare reform was needed. Certainly, Republican women could not and did not influence all aspects of welfare reform, and they did not determine or fundamentally alter the predominant tone or intent of the legislation that was passed.

Nevertheless, the provisions of the legislation which Republican women did influence in the areas of childcare, child support enforcement, and child protection were important ones. Moreover, provisions in at least two of these three areas—childcare and child support enforcement—were central to the overall welfare reform package. Speaking at a conference on "Women and Welfare Reform," sponsored by the Institute for Women's Policy Research and held in Washington, D.C. in October 1993, David Ellwood, Assistant Secretary in the U.S. Department of Health and Human Services, reviewed four elements that President Clinton had identified as essential to welfare reform. One of these elements was child support enforcement. A second element was described by Ellwood as "making work pay"—making sure that people who work are able to make it on their own financially. According to both Ellwood and President Clinton, "making work pay" requires adequate childcare (Mink 1994, 58–59). Thus, Ellwood's remarks clearly suggest that child support enforcement and childcare, two of the three areas where Republican women had the greatest impact were hardly peripheral or unimportant aspects of welfare reform.

Ultimately, however, an assessment of whether the presence and efforts of women in Congress made an appreciable difference in welfare reform legislation must be based in large part on the answer to the question: Are the lives of women and children who are affected by welfare reform legislation better than they otherwise would have been because of the efforts of women members of Congress? We believe the answer to this question unequivocally is "yes."

Notes

1. In other work we have explored more fully the efforts of Democratic women members of Congress to influence welfare legislation; see Casey and Carroll, 1998.

2. A few scholars have focused on debates that took place internal to decision-making units of the U.S. state; see, for example, Kessler-Harris 1995. The literature on "femocrats," much of which focuses on Australia (e.g., Eisenstein 1996), also looks at politics internal to the state.

3. This paper is part of a larger project, conducted by the Center for American Women and Politics, focusing on the impact of women members of Congress on major areas of legislation considered by the 104th Congress. The study was made possible through the support of the Ford Foundation.

   To construct a list of congressional staffers and lobbyists to be interviewed, we began with several key staff and lobbyists we knew had worked on one or more of the policy issues we were examining. From these people we then solicited suggestions of other staff members and lobbyists involved with the issues. Each time we conducted an interview, we asked for the names of other sources to add to our list of potential interviewees. Our goal was to construct as complete a list as possible of the population of relevant, knowledgeable staffers and lobbyists, including Republicans and Democrats, feminists and antifeminists, liberals and conservatives, and allies and opponents of the women members on specific issues. Interviews were conducted from fall 1996 through spring 1998. Interviews with women members of Congress were done mostly in person, averaged about thirty minutes, and were conducted on-the-record. Interviews with staff and lobbyists, which averaged about forty-five minutes, were conducted by telephone, taped, and transcribed. Staff and lobbyists were assured that their names would not be used and that they would be identified only in the most general terms.

4. The main provisions require states to: submit all child support orders to a national registry; develop a new hire registry and collect information similar to what is included on a W-4 form; establish a central registry to track delinquent parents regardless of where they live within the state; and establish a central location for collecting payments. These provisions further require states to distribute payments within two days of collection and unify interstate child support enforcement laws. States are allowed to: order genetic testing; intercept workers' compensation, unemployment, and lottery winnings; and impose liens on property.

Six

Ann Shola Orloff

Ending the Entitlements
of Poor Single Mothers

*Changing Social Policies, Women's Employment,
and Caregiving in the Contemporary United States*

In 1996, U.S. social policy underwent a dramatic change with the passage of the Personal Responsibility and Work Opportunity Reconciliation Act (PRWORA). This act repealed the federal program, Aid to Families with Dependent Children (AFDC), and replaced it with Temporary Assistance to Needy Families (TANF), a system of block grants to the states to run their own welfare programs. The individual entitlement to social assistance, firmly established only in the 1960s and 1970s, was explicitly eliminated. Most striking, there is a lifetime limit of five years of benefits. Moreover, the new welfare legislation mandates TANF beneficiaries, whatever the age of their children, to participate in community service, better known as "workfare," after two months of receiving benefits and to join the workforce after two years.

Although childcare funding has increased, it is notable that caregiving has lost governmental backing if not accompanied by employment. What has been called welfare reform, actually the elimination of a program, is only one part of the political changes concerning gender relations, women, and poor mothers, even within the system of income support, in the United States. Of particular importance is the Earned Income Tax Credit (EITC), which is both raising the employment rates of single mothers and having noticeable and positive effects on the incomes of poor employed parents, especially single mothers (Meyer and Rosenbaum 1998; Weaver 1998). Unlike AFDC, the EITC has been expanded several times over the course of the 1980s and 1990s. Claims for support are made in the course of filing tax returns and are conditional on both low income from employment and supporting children.

What is the significance of these changes? What forces might account for these policy shifts? Political commentary on welfare reform has been extensive but, as yet, analyses of welfare reform in terms of gender relations have been few (one exception is Mink 1998). After briefly assessing the character of the changes and their significance for gender relations, I evaluate some possible explanations for the timing and character of these policy developments.[1]

Welfare reform incorporates at least three distinct components: (a) it eliminates a social right, simultaneously eliminating caregiving as a base for making claims; (b) it expands the role of the market in the provision of income and care; and (c) it marks a shift in patterns of stratification toward gender sameness, in that institutionalized expectations for mothers no longer are distinguished from those for fathers—both are required to be employed, and programmatic distinctions now follow lines of differentiation in labor markets, rather than a family/employment dualism. Meanwhile, the expansion of the EITC reinforces these changes from a more positive direction: it channels resources to poor parents, but only if they are employed, linking support to reproduction and caregiving to participation in the labor market for both men and women. Yet, both eliminating AFDC and expanding the EITC can also be read as supporting the functioning of the low-wage labor market.

How can we explain this set of changes? Electoral and legislative politics were obviously significant (Myles and Pierson 1997; Weaver 1998; Weir 1998; Casey and Carroll, this volume). But my interest here is slightly different: I want to explore the structural conditions and processes of policy feedback that allowed political actors committed to welfare reform and the end of entitlement to gain power, and how long-term shifts in expectations about women's employment—reflecting changing patterns of paid and unpaid work—came to be institutionalized in work requirements that were coupled with the elimination of a (categorical) social right to full-time caregiving in the new welfare legislation.

According to a variety of explanatory approaches that one could loosely group under the rubric of "power resources," the elimination of a social right or entitlement can be linked to changing social balances of power in class, race, and gender relations. Employers, more hostile to social spending than before, have gained strength in the last two decades while labor, which traditionally supported social programs, has declined. As racial antipathies have sharpened, social programs identified with people of color have come under attack. In addition, while women may have scored gains in other areas of policy, public support for the traditionally feminine activities of caregiving has been cut away. How these power explanations bear on the question of newly institutionalized expectations about mothers' employment is not, however, clear. The new work requirements reflect changes in gender relations, especially women's labor force participation and related attitudes. This does not, however, bear on the question of social rights.

Finally, some analysts bring issues of power and the gender division of labor together in the context of relations of race and ethnicity, pointing out that models of motherhood and employment have differed for women of color and white women; women of color have long been expected to be employed, even when they have children, and often as caregivers for others (Glenn 1992). Mink (1998) invokes these racialized models of motherhood and employment to explain why welfare was changed to include work requirements and to eliminate individual entitlement.

That these forces of change are significant is clear. But, constituencies defending welfare, with the exception of a brief period in the 1960s and 1970s, have never been politically powerful (Weir, Orloff, and Skocpol 1988). Racial antagonisms, expressed via the codes of welfare politics, too, have been building for some time (Gilens 1996). And women's labor force participation has been increasing steadily in the postwar decades. Thus, these factors do not fully explain why welfare reform occurred when and in the form it did.

To understand the sources of change in the welfare regime, both social balances of power and changes in gender relations can be looked at within a historical and institutional context. Relations of race, class, and gender shaped welfare reform, to be sure—but as mediated by the policy legacy and the larger political-institutional context. This approach fits within the rubric of historical institutionalism and policy regime analysis, which focus on the characteristics of policy regimes and the politics engendered by these patterns (see e.g., Weir, Orloff, and Skocpol 1988; Esping-Andersen 1990, 1999; Skocpol 1992, 1995; Weir 1992, 1998; Orloff 1993a, 1993b; Pierson 1994, 1996; O'Connor, Orloff, and Shaver 1999).

By "policy regime," I mean to imply more than the welfare *state* because both private and public institutions are involved in the production of income and caregiving (welfare, broadly understood); it makes sense to analyze the ways in which welfare is produced and distributed across the state, market, and families (Esping-Andersen 1990, 1999; O'Connor, Orloff, and Shaver 1999).

The institutional analysis of regimes is critical to understanding the politics of social policy. The concept of a regime encompasses a number of dimensions (Esping-Andersen 1990; Orloff 1993a; O'Connor, Orloff, and Shaver 1999); these include (a) the character of social provision in terms of eligibility, ongoing requirements, duration, generosity and coverage—this determines whether provision takes the form of social rights or discretionary assistance, and influences individual and group outcomes such as income or time poverty, affects power relations and the very stakes of politics; (b) the institutional relationships among state, market, and family, and their capacities for delivering welfare; and (c) the patterns of stratification shaped by welfare arrangements. This last dimension refers to regimes' effects in terms of both (in)equality in access to valued resources and the social and political identities and interests created, supported, or transformed in the context of claiming benefits or services among individuals, and by differences among programs on the institutional level. The regime shapes political and social identities and interests, particularly through resourcing certain statuses and activities, and thus the characteristics of the "universe of political discourse," which Jenson and Mahon (1993, 79) define as the set of accepted meanings about who are legitimate actors, what is their political role, what issues are legitimate targets of political action, and what is ideal form of social relations. (Esping-Andersen [1999] refers to the "path dependency" of the social politics of distinctive regimes; Orloff [1993b], Pierson [1994], and Weir, Orloff, and Skocpol [1988] refer to this process of policy shaping politics as "policy feedback.").

In terms of specific policy areas, existing policies provide the context within which policymakers define problems and construct remedies; certain episodes—and I would include the elimination of AFDC—reflect a policy crisis, which I earlier defined as a situation in which policies no longer work politically, fiscally, or administratively (Orloff 1993b). Indeed, by the mid-1990s, both policy elites and the public believed that anything was preferable to the status quo of AFDC (Weaver 1998).

A number of feminist analysts (e.g., Fraser 1989b; Nelson 1984, 1990; Mink 1998) have highlighted the bifurcated form of the U.S. welfare state, in which women are the principal clientele of the "lower," social assistance tier where claims have been based on caregiving. The implicit assumption is that because women are disproportionately responsible for care and domestic work, all women should have had an interest in preserving and improving the treatment of such claims. But these analyses, while highlighting the significance for social policy of the gender division of labor and the concomitant unequal valuation of caregiving and employment, fail to attend to the overall shape of the social policy regime—particularly neglecting the large role of private provision and the market. For most mothers, even single ones, are employed, and they must get by without significant public support.

Many aspects of the U.S. policy regime—the interventions around employment and reproduction especially—are based on women as well as men being employed (even if patterns of employment differ). The significant policy successes in opening employment opportunities for women which, along with rising real wages and employers' demand for women's labor, have strengthened the forces, including women's own aspirations, leading to women's increased rates of paid employment. Furthermore, many women—especially single mothers—have benefited over the last decade from the enhanced economic possibilities of employment due to the expansion of the Earned Income Tax Credit and the rise in the minimum wage (Meyer and Rosenbaum 1998).

Finally, to the extent that state interventions are tied to equality projects, they are informed by understanding women's equality as tied to employment and economic independence rather than on rewarding women based on their distinctive caregiving activities (Fraser 1994; O'Connor, Orloff, and Shaver 1999). Several aspects of the policy regime influenced the politics that undermined AFDC: the tightly targeted character of public income support combined with its explicit support for full-time caregiving and nonemployment, in a context in which most women are employed, and the racialization of welfare. Even for many political actors generally committed to women's equality, it was at best difficult or, more often, not politically compelling to defend AFDC strongly.

Both the generally market-supporting and market-enhancing character of the U.S. policy regime and the particular articulation of gender equality projects with women's labor market participation helped to create a context within which welfare reform was likely to support employment. And the neoliberal thinking in favor among political elites ensured that welfare reform would encompass some shift of responsibilities from state to labor market and tie assistance to work activities or to employment—so as to support, rather than undercut, the low-wage labor market. But these ideas did not necessitate ending entitlement—social rights could have been made conditional on employment, as has been the case in Sweden or France for some time; indeed, even the Netherlands, where welfare benefits had allowed single mothers to undertake full-time caregiving and where housewifery still enjoys widespread cultural legitimacy, has adopted employment mandates, but within a context of continuing entitlements to social protection (Knijn 1994; Eardley et al., 1996).

What Kind of Welfare Reform?

Before turning to an assessment of alternative explanations for welfare reform, let us briefly examine the characteristics of the U.S. welfare reform of 1996—the Personal Responsibility Act and its gender effects. As a counterpoint to the major features of this act—provisions eliminating entitlements, the valuation of work over caregiving, and provisions regarding the collection of child support—the Earned Income Tax Credit will also be included.

Eliminating Entitlement

The new law eliminates AFDC and the entitlement to social assistance. Temporary Assistance to Needy Families (TANF), which gives states block grants for new state-run welfare programs grant has replaced AFDC; it is accompanied by a child care block grant.[2] The law mandates that adults receiving assistance engage in work after two years of receiving benefits (less, at state option) and that there be a five-year lifetime limit on cash benefits (less, at state option). States decide eligibility criteria, benefit levels, and specific work requirements but, crucially, there is no guarantee of assistance even if these criteria are met, as funding is neither assured nor mandated.

Caregiving and Work

A key difference between the original AFDC and TANF is that the latter makes few concessions to caregiving in imposing work requirements. The original program, enacted in 1935, was designed to support full-time caregiving. Provisions encouraging employment for some segments of the clientele began to appear in the mid-1960s. In the 1988 Support Act (FSA), all AFDC parents— mothers as well as fathers—with children three years of age and above were required to work or undergo training, and states had the option of imposing the work requirement on parents of children as young as one year. Clearly, women were expected to combine parenting and paid work, a dramatically different "model of motherhood," to use Leira's (1992) phrase, than the original. But states did not uniformly enforce the requirements, partly because of states' lack of fiscal resources, partly because political leaders were reluctant to spend funds for child care and transitional health care or were ambivalent about requiring mothers' work (Gordon 1988; Kane and Bane 1994).

The change concerning mothers' employment has become clearer still in the new welfare legislation, with the elimination of any exemption from work requirements for parents of children beyond an initial two-month period of receiving benefits. (Basically, parents get a little less than the equivalent of the twelve-week [unpaid] family leave mandated by the federal government on large employers.) Thus, unless they explicitly opt not to, states must require parents receiving TANF benefits for two months to engage in community service employment (popularly called workfare) unless they have a preschool child and are unable to find child care. States may exempt parents of children under age one, but they may also require immediate work activities or employment search. Moreover, the economic incentives under TANF—as well as in the EITC—favor employment, even part-time, low-wage work—over stay-at-home motherhood (Greenstein and Shapiro 1998).

Child Support and Family-Related Provisions

While the most onerous proposals of the Republican Right, such as the lifetime ban on benefits to unmarried teenage mothers, were not enacted (compare Carroll and Casey, this volume), the law included some measures such as bonuses to states that most reduce their rates of nonmarital births without raising abortion rates. And states were allowed, though not mandated, to establish family caps, under which benefits are not increased if beneficiaries have additional children—most states have done so (U.S. Committee on Ways and Means

1998, 515–518). Child support enforcement and paternity establishment were also strengthened; these measures require custodial parents to cooperate with state efforts to establish and enforce child support obligations and, if necessary, paternity.[3] There are sanctions for noncooperation by clients, but no guarantee that funds will be collected nor that any collected payments will be passed to custodial parents (*Focus* 1998).

Counterpoint: The Earned Income Tax Credit

While the situation for many, though not all, people receiving welfare has declined with welfare reform, the situation of some poor employed parents outside the welfare system—including single mothers—has actually improved over the last few years. Certainly, provision for those who are not employed remains minimal; in addition to TANF, there are federal Food Stamps (with requirements to engage in employment search or work-like requirements if not employed), unemployment insurance for a minority of the unemployed, and inevitably uneven and discretionary private charity. The economic boom of the mid-1990s, however, has reached many low-income workers, boosting wages and reducing unemployment, even as increased income inequality and employment instability remain problems. And returns to employment for low-income people, both women and men, have been increased by policies outside of the welfare framework, most significantly, the Earned Income Tax Credit (Meyer and Rosenbaum 1998).

Parents who have low earnings—the working poor, mothers or fathers—are eligible for a modest benefit, claimed through the tax system (and operating along lines similar to Negative Income Tax proposals; on EITC and NIT, see Myles and Pierson 1997). The logic of EITC is a quite different one than that of AFDC: the EITC is designed to provide incentives to work, especially low-wage work. Recent studies show that the EITC, alone or in combination with incentives and subsidies under TANF, makes even half-time work at the minimum wage a better economic choice than welfare benefits (Acs et al., 1998; Greenstein and Shapiro 1998). EITC expansion, along with the increased minimum wage, has contributed since 1989 to a 42 per cent increase in the (real) earnings of single employed mothers with two children and a 27 per cent increase for single employed mothers with one child (Dionne 1998), and has raised income for other families with children as well, moving more children from poverty than any other government program (Greenstein and Shapiro 1998). In giving gender-neutral help to employed parents, U.S. policy links income support for families to participation in employment for women as well as for men.

By ending AFDC, mandating work and time limits, and strengthening child support, many politicians were hoping to decrease the government share of families' income in favor of private sources. And spending on "welfare" is slated to decrease. But, the EITC, unlike other elements of the U.S. system of social provision, was expanded several times in the 1980s and 1990s, most recently and significantly in Clinton's 1993 budget package (Myles and Pierson 1997; Weaver 1998, 398). Indeed, the EITC outpaced spending on AFDC by the early 1990s; in fiscal 1996, EITC expenditures were double what the government spent on AFDC (Weaver 1998, 398). Forecasts for federal and state spending on low-income families with children—excluding immigrants—show continued increases despite the freeze on AFDC expenditures (Weaver 1998, figure 1; much of the increase, but not all, comes from Medicaid). And this expansion brings public income support to new categories of workers: the EITC represents new commitments to assist employed single mothers and fathers and two-parent families in which one or both parents work, all of whom had been excluded from state assistance under AFDC and associated policies. But unlike AFDC, the EITC does not undercut, but reinforces, the labor market.

Eligibility for the EITC is based on family income; some have therefore surmised that it is a new prop for traditional families, with husbands earning and wives caring. In fact, while such families can receive funds, as could other poor two-parent families with both parents earning wages if their income were low enough to qualify, it has most noticeably helped single mothers. Indeed, about 70 percent of the recipients of the EITC in 1997 were single heads of household and single people, and they received about 70 percent of the amount distributed (U.S. CWM 1998, 871; singles are a very small proportion of this group).

Since the PRA was signed in August 1996, over a third of the caseload has left welfare, encouraged by the buoyant economy of the late 1990s (Pear 1999). In the early phases of the new policy, states have been helped by an unexpected fiscal bonus as block grants were pegged to earlier, higher caseload levels. But recipients are now beginning to hit up against time limits; initial reports suggest that while the majority has found work and seems to be as well off as when receiving welfare, a substantial minority of those who have lost benefits has not found work (Goldberg 1999). Moreover, many welfare recipients face instability in their employment (Pavetti 1997). EITC can only help those who are employed, unemployment insurance only those recently employed (and sufficiently long enough to acquire coverage). When the business cycle next brings recession, there will also be challenges for the states, for unlike the old AFDC program under which the federal government funding to the states automatically expanded as demand grew during downturns, TANF's block grants are fixed and can only be expanded with explicit Congressional approval, in a context of budgetary constraints.

The Gender Effects of Welfare Reform

There are three major effects of this social policy reform on gender relations that will be emphasized. First, the Personal Responsibility Act eliminated an entitlement—a conditional social right for poor single mothers to care for their children full time. This withdrawal of social rights affects all citizens, but especially groups which historically have depended disproportionately on public assistance: single mothers with poor earnings capacities and heavy caregiving burdens, and racial and ethnic minority people, who suffer from relatively high rates of poverty and unemployment. AFDC gave poor women the capacity to form and maintain autonomous households, an exit option from marriage or partnerships, and a safety net against unemployment that paralleled the exit option based on employment enjoyed by women with better labor market prospects. If social rights offer disadvantaged groups greater leverage vis-à-vis advantaged groups, this withdrawal diminishes their power. The EITC does offer public support to families in a nondiscretionary manner, but only to those who are in the labor market and earning wages.

Second, the PRA accomplished a shift in institutional relationships. By replacing an entitlement, or social right, to assistance, however encumbered with restrictions, with benefits granted on a discretionary basis, the state forces citizens and residents toward reliance on private sources of support—the labor market, families, and charities. In terms of how care is organized, the new policy arrangements eliminate support for caregiving and reproduction when they are not linked to participation in the labor market, again emphasizing the importance of the market. While funding for childcare services has expanded, it remains insufficient to meet demand, and support for high-quality services has not yet been forthcoming. For those who do not gain access to the limited public support for care services (either subsidies or direct provision of services), the availability and quality of care depend on market resources, thus disadvantaging those with jobs paying poorly, with a clear bearing on gender, race, and class relations.

Third, this round of welfare reform accomplished a shift in the institutionalized expectations about the gender division of labor, in that women or, more to the point, mothers as well as men are now to be subject to the requirement of employment or work activities in claiming social assistance. Caregiving has been shifted to an even more marginal status within the U.S. policy regime, as claims based on the status of family caregiver have been eliminated. The identity of worker has been strengthened, and the overall pattern of gender stratification reflects a greater emphasis on gender sameness—men and women both work for pay. Remaining gender differences in responsibilities for (unpaid) caregiving are occluded.

Why Welfare Reform?

Why has the United States eliminated certain social rights of poor mothers? Why is employment to be expected of women—mothers—as well as men? Why has the state withdrawn support to caregiving and reproduction, except when it is accompanied by paid labor? Alternative factors commonly invoked to explain welfare policy outcomes include: (a) power resources, and particularly the weakness of constituencies relying on welfare; (b) changes in gender relations, specifically women's increased labor force participation and increasing proportions of single-mother households; and (c) racialized models of motherhood and employment. These were certainly all implicated in the recent policy shifts around welfare. But, the "gendered dual channel" analysis of U.S. welfare has in fact mischaracterized the political interests and identities of women. To understand fully the changes involved in PRA, these factors must be understood in the context of preexisting policies and processes of policy feedback. With regard to this, three factors must be considered: (a) the residualism of U.S. social provision, reflecting the weakness of the public safety net for the working-aged population; (b) the institutionalization in AFDC of a model of motherhood based on full-time caregiving when most women have had to enter employment to sustain households with or without partners, with little support from government programs; and (c) the racialization of welfare. These factors gave rise to a politics in which work requirements were increasingly accepted, but also in which social rights to be supported while caregiving full time became increasingly tenuous.

Many analysts of the welfare state look to the strength, or power resources, of working-class forces as the central factor in the development of social rights. More recently, as race and gender have come to be understood as significant for policy outcomes, the strength of racism and gender discrimination as part of the overall constellation of power resources has figured in explanations for the character of U.S. social policy (e.g., Abromovitz 1988; Boris 1995; Mink 1995).

The relative weakness of social rights, the lack of generosity of American social programs for nonelderly people, and the tight linkage of benefits to employment is often understood as reflecting the political and organizational weakness of working-class forces and the strength of employers vis-à-vis workers and states. Unions have been relatively weaker than in Europe or the Antipodes, while the lack of a major labor, social-democratic or socialist party has been a notable feature of U.S. political development. And indeed, the United States has had a relatively less-developed public system of supports for the working-aged population than has existed in other Western countries since at least the Second World War. Moreover, increased capital mobility and the opening of new low-wage labor markets in the developing economies has strengthened the position of employers vis-à-vis workers and organized labor over the last two decades or so (Rhodes 1996; Esping-Andersen 1999).

Also significant is the rise of (neo)liberalism as an ideological and cultural force—a preference for private provision and for minimizing state interventions, reflected in pressures to keep taxes and social spending low. These factors have led to the retrenchment and restructuring of social programs everywhere to make income support more closely conform to the "demands" of the new global economy—which is to say, of the employers in that economy. And in the United States, in contrast to other Western countries, employers have not been countered by a particularly strong labor movement, or a well-developed social-democratic, or labor party that might oppose the harshest aspects of policy restructuring.

But where those who take a simplistic view of working-class strength and policy demands as the key factors in expanding social rights might expect such a system to engender continuing but unfulfilled political support for the expansion of rights, this has clearly not been the pattern of U.S. social politics. Rather, limited social assistance has gone along with popular antipathy toward welfare. Historical institutionalists and policy regime analysts have examined the political effects of the relatively strong private provision that characterizes the United States and other liberal welfare states (Weir, Orloff, and Skocpol 1988; Esping-Andersen 1990). Because U.S. labor organization has been uneven, some sectors of the working class were able to wrest protections from their employers, creating a private welfare state for the better-organized segments of workers and their families (Stevens 1988), while leaving those who cannot get private coverage to a residual public system. This situation has produced weak political support for welfare provision aside from Social Security, the one U.S. social program that covers almost the whole population.

Poor single mothers, disproportionately women of color, on AFDC were a weak group, partly because the programmatic structure of the U.S. welfare state politically isolated them. While Medicaid involved the interests of medical providers or Food Stamps the concerns of agricultural interests, AFDC drew on no middle-class or well-organized interests. This was particularly the case after the mobilizations of poor people, especially women welfare recipients, died down after the early 1970s (Piven and Cloward 1988). Poor single mothers on welfare, however, have been a weak constituency for a long time, so one still needs to ask why in 1996 AFDC was vulnerable not just to cutbacks and the addition of deterrent provisions, but to elimination.

Why, given the overall weakness of social rights, was the categorical social right to assistance for single mothers to be full-time caregivers the one eliminated? Three different views contribute to its explanation. One answer lies in the very limited—residual—character of provision. While other countries have targeted the long-term unemployed—mainly men—in efforts to restructure social provision, the United States has gone after single mothers (Eardley and Thompson 1997; O'Connor, Orloff, Shaver 1999, chap.4).

Second, it has also been suggested that welfare reform reflects an androcentric bias. Caregiving, while socially necessary, is culturally and institutionally denigrated (Knijn and Kremer 1997; Kittay, this volume; Tronto, this volume). Conservative thinking—sometimes espoused also by "liberal" policy experts—has strengthened political forces hostile to AFDC through the occlusion of the significance of unpaid, caring labor (especially but not only when performed by women of color); the vilification of welfare programs; and the construction of any sort of dependency, or even interdependence, as pathological (Fraser and Gordon 1994b; Roberts 1995; Naples 1997; Fineman, this volume).

Indeed, for some feminist analysts (e.g., Mink 1998), the elimination of AFDC and the associated requirement for mothers to be employed coupled with the elimination of caregiving as a recognized basis for claiming social assistance is the ultimate act of institutionalized gender discrimination. Others—myself included—are more sympathetic to the notion of expecting work from all adults, but remain concerned about the inattention to real dilemmas of caregiving and employment, the lack of support to caregiving work, and the poor quality and inadequate funding afforded child care services. Regardless the unequal valuation of caregiving as compared to employment, both understand welfare reform as reflecting a gendered imbalance of power. This complex of cultural valuations and power resources helps to explain the undermining of support to caregiving reflected in the PRWORA.

A particularly influential view on how state social provision reflects gender inequality is that which sees welfare as bifurcated into two gendered "streams," tiers or "channels." The feminine tier is made up of inadequate social assistance programs, AFDC paradigmatically, serving a predominantly female clientele who made claims based on their family status, while the masculine tier is made up of relatively more generous contributory social insurance targeting a male clientele who made claims based on their status in the labor market (see, e.g., Pearce 1986; Fraser 1989b; Nelson 1984, 1990). The changes of the 1990s have left the system even more deeply bifurcated between Social Security and welfare, as TANF represents a worsening of social assistance by undercutting its already limited entitlement, imposing time limits, and the rest. Based on this description of U.S. social provision, these scholars imply that a gendered pattern of political support should have emerged around social policies, with women more sympathetic to welfare than are men. To some extent, this has occurred and is represented in a gender gap in which women, particularly nonmarried women, vote Democratic (partly because of their stand as a more prosocial spending party than the Republicans) at rates higher than do men (Manza and Brooks 1998). Thus, the elimination of welfare rights could reflect the political weakness of women (e.g., as one might surmise from Piven [1984] who does not, however, subscribe to the gendered "dual channel" thesis).

This view of the lack of women's power is hard to sustain in a period when politicians recognize a gender gap in voting and competition for women's votes has been intense. Moreover, the Clinton administration has been supportive of the agenda of women's groups in many ways (e.g., personnel appointments, parental leave legislation, abortion rights). Programs of social protection aimed at covering the risks faced disproportionately by women, such as paid maternity or parental leave, are not well developed in the United States (Gornick, Meyers, and Ross 1997). But by many other indicators—declines in occupational sex segregation; the strength of regulations prohibiting sexual harassment; and the recognition of bodily, reproductive, and sexual autonomy for women—at least a good many U.S. women are relatively advantaged compared with their counterparts in other Western countries. Perhaps it is not that women are politically weak, but that it is incorrect to characterize women's interests as united around welfare, or to assume that AFDC captured the procaregiving sentiments that many women express. And, in fact, few women or women's equality organizations mobilized to protest welfare reform.

Why did the proposed or actual elimination of AFDC not call forth popular protests similar to those which followed the 1989 Supreme Court *Webster* decision, when hundreds of thousands of women turned out to defend abortion rights? The Women's Committee of One Hundred, one of the few prowelfare, feminist lobbying groups to appear when welfare was being debated, tried to mobilize under the slogan "a war against poor women is a war against all women." It succeeded in drawing out only hundreds during several demonstrations. In defending abortion rights, women across the social spectrum saw this as an issue that engaged their interests; in the case of welfare reform, this did not happen.[4]

Feminist descriptions of the dual channel U.S. welfare state have tended to neglect the overall shape of the U.S. welfare regime, with the large share of private provision for working-aged people. It is true that almost all adult recipients of AFDC and TANF were and are women and, in fact, women make the majority of family-based claims, while men's claims are almost all as workers (Meyer 1996; O'Connor, Orloff and Shaver 1999, chap.4). Women in the upper-tier social insurance programs, principally old-age insurance, however, make most of these family-related claims. Before reaching retirement age, the majority of women, like most men, must rely on employer-provided or privately financed services and benefits, or do without. This includes the majority of single mothers (72% were in the labor force in 1984, 84% in 1997; Meyer and Rosenbaum 1998).

Women, particularly mothers of young children, do sometimes depend at least partially on male partners' income, but labor force participation (albeit sometimes part time) has become the norm for women as well as men—even among women with children less than a year old, half are in the work force. Women who identified their political interests and identities as those of "working (employed) moms" or taxpayers did not see themselves as potential welfare recipients. And while women exhibit more generous attitudes than do men vis-à-vis social spending, they have not defended "welfare as we knew it." Rather, there is sentiment for helping those who try to work for pay, but cannot, expressed through supplying affordable child care and health care, and the like (Gilens 1998).

Third, there is the thesis on the racialization of U.S. welfare based on the premise that the U.S. welfare state owes much of its distinctive structure and character to racial divisions that shaped the economy and polity.[5] Many people of color were initially excluded from social provision, but were incorporated into social programs by a series of changes made between 1950 and the 1970s. However, the political processes by which these groups gained access to social assistance were hotly contested, and the terms of their inclusion never fully accepted by many whites. President Reagan mobilized these sentiments in the campaign against AFDC and "welfare queens" in the 1980s; this was the context for the Democrats move to the right on wedge issues (Edsall and Edsall 1991; Dawson 1994; Skocpol 1997b; Wilson 1997; Williams 1998).

Quadagno (1994) has described how racism and the competition for favorable positions and access to public resources undermined struggles for racial justice and weakened public support for the welfare system in the 1960s and 1970s, as that system came to be understood as a system for minorities—a process she calls the "racialization" of welfare. Lieberman (1998) has demonstrated that racial politics, in both Northern and Southern versions, shaped AFDC practices and provisions. While southern political practices meant African Americans were often excluded from AFDC, in the North, African Americans were brought under the umbrella of AFDC coverage through patronage politics, but in ways that fed resentment by other ethnic groups. Both Lieberman and Quadagno argue that race shaped the U.S. welfare regime, which in turn constitutes racial categories and divisions. Thus, social politics cannot be understood as a simple reflection of some underlying racial order, but rather must be seen as an active agent in producing that order.

Today, there is little doubt that welfare politics has served as a mechanism for some whites' expression of racial antagonisms toward African Americans (Gilens 1996, 1999; Bobo 1998). Indeed, African Americans' political leverage has been blunted by the lack of competition for their votes, as Republicans assembled winning coalitions based primarily on suburban and rural whites (Weir 1995). The media emphasized—to the point of distortion—African American images in discussions of both poverty and welfare, contributing to racializing welfare politics (Gilens 1999). Yet, because of other features of U.S. social provision, particularly the lack of active labor market measures (Weir 1992), AFDC recipients have been, since the 1960s, disproportionately members of racial and ethnic minorities. Indeed, policy analysts have uncovered racial differences in patterns of welfare use that reflect the deeper and more chronic poverty of people of color and their disproportionate share of unemployment and underemployment (e.g., Bane and Ellwood 1994; Spalter-Roth et al. 1995; Pavetti 1997).

Compared with white women, African American and Latina women were more likely to depend on welfare for longer periods of time, either alone or cycling between welfare and employment, which, because of the character of jobs in the low-wage labor market, the absence of services, and the lack of medical coverage, provided insufficient resources for them to leave welfare permanently. Whites tended to use welfare more intensively, for shorter periods in response to crises. Welfare reform was designed to chase short-term would-be recipients to private sources of support, while subjecting potentially longer-term recipients to stringent new requirements.

Politicians did not have to discuss race explicitly for all to understand the racial impact of the new welfare legislation (Williams 1998). Since the PRA was passed, whites have been leaving the system faster than have minorities, with the consequence that the majority of welfare recipients are now African American and Latino (DeParle 1998). Although driven partly by racial politics, welfare reform affects race relations through a formally race-neutral legal apparatus that eliminates social rights and support to full-time caregiving for all and imposes work requirements on all those who apply for state assistance, abetted by what Larry Bobo (1998) calls "laissez-faire racism."

Against this line of analysis, however, there are some objections. The beneficiaries of sole-parent programs in other Western countries, where provision for single mothers has not been so seriously cut, are overwhelmingly white.[6] Yet, the fact that neighboring Canada eliminated social assistance as a social right should make us pause before assigning all explanatory power in the end of AFDC to racial animosity in the United States.[7] However much Quebecois-Anglophone Canadian divisions condition politics, Canadian welfare politics are not racialized U.S.-style, but social assistance was still vulnerable to retrenchment.

The timing of welfare reform in the mid-1990s is especially interesting given that elimination of AFDC was politically not possible under President Reagan who was certainly hostile to welfare.[8] Democratic control of the House was a bulwark against the most radical retrenchment under Reagan; a Democratic President in 1995-1996 was not a bulwark against the attempts of a Republican Congress to eliminate AFDC, however. Thus, it is not simply a matter of divided government, but a question of what deprived AFDC of political protection even among Democrats in 1996.

Pierson (1998; Myles and Pierson 1997) contrasts the demise of AFDC with the expansion of the EITC; yet, he did not pinpoint why elimination of AFDC became possible in 1996. Like others, Pierson fails to take into account the gendered dynamics—most important, the increases in women's employment—

that made AFDC politically indefensible at worst, unattractive at best, even among many committed to women's equality (or racial justice). Having lost the commitment of forces traditionally favorable to social provision, welfare became vulnerable to the Right's campaign for repeal.

A comparison with Britain is instructive to support this explanation. Both the UK Income Support system, which supports poor lone mothers among other groups, and U.S. AFDC were subjected to similar tinkering in the 1980s, but the programs' fates diverged more considerably under Clinton and Blair. Clinton's initial election promise to put welfare mothers to work was popular, and even the elimination of AFDC in 1996 did not incur widespread popular or political outrage. In contrast, Blair's less radical proposals to cut lone mothers' benefits and to expand work incentives were greeted with resistance—in the former case, sufficient to force the administration to back down (on the British case, see Millar 1996; O'Connor, Orloff and Shaver 1999, chaps.3–4). Mothers' full-time caregiving, at least until children are in school, remains legitimate and politically defensible in Britain, where mothers generally are more likely to stay at home full time or work part-time than in the United States. In the United States, the clamor for reform remained high through the 1980s and 1990s despite U.S. single mothers exhibiting relatively high rates of labor force participation and low rates of welfare receipt and many U.S. mothers cycling between paid work and welfare, in effect using AFDC as an unemployment benefit (Spalter-Roth et al. 1995). Yet in the United States, a program assisting poor full-time caregivers could not call upon such popular and elite support. Why? I contend that a significant part of the answer lies in the specific character of U.S. gender relations, especially patterns of women's labor force participation, in the shape of the welfare regime, and in the racialization of welfare.

Changing Gender Relations: Single Motherhood and the Gender Division of Labor

Women's increased labor force participation and changing family and household forms are relevant for policy outcomes, specifically because social assistance for mothers increasingly has been conditioned on work activities or employment (e.g., Ellwood 1988) and has included provisions designed to discourage nonmarital childbearing and to encourage payment of child support. Rhetoric championing the traditional family and attacking illegitimacy featured heavily in the welfare debates, drawing on reservoirs of hostility toward single mothers—particularly women of color. These sentiments were most notable on the political Right, although liberals, too, claimed that single-parent families were harmful for children (e.g., McLanahan and Sandefur 1994). But I would argue that the gendered changes around households were not the decisive feature which led

Democrats, liberals and feminists to desert AFDC—rather, it was the change in women's employment patterns.

Clearly, the gender division of labor today is quite different than when AFDC was established in 1935, with far fewer women staying home full time to care for children and large increases in women's, especially mothers', labor force participation. This largely explains why work requirements for single mothers came to be seen as reasonable by policymakers, academics, and the public. Benefits for single parents—both AFDC and Survivors' Insurance—were established with the aim of allowing white single mothers to pursue the distinctive, noncommodified life pattern deemed appropriate for other white mothers to care for their children. Public provision construed single mothers as unemployable, as full-time caregivers rather than as potential workers, even after court decisions and political challenges of the 1960s and 1970s broke down exclusionary provisions and the clientele of AFDC expanded to include women of color. Yet, women's labor force participation, particularly among married mothers of children under age six, was accelerating at this time (Reskin and Padavic 1994, 143–145). And indeed, one can perceive changing attitudes about mothers' employment in changes to AFDC from the 1960s through the 1980s, in which first work incentives and then, some limited work requirements, were put in place.

The emerging model of motherhood—as encompassing paid work—which we see expressed in U.S. policies may also relate to U.S. women of color having been held to requirements about combining motherhood and paid work that have differed historically from those applying to whites (Collins 1990; Glenn 1992). In the early years of AFDC, many women, particularly in the South, were excluded from the right to care for children full time, as they were classified as "employable mothers"—this exlusion had an unmistakable moral and racial cast, for it was unwed mothers and women of color who fell into these categories (Bell 1965; Lieberman 1998). As these women came to be included in AFDC and its clientele was perceived as less white, the standards applicable to women of color were being made requirements of all welfare programs, a trend reinforced by the increasing proportions of women of all races and ethnic groups entering the labor force. Perhaps the expectation that women of color should work for pay also reflects a lack of cultural valuation of their caregiving work, and of the reproduction of people of color (Roberts 1995; Mink 1998).

Mink (1998) has argued that single mothers are being singled out for harsh treatment in the new work requirements of TANF and that this reflects not a commitment to employment for all women, but special punishment for women who flout conventional household and sexual mores, with clear racial implications, given that women of color are far more likely to be unmarried mothers than are white women. She notes of the earlier welfare regulations forcing certain women—those who were "immoral," because unmarried (and therefore more likely to have been African American)—to work for pay, "wage work became penance for illegitimacy" (Mink 1998, 37). And she argues that this is the impetus behind current welfare reform; women of color are being punished—by being forced to work—for their household and reproductive decisions and because their caregiving work is not valued. This, she says is reflected in the PRA creating a mandate for single parents to be in work activities, while requiring only one parent in two-parent families to be working, thus allowing housewifery in two-parent families receiving assistance (Mink 1998, 105–107). Indeed, unless a two-parent household claims childcare benefits, one or both parents together must work the equivalent of thirty-five hours per week, while single parent households are required to be in work activities for thirty hours by 2000 (although states may limit this to 20 hours).

Do such regulations simply reflect racism?[9] Or are they also affected by the residualism of U.S. social provision and the fact that employment is the basis for most households' support? It does appear that two-parent families are to be allowed somewhat greater flexibility in making work and caregiving arrangements than are single-parent families—echoing the greater flexibility such families have outside the welfare system. Because of the very small proportion of two-parent families that are even eligible for and receiving welfare assistance—never more than about 5 per cent of the caseload (U.S. CWM 1998, 410, 413, 431), the majority of two-parent families are forced to conform to labor market and economic exigencies in determining caregiving arrangements. Again, the residualism of the system is significant. U.S. families—in contrast to some of their European counterparts—do not receive any direct subsidy for full-time caregiving (Pedersen 1993; Wennemo 1994). If a household's income permits, one parent can opt out of the labor market or cut back her or his hours. However, many fewer people are in this category than previously because of the decline in jobs with family-supporting wages; of course, we see these economic exigencies reflected in increasing numbers of dual-earner families and the concomitant sharp decline of single-earner ones (Reskin and Padavic 1994; in 1940, one-earner households made up more than 70% of U.S. families, by 1980, only 28%).

I argue that we should understand the strengthening of institutionalized expectations that women on welfare be employed as reflecting the social changes outside welfare—that the majority of women, including mothers, are employed—and the limited character of the system of social provision itself—that caregiving receives little public support and that households must rely on employment for their support. Racial models of motherhood likely hastened shifts in the character of work requirements. In other English-speaking countries, there have been similar shifts toward encouraging employment, but the outcomes have been less severe given competing concerns about caregiving among policymakers and the public. But in the United States, racism probably weakened the force of such competing concerns.

Work Incentives, Work Requirements, and the Logic of Gender Equality

Work incentives were introduced into AFDC in 1967, in the wake of successful campaigns to expand coverage, and in line with increases in women's employment. In the 1970s, work requirements actually allowed women to combine employment earnings and welfare benefits, while retaining health coverage under Medicaid. While this was probably the outcome most favorable for beneficiaries in the short run, this line of policy development continued to leave the employed poor and most two-parent families outside the umbrella of social protection, which in turn left AFDC politically vulnerable (Weir, Orloff, and Skocpol 1988). Then new restrictions against combining paid work and welfare, causing over a tenth of the caseload to lose eligibility, were brought in during the early Reagan administration (Blank 1997, 137). These changes left in place a formal model of motherhood based on full-time caregiving, which over the course of the decade was increasingly out of sync with the behavior of most mothers, married or not (Reskin and Padavic 1994, 49). Furthermore, the welfare poor and the working poor were more clearly distinguished.

The Family Support Act of 1988 at first glance might appear to have changed this formally institutionalized model of motherhood. Many argue that there was a new consensus involving welfare recipients' employment by the mid-1980s, as the FSA mandated work or training for mothers as well as fathers, with some exemptions (Naples 1997). Single parents were required to be at work or in training after their youngest child reached three years of age, and states had the option of requiring work or training for parents of children as young as one year (U.S. Social Security Administration 1993, 83–97). Still, welfare remained an entitlement under the FSA—the new work requirements in this case were not coupled with loss of entitlement. But one might well argue that the FSA helped to bring about the elimination of AFDC—because it did not effectively promote employment among most welfare recipients. The Family Support Act was, hence, "welfare reform" within the parameters of the AFDC: the clientele remained limited, work requirements had little impact, and implementation was slow, largely reflecting fiscal constraints due to conservatives' campaigns against taxation and public social spending.

The particular patterns of American women's labor force participation, the policy context within which these occur, and the disjunction between formal models of motherhood in AFDC and labor force participation patterns among women not on welfare made AFDC more problematic politically than sole-parent provision in other countries. American women are likely to work full time—about three-fourths of all employed women are working full-time—and year round (O'Connor, Orloff, and Shaver 1999, table 3.3). Perhaps most critical to the lack of political support for AFDC was that American women work with less public support, such as child allowances, child care, or paid leaves, than do their counterparts in other parts of the West, where women's employment is institutionalized in the policy regime (e.g., Scandinavia) (Gornick, Meyers, and Ross 1997). The United States has not had programs of universal support for mothering or reproduction while in much of Continental Europe, Britain, and Australia, nationalism and pronatalism helped bolster social provision, creating a safety net in which motherhood was supported through near-universal programs—a set of provisions that in some places has been used by employed mothers in recent decades to ease caregiving-work conflicts.[10]

In the United States, there is widespread sentiment that mothers as well as fathers must work for most families to maintain households, or, among the more affluent sectors of the population, to maintain a middle-class standard of living, including education for children and the like. Staying at home full time to care for children has come to be understood as something to be earned through one's efforts in the labor market—as a reward from an employer who gives paid leave—a benefit usually reserved for the best-off women, or supported through savings, help from parents, or at the price of a normal consumption pattern (e.g., Christian conservatives argue that upholding family values, including housewifery, requires resistance to middle-class consumerism). AFDC rules seemed to make possible staying at home to care for children at public expense for poor women—exactly what is not guaranteed to any other mother or father.

Welfare reform aimed to extend the compulsion of the market to welfare recipients. For example, in the course of debates about family caps (e.g., Magyar 1998), proponents argued that wage earners get no supplement when they have another child, so why should welfare recipients? It was difficult for critics to mount an effective response to this logic of the market.

Feminists' interventions tended to support this premise that employment is to be expected from all. A maternalist option—support for full-time caregiving—has been the preference of only a minority of activists and academics, even as most feminists, coming from left-liberal positions, opposed most of the provisions of the 1996 welfare reform bill, especially the end of entitlement and lifetime limits and the targeting of illegitimacy. But the main focus of activists' attention around the 1996 legislation was the Domestic Violence Option (DVO), which permits states to exempt women fleeing battering from work requirements. It seems that here the premise is that absent such circumstances, and given proper supports such as childcare, women's paid work is reasonable (compare Institute for Women's Policy Research 1997; Casey and Carroll, this volume).

Situating welfare reform in this context of wider policy developments relevant to gender relations—such as the regulation of labor markets and policy on reproduction—makes clear that it reflects broader patterns characterizing the U.S. policy regime and gender politics (Hobson 1994; O'Connor, Orloff, and Shaver 1999). Gender equality forces have defined employment and educational opportunity as central to women's emancipation. Employment-equity legislation has, in combination with strong employer demand for women workers, helped to create much-enhanced possibilities for women's economic independence (Bergmann 1986), despite the continuation of a pay gap and occupational sex segregation. Reproductive rights are also understood as central to the equality project, at least partly because control of one's reproductive capacities is necessary to competing more equally in the labor market. In contrast, social protection has been much less significant in post-World War II U.S. gender policy than in almost any other industrialized country.

Yet, especially on the center-left of that spectrum, supporting the employment of women, on or off welfare, was not simply a matter of conforming to the exigencies of the labor market. Rather, employment was defined as central to the strategy of achieving women's equality, and also as the proper mode for supporting families and caregiving. The logic is that if all must work to support households—and this furthers women's prospects—women on welfare, too, should be employed. I would argue that this is why women's organizations and organizations of African Americans, including the Congressional Black Caucus, did not, in the end, make preventing welfare reform a high priority (Williams 1998). Indeed, Mink (1998, 1) admits that AFDC had come to be "viewed less as an alternative to wages than as a safety net for mothers when wages were not available to them" (see also Piven and Cloward 1988, 1997). If this is the case, then AFDC was a type of unemployment compensation—and there is no capitalist country that gives unemployment compensation without conditions mandating that recipients take available employment. There is no doubt that the conditions under which they take employment (including wages, hours, access to care services, and so on) differ widely. But once women, including mothers, are understood as workers, the logic of supporting their "choice" between employment and unpaid full-time caregiving collapses.

The End of Entitlement

Many of the characteristics which undermined welfare politically were present in the initial legislation of 1935 (Skocpol 1988). But probably the turning point from which we can trace the developmental trajectory which has led to the demise of AFDC was the failure of Nixon's proposed Family Assistance Plan in 1974, following the politically contentious and unevenly successful efforts of the War on Poverty and the drive of the National Welfare Rights Organization to recruit the poor onto the welfare rolls (Quadagno 1994; Myles and Pierson

1997). Since the Reagan administration, the "reform" of welfare has meant increasing restrictions and work requirements, occasionally with enhanced childcare services or training, or even elimination of the program.[11] This closed off the political possibilities for more generous and more universalistic provision.

Welfare was a key wedge issue used by Republicans against Democrats throughout the 1980s, a key part of their strategy to separate white voters from African Americans and Latinos. Democrats were put in the unenviable position of defending a deeply flawed welfare program in order to defend poor people and a safety net, and lost support among traditional white working-class constituencies, among others, because of it (Edsall and Edsall 1991; Williams 1998).

On the intellectual and discursive front, conservative analysts who helped to shape the Republican policy agenda reframed the debate about welfare: above all, welfare was creating and reinforcing dependency, and this was linked to crime, poverty, and illegitimacy, particularly in the inner cities—the coded term for communities of color. Many liberals, too, came to agree that creating dependency was the problem with welfare. As a number of analysts have pointed out, the pathologizing of dependency obscures the inevitable interdependency of social life, especially the caregiving responsibilities for children which figure so prominently in women's lives (see, e.g., Fraser and Gordon 1994b; Fineman 1995 and this volume).

While, among elites, conservative thinking about welfare was gaining sway, there was not a public consensus on needed changes—but public opinion polls after the 1994 election "showed that the public preferred *any* possible package of reforms over the status quo" (Weaver 1998, 375; see also Gilens 1999). Thus, there was a continuing demand for reform and mounting receptivity among the electorate for radical solutions to the "welfare mess." And by the 1990s, both Democrats and Republicans took advantage of the electoral popularity of welfare reform.

The political fact of the Reagan Democrats helped propel the Democratic Leadership Council and then-candidate Bill Clinton to a new domestic policy and political strategy. These centrist Democrats wanted to "inoculate" their party on welfare (and other wedge issues) by adopting a different approach. And Clinton did manage to turn around his party's vulnerability among white voters with his famous 1992 campaign pledge to "end welfare as we know it," while promising to "make work pay." Clinton entered office willing to consider radical change in AFDC, and committed to an approach to social protection that would more easily accommodate EITC expansion than the defense of the existing welfare system.

The key aspect of Clinton's approach to welfare was to require welfare recipients to work for pay, or engage in work-like activities, training or education, after two years of receiving benefits, although with various guarantees of child care and public employment if jobs were not to be found (Ellwood 1996). Two components of the Clinton plan were novel: time limits and employment requirements that applied to mothers as well as fathers among all segments of the population—a shift towards gender "sameness." Caregiving by mothers (or others) was minimally supported—the choice to stay at home full time would be limited to caregivers of very young children. Poverty would be fought not with higher welfare benefits or expanded coverage, but by getting everyone—including mothers—into employment, then improving pay and conditions. In essence, Clinton Democrats wanted to make AFDC more like unemployment insurance or active-labor-market programs—a short-term benefit to help claimants get on their feet but premised on labor market participation; in fact, this is how many women were using the program, although the formal rules obscured this (Spalter-Roth et al. 1995; Edin and Lein 1997). This policy orientation complemented other policies designed to "make work pay" (the phrase was originally Ellwood's), such as enhancing the Earned Income Tax Credit and increasing the minimum wage; had the Clinton administration prevailed with proposals to expand job training and job creation efforts and to establish universal health insurance, this approach to welfare might have been more viable (Ellwood 1996).

Meanwhile, precisely because the FSA incorporated what expert opinion had argued was needed to reduce dependency and associated social problems, but did not do so, it created ground for more radical reforms to be considered. Thus, experts were struck by the rise in welfare receipt after passage of the FSA; popular opinion was influenced by the picture of an essentially unreformed welfare system that was clearly not working, as reflected in continuing social problems. All of this contributed to the emergence of a policy crisis—the perceived failure of existing policy and the opening of possibilities to include heretofore excluded policy options. Clinton was committed to time limits and work requirements—policy options that had been unthinkable within Democratic circles a decade earlier, and which in themselves would have represented a sharp change from previous policy (Reich 1999). Republicans' power in Congress after 1994 forced the issue of eliminating AFDC; yet Clinton, in the end, accepted this.

Indeed, one might argue that the elimination of AFDC became almost inevitable once Clinton made his famous promise. Although Democrats sought to retain control of the welfare issue, the call to end welfare was seized on mainly by Republicans, who moved the debate far to the right—to outright elimination of a right to assistance. After the Republicans captured the House of Representatives in 1994, they challenged President Clinton to sign welfare bills much more restrictive and less generous than his own, unsuccessful plan. After vetoing two bills, he ultimately signed the third, which, significantly, excluded Medicaid from radical changes. Did he have to do it? Critics point out that he could have continued his opposition; the Republicans probably could not have overcome a veto. Yet, Clinton apparently worried about losing his healthy margin in the polls in the 1996 presidential race with Republican candidate Bob Dole if he were to come before the electorate having failed in his promise to "end welfare as we know it" (Reich 1999). One might also plausibly argue (as does Mulé [personal communication 1999]) that Clinton wanted to pass welfare reform to undercut the power of the liberal wing of the Democratic Party.

Summary

The end of the entitlement to social assistance in the United States in 1996 coincided with a shift in formal expectations about women's employment and a withdrawal of (residual) support to full-time caregiving. While some see work requirements for single mothers as indistinguishable from ending the social assistance safety net, one can imagine social rights based on employment for mothers as for all citizens and encompassing protections for caregiving, as for example, in Scandinavia or France (Hobson 1994). But in the United States—as in the other predominantly English-speaking countries often called liberal regimes—there has been emphasis on the importance of "choice" for women, not just in the arena of reproduction, but vis-à-vis arrangements for employment and caregiving. And clearly, these policy changes have brought about an end to publicly subsidized choices for poor mothers as to their employment and caregiving arrangements in the United States (compare Hirschmann, this volume).

Why were work requirements and the loss of social rights connected within the shifts in the U.S. welfare regime? Almost all who would reform welfare by the 1990s accepted requirements for recipients to seek employment; the only questions left concerned the conditions under which they would do so. But while work requirements of some sort seem to have been heading inevitably for adoption in some form, there was more contingency in the linkage of such requirements and the end of entitlement. American political and policy dynamics in the 1990s featured electoral pressures to move to the right on social spending and a policy crisis around AFDC. Quite simply, AFDC was utterly discredited among both policy and political elites and the public, opening the way for consideration of such radical reforms as work requirements without exemptions, time limits and, ultimately, the elimination of AFDC and its replacement by discretionary state-level programs under TANF. The electoral victories of Republicans, along with a Democratic president determined to pass some version of welfare reform, created the conditions for the repeal of AFDC.

The elimination of an entitlement to social assistance in the United States reflects a complicated conjuncture of forces, including the increased power of employers, racial antipathies and the devaluation of caregiving in a political moment marked by significant shifts to the right of the political spectrum by both parties. In addition, changes in the gender division of labor, in which women's employment has increased, have been critical in shifting political sympathies toward expecting employment from all adults. But the passage of the Personal Responsibility Act cannot be fully understood apart from the context of a welfare regime which offers little public support to caregiving or to easing the reconciliation of employment and care for most women. This case of U.S. welfare reform demonstrates the usefulness of a gendered historical institutionalist analysis of policy regimes.

Notes

1. Before I go any further, let me clarify for non-U.S. readers some of the terminology used in these political debates. U.S. politics is correctly seen as heavily focused on rights. Yet political and civil rights have been more prominent in U.S. political discourse than have *social rights*, a term that is not widely used outside of some academic discussions of welfare states. Indeed, the term *welfare state* is not used in popularly, or even in many academic discussions—those of economists, for example. Rather, Americans differentiate between "welfare," meaning means-tested social assistance, particularly AFDC, and "Social Security," near-universal contributory retirement and medical coverage for retired elderly workers and their dependents—Old Age, Survivors' and Disability Insurance, and Medicare (Skocpol 1988; Orloff 1993a, chap.1; Gordon 1994). While Social Security has much of the positive connotation attaching to social rights elsewhere, welfare has been politically vilified, particularly over the last two decades, and is a very unpopular set of programs. Thus, "reform" of welfare came to mean cutbacks or the elimination of AFDC. Many conservatives have been opposed to any type of social spending. However, elite attempts to deprive Social Security of its legitimacy as a part of a drive to privatize retirement provision have been less successful than attempts to scale back social assistance for the working-aged population. One aspect of their campaign has been to popularize the term *entitlement* to refer to legislated government commitments to particular constituencies. Conservatives blame entitlements for causing budget deficits, current and projected, and for threatening the bankruptcy of Social Security by giving benefits to middle-class people who do not need support at the cost of high (and unfair) payroll taxes on younger people (Skocpol 1995, 297–312). But while Social Security's popular support has not been substantially undermined, the term *entitlement*, with its whiff—however faint—of undeservingness, has come to be the preferred term for all benefit programs in which spending is automatic, based on legislated criteria, rather than being subject to Congressional approval in each budget cycle (as is so-called discretionary spending). Finally, let me note that reformers interested in rolling back the role of the state in social provision are called neoliberal in many places, but are usually referred to as "conservatives" in the United States. Those defending some role, albeit a residual one, for the state in alleviating market failures or pursuing public purposes outside national defense and crime control are "liberals" in the United States, while elsewhere they would likely be referred to as "social liberals" (as distinct from social democrats, who favor a more expansive state role).

2. Basic information on the PRA is obtained from the *Green Book* published by the U.S. House of Representatives Committee on Ways and Means [US CWM] in 1996 and in 1998, supplemented by coverage from the *New York Times* and *Washington Post,* and materials published by various think tanks and advocacy groups, liberal and conservative.

3. These measures were included largely due to the efforts of moderate Republican congresswomen, who saw child support as important in enabling single mothers to survive without welfare and argued that it would be unfair to toughen work requirements for mothers without simultaneously going after "deadbeat dads" (Casey and Carroll this volume). But others (e.g., Mink 1998) argue that these provisions (both in the PRA and in earlier legislation) undercut poor women's citizenship rights by enforcing contact with ex-partners. While there are good cause exemptions to prevent contact with violent partners, these may not be properly enforced, especially given the context of radical devolution of administration and lack of entitlement.

4. Here, one might make the parallel to Sweden's recent experience of the lack of an explicit defense of spousal pension benefits when these were cut back. Apparently, many women felt they might need such benefits, as a much higher-than-average number of marriages were registered before the deadline (after which the provision granting them would no longer apply). Yet no public protest emerged around the issue. Barbara Hobson (1998) explains this with reference to the strong assumptions about women's employment in the Swedish policy regime, which undercut claims based on spousal status.

5. The political bargains between President Roosevelt and Congressional leaders led to the exclusion of most people of color from coverage in the initial period of Social Security and welfare, albeit by different mechanisms (Bell 1965; Quadagno 1988; Orloff 1993a, chap. 9; Lieberman 1998). They came to be included in the 1950s, 1960s and 1970s. The universalization of coverage in the programs of Social Security successfully incorporated people of color (Skocpol 1995).

6. Many indicators about welfare use point to a greater problem of social exclusion in the United States, tied to the history of race and racial labor markets, as well as to higher levels of economic inequality. Analogous problems exist in the other settler nations among the advanced industrial countries, New Zealand, Australia and Canada—indigenous populations in these countries are terribly deprived and marginalized, but they form a very small proportion of the population and, moreover, are geographically concentrated away from the biggest urban centers. Consequently, racial issues have not been central in their debates over welfare (O'Connor, Orloff, and Shaver 1999, chap.4).

7. The Canada Assistance Plan was replaced by the Canada Health and Social Transfer, a block grant, in 1995 (Myles and Pierson 1997).

8. Pierson (1994) has argued that even with the decline of groups such as trade unions whose power resources were central to initiating and expanding welfare programs, cutting back welfare provision was difficult because the institutionalization of particular policy features raises the costs of radical change. Even in the case of a marginal constituency like poor single mothers, there were constraints on political elites that made the complete elimination of AFDC difficult. True, to the extent that retrenchment occurred in the 1980s, it fell disproportionately on AFDC and allied programs, rather than on those programs which served larger constituencies (Weir, Orloff and Skocpol 1988; Pierson 1994). But President Reagan and like-minded governors were unable to eliminate AFDC, and in fact found it politically useful to subject welfare to numerous new and widely-publicized sanctions and attacks. This also had the merit of being cheaper than what most analysts considered to be "real" reform, that is, getting recipients into the labor force, with concomitant supports like child care and health insurance. Pierson relied on the Family Support Act of 1988 to make his case—the

FSA did not break out of the AFDC framework, but added provisions to encourage employment that looked more radical than they were in reality. Few expected that AFDC could be eliminated without any kind of government back up, as it was in the PRA.

9. Like many, Mink puts great store in the statement of purpose of the PRA, which sets reducing "illegitimacy" as a primary goal, and thus interprets work requirements in this light. While admitting that the "PRA does not actually compel mothers to marry," Mink (1998, 43) argues that "its work requirements give them strong incentives to do so. . . . A mother who wants to meet her caregiving responsibilities in the home would thus be wise to trade her welfare check for a husband's income. Given the defeat of proposed coercive profamily provisions, the statement of purpose might well be interpreted as a sop to social conservatives (as Piven and Cloward [1988] argue has often been the case with profamily rhetoric). More serious, this interpretation seems to misconstrue the actual conditions of most U.S. households. Are there husbands with incomes sufficient to support women as stay-at-home mothers available? Even where two parents are present, few can afford to support full-time caregiving for any length of time. Most American women, single or married, now deal with their caregiving responsibilities in combination with paid work, although white married women with young children are likely to be employed part time.

10. Even unpaid parental leave is guaranteed only for workers in firms with more than fifty employees; in contrast, in Scandinavia, most mothers of young children remain formally in the labor force, but are enabled to be home caring for children by generous paid parental leave systems (Jenson 1997, 183).

11. Reagan was also able to affect future social policy developments by defunding the welfare state through tax cuts, and defense spending that created a huge deficit. But while welfare reform was shaped by fiscal austerity, it was certainly not necessary for budget reduction.

Seven

Heidi Hartmann and Hsiao-ye Yi,
with Megan DeBell and Jacqueline Chu

The Rhetoric and Reality of Welfare Reform

In recent years, we have witnessed a major shift in the poverty debate, away from the Great Society ideal of providing relief for the poor, toward the "New Federalism" vision of smaller government and reduced dependence on government. The rhetoric has also shifted from alleviating or eliminating poverty to reducing illegitimacy and "ending welfare as we know it." Despite these changes, women have remained at the center of the poverty debate, and public assistance programs, formerly Aid to Families with Dependent Children (AFDC) and its current replacement, Temporary Assistance to Needy Families (TANF), which provides assistance primarily to single-parent families, are the focus of copious media attention. The Clinton Administration, the Congress, and the National Governors Association all offered welfare reform proposals to end the safety net features of AFDC and decrease dependency on federal public assistance. With the passage of the Personal Responsibility and Work Opportunity Reconciliation Act of 1996 (which provides block grants to the states to fund TANF), each individual state is now developing its own welfare programs in response to the federal time limit on benefit receipt and the requirement to participate in the labor force.

In this chapter, we take a closer look at the subpopulation of the poor that currently preoccupies policymakers—single-mother families. One reason this group is central to the poverty debate is their sizeable presence among the poor. Single-mother families make up 60 percent of all poor families with children, and people living in these families make up 22 percent of all poor people. Single-mother families are more likely to experience poverty than almost any other group. For example, in 1994, 44 percent of single-mother families were poor, compared with 8 percent of married-couple families with children and 12 percent of people over age sixty-five (U.S. Bureau of the Census 1995). Over the past two decades, the number of poor female-headed households grew by 45 percent, faster than all poor families and poor married-couple families (which grew by 39 and 24 percent, respectively). The higher incidence of poverty among single mothers results from several causes: (a) single mothers lack access to the income stabilizing effect of an additional earner that many married-couple families enjoy, (b) they receive only small amounts of child support from the absent fathers, and (c) they earn substantially less than male breadwinners.

Since former President Reagan's characterization of welfare mothers as "Welfare Queens," poverty has come to be viewed as the result of pathological behavior of individuals rather than as the result of structural flaws in the economic system or even simply misfortune or bad luck. Those who received AFDC benefits were viewed as lazy, preferring to sit at home and have more babies instead of acquiring the skills they need to obtain jobs to lift them out of poverty. And welfare benefits themselves were seen as encouraging this pathological behavior (see Hirschmann, this volume). According to one opinion poll, more than two-thirds of Americans believe that welfare does more harm than good (Davidson 1995). Because of this perception, the dominant theme of the 1996 federal welfare legislation and the state programs being implemented now is to put the able-bodied to work. No one argues against the value of work: in fact, another poll shows that fully 94 percent of Americans believe welfare mothers will gain self-respect by working.

If policies requiring work are to succeed, policymakers must look realistically at two assumptions underlying the new programs: (a) single mothers who are the primary caretakers of their children can work outside the home and (b) they will find work that enables them to support themselves and their children. Policymakers newly charged with getting women off welfare and into work must also deal with the legacy of the bad rap these women had while on welfare. If they were such pathological people, how will they be able to work now?

Debunking the Stereotypes

In a series of studies over a number of years, to bring empirical evidence into a debate largely governed by ideology and politics, the Institute for Women's Policy Research (IWPR) has examined the actual patterns of receipt of welfare benefits and labor force participation of single mothers who receive AFDC benefits. The data for IWPR's studies are generated from the U.S. Census Bureau's Survey of Income and Program Participation, a nationally representative sample of individuals and families who are interviewed repeatedly over a thirty-month period.[1] IWPR's research first studied single mothers who had received AFDC for at least two months over a two-year period and, more recently, have included all low-income families with minor children living at home (IWPR, forthcoming). The data cited in this chapter are from 1984 through 1992.

The Myth that Welfare Breeds Dependence and Fertility

IWPR research using the first four panels of the SIPP and covering the years 1984 through 1989 found that only a minority, 26 percent, of single-mother families who receive welfare are totally dependent on welfare.[2] Three-quarters of the single mothers had substantial income either from their own earnings or from their families or both. Moreover, of those who appear to depend exclusively on welfare (because they report no other substantial income source), virtually all (98%) have family incomes that fall below the federal poverty line. Far from supporting welfare recipients at a "queenly" level, welfare provides only the barest subsistence. It should not be surprising, therefore, that welfare mothers package income from as many sources as possible in an effort to increase their well-being. More than half (57 percent) of single mothers are helped financially by their families. Of these, 26 percent work for pay as well, while 31 percent receive only family help to supplement their AFDC benefits. In addition to those who receive help from their families, another 17 percent who receive little family help work outside the home to bring in earnings to supplement their welfare benefits. Those mothers who have additional sources of income are substantially less likely to be poor (see Table 7.1). It can hardly be said, then, that welfare mothers are actually dependent on welfare in the sense of total dependence that the critics of welfare seem to take for granted.[3] Research also shows that women who receive welfare benefits are no more fertile than other women are. In fact, at least one study (Rank 1989) found that women receiving welfare have fewer children than similarly situated women not receiving welfare benefits. It is there-

———— Table 7.1 ————
Types and Impact of Income Packages Among AFDC Recipients

	Total Number	AFDC Only*	Family and AFDC**	Employed and AFDC***	Employment, Family, and AFDC
Total	2,797,285	732,335	865,995	484,511	714,444
As Percent of Total	100%	26%	31%	17%	26%
Total in Poverty	2,027,494	716,9837	634,878	372,565	303,114
Percent in Poverty	72%	98%	73%	77%	42%

* To be included in this study of AFDC recipients, a woman must receive AFDC for at least 2 months out of the 24-month study period.

* To be included in this category, recipients must live with relatives contributing at least $1,500 in family income over the 24-month study period.

*** To be considered employed, a welfare recipient must work at least 300 hours during the 24-month study period.

Source: IWPR calculations based on the Survey of Income and Program Participation, 1984 and 1986–1988 panels.

From: Spalter-Roth, Burr, Hartmann, and Shaw (1995).

———— Table 7.2 ————————————————————————————

Welfare Mothers' Time Use Over a Two-Year Period

Percent of time receiving welfare	77%
Percent of time not receiving welfare	23%
Percent of time receiving welfare	100%
Working	13%
Looking for Work	18%
In School	8%
Caring for baby (under two years)	18%
Caring for preschool children (ages 2–5)	22%
Caring for children (ages 6–12) during summer months	4%
Disabled, doing none of the above	8%
Able-bodied, doing none of the above	9%

Source: IWPR calculations based on the Survey of Income and Program Participation, 1984 and 1986–1988 panels.

From: Spalter-Roth, Burr, Hartmann, and Shaw (1995).

fore extremely unlikely that either of the widely held beliefs that welfare mothers have babies in order to collect welfare or that they have one baby after another to increase their welfare benefits could be true. In the IWPR study sample, the average number of children for each welfare mother is 2.1, slightly below the average for all U.S. Women (Spalter-Roth et al. 1995).

The Myth of the Lazy Welfare Mother

Despite the popular perception that welfare mothers do not work, half of all single mothers who spend any time on welfare also work in the labor market (at least 300 hours, over a two-year period): 20 percent combined work and welfare; 23 percent cycled between work and welfare; and another 7 percent worked limited hours, spending more time looking for work than actually working. An additional 23 percent were not employed but spent substantial time looking for work. In other words, more than seven out of ten AFDC recipients spent significant time in the labor force, either working or looking for work, but not finding it. Severe disabilities prevent nearly one in ten welfare mothers from working or seeking work—these women compose one-quarter of welfare mothers who neither work nor look for work (Spalter-Roth et al. 1995).

Table 7.2 shows that only 9 percent of the time spent on AFDC during the two-year study period is spent by able-bodied mothers who are neither working at paid employment, looking for work, attending school, nor caring for babies or preschoolers year-round or pre-teens during the summer. Few welfare dollars are "wasted" on able-bodied women who are not caring for children too young to care for themselves. These data suggest that the AFDC system achieved its

————— Table 7.3 —————
Results from Multivariate Logistics Models

Factors That Significantly Improve The Changes That an AFDC Recipient Works	Factors That Significantly Improve the Chances That an AFDC Recipient Escapes Poverty
Human Capital Able-bodied Has completed high school Has work experience Has had job training	**Human Capital** Has completed high school Has work experience Has had job training
Additional Income Another earner in household Gets married Receives child support recipient	**Additional Income** Income from other family members
Children Fewer children No infants or toddlers	**Children** Fewer children
State-of-Residence Characteristics Low unemployment rate (3.5%)	**State-of-Residence Characteristics** High welfare benefit per person Per month Low unemployment rate
	Employment Conditions Stable work Union coverage

—————

Source: IWPR calculations based on the Survey of Income and Program Participation, 1984 and 1986–1988 panel

From: Spalter-Roth, Burr, Hartmann, and Shaw (1995).

original goal of enabling women without other means of support to care for their own children (rather than send them to orphanages while the mothers worked). But they also suggest that if all these mothers are required to work, a great deal of childcare will need to be done by others.

What Factors Increase the Likelihood of Working for Single Welfare Mothers?

While most of the single mothers in IWPR's study participated in the labor force, many spent their time unsuccessfully looking for work or experienced periods of unemployment between spells of welfare receipt and work. IWPR research suggests that employment at stable and long-term jobs provides the greatest likelihood of escaping poverty, although the odds of escaping poverty by work alone are small for this group of women. Generally, as noted above, earnings from employment are packaged together with other income sources such as AFDC and income from other family members. Nonetheless, paid employment does improve the economic wellbeing of these single mothers and their families.

Not surprisingly, the factors that predict whether an AFDC recipient works are the same factors that predict employment for most women, regardless of income level: such as not having a disability; the availability of jobs; not having infants or toddlers in their care; access to family supports (i.e., child care or earnings from other family members); and greater levels of accumulated human capital including high school education, job training, and past work experience (see table 7.3). For instance, having a work-preventing disability makes it seven times more likely that these single mothers will not find employment. AFDC recipients are more likely to find work if more jobs are available (i.e., if they live in states with low unemployment rates), while mothers with older children who have lower childcare costs and fewer demands on their time and are much more likely to work. Additionally, family supports ease the costs of working, which significantly increases the likelihood of working. Obtaining more work experience or job training and completing high school makes the mothers more attractive to employers and more likely to find work—these factors double the chances of finding work.

Contrary to stereotypes, average state benefit levels, the amount of time spent looking for work, the mother's age, and the mother's welfare history were insignificant in distinguishing between mothers who engage in paid employment and those who do not. And being African American had little bearing on predicting whether an AFDC mother engages in paid work.

Job Prospects Of Mothers Receiving Welfare
Low-Wages and Unstable Jobs: Can Single Mothers Rely on the Low-Wage Labor Market?

If low-income single mothers succeed in finding work, do their jobs provide sufficient earnings to raise their families out of poverty? Tables 7.4 and 7.5 compare single mothers who receive AFDC with low-income employed mothers who do not receive AFDC (whom we call the "work reliants").[4] The work-reliant group represents a best case scenario for what we can expect to happen to welfare recipients who, because of time limits and work requirements, will likely rely more on the labor market for their livelihood. Given the often inadequate wages and intermittent work that characterize the low-wage labor market, however, it is unlikely that single mothers can achieve above-poverty incomes based on their earnings alone. Moreover, the work reliants, who by definition have incomes up to 200 percent of the poverty level and receive welfare for one month or less, have demographic and human capital characteristics that enable them to work more hours and earn more per hour than those women still receiving welfare assistance.

Table 7.4

Characteristics of Low Income* Single Mothers

		AFDC Recipients		Non-AFDC
			Work/	Work
		Welfare	Welfare	Reliant
	Total	Reliant	Packagers	
Sample Size (Unweighted)	2,554	688	474	1,392
Sample Size (Weighted)	5,735,793	1,536,332	1,117,029	3,082,432
Percent (Weighted)	100.00%	26.80%	19.50%	53.70%
Demographic				
Age (mean years)	32.2	30.3	29.3	34.3
Teenage (Age 19 or less)	9.70%	11.40%	10.70%	8.50%
Youth (Age 20–24)	16.40%	20.60%	24.50%	11.50%
Young (Age 25–34)	38.10%	40.70%	40.90%	35.90%
Prime (Age 35+)	35.60%	37.30%	23.90%	44.10%
Percent Recently Married	57.10%	44.10%	49.90%	66.20%
Race and Ethnicity				
White	43.20%	32.50%	42.10%	48.90%
African-American	40.70%	48.70%	44.00%	35.50%
Hispanic	13.90%	16.90%	11.20%	13.40%
Other	2.40%	2.80%	2.60%	2.20%
Family and Household Structure				
Number of Children	1.6	2.0	1.8	1.4
Age of Children (monthly average)				
Percent of Children under Age 3	24.30%	29.90%	30.70%	19.20%
Percent of Children Age 3 to 5	16.30%	20.30%	18.20%	13.60%
Percent of Children Age 6 to 12	34.00%	32.00%	33.80%	35.00%
Percent of Children Age 13 to 17	25.40%	17.90%	17.20%	32.20%
Number of People in Household	3.7	4.1	3.9	3.5
Human Capital				
Education and Job Training				
Years of Schooling	11.3	10.6	11.4	11.6
Educational Attainment				
Percent High School Diploma Only	41.00%	31.80%	43.40%	44.70%
Percent Some College	17.70%	11.40%	18.80%	20.50%
Percent 4 Year College or More	3.10%	1.30%	1.80%	4.60%
Percent Enrolled in School During				
Survey	26.10%	32.70%	32.70%	22.10%
Percent Ever Received Job Training	27.10%	22.50%	33.30%	27.10%
Percent Ever Received Federal				
Job Training	9.70%	11.00%	15.20%	7.10%
Work Experience				
Years of Work Experience	7.2	3.7	5.8	9.4
Current Job Tenure (Years)	3	1.3	2.1	4.2
Physical Limitation on Work				
Percent Disabled	17.00%	27.20%	13.90%	13.00%

* Family Income is less than 200 percent of the federal poverty line.

Source: IWPR calculations based on the Survey of Income and Program Participation 1986, 1987, 1988, and 1990 panels.

From: IWPR (forthcoming).

———— Table 7.5 ————
Poverty and Employment Characteristics of Low-Income Single Mothers
(Over the 24-Month Study Period)

| | Single Mothers | | |
| | AFDC Recipients | | Non-AFDC |
	Welfare Reliant (a)	Work/Welfare Packagers (b)	Work Reliant (c)
Sample size (Unweighted)	688	474	1,392
Sample size (Weighted)	1,536,332	1,117,029	3,082,432
Poverty (modified definition) (d)			
Percent in Poverty	79.1%	52.7%	29.2%
Months in Poverty	19.8	14.7	8.4
Labor Force Participation			
Percent in the Labor Force (monthly average)	11%	65%	74%
Percent Ever Worked During the Survey	11%	100%	84%
Weeks of Employment	8.5	53.5	84.1
Weeks of Unemployment	20.3	14.1	5.9
Total Hours Worked	140	1,862	3,232
Number of Jobs per Recipient	1.09	1.71	1.69
Earnings (in 1994 dollars)			
Total Annual Earnings	$327	$5,419	$11,134
Annual Earnings in Primary Job	$309	$4,713	$9,955
Hourly Wage Rate at Primary Job	$4.42	$5.29	$6.60
Work Experience			
Total Weeks Worked	9	54	84
Weeks in Primary Job	9	47	77
Weeks in full-time at the primary job	1	29	57
Weeks part-time at the primary job	8	18	20

(a) Welfare Reliants received AFDC for at least two months during the 24-month survey period but had less than 300 hours of paid work.

(b) Work/Welfare packagers received AFDC for at least two months during the survey but had over 300 hours of paid work.

(c) Work Reliants received AFDC for fewer than two months. Only 1 percent of these women received AFDC during the 24-month survey period, for spells of a maximum of one month.

(d) Includes the cash value of Food Stamps and Women, Infants, and Children (WIC).

Source: IWPR calculations based on the Survey of Income and Program Participation, 1986, 1987, 1988, and 1990 panels.

From: IWPR (forthcoming).

The work reliants are the most likely of the low-income single mothers in our study to have a high school diploma; only 30 percent of the work reliants lack a high school diploma compared with 36 percent of the work/welfare packagers (those who both receive welfare and work) and 56 percent of those who rely mainly on welfare. As table 7.4 shows, work-reliant single mothers have more work experience and more years on their current jobs. They are also older, have

Table 7.6

Jobs and Wages of Work/Welfare Packagers
(average hourly wages in January 1997 dollars [a])

	% in Occupation	Hourly Rate (b)
Service	37.80%	$5.86
Administrative Support	19.00%	$6.69
Operator/Laborer/Farming (c)	18.50%	$4.90
Sales	14.30%	$5.67
Managerial	3.80%	$7.39 (d)
Professional	3.70%	
Technicians/Related Support	1.90%	
Precision Production	1.10%	
Total	100.10%	$5.96

(a) Wage rates were CPI-adjusted to the January 1997 dollar value from their original amount in the current dollar value at the time of the survey.

(b) The wage rates are for the primary jobs held by the respondents during the two-year survey period. A primary job is the job at which the respondent worked the longest hours, including wage, salary, and self-employed jobs. The hourly wage rate is calculated from total earnings and total hours worked at the primary job.

(c) Including 2.1% in farming and forestry.

(d) Average for four occupations: managerial, professional, technicians and related support, and precision production, due to small case numbers.

Source: IWPR calculations based on the Survey of Income and Program Participation, 1990 and 1991 panels.

fewer children, and have older children. They and the work/welfare packagers are much less likely than the welfare reliants to have a physical work-limiting disability. As table 7.5 shows, the work reliants work substantially more hours than the work/welfare packagers, for a total of 3,232 hours, or about three-quarters time, over the two-year study period. They have the highest hourly wages among low-income single mothers—an average of $6.60 per hour and total annual earnings of $11,134 (in 1994 dollars). Although low-wage service jobs constitute the largest source of employment for both the work reliants and the work/welfare packagers, a comparison of tables 7.6 and 7.7 shows that the work-reliant mothers are more likely to be in better jobs (managerial, professional, technical or precision production jobs).[5] (Of work-reliant single mothers, 33 percent work in the service occupations and 14 percent work in the higher-skilled occupations, while for the packagers, 38 percent work in the service occupations and 11 percent work in the higher-skilled technical, professional and managerial occupations.) Work-reliant single mothers earn more per hour in each occupation than do work/welfare packagers—an average of $7.43 per hour versus $5.96 per hour, (in January 1997 dollars) consistent with their higher levels of human capital. For welfare mothers who work, the most common occupations are do-

_____ Table 7.7 _____

Jobs and Wages of Market Reliant Single Mothers in Low-Income Families
(average hourly wages in January 1997 dollars [a])

	% in Occupation	Hourly Rate (b)
Service	33.00%	$6.60
Administrative Support	22.30%	$8.39
Operator/Laborer/Farming (c)	17.10%	$7.05
Sales	13.40%	$6.49
Professional	5.30%	$9.17
Managerial	3.40%	$9.55
Technicians/Related Support	2.50%	$10.63
Precision Production	3.00%	$7.41
Total	100.00%	$7.43

(a) The amount of the wage rates were CPI-adjusted to the January 1997 dollar value from their original amount in the current dollar value at the time of the survey.

(b) The wage rates are for the primary jobs held by the respondents during the two-year survey period. A primary job is the job at which the respondent worked the longes hours, including wage, salary, and self-employed jobs. The hourly wage rate is calculated from total earnings and total hours worked at the primary job.

(c) Including 0.7% in farming and forestry.

Source: IWPR calculations based on the Survey of Income and Program Participation, 1990 and 1991 panels.

mestic workers, cashiers, nursing aides, childcare workers, and wait persons (data not shown).

Despite their greater work effort and slightly better occupational status, work-reliant single mothers experience significant levels of job instability, holding an average of 1.7 jobs during the two-year survey period, the same as work/welfare packagers (see table 7.5). Though work-reliant single mothers spend significantly fewer months in poverty than other low-income single mothers, they still earn less than the $14,916 that Edin and Lein (1997) estimate is necessary for working single mothers to survive at a minimal standard of decency.

What Factors Increase the Chances of Escaping Poverty for AFDC Single Mothers?

Stable jobs, more human capital, union membership, and access to means- and non-means-tested benefits increase the chances of escaping poverty (see table 7.3). Among all single mothers who package work and welfare, the more months during which a mother pools income with other family members, the more likely she is to escape poverty. Single mothers who have access to income from family members on a continuous basis are eight times more likely to escape poverty than women who do not have this steady income source.

The majority of working welfare mothers lack access to significant family resources—for these mothers, earnings from employment and stable jobs become a more important ingredient of an antipoverty strategy. Of primary importance is job volatility (the number of times they change jobs). Regardless of the reasons for job loss, the more times the mother starts and stops working, the more likely she is to be poor. Mothers whose jobs are covered by union contracts generally enjoy more job stability—union coverage triples these mothers' chances of escaping poverty.

Working welfare mothers with a high school education and job training are more likely to escape poverty. Although previous work experience is also significant, it takes ten years of work experience to raise a family's chances of escaping poverty by two-thirds. Living in states with higher AFDC benefits is also a significant antipoverty factor, as is receiving non-means-tested benefits, such as unemployment compensation, social security, or workers' compensation.

How Significant are Childcare Costs for Single Mothers?

As noted earlier (table 7.3), the presence of young children is an important factor in reducing the likelihood of a low-income single mother's employment. Underlying this negative association is the lack of affordable, quality childcare (Kimmel 1994; Hofferth 1995). Recent research at IWPR has analyzed childcare usage among working mothers in low-income families (those within 200 percent of the poverty line) with children under thirteen to investigate both what type of childcare these families use and how much they pay for it.[6]

Both working single mothers who receive welfare and those who do not use relative care most often, followed by center-based care and non-relative family-based care. Working single mothers who receive welfare are considerably poorer than those who do not; they use much more care provided by grandmothers and other relatives than do the work-reliant mothers, who use more center-based care (see table 7.8). Despite their greater use of relatives, AFDC working mothers and work-reliant mothers pay for childcare about half the time. Among AFDC working mothers, 33 percent who use grandparent care, 71 percent who use other relatives, 83 percent who use family care by nonrelatives, and 68 percent who use center-based care pay for it. Among the work-reliant single mothers, lower proportions pay for relative care but higher proportions pay for nonrelative and center-based care (data not shown).[7]

To determine the burden of cost to single working mothers, the childcare cost in relation to mothers' earnings, to total family incomes, and to the families' poverty status (see table 7.9) was analyzed. Both AFDC and non-AFDC single working mothers are about equally likely to pay for childcare (ranging from 38.6 to 40.9 percent; these proportions are lower than those noted earlier for children under six, because children up through age twelve are included in this analysis—it is easier to find unpaid care for older children). Furthermore, low-income

_____ Table 7.8 _____

Child Care Arrangements of Children Under Six for Low-Income*
Single Working Mothers

	AFDC Mothers	Non-AFDC Mothers
Sample Size (Unweighted)	78	208
Sample Size (Weighted)	306,007	799,579
Average Number of Children Under Age 6	1.3	1.2
Primary Care Arrangements (percent of total children)		
Relative Care	53.40%	36.70%
Other Parent	10.40%	8.90%
Siblings	0.60%	1.50%
Grandparents	25.70%	17.50%
Other Relatives	16.70%	8.80%
Non-Relative Family-Based Care	16.50%	20.90%
Center-Based Care	19.80%	30.00%
Other Care**	10.20%	12.40%
Percent of Children in Paid Care	46.70%	52.90%
Percent of Children with More than One Arrangement	19.10%	30.50%

*Family income is less than 200 percent of the federal state poverty line.

**Other care includes child in school, child caring for self, and child care by mother while mother is working.

Source: IWPR Calculations based on the 1998 and 1990 panels and Topical Module 3 of the Survey of Income and Program Participation

non-AFDC mothers and AFDC mothers paid about the same amount for childcare monthly, with the AFDC mothers paying slightly more ($222 per month versus $204 per month). Since the AFDC working mothers earn substantially less, the cost of childcare is a much higher burden for these mothers than it is for the non-AFDC working mothers. AFDC mothers spend $1.72 per hour of employment on childcare, amounting to 34 percent of the mother's earnings overall. Work-reliant mothers pay $1.36 per hour of employment and 19 percent of their earnings overall on childcare. Work-reliant mothers have lower childcare costs (per working hour) because, among other reasons, they have older children and fewer children. Their lower childcare costs undoubtedly contribute to their greater work effort.

To what degree would childcare subsidies help poor employed mothers escape poverty? These findings suggest that about one-third of the below-poverty AFDC families would benefit from childcare subsidies (up to the amount of their current childcare cost, $214 monthly, on average) and escape poverty, that is, their poverty rate would decrease by one-third (from 52 to 34 percent). The poverty rate for families of low-income, non-AFDC, single mothers would decrease by

_____ Table 7.9 _____

Child Care Costs for Single Mothers with Children Under Age 13 in Low-Income Families, 1994 Dollars

| | Working Mothers (a) | | | |
| | AFDC (b) | | Non-AFDC | |
	Paying	Not Paying	Paying	Not Paying
Sample Size (Unweighted)	70	49	234	160
Sample Size (Weighted)	272,000	180,000	868,000	601,000
Average Number of Children	1.7	1.9	1.5	1.6
Average Size of Household	4.5	4.1	3.6	3.4
Distribution of Families by Paying and Not-Paying	60.20%	39.80%	59.10%	40.90%
Monthly Child Care Cost		$222		$204
Mother's Hourly Wage Rate (c)	$5.81	$5.92	$6.81	$0.79
Mother's Hours Worked	132	141	161	164
Cost per Mother's Employment Hour		$1.72		$1.36
Mother's Monthly Earnings	$735	$813	$1,088	$1,281
Cost as a Percent of Mother's Earnings		34.30%		19.20%
Monthly Family Income	$1,491	$1,586	$1,089	$1,881
Cost as a Percent of Family Income		19%		13%
Percent in Poverty (d)	48.70%	51.50%	28.40%	15.10%
Percent in Poverty if Child Care Costs are Subsidized		34.50%		8.10%

_____

(a) Mothers who were working as well as enrolled in school are not included in this table to avoid over-estimating childcare costs in relation to mother's earnings and family income. All data are for Month 12 in the 24-month study period.

(b) Women in the AFDC group may or may not be on AFDC in Month 12, but receive AFDC for at least two months of the 24-month study period.

(c) Mother's hourly wage rate is for her primary job (the job at which she worked the most hours) during Month 12.

(d) A modified poverty measure, which includes the cash value of food stamps and WIC in family income for Month 12 is used.

Source: IWPR calculations based on the 1988 and 1990 panels and Topical Module 3 of the Survey of Income and Program Participation

nearly half (from 15.1 to 8.1 percent). Along with this simple effect on family well-being, childcare subsidies might have further positive effects that would help mothers stabilize their employment and improve their earning capacity in the long run.

Conclusions

Continuing research at IWPR strongly suggests that welfare recipients required to work as a result of welfare reform will likely do worse in the labor market than those already working. They have less education and work experience, which are likely to lead to lower earnings and higher childcare costs per employment hour because they have more and younger children. Their earnings will be low, well below the poverty level, and their childcare costs will be high. They will therefore need considerable ongoing financial assistance to enable them to work and maintain their current standard of living, which is already quite low. It appears from this analysis that when conditions improve for single mothers on welfare, when they have completed their schooling and their children are older, they begin to work and increase their work hours over time. These are the women who have been most able to leave welfare, and many have done so. The welfare reforms underway amount to pushing women off welfare before these basic, work-enabling conditions have been met.

Government data for 1996 saw no change in overall poverty rates but a large increase in the proportion of families living below 50 percent of the poverty standard. It is possible that this is an early result of welfare reform. The welfare rolls have fallen quite dramatically in many states, frequently by 40 to 60 percent, in the past several years. According to the President's Council of Economic Advisors, reduced rolls are a result of state-based welfare reforms undertaken under the previous waiver programs (which allowed states to experiment with AFDC eligibility rules and benefit levels), the 1996 welfare reform, the strong economy which has provided many new jobs, and decreased applications for welfare assistance even among those eligible (possibly as a result of the intense public discussion about changes in the welfare system).

Currently, because the strong economy is providing employment opportunities and because the federal block grant funds to the states, which are based on previous caseloads, are high relative to current caseloads, many states have large budget surpluses. Some states, not all, are spending increased amounts on childcare, job placement, and job training to facilitate the transition of these prejob-ready single mothers from welfare to work. Few are saving for a rainy day, raising great concerns for what might happen to poor families when the economy turns downward again.

As Nancy Fraser has pointed out, the United States is nearly unique among advanced industrial countries in having no ongoing financial support for mothers, either in the form of paid maternity leave for workers (which is strictly voluntary in all but five states in the United States) or in the form of child allowances. While most industrial nations have both maternity/child rearing financial aid and poor relief, the United States rolls both programs into one, providing maternal support only for those women who are desperately poor and lack other resources. Consequently, there is a stigma attached to the poor stay-at-home mom, the only mom who is obviously subsidized by taxpayers.

Policy Recommendations

Policymakers must recognize that there are no simple or inexpensive ways to make welfare mothers more self-sufficient over the long term. Not investing in these women now will likely doom most of them to more intense and long lasting poverty, even if more of them are working.

The five-year lifetime limit on benefit receipt will work against enabling women to complete high school or enter college, education they sorely need to increase their earnings capacity. Time limits may also make it difficult for these women to use welfare as unemployment insurance: given the instability in the low-wage labor market most of them will likely enter, income to fill the gaps between jobs will be necessary. While unemployment insurance should theoretically cover them in between jobs, in many states, low-wage workers who have not been able to work full-time for enough weeks of the year will not qualify for benefits; benefits are likely to be low for low-wage workers and may not be high enough to tide a mother with children over a jobless period. IWPR research has shown that when women who had left welfare lost their jobs, they were more likely to go back on welfare than on unemployment insurance.

Also, mothers who care for children will continue to have the kinds of family emergencies that put many of them on welfare in the first place. Lacking any other source of income in periods when they cannot work because of family needs, women who have exhausted their time limits will likely suffer great hardship. Expanding Temporary Disability Insurance programs, now required for workers in five states, to the rest of the states and enhancing them to provide paid family leaves would help women at all income levels, but would be especially important for low-income women. Alternatively, unemployment insurance could be expanded to provide paid family leave.

Finally, the presence or threat of domestic violence often prevents these women from entering the workforce or completing job-training programs. Women suffering from domestic violence will often need more than five years of benefits. Though states can exempt such women from the time limit, they are not required to do so. Recent estimates show that from one-fifth to over one-half of all AFDC recipients are current victims of domestic violence (Raphael 1996).

Time limits on benefits will be especially difficult for this group of women, since repeated attempts to leave abusive relationships are usually needed. For many reasons, the issue of time limits in benefit receipt should be reexamined.

Efforts to increase single mothers' earnings in the labor market are also needed. A higher federal minimum wage (even with the recent increase, the minimum wage is still below its historic relative average), greater support for unionization among low-wage workers, and discouragement of the contingent work phenomenon would all improve the earnings prospects of welfare mothers. Stronger enforcement of antidiscrimination laws and new laws requiring pay equity would also help. In the interim, welfare reform should encourage welfare recipients, who already exhibit substantial work and job search effort, to package earnings along with their benefits so that they can stabilize their family income at a higher level. Given low wages and low benefits, the average single-mother family needs both to survive. Although many states have liberalized their welfare programs in this way, these work/welfare packagers could face hardship when their five-year lifetime limits have been reached if, in the interim, they have not been able to find higher wage jobs that allow them to survive without welfare.

Childcare and healthcare are especially important for this group of newly working mothers who will lose welfare benefits. By providing childcare subsidies to low-income mothers and mothers who formerly relied on AFDC, policymakers could improve the likelihood that low-income families could work their way out of poverty. Recent Congressional action has provided more funding for health insurance for the children of the working poor, but has done little to provide it for their mothers (and fathers).

Reforms such as childcare and healthcare subsidies for the working poor, higher wages, more unionization, reduced contingent work, improved unemployment insurance, and paid family leave would help all working women, though they would help the poor disproportionately more. The only potentially good thing about welfare reform is that it could lead to a changed perception of welfare mothers as working mothers, enabling them to have more in common with all mothers. Cross-class coalitions in support of these workplace reforms could become more possible. Alternatively, competition for scarce resources, such as subsidized daycare slots, might intensify between the welfare working poor and the working poor not moving off welfare and opportunity for unity could be lost.

Despite the prevailing perception that social policies have failed to achieve their goals, federal programs for the elderly have resulted in dramatic improvements in their economic status, primarily because of increases in real Social Security benefits (which grew by 57 percent between 1970 and 1986; Moon and Juster 1995) and Medicare and Medicaid programs, which cover more of the costs of medical care for the elderly. The poverty rate for the elderly in the United States fell from a high of 30 percent in 1967 to 12 percent in 1994 (U.S. Bureau of the

Census 1995). These programs, which have broad benefits, also have broad support. They help all the elderly, but they help the poor elderly more.

While it is unlikely that programs targeted only at poor single mothers and their families will ever achieve the scale of the Social Security programs, current reforms and cutbacks will almost certainly result in *increased* poverty for many single mothers and their children. Sensible policies, targeted at increasing education and training, providing subsidized childcare and healthcare, establishing paid family leave, and reforming the low-wage labor market should be designed to help a broad group of women workers. Such programs could help poor single mothers lengthen and strengthen their labor market participation, improve their earnings, and perhaps, eventually, move beyond the need for welfare assistance from the public.

Notes

1. Each year, a new panel of the SIPP, usually consisting of about fifteen thousand households goes into the field. IWPR staff continue to study the population of low-income families and welfare mothers as each new panel of the SIPP becomes available for research.
2. The sample size for this study was 1,181 single mothers who received welfare for at least two months of the twenty-four-month study period. They represented about 2.8 million women in the U.S. population, or 80 percent of all adult AFDC recipients; see Spalter-Roth et al. (1995).
3. It should be noted that the percentages of women identified as working or receiving help in the EWPR study are higher than those so identified in administrative data. The administrative data are generally cross sectional and refer to a given point in time, for example, a single month. Although in any one month the average percentage receiving income from other family members may be small, the proportion receiving substantial family help over the twenty-four-month study period is much larger.
4. The data for these comparisons are drawn from an as yet unpublished IWPR study of the 1986 through 1990 SIPP panels, which includes analysis of all low-income families with minor children at home.
5. These data are from a recent unpublished analysis of SIPP data from the 1990 and 1991 panels (containing data up through 1992).
6. The 1988 and 1990 SIPP panels were used in this analysis.
7. All data in this paragraph pertain to children under age six.

Eight

Lisa Dodson

At the Kitchen Table

Poor Women Making Public Policy

In the last few years, longstanding national policy for poor child-raising families has been fundamentally changed and consequently about four million poor women and children—and some men—no longer receive cash support or welfare. Swept away by a startling coalescence of bipartisan interests and facing politically insignificant opposition, welfare was not so much reformed as dismantled and thrown out altogether, at varying paces around the country. With new-found freedom, states experimented with strict criteria for welfare eligibility and tough sanctions, all steps along the way to reducing the number of families on assistance. Such efforts proved surprisingly effective and thus national policy for poor families changed not only rhetorically but also in fact. The impressions that such change is having upon individuals, families, communities and, indeed, on our whole society are still unfolding, with a legion of evaluative efforts underway. Yet, political leaders and much of the media have already declared victory simply with the disappearance of people from the welfare count, with only soft early rumblings of concern about subsequent job losses and intractable poverty.

In the first part of this chapter, early effects of welfare reform are considered. The precipitous decline in caseload is contrasted with the continued increase in child/family poverty, nationwide. In this context, the political affirmation that welfare reform is a success is examined as a significant expression of contemporary American social thinking.

The second part of this chapter explores a divergent perspective that, it is argued, can be found in low-income America. The analysis of conversations and anecdotal data from low-income mothers and others whose work is rooted in low-income communities challenges mainstream policy thinking. The words of these women suggest a divergent social thinking characterized by judging public choices as "good" if the people, in particular children, who are directly affected by such choices do better as a result. While by no means a universal practice in poor America, nor nearly adequate to meet the needs of millions of fellow poor travelers, still this view of social engagement is posited as a source of alternative policy. Described by one woman as values learned "at my mother's table," a common forum for many mothers (and some fathers) to guide their children's ethical development, this social thinking is contrasted with mainstream policy.

Using qualitative data, the argument is made that such social thinking and practices are ongoing in poor America, expressed as spontaneous gestures to fragile people but also as principles known and understood to belong to people living in America's economic outback; kitchen table lessons as nascent policy. With the withdrawal of millions of dollars of public aid to families and children, overburdened local networks and individuals find themselves facing even more desperate need and tougher decisions. Their views of changing conditions and their complex, largely hidden practices in response, offer the possibility of revolutionizing social policy, sparking an investment in human development, thus veering away from the current trend toward institutionalized social exclusion.

Ending Welfare

Early evaluation of welfare reform is emerging and, as expected, the results are debatable. Above all, the number of families nationwide who are currently receiving cash support has declined dramatically, by 1.8 million families, and this decline alone has been widely heralded as a success story. Yet, state surveys following former recipients who exited welfare in the mid-1990s found that only just over half were employed when they left and that much of the employment is temporary and or part time (Venner and Brown 1999). The National Conference of State Legislatures reported that states had varying rates of postwelfare employment of any sort, as high as 64 percent in Indiana and as low as 30 percent of parents terminated from welfare in New Jersey (Tweedie and Reichert 1998).

The kinds of jobs that most parents find after welfare are in sales work, food services, and retail: notoriously unstable, low-paid occupations that offer few if any benefits or opportunities for advancement and in which high turnover is commonplace (Hershey and Pavetti 1997). As Susan Lambert (1999) puts it, "The fact that most low-skilled jobs do not pay enough to pull a family out of poverty even when workers work full time, year round has been well known for some time" (178, 117).

Of the hundreds of thousands of families that left welfare and do not have any or adequate employment, even less is known. A New Jersey survey reported that while "only" 23 percent of parents expected to turn to their own families for support after welfare, 47 percent did so, suggesting that family members are picking up a large part of the loss of public income (Tweedie and Reichert 1998). The effect this has on extended families, particularly grandmothers who are most likely to assist, is not fully known. But anecdotal evidence suggests that grandmothers, often themselves employed, are exhausted by the demands of young children and may experience a significant loss of quality of life when trying to care for grandchildren.

Housing instability is a major aspect of poor family life. While the mean income of people eligible for welfare also makes them eligible for housing assistance, in 1996, only 29 percent of welfare recipients received housing assistance (US GAO 1998). Thus, even before welfare reform, housing was a critical problem for poor families. With deteriorating public housing stock and the transfer of some public housing into the rental market, the actual number of units available to low-income families continues to decline (GAO 1998).Thus Nichols and Gault report that "[e]arly findings on the effects of welfare reform suggest that benefit loss makes it more difficult for families to pay rent" (1999, 1).

In response to this housing scarcity, families commonly "double up" with relatives to avoid moving into a shelter. One telephone survey of 349 former welfare recipients in New Orleans found that 21 percent had to move in with someone else within five months of losing benefits (Mancoske, Kemp, and Kindlhorst 1998). Of course, as in all of the postwelfare follow-up, particularly using telephones as the mode of tracking people, the data collected are limited and tend to understate the problem. In interviews in Boston and Cambridge Massachusetts in the summer of 1998, homelessness was stated as the greatest fear among mothers slated for the December "cut off" (Dodson, Joshi, and Pavetti 1998).

Healthcare access is another issue that hangs over low-income families as the low-wage jobs parents tend to find do not include health insurance, and those who have left or lost welfare may believe they have also lost Medicaid. Exacerbating a lack of health care, poor families tend to suffer from a high prevalence of acute and chronic maternal- and child-health problems (Olson and Pavetti 1996). A Massachusetts study conducted six months before time limits became effective revealed that of 100 mothers who were scheduled to lose support, more than 60 percent had at least one child with a chronic health condition (Dodson et al. 1998). Ill health, morbidity, and chronic health problems among children have long been associated with family poverty. "Research indicates strong correlations between poverty and poor health outcomes for children," according to Hudman and Starfield (1999), and the loss of welfare is likely to exacerbate those conditions. Though hundreds of thousands of people who left welfare remain eligible for Medicaid, many have lost that health coverage as well due to misinformation; lack of access to the reapplication process; and fear of reprisal, particularly among legal immigrants. Recently, Families USA conducted a study which found that along with the precipitous decrease in families receiving welfare is an associated drop in families on Medicaid; some 675,000 people, most of them children, have lost their health insurance along with their income. As Susan J. Golonka of the National Governor's Association commented, "It's true that there are unintended consequences of the 1996 welfare law" (*New York Times* April 14, 1999).

Ancillary to these changes, an associated effect within the communities in which many low-income families reside has occurred. Community-based organizations and services are the very first places that mothers and children go when they are in crisis. Thus, the volume and the intensity of service needs (and the effect of that upon service providers) in low-income America has only escalated, undermining the fragile networks of care (Withorn and Jons 1999). Teachers in urban neighborhoods where welfare reform has had a monumental effect report increasing distress and distraction behavior among very young children, turning efforts to teach reading into "just trying to keep them feeling safe, calming them down, letting them know there's still one place where things are routine" (Dodson 1999 interview, see note).

Of course, many basic troubles facing the health, stability, and well-being of poor families could gradually be resolved if they earned an adequate postwelfare income. Yet, here too low-income families have been only losing ground. While the number of jobs available has increased, the number of good jobs based on wages, wage growth, and benefits has been deteriorating (Kramer 1998). By these criteria, jobs that are open to less-skilled workers have only worsened (Blank 1997). The National Governor's Association reported in 1998 that, of those people leaving welfare who found jobs, earnings were between $5.50 and $7.00 an hour, placing many of these families well below the federal poverty rate. Numerous reports have already documented that many families return to apply for welfare (if they can) and as many as 20 to 30 percent of those who leave welfare return to reapply after just three months, suggesting their postwelfare plans are unsuccessful almost immediately (Tweedie and Reichert 1998).

Yet, none of this is new it is only worse. The extreme difficulties that parents/ families have as they attempt to care for their families without welfare support is similar to problems hundreds of thousands of families have faced in the past (Pavetti 1993; Spalter-Roth et al. 1995). The major reason for this is simple: the overall economic and social conditions for low-wage families have only worsened. The cost of housing, health care, and childcare has skyrocketed, while average wages have lagged, particularly in the lower-income labor market. Today as in the past, many women do not have a partner who is able to provide entirely or even largely for a family and most single mothers do not have the prerequisite education and skills for an occupation that will pay enough to cover family expenses. Further, even if they did land a job that paid well over minimum wage, the need to purchase replacement services for caretaking labor, presumed to be supplied by two parents, would simply overwhelm the budget of a single parent making even twice the poverty level.

Why did we not revolutionize rather than terminate poor-family assistance? From early retrospect, it may be postulated that reform was never proposed as a first step in replacing welfare with an innovative, more effective approach to support the advancement of millions of low-income people. Rather, reform was implicitly, if not explicitly, constructed as a way to end welfare benefits altogether.

Yet, an alternative approach could have pointed to copious documentation that, despite welfare's long history, over the last two decades poverty has been deepening and is more concentrated in children and family life. Clearly, no other social program could be called successful if the people it has served are experiencing greater hardship, particularly developing children. This approach would have been a sound position to take, easy to validate, the heart of it being that however we have been investing in the economic bottom-third of our families, it has not worked. One might simply pull in the cost/benefit economists to point out that the costs of managing the products of poverty are indeed higher than investing in people. Such costs include a high prevalence of chronic diseases, trauma, and early mortality among poor families; troubled children who are displaced and need intensive, residential care; critical need for rehabilitative educational and career services; homelessness; prisons; school dropouts; and premature parenting. The monumental, long-term cost of not investing in families could be set against the alternative of building well funded and well designed human development policies—a more rational policy option.

But welfare reform never had a mission of bringing poor children and families into their own, into any part of the economic and social mainstream of American society. Under welfare reform, the devil is offered up the hindmost. Those who are now losing long-standing assistance through welfare reform most profoundly feel the effect of this economic triage. The escalation of Darwinist policy, however, goes beyond those millions who are actually losing assistance, effecting a much larger circle of friends, kin, neighbors, schoolmates, service providers, teachers, and institutions. Human effects are spreading far afield and will be felt in all kinds of obvious and unpredictable ways over decades.

At the Kitchen Table

While federal and state governments were busy ending former welfare and associated poverty policies, obscured from mainstream view, other people were also engaged in dealing with this transformation. As the phenomenon of increasing economic instability changed the lives of millions of child-raising families, those families and all those intertwined and coexisting with them faced changed political and philosophical currents. In 1998, almost one third of America's children lived at or below 150 percent of poverty—almost one in three of all of our children lived with a sibling and mother who must cover all of her family's expenses on $300 per week (Interagency Forum on Families and Children 1998). Others estimate that nearly 40 percent of the nation's children are poor or close to poor (Hernandez 1997). The significance of this, not only the staggering proportion of children (and their kin) who live poor but also the disparity of their status relative to the top 10 percent of the population, is intrinsically connected to poverty policies and a national social ethos.

At least one third of all children who will become adults in the next decade in America may as well have been raised in another country; their experiences and knowledge of life are so divergent from that of the middle class. Adults connected to these children, those who raise them and those who have routinely worked with them, are absent from a discourse filled with politicians, policymakers, researchers, and social critics. Yet, many of the people who tend to poor America have also been pondering changing poverty policy and are doing so while daily watching the human effects of poverty.

April 1999—A kindergarten through 8th grade school in Boston. On this sunny day, the old school building is quiet, children are in the classrooms and, as always, in the nurse's office more than one child is holding up a cupped plastic breather to sucking mouths. Asthma is endemic in this neighborhood and the largely Latino and African American children who suffer from this chronic illness have a whole cabinet of ventilation equipment. The nurse smiles, but she is clearly worried about one of the two boys. "You have a fever honey, it's not just asthma this time. You can stay here a while but I have to call your mom." The African American boy of seven, Tony, is shaking his head as he sucks, he pauses to say, "Don't call, she can't miss no more work." The principal comes out of her office next door with a little white boy, and the two boys nod at each other. "I'm keeping Adam here for an hour or so; he has to write up what started the fight and how he could have handled it differently," Adam has been crying, but at her words, he and Tony exchange a quick grin and then look away.

"You're not sending him home?" a teacher's aide, Yvette, asks as she comes in the office. She is the mother of two children in the school and she knows the rules: you fight, you go home. "His mother will definitely lose her job with one more call. I think you know that Adam, and you want her home again," Adam said nothing to this. His mother received welfare until six months ago, and he has been difficult since she started work. He goes home to an empty apartment with periodic checks by a neighbor, but his teacher believes he is frightened. Yvette turns. "What about Tony, how you doing baby? Oh he *is* hot, you sending him home?" The nurse looks at the principal who looks up at the ceiling. Speaking almost to herself the principal says, "I got no choice. If it was just asthma, I'd keep him, but a fever . . . ."

The three women stand looking at the two boys as though they might come up with a suggestion. Then Yvette says, "I know DeeDee, let me call her, she'll give you permission to let me take him home with me, I'll give him Tylenol, let him rest and then bring him back for my afternoon period. By then the fever will be down. . . . "

The nurse is unhappy. "He's got something going, he may get worse." Yvette answers quickly, "What's worse is his mama losing that job and them being on the street again." Tony has heard bits and pieces of this conversation and he comes over, still hugging his breather. He looks at the boss, the principal. She looks down at his flushed face, runny nose, and anxious eyes. "Ok, Yvette call DeeDee. Tell her she has to sign a note when she gets in, ok. You check his temp too, ok?" Yvette is already bundling Tony out the door, telling him he will speak to his mom when she calls and get a Popsicle at her place. The principal mutters, "I'm gonna go too far and lose my own job." The nurse starts to say something but a big girl comes bursting into the office breathing laboriously, and she turns her attention to getting out this child's asthma gear.

In public city schools, childcare centers, and services serving a high population of low-income children, such ethical paradoxes are routine. Parents and those who work with parents face complex and incoherent rules and laws that circumscribe family life, social policies from Babylon. Poor parents are always juggling and trying to manage this snarl yet, increasingly, so too are the adults to whom they must turn or who try to help them manage their children. Yvette displayed almost no concern about liability for Tony, a sick child not her own yet in her care, without written permission. What Yvette knows from life is that for Tony and DeeDee to be homeless is worse than some abstract law or liability. The school principal is aware of how precarious such an arrangement is and still participates in a ruse to get around the rules. She makes individual judgements constantly and, even with years of knowledge about the reliable character of the people involved, she knows that if "anything should happen" it would fly back to her in a flash. Nevertheless, she says, "I will not call these mothers out of jobs if there is some way we can avoid it, one way or another." She believes that the "law" forced mothers to get out of their families and go and obtain paid work— of any kind. The ramifications of this are evident in her school, and she and the twenty teachers who work there refuse to take a neutral position. Often taught counter strategies and policies by local mothers, these teachers and other school workers who do not live in the community find they must choose sides.

In a potluck dinner discussion the same year, at another grade school, an older woman raising her own and foster children explained the ethical paradox of America today. "They start with their plan, for getting people to do this or do that. We start with the child, 'cause if the plan don't do for the child, it's no kind of plan at all. Just look around, just use your eyes and look. Is the plan a good plan? Are these children doing, as they should be? I say 'no' so I don't cooperate with the plan." The room full of parents and teachers nodded.

Other Peoples' Social Ethics

For decades, some researchers examined alternative norms, social practices, and what arguably are indigenous social policies. Carol Stack (1974) carefully documented kinship norms in an urban African American community, a place where people had long designed ways of managing hard lives that were unknown in the larger, white society. She traced peoples' ways (in fact, they were largely reported as women's ways) of offering assistance to those in need within extended families, more than twenty-five years ago. Human resources, particularly the caring work of women in families, was passed around, usually coming back home and creating mutual care networks. Those findings are as pertinent now to survival ways of low-income families as they were then.

Patricia Hill Collins (1994) examines the power and significance of a role that she (and others) would argue is ubiquitous in low-income communities of color. She calls this the "community othermothers," the extending of social and caretaking connections beyond one's biological own. Not only do motherwork and community othermothers provide for, and are critical to, the survival of their immediate kin, but that commitment is part of a larger mission, a whole people's resistance to being crushed by another culture, race, or class that holds sway. Unlike the practice of adopting and bringing a child into one's own household or reinventing a child as one's own, this approach is centered upon extending care outwardly to the community so families and children dwelling there may do a bit better. "This type of motherwork recognizes that individual survival, empowerment, and identity require group survival, empowerment, and identity" (59).

Nancy Naples (1991) takes these ideas on a different but related course. She calls "activist mothers" those women who extend their caregiving knowledge and experience into their community, consciously engaging in social care rather than private mothering. She recognizes such labor and the social philosophy behind it as activism, not just acting in the interests of someone in trouble but by doing so, challenging mainstream norms. Naples argues that low-income women challenge the delineation between paid and unpaid work, or between "social reproduction [and] so-called productive labor and show the interlocking and reinforcing connections between political activism, mothering, community work, and paid labor" (224).

In the late 1990s, just before and during welfare reform, some activist mothers found themselves involved helping others face the complex rule changes and the loss of welfare. As with the principal and teacher's aide above, such arrangements are often found to require crossing over from what is strictly legal to what seems to be imperative, legal or not.

Othermothers, Activists, and Subversive Advice

When they ask why you don't have job, you got to talk about how sick your childrens are, listen . . . you may not like it but that counts with them. Anyway, how're you going to keep that job with two babies under three?

Anna is helping Lorna figure out how to deal with losing welfare in three months. In several focus groups of women in the Dorchester section of Boston in fall 1998, strategies learned by those who had already left TANF were offered to those about to.

"Lorna, it's not like you can just up and walk out of the door (of a job) if you sister (who is supposed to provide childcare) calls and says you got to come home," Anna adds.

"I don't like this," Beatrice says before Lorna can answer. "It's teaching us to be sick, so as to keep welfare, but we're not sick, we just got all these responsibilities. The lady from the health center (a community health advocate) come and gave lessons 'bout how to get the exemption (Massachusetts has waivers for families with chronically ill members) but I don't like telling my children we are sick."

Anna is quick to defend her advice. "But Bea, you kids are all in school . . . your youngest is eight. Remember when they was little? You couldn't keep the job you got now if they was little like Lorna's."

Bea doesn't disagree, but she repeats her feelings afterward in a private conversation. To this proud woman of forty years who has raised four children off and on welfare for ten years, advising another woman to convince authorities that she or that child is chronically ill is a distortion of one's character and is unhealthy. Yet, she lays the problem at the feet of the policymakers.

What if you've got some young mother who's got problems and she is real scared about going out to find a job . . . she got no confidence and she's depressed or some man is beating on her. Now, she going to *feel* sick isn't she? And maybe she going to think her baby is sick too . . . and maybe in a way they both are sick, but that's not something to reach for. Why can't they see that folks need help getting healthy, not saying we're sick so's we don't lose that little bit of money.

In fact, Anna agrees with Beatrice, but she is a pragmatist. "I know a lot of ways to get around them people and I use them all and I teach mine how to use them. Bea's forgotten 'cause she don't want to remember those times. They shame a woman you know? But when you're there in that mess, you do what you got to."

Her "mother's table," according to Adrienne, a white woman in her thirties who previously spent several years on welfare, was the location where she, her sisters, and brothers would sit and listen to their mother. It was a sturdy female forum for monitoring homework, serving meals, sharing jokes, and shouting at children when they "messed up." Above all, it was the place where Adrienne's mother tried to tell her children about the world that they inhabit—the tough world of low-income America.

Adrienne's mother taught the lessons of individual responsibility for survival and included in her teaching the idea of responsibility for others as well as one's own. Whether rooted in her religious faith, her identity as an activist mother, or a simple belief in decent behavior, Adrienne's mother would practice her kitchen table philosophy. During Adrienne's childhood, her mother adopted and raised a child that his family had abandoned. "We called it a street adoption," Adrienne explained, and she remarked that, at her family's kitchen table, they practiced their own child-welfare policy. At that forum, Adrienne grew into a person who believes that the government is morally bankrupt—that the only justice a poor person will ever find is of her own creation.

Adrienne's home was similar to Jacquie's family life. At each summer's end, Jacquie, an African American woman, also in her thirties, would sit with her three children and figure out which child *had* to have new shoes before school started. While doing so, she would explain to them why this did not mean one child was more loved than another, nor that they should be ashamed to go to school with old shoes, and should stand up for each other if anyone was disrespectful. "I spent time telling them we were not poor on the inside and 'cause other children have much more, 'specially all the [white] kids in other neighborhoods, and around, you know. . . . I spent time telling them it was not something to take hate into you character. But sometimes it was hard, for me too, 'cause I wanted better for mine."

Jacquie suggested that part of the work of mothers in a society in which children grow up poor in the midst of very public wealth, is to explain that dichotomy . . . "'cause you got to make them learn to feel ok about it, even when you don't." Jacquie suspects her children understand more than just her words spoken. She suspects they know that their mother is trying to reassure them yet resents the inequality—largely spoken of as race inequality—just as much as they do. Jacquie concluded her soliloquy: "I wonder how those folks [wealthy white politicians and policymakers] sleep at night knowing of all the children that has so little while they have so much."

Both Jacquie and Adrienne believe that, particularly in the wake of welfare reform, table thinking has spread beyond the private kitchens of poor America and has crept into public places wherever parents congregate. Tales, critiques, and strategies are exchanged where mothers rock babies, where parents line up at food pantries, at health clinics, and in schoolyards. It is part of the inevitable response to living in extreme hardship in a nation that boasts astonishing prosperity and economic well being. As one young woman asked others in a 1998 focus group about welfare reform, "I don't understand what they are thinking, how can a woman make it with two small kids and making that little money and no place to leave her babies?"

An older woman in the group answered her, "This here isn't about 'how you going to make it.' It's about we don't want your kind to make it, you're not the citizens we want here. So you'd best get ready in your own way cause that what it is." Her words disturbed most of the women in that and several other groups . . . you are not wanted so you had best make your own way, your own rules for survival.

The principal who broke the rules to assist a mother facing untenable choices is not alone. In 1998, in several interviews with employers of former welfare recipients, work/family paradoxes came into the workplace along with the people who live them. One head of a food service franchise in downtown Boston said:

> I have a work schedule that, if I wrote it all down, would show women coming in and out during the day so they can meet their child's bus or get that child to his aunt's or whatever. Then she [they] comes rushing back in. The others [employees at the food service] cover for her because their turn is next. I don't tell them [the franchise upper management] because you're not supposed to . . . but we have worked it out and it is the only way I can sleep at night.

This supervisor was not alone amongst employers who—in nonrandom pilot interviews in Boston—reported making self-styled arrangements for low-income single mothers. Those who did suggested that these employees were more invested and comfortable in a workplace that seemed to acknowledge the complex family issues workers bring. Public recognition of these self-styled or kitchen table employment practices might reveal to what extent they are practiced and the benefits that emerge; yet, they tend to hide their work practice unorthodoxy.

Anna, who advised her younger friend Lorna above, counsels others about survival in postwelfare America. She believes in acknowledging that there is a dichotomy in how families are treated in this nation; she calls it "two-faced." Anna believes that raising some American children is considered admirable and valuable but raising poor children, particularly children of color, is treated as worthless and, therefore, is not work. In the face of this dichotomy, Anna has come to believe a mother should do all she can to reclaim her right to parent, and if that means lying about illness, about cash received from fathers, or about other routes to strengthen the family's resource, "So be it. Some people may not like it but it is what you have to do to get by. It's not like this is what a person asks for, but it is what you get around here, so ok, so be it."

On the other hand, Beatrice, her neighbor, is walking the thin pink line. She is the female image of a welfare success story and wants to believe there is a way through the channels of government offices. As have numerous women around the country, she has been in the spotlight as an example of the good welfare mother. Sometimes sounding similar to mainstream politicians, she counsels hard work and schooling, yet she admits that when her children were young the possibilities were very different. Bea admits, "If I didn't have a mother and father who was always there to help out . . . well . . . they might of ended up in care [foster care]."

Adrienne has given up on trying to enter mainstream America. Like her mother before her, she has informally adopted the son of a woman friend who lost control of her life. Adrienne, too, ignored the legal adoption process. She makes no bones about her beliefs and practices, her rejection of laws or rules that "are not meant to help people like me, just hold us down." Adrienne is passing her ways onto her children and others within her social network because she truly believes that rejecting rules is the first step to surviving in a country that does not seem to care if you do.

And young Lorna, who said hardly a word throughout the discussions, seems muted by fear, confusion, and increasing depression. In the wake of welfare's end, tens of thousands of Lornas are seeking a way to survive and rise. What they observe around them are individual examples of what nationwide data suggest, that the wages of most poor single mothers do not pull the family out of poverty. They simply take a mother out of the home for long days or nights—not for employment that leads up the ladder but for minimum wage, no benefits, no future jobs. Lorna observes that many children are left alone, perhaps watched by a sibling only few years older. She sees women who were trying to complete their education so they could get a decent job forced to drop out of college with welfare's demise. Lorna hears different kinds of advice—some crafty and duplicitous, some filled with cliches that do not ring true, some desperate and demoralizing. What is missing for tens of thousands of parents such as Lorna all across the country is a national voice, a place in their own government committed to investing in safe and stable family life—for the families in poor America.

Many low-income people, particularly mothers, integrate the lessons given at the kitchen table in the school lobby or daycare center hallway, at the bus stop, and on long lines that eat up poor people's time every day. Kitchen-table policy assumes choices are not clear cut, no black and white, gray is all that is real. Raising families on poverty wages; transcending stigma; managing complex households that have a high rate of health problems, disruptions, and stresses—none of this labor can be crammed into crisp and polished work schedules. Yet one clarion imperative emerges: If you are a healthy and self-respecting woman, your family *will* survive.

Postwelfare America is a land of juggling economic hardship, facing the changing rules of public assistance, entering low-wage, short-term jobs, and dodging regulations that are nonsensical and even destructive. It is a place where some find jobs supervised by individuals who attempt to recognize and respond to life issues that poor women face and where others cycle in and out of jobs as their families, personal problems, and conventional work practices overwhelm them. It is a place where life was already hard and with the loss of cash support (and for many, food stamps and Medicare as well), is undergoing rapid change. Policymakers from around the country report caseload decline, jobs filled, and expenditures for welfare drastically down. Others, though, are reporting ongoing poverty, job losses, increased foster care placement, and increased maternal and child hunger, with little calculation of the cost. Systematic evaluations of the various impacts of welfare reform continue; the debate goes on.

Yet, in the economic outback of America, the neighborhoods, inner cities, and counties where millions of low-income families cope with poverty, both welfare poverty and low-wage poverty, this debate is urgently underway as well. In those places, as mothers and involved others raise children to understand their world, they must try to reconcile the bifurcation of a democracy, a land of extreme wealth for some and grinding hardship for others, particularly child-raising families. For many, these "two faces" have become irreconcilable. In the postwelfare transformation of poor America, kitchen-table policies spring up and spread out as they always do when people perceive unequal treatment. Allies, local service providers, and neighbors will join in, coconspirators in an effort to support the survival and development of many of the nation's children and parents, largely the women, who tend them.

The lessons from the kitchen table speak of another America; a place where millions of families—which women largely head—are left out of the comfort and opportunity that national wealth has created. These lessons bring with them stories of terrible hardship, despair, and loss, but also offer ethical guidance, the obligations of kin, community, and of decent human behavior. They tell of strategies, creative management of bureaucracies, and of the moments when a lie is less terrible than the truth. Whether these lessons and their policy makers are ever offered a seat at the formal public policy table is, ultimately, a decision about democracy. Regardless of exclusion from mainstream institutions and processes, under current conditions, divergent social thinking abounds; kitchen-table policy is already underway.

Note

All references to Dodson's 1999 findings come from ethnographic research, interviews, and focus groups from current research in Boston Public Schools with parents, teachers, and representatives of local community groups.

Part 3

Realigning Social Welfare Regimes

Nine

I tell people in Eastern Europe that pension policy is impoverishing their children. The demands of pensioners are taking food out of the mouths of working people's children.
                                                Louise Fox, World Bank

Joyce Marie Mushaben

Challenging the Maternalist Presumption

The Gender Politics of Welfare Reform in Germany and the United States

Constraints of both the structural and ideological sort determine not only the ways in which women are affected by welfare policies in diverse national settings—they also provide many clues to the strategies women can use in redressing persisting inequalities. The gender-politics approach employed here does not focus on the ways in which women per se are mobilizing to protect their self-defined welfare interests, but rather on the ways in which gender roles are being de- and reconstructed under changing but still male-defined global parameters.

The first part of this chapter outlines the gender-neutral crises that have been afflicting the two systems since the 1990s, as well as the reform goals espoused by officials on both sides of the Atlantic; subsequent sections explore the gendered impact of the welfare courses pursued to date. I argue that cutback politics in the United States are affecting a much more substantial paradigm shift regarding women's place in society than recent changes in the Federal Republic of Germany. American reformers have made a critical break with the past insofar as they have redefined the image of deserving women along commodification lines: U.S. welfare recipients are to be viewed henceforth as paid laborers first, as mothers second.

Recent changes in the German *Sozialstaat* are geared toward reinforcing arcane notions of gender dependency and women's worthiness as mothers or homemakers first, and as members of an economic reserve army second. A partial commodification of women's care work in Germany does not substantially challenge their traditionally precommodified status within the welfare state, despite widespread evidence that this is not the place women themselves want to be.

Political-Economic Dynamics: Common Causes for Change

Although Helmut Kohl was philosophically attracted to Ronald Reagan's and Margaret Thatcher's cutback politics when he assumed office in 1982, historical factors rendered a major rollback of Germany's generous social programs politically taboo prior to 1990. The last several years have nonetheless provided both American and German policymakers with new windows of opportunity for making substantial cuts in their respective welfare programs.

At issue in both countries is, first, the problem of mounting national debt. U.S. and German politicians have instrumentalized a string of economic crises to weaken the pillars of their own welfare states over the last ten years, though their respective fiscal problems are due to different causes. Beginning his first term with promises to balance the budget, Reagan did not discover welfare as a target for outright dismantling until a combination of major tax cuts and exponential increases in defense spending left the budget with no place else to go. One million residents lost access to Food Stamps, while AFDC funding was cut 24 percent (1981–1984): at that time, 93 percent of the AFDC recipients were women. Programs for the poor, amounting to 18 percent of all nondefense spending, took 44 percent of the hits in Reagan's first round of cuts alone. The self-precipitated debt crisis left successor George Bush with no alternative but to break his now infamous promise of "No new taxes," exacerbating public ire over welfare handouts despite corporate downsizing and high unemployment.

In 1993, anti-big-government forces rallied to defeat Clinton's proposed national healthcare reform, which could have given new impetus to proactive welfare reforms (Hacker 1996; Skocpol 1997a). So-called "angry white men" enabled a new breed of Republicans to take over both Houses of Congress in 1994. The paradox inherent in the broader U.S. welfare package adopted in 1996 is that the mentality of cut-cut-cut has assumed a new quality, though the economy as a whole is booming and a balanced budget as of 1998 might have revitalized the belief that "there's enough to go around" typical of the late 1960s. Instead of returning to the vision of a "kinder, gentler America," U.S. elites embraced the leaner and meaner forces of globalization. The break in elite/public consensus over the legitimacy of welfare programs, perhaps the most significant change of the 1980s, has redirected the course of reform processes in Britain, the United States, Germany, and Canada (Borchert 1995).

German antiwelfare forces first experienced a fundamental shift in their political opportunity structure in 1989 through 1990, when the fall of the Wall eliminated the Federal Republic's most salient domestic policy competitor, the socialist-welfare state next door (the G.D.R.). East German accession under Article 23 of the Basic Law left the Western model intact, and thus unreformed in terms of its built-in social inequalities and design flaws. The July 1990 Treaty on the Social and Currency Union promised only to make things better than they were before. Though its social policies advancing equal rights left much to be desired in practice, the G.D.R.'s demise as an alternative welfare-state model brought the simultaneous loss of a moral imperative: the belief that *the better Germany* would ultimately provide the widest array of socioeconomic rights to women and men as parents and workers.

Mounting state debt in the German case is tied to the rehabilitation of the Eastern economy, as well as to the misappropriation of contributory social-insurance funds in treating unity's disruptions. More than DM 700 billion (US400 billion) has been spent to date, but little investment capital has remained in the East-Länder. Privatization turned into a production and real-estate boom for West Germans: 85–90 percent of the Eastern commercial/industrial property now rests in Western hands (Dahn 1994; Merkl 1996; Misselwitz 1996).[1] Bonn's decision to uphold (personal) property restitution before monetary compensation has resulted in countless evictions and skyrocketing rents for East residents. Roughly one-fourth of the insurance premiums (monthly, earnings-related payroll deductions) collected from Westerners to cover their own health, retirement, and unemployment needs are being used to finance Eastern benefits, to obfuscate the real costs of unity, which should have been covered by tax increases substantially higher than the current solidarity surcharge (which Easterners also pay). Privatization became an exercise in industrial downsizing, triggering an immediate unemployment crisis in the former Workers' State: 35-40 percent of all G.D.R. workplaces were eliminated by way of the Currency Union and sales contracts underwritten by the *Treuhand* (Knappe and Jobelius 1997). Most job creation (ABM) programs ran out in 1995, including short-time work contracts, temporary positions, and retraining courses. By 1996, 3.7 million Germans were officially jobless (9.7 percent West, 16 percent East); 4.6 million were registered as unemployed in mid-1997 (the de facto figure is 6.5 million).[2] The state's decision to break openly with the precept of full employment in 1990 has affected Eastern women more negatively than any other group.

A second force driving reforms in both countries is the unprecedented impact of demographic change. As of 1996, one American, statistically speaking, is turning fifty years of age every seven seconds, a trend that will continue through 2014. The aging U.S. baby boomers (born 1946–1964) has produced its own boomlet, however: 1997 saw the highest number of school matriculations in the nation's history. The U.S. population is expected to increase 50 percent by 2050, implying that Social Security contributions will not dry up, as long as future generations of workers make a living wage. Average fertility among American women stands at 2.05 children; as of 1990, 25.7 percent of U.S. residents were under 25, 12.5 percent were sixty-five or older. The Census Bureau estimates that the share of persons over sixty-five will reach 10.8 percent by 2040, when those over eighty-five will account for 19 percent (White House Conference on Aging 1995; Seelye 1997).

Ethnic newcomers continue to produce children at higher rates than established white non-Anglo groups. This part of the demographic equation makes angry white males quite nervous, though it is ultimately the nation's women who will witness a real shift in the country's ethnic composition (because they will outlive male cohorts by six to eight years). The white share of the population, which declined from 87 percent in 1950 to 76 percent in 1990, may fall to 62 percent by 2050 (Isbister 1996). As long as the United States remains not only a land of immigration but also a country which believes in turning legal aliens into citizen-taxpayers as quickly as possible, in stark contrast to Germany, it should be able to master the crisis.

By 2030, half of all German voters will be over fifty-five, implying a crisis of a different magnitude. The proportion of citizens over sixty-five rose from 21.6 percent in 1987 to 24.1 percent by 1995; projections for the years 2010 and 2020 stand at 31.3 percent and 35 percent. The number of live births per West German woman fell from 2.37 in 1960 to 1.37 in 1987, though it has risen slightly since unification (the biological clock among baby-boom women has reached 5 minutes before 12). While women from the former German Democratic Republic evinced higher fertility rates prior to unity (90 percent vs. 60 percent), births in the east plummeted nearly 60 percent after 1991 (despite recriminalization of abortion in 1993). The immediate decline is due largely to mass unemployment among females and to the cancellation of maternal support services.

Feminist writings on the welfare state rarely mention a critical normative factor inherent in the sweeping demographic changes just noted. A majority of U.S. and West German citizens has grown up under conditions of affluence; few recall the society-wide hardships of the 1920s, 1930s, and 1940s that gave rise to the modern welfare state. It is hard to generate a sense of societal commitment to its preservation among citizens unable to imagine the prospect of disease/epidemics or destitution in old age as the fate of whole generations. At the same time, spending and saving patterns in both countries have increasingly pitted the old against the young. The current generation of retirees derives greater benefit from the system than past and future generations of elderly could ever begin to imagine. Older citizens vote more faithfully than youth, lending pension programs their sacred cow character. Fiscal crises have taken their toll on public schools across the United States and have wiped out youth culture centers in the East German states. The best funded youth programs focus on drug-addiction, boot camps, gang- and anti-foreigner violence. All told, policy changes in both countries are giving rise to a serious break in the generational contract.

A third force for change is the increasing polarization of haves and have-nots and, with that, a breakdown in the specific culture of solidarity that has historically emerged in each society. The United States and the Federal Republic of Germany count among the world's ten wealthiest nations, yet both countries have witnessed troubling increases in their overall poverty rates as well as in the spread of deep poverty over the last ten years. Economic polarization at home has led many analysts to characterize the United States of the 1990s as the "winner-take-all society" (Phillips 1991). The United States ranks last among the OECD states in income inequality, meaning that it tolerates the greatest gap between its best and worst paid workers; in 1995, the lowest (10th) percentile received 35 percent of median income, while its wealthiest earners (90th percentile) drew 206 percent.

Quantity is not the only critical concern here; major shifts in the quality of poverty began to surface during an era of welfare-state consolidation. The first, characterized as the feminization of poverty, found elderly women sinking more rapidly into poverty than most men through the 1970s, due to the cumulative impact of lower pay, shorter work lives, and longer life spans. The second shift, rooted in the 1980s but intensifying in the 1990s, is known as the infantilization of poverty, extending well beyond U.S. and F.R.G. borders (Sorenson 1994; Duncan and Edwards 1996).

Family policy has never been an explicit component of welfare discourse in the United States, despite the fact that any elected official will take to the soap-box when the topic of family values is raised. Changes in AFDC eligibility requirements in 1981 had a double whammy effect for many U.S. families, tied as they were to cutbacks in Medicaid: 500,000 families lost their access to healthcare. Although Medicare is recognized as an entitlement program for all citizens over the age of sixty-five (and thus not stigmatized, like means-tested Medicaid), it is increasingly hard to distinguish between the two programs in relation to long-term elder care.[3] Once they have exhausted Medicare benefits, older Americans become eligible for Medicaid; in fact, 71 percent of all Medicaid funds now go to the elderly, the blind, and the disabled. Only 26.1 percent go to the poor in general, that is, AFDC recipients (Healthcare Financing Administration figures). The real value of AFDC payments dropped from $675 per month in 1970 to $378 in 1994; at the same time the share of female-headed households in the United States rose from 13 percent to 24 percent (O'Hare 1996, 16). During the 1960s, destitution among the elderly exceeded poverty among children, 12 percent compared with 15 percent; by 1994, child poverty rates were nearly twice those of seniors, 22 percent compared with 12 percent. Children less than eighteen now account for 40 percent of America's poor but comprise only 25 percent of the population (Abrahamson 1991; O'Hare 1996). This is not the whole story, since child poverty in the United States is clearly delineated by race; while 39.6 percent of white female-headed families were counted as poor in 1993, figures among black female-headed and Latina families were 57.7 percent and 60.5 percent, respectively (U.S. Census Bureau). Nor is the infantilization of poverty restricted to single-parent households: the poverty rate for married couples with children also rose, from 6 percent in 1974 to 8.3 percent in 1994 (Clymer 1997).

Described as the Two-Thirds Society (implying some redistribution still occurs), Germany placed sixth among the fifteen OECD countries in income equality, its least privileged earners receiving more than 50 percent, its richest 10 percent taking home 175 percent of the median income (Brasher 1995). Average salaries in the East still fall 15–20 percent short of their Western equivalents; yet a closer look reveals that Germany's growing income gap has little to do with the disruptions of unification. The number of West German households with a monthly net income exceeding DM 8,000 (US 4,500) doubled between 1980 and 1988; the proportion of *Sozialhilfe* (SH [Social Assistance]) recipients meanwhile rose from 3.5 percent in 1980 to 5.9 percent in 1990 (Textor 1997, 5–7). Though Hamburg boasts the greatest number of millionaires per capita (1,360 in 1992), its other residents are second only to Bremen in per capita welfare dependency (9 percent); the highest rates nationwide are found in the Western city-states. The segment of West Germans dependent on *Sozialhilfe* grew from 1.3 percent to 4.7 percent between 1963 and 1992 (809,000 persons in 1972; 1,769,000 in 1984; 2.8 million in 1990); one-third of all West Germans were classified as "poor" at least for short periods, 1984–1992 (Eckardt 1997, 60). Two-thirds of all single parents in West Germany fell beneath the poverty line in 1989; by 1992, 11.7 percent of all one parent/one child households, and 24 percent of one-parent homes with two or more children were drawing social assistance in the West alone (Voges 1996, 85). In 1994, 42 percent of the Federal Republic of Germany's 1.5 million single parents had monthly incomes of less than DM 1,400 (not enough to be taxed); 23 percent of all SH recipients are single mothers (Zwicker-Pelzer 1997, 98). Calls for cuts in capital gains taxes (as a stimulus to investment and job creation) are a persistent feature of conservative political discourse in the United States and the Federal Republic of Germany.[4] Still, mass unemployment in the Eastern states is clearly not the predominant cause of poverty in Germany.

Reform Goals and Retrenchment Strategies

Policymakers in the United States and the Federal Republic share a set of common goals with respect to entitlement programs such as healthcare and pensions. One is cost containment, especially in view of long-term demographic trends. The main aim of the 1992 and 1997 pension reforms in united Germany was to slow increases in retirement payments by tying them to net rather than gross wages. As of 1997, benefits will decrease from 70 percent to 64 percent of former gross income for most workers (civil servant pensions will not be affected until 2030). Though U.S. Social Security benefits are far less generous (less than 38 percent of gross wages), proposals to tax benefits above certain income levels, increase copayments for Medicare, and altering the cost-of-living formula not only threaten to undermine the universal nature of these programs but also preclude increases in benefits.

A second shared goal centers on the need to stabilize average contributions to insurance programs as a percentage of wage income, though both governments have increased such burdens as they apply to individual workers. Reagan's tax cuts of the 1980s benefiting upper income brackets were offset by higher Social Security taxes for lower- and middle-class workers, as well as by tax increases at state and local levels (suddenly faced with growing service burdens but shrinking revenue bases under New Federalism). Tax advantages for the well-to-do in Germany have also come at the expense of higher withholdings further down the wage scale. Mass unemployment coupled with demographic change means that ever fewer wage earners are required to carry an ever-expanding burden, insofar as whole professions are exempt from contributions to unemployment and pension funds (e.g., civil servants and the self-employed).[5]

In Germany, the proportion of social policy expenditures financed through payroll withholdings rose from 61.8 percent to 63.9 percent from 1980 to 1993, while the share of benefit programs financed through direct taxation fell from 36.1 percent to 33.9 percent. Health insurance withholdings alone rose from 12.2 percent in 1960 to 16.2 percent in 1980 to 19.65 percent in 1995; had unification been financed through tax increases—not by sending jobless Easterners more than fifty years of age into early retirement—the contributory rate could have been reduced by 8 percent (Hinrichs 1995). Healthcare in Germany and, to a degree, Medicare/Medicaid in the United States, are the only welfare programs that distribute benefits based on need, irrespective of contributions, which could be achieved more equitably through tax-based financing.

A third common objective centers on fostering choice and individual responsibility. Here the two national paths diverge, not so much in relation to the degree of gender dependency they have historically promoted but in regard to the day-to-day impact choice has on the quality of women's lives. Hanging on to what may have been rational choices between the 1870s and the 1930s (when basic program structures first took shape) can only lead to greater inequities and perversions under conditions of the 1990s.[6]

The title of the 1996 U.S. welfare reform bill says it all: the Personal Responsibility and Work Opportunity Reconciliation Act (PRWORA), except for the fact that the emphasis falls a lot more on personal responsibility than on work opportunity. An American woman's ability to reconcile paid labor and mother-hood (the thrust of many G.D.R. policies up until 1990) will henceforth depend on whether her state of residence sees fit to provide the necessary infrastructure, such as daycare and transportation. PRWORA dropped its original dictum of "two years and you work" in favor of "two years and you are off" with regard to AFDC (now TANF). Because the clock began ticking before recipients learned about the new federal constraints, many will exhaust the lifetime limit of five years more quickly than they might have expected.

Constraints on choice and stress on personal responsibility in Germany have thus far been limited to the state's most costly program, national health insurance. Prior to 1997, only persons above certain income levels could select private over public insurance funds; privatization initiatives of the 1980s were not very successful, since those who dropped out could not reenter the public system (the GKV) in the event of a significant loss of earnings. As of January 1997, all GKV members may choose their own insurance fund—an attempt to push the major providers into greater competition; yet all insurers are required to offer a minimum package of benefits—limiting their cost-cutting options. Copayments for some services, such as prescriptions, increased for all users in July 1997, though they cannot exceed 2 percent of gross income (1 percent for chronically ill).[7] A corresponding 20 percent reduction in the wages paid during short-term illnesses has been coupled with a 10 percent cut in sick pay (*Krankengeld*) for long-term or chronic illnesses.[8]

Insofar as health and pension programs have a universal character, German women are not forced to make the existential choices their American counterparts have traditionally faced. Nor has postwar Germany subjected its women to determinations of worthiness based on race, which enables U.S. policymakers to pit one group against another. While the German social net is not without its holes, any attempt by legislators to deny citizens a basic quality of life would soon lead to a direct challenge before the Constitutional Court (see discussion below). It may be a very uncomfortable net for some, and German society is still very patriarchal—but the state provides a real net nevertheless. Having lived in Germany, East and West, for some ten years since 1971, I have never encountered pockets of poverty that begin to compare with the urban nightmare known as East St. Louis (Kozal 1992).

Last but not least, both sets of national policymakers seem bent on reducing labor costs to employers while simultaneously increasing the latter's flexibility vis-à-vis the labor market. At issue are changes in the meaning of paid work as well as new questions regarding the value of women's unpaid work. Both countries have seen phenomenal growth in the part-time/temporary employment domains, though much of this has bypassed sectors critical to a decommodification of women's unpaid labor, like childcare and elderly/disabled services.

Not so Neutral Consequences

West German women with children have always had to rely heavily on part-time employment opportunities, because full-day schools were the exception to the rule (but the norm in the East). United Germany's chronic shortage of preschool childcare facilities (in contrast to nearly universal access under the G.D.R.) will not be remedied until after 1999; guaranteed places were postponed for four years as a cost-cutting measure after abortion was declared illegal for all Germans.

The share of part-timers among all gainfully employed laborers in Germany rose from 11.6 percent in 1984 to 12.9 percent in 1989 to 16.6 percent by 1993, albeit without the proportionate benefits package found in the Netherlands; 89 percent of those slots were filled by women (Deutscher Bundestag 1996; Walwei 1996, 29). Half of all jobs allocated by state employment offices in 1996 were of a temporary nature: 54.3 percent of those in the young states, 46.4 percent in the old ones; 36.4 percent of the Eastern positions were limited to six months, 8.2 percent in the West (*Leipziger Volkszeitung*, 11 February 1997). F.R.G. citizens temporarily unable to engage in paid employment (due to maternity, for instance) could permanently lose their place on the career track.

Another factor worth noting is the role of the German welfare state as a direct user of women's work, as an employer (Meyer 1994). By 1990, 58 percent of all Germans holding jobs in the fields of health, education, and welfare (pink-collar domains) were state employees, compared with 93 percent in Sweden and 38 percent in the Netherlands (Alestalo, Bislev, and Furaker 1991). Program cuts impel cuts in the number of persons paid to deliver social services; new limits on health cures may result in the loss of 18,000 positions in rehabilitation services. G.D.R. women were driven out of the banking, insurance, and social service sectors after 1990; the first two were remasculinized thanks to privatization.

The plight of U.S. women, in contrast, is best illustrated by a joke making the rounds in Missouri: *A booming economy, with millions of new jobs being created? Yes, I know all about it; I have three of them.* Even female social workers are now expected to do three jobs for the price of one: that of caseworker, job coach, and employment agent. Though the number of part-time jobs in the United States has only grown 30 percent in 30 years, temporary jobs have increased 500 percent in the last fifteen years (Weiss 1997). The job problem in the United States is not one of availability but rather one of actual pay; temps are often workers who have replaced regular employees long term without their respective benefit packages.

Based on 1991 statistics, about half of all women employed full time and year round earn too little (under $6.67 per hour) to raise a family of three out of poverty, once they have subtracted daycare costs. The median wages of full-time female laborers declined 1.5 percent in 1995 to $22,497; male wages held steady at $31,496 over 1994. The share of workers with below poverty wages rose from 24 percent in 1973 to 30 percent in 1995: 23 percent for men, 37 percent for women (O'Hare 1997, 10). Women now bring home 76 cents for every dollar, or 72 pfennigs for every D-Mark a man makes, largely because deindustrialization has led to a decline in male earnings since 1980.

Boasting of Wisconsin's so-called success in striking people from the welfare roles under the *W-2* program (a 65 percent reduction), Governor Tommy Thompson insisted during a 1997 television interview, "the only way you get out of poverty in America is by working" (*ABC-Nightline,* 4 September 1997). Working may be a necessary condition for escaping the grisly hold of poverty in America, but it is certainly not a sufficient one in a labor market grounded in a part-time/ temporary, low-pay/no-benefit wage structure. An individual can do little to remedy a gendered, racialized distribution of job opportunities, or to compensate for a dearth of support services.

As to unpaid labor, changes in Germany offer some recognition of care work by way of pay for home care and credit toward retirement. By 1992, more than 1,123,000 citizens residing in private households required regular care (70 percent of whom were over sixty-five); 73 percent received that care from daughters or wives (Naegele 1997). The 1995 adoption of long-term care insurance (*Pflegeversicherung*) ads a new fly in the ointment to the state's reliance on women's private care work, however. Compensation under Care Insurance ranges from DM 750 to 2,800 per month for persons receiving professional in-home care, while caretaking relatives will receive payments of DM 400–1,300 for providing personal care, clearly unequal pay for equal work.[9]

Conservatives' preference for private eldercare solutions raises the question as to who will care later for women of the so-called sandwich generation, already tending their own children and their parents. Expecting jobless women to pick up the slack may lower unemployment statistics in the short run, but it will not mitigate the looming costs of long-term care and demographic deficits. Germany already lacks sufficient care personnel, having long relied on alternative-service obligated Conscientious Objectors to fill the gap.

New welfare-to-work programs in the USA do nothing to reward women's labor in these areas. Indeed, recent changes in federal welfare law imply that maternal caretaking is no longer viewed as real work for any woman falling beneath the poverty line. Under the PRWORA rules, as interpreted by Wisconsin officials, women must look for or return to paid labor once their newborns are 12 WEEKS OLD (the maximum of *unpaid* care time guaranteed by the 1993 Family and Medical Leave Act). The ramifications are still a big unknown (Chris Bury, *ABC-Nightline,* 4 September 1997). U.S. officials have terminated Social Security Insurance benefits for parents with disabled or chronically ill children and family members whose conditions are no longer considered serious enough to warrant full-time home care; they are likewise cutting more than 500,000 elderly legal immigrants from the welfare roles.

Philosophical Contrasts: Models under Fire

Theda Skocpol (1995, 1996) has shown how a rudimentary U.S. welfare system of the late 1800s came to embody the maternalist presumption, the idea that as preservers of the race qua nation, women and their children deserved help from the state if cut off from male support through no fault of their own. Progressive forces aligned with first-wave women's movements charted a reform course that led to their own political enfranchisement. State programs extending from the Widow's Pensions of the Civil War era to the 1921 Sheppard-Towner Act provided many services to women, albeit only in their traditional roles as wives and mothers.

For a country so fundamentally antistate, the adoption of policies assisting women and children symbolized a great leap forward in social consciousness, though a framework of woman's worthiness rooted in conformity to predetermined, natural roles quickly lent itself to outright discrimination. The good intentions of nineteenth-century reformers notwithstanding, an expanding network of state programs eventually "evolved into one of the most socially demeaning and poorly funded parts of U.S. social provision" (Skocpol 1995, 255). In addition to establishing benefit levels well below an existential minimum, these programs excluded most nonwhites well into the 1960s (Mink 1990). Federalizing a multiplicity of state-level benefit schemes between 1935 and 1939, national policymakers continued the practice of inadequate funding under the new ADC label but moved what they considered to be the very worthy widows—surviving dependents of contributing workers—directly onto Social Security's Old Age and Survivors' Insurance track. Occupations encompassing predominantly nonwhite workers were deliberately excluded from Social Security coverage.

While white wives derived increasing benefits under an emerging breadwinner model, women of color had little choice but to use the maternalist-oriented AFDC as a parallel entitlement program (Amott 1990). The War on Poverty programs, coupled with a slow mitigation of direct discrimination following the passage of the 1964 Civil Rights Act, began to lift many families out of poverty through 1973 (an all time low of 11.1 percent). Southern states found new ways to discriminate, for example, by keeping benefit levels inordinately low, but even here poverty rates were cut in half (O'Hare 1996). Poverty did not decline fast enough to counteract the blows that would befall the system in the 1980s, however; each wave of recession has broadened the base, leaving many families literally one paycheck away from poverty.

Like German Social Assistance, AFDC was never designed to provide a long-term wage substitute. The temporary nature of AFDC has nonetheless created permanent dependencies to a greater extent than *Sozialhilfe*, because German benefits are indexed, based on cost-of-living statistics.[10] Roughly three-fourths of AFDC applicants turn to public assistance as a result of a relationship change (abandonment, divorce, death of a partner), not because women have given birth in the hopes of receiving a state hand-out. States offering higher benefit payments do not have larger welfare families (1994 *Green Book*). If marital break-up marks the onset of poverty for many women, pushing pregnant teenagers and single mothers into marriage will hardly solve the problem; it will only postpone applications for assistance until they are divorced (likely to ensue quickly). One of the most effective mechanisms for keeping married parents and their offspring out of poverty, the Earned Income Tax Credit, has been under Republican attack since 1993.

The (misnamed) Family Security Act of 1988 did little to remedy many of AFDC's internal contradictions, though it did enable some married families to seek aid. Nor did it plug many of the gaping holes in the overall system, for example, the lack of health insurance for the working poor. What the FSA did do was to push recipients into short-term training and paid-work opportunities, setting the stage for their permanent elimination from the welfare rolls under the 1996 legislation. The 1988 bill thus signals an incipient break with the belief that women merit the support of the state in their capacity as mothers.

Analogous to the prejudicial effects of marital tax-splitting and dependent benefits in Germany, the current Social Security structure privileges not working women but rather middle-class and upper-class married white women who have never contributed to the system (Meyer 1996). Fewer women received retired worker benefits based on their own contributions in 1992 than in 1960, despite dramatic changes in divorce rates and female labor market participation (Meyer 1996). U.S. claims filed as wives or widows ensure a higher payoff than do benefits accrued through women's paid labor (due to lower wages and interrupted work lives). Nor can U.S. women expect pension supplements based on the number of children they have reared; childless women not only enjoy a life of less work and higher disposable incomes but also one of equal entitlement to noncontributory health and pension benefits.

Since the 1880s, Germans have relied on a social security system built on the breadwinner model, and thus on the normal biographies of men. Tightly coupled with the Catholic social teaching of subsidiarity, the system promotes care by the smallest societal unit over provision by the wider public community. Translation: family members or relatives are obliged to ensure care for persons in need; the state intervenes, temporarily, only when the family is unable to meet its obligations.

A profamily system in the traditional sense turns out to be not as family friendly as the F.R.G. constitution posits: The Basic Law mandates sexual equality (Art. 3) as well as special protection for mothers and their children (Art. 6 GG) within the framework of a regulated social-market economy (Art. 20). Grounded in an arcane family model (father, mother, two or more children), the insurance system supports marriage *an und für sich*, excluding mothers and children who do not fall under the cover of holy matrimony; it provides full health, long term-care and pension coverage to dependents at no extra cost to the breadwinner, profiting high earners with children and childless couples the most. Efforts to operationalize either the household or individual entitlement as more appropriate units of analysis were put on hold by the 1996 Savings Package that privileges high earners even further.

The breadwinner model institutionalized discrimination against women as paid workers in West Germany well into the 1970s. It upheld a system of low-wage labor and mandated a shorter working life (paid work) for many women; wives needed husbands' permission to seek work and had to document access to childcare as a condition of employment until the mid-1970s. By 1987, 52 percent of Western women had joined the paid labor force, 30 percent part-time, despite the double burden this implied; 90 percent of East German women engaged in paid employment prior to unity, backed by a wide array of social rights. The old F.R.G.'s first compensation for years invested in childrearing came in 1986 with the so-called Baby-Year Pension. Initially Chancellor Kohl (born 1930), CDU-Chief Geissler (born 1930), and Labor Minister Blum (born 1935) sought to exclude the generation which would have benefited most: their own mothers, born prior to 31 December 1920! This group included countless *Trümmerfrauen* (a majority of the retirees by 1986), who had not only dug the shattered republic out of its own rubble after 1945 but also bore the 11.2 million children who produced the Economic Miracle.

A comparison with G.D.R. women who enjoyed individual rights to social security, along with many more maternal (as opposed to wifely) support services prior to 1990, demonstrates the negative impact of a shorter paid-work life. As of 1991, more than 70 percent of the eastern women had registered 31 or more years of active employment (and a commensurate level of full insurance contributions); 46.9 percent had completed more than 40 years. In contrast, 76.5 percent of the Western women had accrued fewer than 30 years of benefit time, 10 percent had worked less than one decade, only 10 percent more than 40 years. Among blue-collar workers, the average pension paid out to West women was DM 572 in 1992, with DM 819 to East women. Benefits for surviving spouses of white-collar workers (a category which hardly existed in the G.D.R.) were substantially higher: West widows could count on DM 1,147 per month, their Eastern counterparts only DM 472, testifying to the privileged status of marriage dependency in the West Germany (Scheiwe 1994, 143).

The maternalist model is fraught with its own perils, but the breadwinner model is also one whose logical consistency can no longer be sustained, irrespective of its violation of a woman's right to occupational choice under Art. 12 of the Basic Law. The 1990s have added three new twists to the unequal protection that flows from women's dependency on a male breadwinner. First, marital union can no longer be construed as a permanent condition, thus eligibility requirements for many programs are sorely out of synch with the real needs of *womenandchildren*. Second, German women find themselves increasingly out in the cold with the spread of long-term or structural unemployment, insofar as the adequacy of contributory retirement benefits (direct for men, derived for women) is premised on an unbroken span (35–40 years) of male work activity. Third, even women who choose to take refuge in the breadwinner model will quickly learn that it only works as long as employers are compelled to provide job security and to pay their male workers a real family wage, two preconditions they are no longer intent on meeting.

Building on Constitutional Rights: Potential Strategies for Change?

In stark contrast to German law, the U.S. Constitution does not mandate the legal equality of women and men, nor does it formally oblige the state to accord special protection to mothers and children. The Supreme Court has yet to apply the same *strict scrutiny* to equal protection cases involving sex that it routinely employs in cases based on race or religion. The High Court has moreover proved unremittingly hostile to equal protection claims by the poor, particularly where welfare benefits are involved (Weiss 1997, 219).

Under the PRWORA, poor women drawing Temporary Assistance (replacing AFDC) no longer have "the right not to engage in paid work, nor do they have the right to receive state support for performing care work" (Michel 1997, 205). That right of choice is reserved for women deemed worthy of Social Security Survivor Insurance (SI): widows and women who survive SS-eligible ex-husbands (dying within five years of divorce). Key PRWORA components may quickly be put to a constitutional test. Past Supreme Court rulings (*Meyer v. Nebraska*, 1923; *Pierce v. Society of Sisters*, 1925; *Stanley v. Illinois*, 1972) have asserted that parents—including single mothers—enjoy a fundamental right to make choices involving their children's upbringing under the Due Process Clause. *Cleveland Board of Education v. LaFleur* (1974) accorded a pregnant school teacher "the right to choose her own balance between employment responsibilities and the demands of pregnancy, a balance which could easily be extended to decisions concerning childrearing" (Weiss 1997, 234).

This recognition of fundamental parental rights does not oblige the government to subsidize those rights in any way. U.S. verdicts concerning female retirement benefits, for example, deal primarily with unequal contribution requirements and payouts on the part of employers. At issue is not the need to recognize women's double burden but rather the fine legal point that while women live longer on average, employers cannot use actuarial data to pay individual women reduced benefits, assuming they will draw compensation for more years than men (Patterson 1996). Some state judges have ordered women to undergo Norplant implants as a condition for continuing public aid. Fundamental parental rights do not include a basic right to become a parent (though U.S. courts have applied *stricter scrutiny* to the sterilization of indigent or mentally incompetent women).

The constitutionally embedded nature of the *Sozialstaat*, in contrast, may raise new hurdles for German welfare reform by way of new rules from Karlsruhe judges and the European Court of Justice. The 1986 Baby-Year Pensions granted one year of work-credit per child to women born after 1921; their fictive pay was calculated at 75 percent of the average wage. Public protest forced lawmakers to phase-in supplementary pension benefits for mothers born before the cutoff year. The last group to be incorporated, born between 1917 and 1920, filed suit, charging sex and age discrimination. In its Mother's Verdict or *Mütterurteil* (also known as the *Trümmerfrauenurteil*) of July 1992, the Court not only sided with the older mothers but also decreed that lawmakers had to find more effective ways of rewarding time spent in child rearing in every subsequent pension reform.

The Constitutional Court had already ruled in 1987 that a woman's ability to retire at age sixty (with at least fifteen contribution years) and still receive full pension benefits was justified in view of the double (actually triple) burden of the worker-wife-mother. Women who stay at home with their children (up to three years) currently receive an educational stipend of DM 600 per month, compared with average male earnings of DM 4,000 per month. Since 1995, mothers can expect to have three educational years per child included as a fictional contribution to their GRV calculations, amounting to DM 543 per month; 380,000 women took advantage of the retirement-at-sixty rule in 1995. The average pension for all women stood at DM 773 per month in 1996, DM 1,847 for men.

Changes adopted in the 1996 *Savings Packet* violate the 1992 *Mothers' Verdict*; the female age for retiring with full benefits has been raised to sixty-five (though public outrage led the Government to postpone implementation by four years). Women who retire early under the new stipulations will have 3.6 percent subtracted from their net benefits for one year, 10.8 percent for three years, and 18 percent for retiring five years early, beginning in 2001. Amounting to a breach of faith vis-à-vis women over fifty who structured their work lives around the age-sixty option, these changes chip away further at the generational contract and reinforce a redistribution from bottom to top: women who assume a double burden ensure the pensions of childless persons and the nonworking wives of high earners privy to tax-splitting. Given that 1.8 million females were involuntarily unemployed in 1996, extending the work life of older women comes at the expense of younger ones.

The last two years have also brought changes in Germany's dual child subsidy system, comprised of direct payments (*Kindergeld)* and dependent tax credits (*Kinderfreibetrag*). As of 1997, the state provides a direct subsidy of DM 200 monthly for the first and second child, DM 300 for third, DM 350 for four or more (the CDU's attempt to postpone this long-planned increase in light of the deficit even invoked the wrath of Kohl's hand-picked, antichoice minister, Claudia Nolte). Parents whose taxes fall into the 26 to 53 percent brackets can use a tax credit of DM 149-305 per month, up to DM 6,264 per year, an option most beneficial for those earning DM 77,000 to 120,000 per year (Kleinheinz 1997, 109).[11] These changes were also mandated by the Family Taxation Verdict (*Familienbesteuerungsurteil*) of September 1992. The High Court insisted that an "existential minimum" for each child must remain tax free, calculating that the amount necessary to maintain a child is DM 600 per month (to keep parents from being forced onto welfare). The estimated cost of raising a child until the age of 18—DM 800,000-900,000—is money which parents cannot invest in private pensions or in other assets (Berghahn 1995). The 1997 increases clearly fall short of the Court's requirements.

Enter the New Federalism: Burden-Shifting versus Burden Sharing

The United States, home to a host of corporations singing the praises of interdependence during the 1960s and 1970s, is once again heading the pack in the race for global competitiveness. Competitiveness (unlike its truly capitalist predecessor, competition) favors a decoupling of economic growth from job creation, as well as a decoupling of productivity increases from wage increases. Owing to stronger unions and collective bargaining rights, the fall in real wages in Germany has not yet matched declines in the United States, but there is a move afoot to expand profit margins by cutting one type of cost, *Lohnnebenkosten* (earnings-related benefit-contributions split between employer and employee). Still, F.R.G. policymakers insist that the last thing they want are "American conditions": deep poverty, urban decay, illiteracy, denial of healthcare for workers, and world-class crime rates.

Change processes in Germany and the United States have another feature in common: fundamental economic decisions (e.g., capital transfers, investment, industrial restructuring, corporate downsizing) are being made at ever higher levels, while responsibility for basic social services is being shifted to the lower levels with the least flexible resource base. Reagan's routine verbal assaults on big government opened the door to the New Federalism, Stage I, in the early

1980s. Promising to restore power to the states, the federal government began to extract itself from the business of financing welfare by extending monies in the form of block grants. Enthusiasm for states' rights quickly waned, as even Republican governors discovered that privatization and workfare programs entail enormous start-up costs.

The Bush Administration encouraged the states to experiment with welfare-to-work initiatives, but the overwhelming majority of federal waivers granted for such purposes was signed by Governor-turned-President Bill Clinton. The 1996 legislation has redefined the contents of the New Federalism, to the disadvantage of state authorities. Neither Democratic nor Republican Governors sought merely to reduce or eliminate public assistance; their aim was to shift federal matching funds toward real job-creation and work-preparation programs, the thrust of most experimentation. Yet "that is what went out the window when the budget-cutters took over PRWORA and essentially capped federal welfare spending at 1994 levels" (McGeever 1997, 12).

Implementation of PRWORA will bring greater differentiation in benefit levels and supplementary support systems than has been the case under federal law. Tax resistance proves much more effective at lower levels, as public school officials know too well. Besides making meaningful comparative evaluations more difficult, it will render program success very dependent on regional economic trends: some are likely to succeed, others will be overstressed from the start (like the rural South). Providing an adequate infrastructure (childcare, state health services, vocational training) will become a priority in some states (Wisconsin, Minnesota) but not in others (Wyoming, Alabama). The potential for social dumping within the national borders of the United States may be greater than the prospect of migrating welfare cases within the boundaries of the European Union, since EU-Members are being driven toward common regulation.

In Germany, the process of shifting the social burden to the Länder and *Gemeinde* began with the dramatic influx of refugees after 1990. Rising Social Assistance costs fall to the communes, which are hardly in a position to turn short-term, last-resort aid programs into long-term wage substitutes for single parents and jobless East Germans. The New Länder have been saddled with an extraordinary debt burden, artificially calculated by Bonn based on the G.D.R.'s deficits. In the western, states privy to a postunity boom, revenues increased by 2.4 percent, while social expenditures rose 8.2 percent in 1994–1995 (cash payments alone), though payment levels were capped in 1993. The 1996 German *Städtetag* reported that, overall, communal revenues have fallen, absolute expenditures have remained stable, but *Sozialhilfe* outlays have increased by 6 percent (Braun 1997). Unity has brought home the need to reconfigure the smallest states into more economically viable units (though the Berlin/Brandenburg attempt failed). Least subject to economic crisis, Bavaria and Baden-Württemberg can afford to block such reforms; the four biggest states retain a veto right over federal issues that the five East-Länder do not possess, though structural unemployment is a regional problem.

Germany's need to keep pace with U.S. competitiveness is one external force for change but even more significant is its dependency on EU-policy directives. The Single European Act, adopted in 1987, offered the Federal Republic few external justifications for major cutbacks during Kohl's first two terms in office. Taxpayer backlash had not yet spilled over its borders, and Germany's historical qua normative preference for security over freedom remained intact. The end of the German Democratic Republic as a competing welfare model coincided with full SEA (Single European Act) implementation in 1992. Like the 1990 Treaty on an inter-German Currency Union, the move toward a European Monetary Union paid little heed to social protection issues. The Social Chapter is nonbinding; efforts to regulate conditions beyond the immediate workplace require the unanimous consent of the Member-States, as does any infringement on employer rights (Commission of the European Communities, 1993).

But the European Union has also generated countervailing forces: The Court of Justice has decreed a few social rights inalienable, for example, equal pay, equal treatment, and the transfer of earned pension benefits (Cochrane & Doogan, 1993; Commission of the European Communities, 1993; Borcherst, 1994). Germany sought to structure its *Pflegeversicherung* in such a way (direct payments to caregivers) as to preclude benefits from leaking across its borders (Leibfried and Pierson 1995), yet a Member-State can no longer restrict the payment of benefits only to native citizens residing within its physical borders.

Women are even less effectively represented in the European Union's key decision-making organs than they are in their home governments (Mushaben 1998). Shifting the actual welfare burden to the states/Länder (a variation on subsidiarity) may afford women a better chance of defining the policy problem, even if it reduces their prospects for increasing welfare budgets. Women are entering state assemblies at a faster rate than is true of national parliaments where party grandstanding takes precedence over problem solving. The proliferation of local Equal Opportunity qua Women's Affairs Offices in Germany gives women greater institutional access to city halls, county councils and feminist-activist networks, critical to the distribution of benefits and public employment subsidies.

Conclusion: Greater Freedom Equals Fewer Rights

As one Eastern woman opined with regard to the West German media attacks on G.D.R. writer Christa Wolf, "it is easier to behead a queen than a king." The lesson applies as much to the world of welfare as it does to the realm of literati. Reagan drew regularly on anecdotal sightings of the proverbial (if empirically unsubstantiated) welfare queen, riding around in her pink Cadillac and randomly producing children for Father-State to support. Because gender, race, and class are often conflated in this image, it is not surprising that welfare queens, not welfare kings, have become the targets of most government cuts (Williams 1995). The U.S. budget reconciliation process of 1995 brought $30 billion in corporate welfare cuts, that is, programs paying Gallo to advertise its wine in France and subsidizing McDonald's promotion of french fries in Singapore; it foresaw $300 billion in social service reductions through 2002. Subsidies to business, the Congressional Budget Office (CBO) reports, amount to roughly $100 billion per year ($70 billion in tax breaks); the Republican-imposed reconciliation deal foresaw a 1 percent cut for business and a 17 percent cut for welfare programs excluding Social Security (Donahue 1994; Kelly 1996).

This comparison of German and American reform trends tells us that despite their fundamental differences, there is something very wrong with the structure of welfare policy in both countries. Disproportionately dependent upon various types of public assistance, women are also affected by a conflation of short-term and long-term needs inherent in AFDC/TANF and *Sozialhilfe*, by obsolete definitions of the family unit, and by changing presumptions that a decision to bear children should be contingent on a *woman*'s long-term economic activity. Motherhood alone does not entitle her to social security, though maternal responsibilities may preclude her from accruing the wages, work hours and savings she needs to secure her well-being in later years.

Gender stigmatization is alive and well in both countries, although the modes/degrees of stigmatization vary tremendously. The United States has never espoused the ideal of an organic national community; though its concept of citizenship has never been absolute or exclusive in a blood-based sense, it has a long history of dividing its own people into deserving and undeserving groups. Mounting U.S. resentment toward welfare stems, in part, from lawmakers' practice of pitting the nation's women and men against each other, giving rise to the rage of men at the edges of the system (symbolized by so-called Promise Keepers, the Million Man March, Fathers' Rights, and other men's movements). The U.S. welfare system was grounded in the historical premise that only women left without supporting men were worthy of public assistance, forcing many to abandon relationships, marital or otherwise, to qualify for aid. Now they are blamed for the fatherless families the system has fostered and rendered the target of crude assaults by youth-music scenes: the misogyny articulated by the hip hop generation comes from its marginalization by a welfare system that defines "family" as a woman with children and a check from AFDC or child support (Stepheny, cited in McGeever, 1997). Policymakers first discovered dead-beat dads when child support became a cost-savings vehicle for the state, just as many divorced fathers evinced little interest in their offspring until they were compelled to pay for their children's upkeep.

In contrast, outright stigmatization was never a salient feature of the German *Sozialstaat*. This owes to the leveling effects of two World Wars as well as to the blood-based nature of German citizenship, leading to organic notions of national community. Unity dynamics have precipitated a break in feelings of solidarity between West and East Germans, preconditioned by a break with migrants and asylum applicants, whose numbers rose from 4.85 million in 1989 to 6.5 million by 1992. The tragedy of unification is that the very process supposed to bring an assortment of ethnic Germans together as a nation has had the paradoxical effect of driving them apart, a condition which extends to the feminists of East and West.

More than a decade ago, Helga Hernes cautioned feminists in other Western countries not to overvalue women's status within the Scandinavian welfare model. Welfare states had liberated women only insofar as they had brought about a "transition from private to public dependence, which brought to light new inequalities of power between women and men (one group as the objects of welfare policy, the other as the makers of welfare policy)" (Hernes 1987a). A decade later, women in Eastern Germany must feel like they have stepped *through the looking glass*: they have experienced their second major paradigm shift since 1949—from private to public back to private dependency—but the *Sozialstaat* they thought they were entering becomes curiouser and curiouser by the year. The German state has redefined women's economic dependency as good dependency, even if it is not so perceived by women themselves.

The good news in the United States is that lawmakers have openly abandoned the cult of true womanhood; the bad news is that they have jettisoned the idea that maternal roles are intrinsically valuable to society. Motherhood becomes a question of personal responsibility, paid labor becomes the precondition for state assistance. Individual states may provide the means necessary to reconcile these two roles, but they are not obliged to do so. For economic purposes, women are to be treated the same as men, expected to take on breadwinner roles for themselves and their children; but they still lack the one magic ingredient which made it all possible for men, namely, a wife. Under the federal five-years-and-you're-out-forever rule, U.S. policymakers have rendered the liberal male creed a universally applicable one: no dependency is a good dependency (Fraser and Gordon 1994a; Showstack Sassoon 1994). The natural roles presumption and the doctrine of separate spheres which gave rise to dependent-benefit systems for U.S. women are now being pitted against the image of a thoroughly modern Milly.

Whereas American welfare reforms shift women from a state of separate-and-unequal dependency to a unified-but-false state of independence, alterations in the German social state offer women restored dependency at lower benefit levels. Most of the caring that goes on in Germany and the United States will remain the task of women, but their resources for carrying out this work will diminish further if globalization continues along its present trajectory (Jenson 1996; Mitchell and Garrett 1996). Globalists such as Louise Fox (World Bank), would have us believe that there is an explicit trade-off to be made between supporting livable pensions for one's parents and providing adequate nourishment for one's children. Can German and American welfare economists really expect women to accept this as the stuff of which rational choice is made?

Notes

1. There is now incontrovertible evidence, added to a few sensational court cases, detailing corruption with regard to *Treuhand* deals and West sabotaging (Südmilch, Dortmund Union) of potential Eastern competitors (Dahn 1994; Merkl 1995).
2. The amount of *Arbeitslosengeld* paid out in 1994 averaged DM 1,581 per men and DM 1,033 for women in the old Länder; males in the new states received DM 1,064, females DM 1,004 per month. *Arbeitslosenhilfe* runs about DM 350 less. Older persons no longer eligible for these payments are shifted into ABM (job creation) programs until they become eligible for *Rentenversicherung* ("training their way into retirement," as one group told me in the summer of 1999). Younger residents wind up on *Sozialhilfe*; 30 percent of the West applicants and 54 percent of the East applicants cited joblessness as their reason for seeking *Sozialhilfe*; another 2.2 million children live in households affected by unemployment. Though only 3.4 percent were classified as poor in 1990, 7.3 percent of the East Germans fit this description in 1995 (Hauser 1997, 143–156).
3. Automatic cost-controls effected by the Gramm-Rudman bill raised the out of pocket expenditures among older healthcare consumers from 12.8 percent to 18.2 percent of their incomes (Pierson 1994, 137–138).
4. Female Bundestag members have testified that under Germany's 1996 welfare reforms, a business executive making over DM 250,000 per year will receive subsidies for household help, a reduction in his (sic) capital gains taxes, higher tax-free per diems for business trips, and a reduced auto sales tax for a net savings/gain of DM 20,000. In contrast, an average worker making DM 3,000 per month net who happens to fall ill for eight weeks will lose DM 900 of her/his earnings during the first six weeks (*Lohnfortzahlung*), followed by a further cut of DM 450 in sick pay (*Krankengeld*). That same worker will need DM 40 more for her or his medication and will see her or his rehabilitation time cut to three weeks (though cures will cost DM 189 more in copayments)—for a net loss of 6.5 percent in that worker's annual disposable income.
5. Implemented in 1995, a new system of long-term/elder care (*Pflegeversicherung*) increases the load carried by payroll contributors still further by way of a surcharge on health and pension premiums.
6. Reporter Katherine Boo (1997), for example, examined the cases of Elizabeth Jones (27 years old) and LaVerne Peeler (39 years old), two Washington D.C. neighbors who both had their first child and went on welfare at age seventeen. Jones, who left the system in early 1997, brings home $687 (after taxes) every two weeks from her job at the nonprofit D.C. Private Industry Council; once she acquired her job, Jones saw her rent in the projects go from $103 to $497 per month, coupled with a loss of $235 in monthly food stamps. She pays $380 per month (the rest is subsidized) for daycare for three children. Her employer provides her with personal health insurance but her children lost all benefits under Medicaid. Subtracting her costs from her monthly

earnings of $1,374 appears to leave her with $497 in discretionary funds per month. Peeler, who cares for six children, received $599 in public assistance and food stamps at the time of the report, along with $2,400 monthly for providing foster care for her sister's three children and a baby belonging to one of the latter. Her total income of $2,999 was tax free, and her rent (in the same project as Jones) amounted to $71 per month. Medicaid provided guaranteed healthcare for herself and all of the children; Peeler's discretionary income thus amounted to more than $2,000.

7. Substantial dental costs have been largely privatized for all born after 1979, opening the door to potential windfall earnings for dentists (*Der Tagesspiegel*, June 13, 1997; *Süddeutsche Zeitung*, June 13, 1997).

8. The idea was to penalize workers who fall ill on Fridays/Mondays surrounding holiday weekends; yet as Ulrike Mascher (MdB-SPD) pointed out during the 1996 Bundestag debate, 44 percent of all registered sick days fall to 3 percent of the cases, implying long-term illnesses are involved (Deutscher Bundestag protocol, p. 9401).

9. The program is financed through a 1.7 percent surcharge on wages subject to insurance withholding for health (which also applies to retirees). Employers render no direct contributions and have one less paid holiday to finance, to boot; as with healthcare, family dependents are insured without an obligation to contribute.

10. Bane and Ellwood found in the early 1980s (using national data housed at the University of Michigan) that AFDC indeed serves two purposes: short-term relief and long-term maintenance. Half of the women who entered the program went off in two years or less; two-thirds were on their own within four years; only 17 percent remained on the roles for eight or more years; as a result, the 17 percent wound up consuming over half of all available welfare funds; three-fourths of all AFDC spells in their study began with a "relationship change." (Kennedy 1993, 271–272).

11. "Youth" as such appeared in longer 1996 *Sparpaket* (Savings Package) text, MdB Kerstin Müller pointed out, only as pensioners in the year 2030.

Ten

Marcia K. Meyers and Janet C. Gornick
with assistance of Katherin E. Ross

Gendering Welfare State Variation

Income Transfers, Employment Supports, and Family Poverty

Although employment has increased among women in all industrialized countries in recent years, rates of employment—particularly among mothers—vary substantially across countries that have similar levels of economic development. Levels of family poverty also vary enormously across the industrialized welfare states, and poverty rates do not correspond neatly to levels of women's employment or earnings. Rates of female employment are relatively high in the United States, for example, but after government taxes and transfers are considered, nearly one out of five two-parent families with a child under age six lives in poverty. Women are also quite likely to be employed in Sweden, but fewer than one in thirty Swedish families with children is poor. The added likelihood of poverty associated with having children also varies cross-nationally, with families in many countries experiencing considerably greater risk for poverty than similar households without children.

Demographic characteristics, including variation in the proportion of families headed by a single parent, can explain some of the cross-national variation in female employment and family poverty. And macroeconomic factors, including differing levels of unemployment and market earnings, explain additional variation. A substantial share of the variation in poverty outcomes may also be the direct result of cross-national variation in the generosity of government policies that transfer income to families or support the employment of parents.

Variable rates of poverty and employment in similarly rich countries raise provocative questions about the effectiveness of modern welfare states in reducing economic insecurity for families with children. Because it is mothers who bear the primary responsibility for child rearing, these questions have particular relevance for understanding the role of the state in promoting women's economic welfare and gender equality. Given that the rearing of children imposes costs on families, mothers who care for dependent children are more likely than other women to live in poor families; government policies that transfer income to families with children have the potential to increase the economic security of these families while reducing economic inequality between women who care for children and those who do not. An elevated risk for poverty among families with children also reflects the fact that women who have young children face more barriers to employment. Government policies such as maternity leave and childcare that allow continuous employment for women during their child-rearing years may reduce economic disadvantage for families with children. These policies may simultaneously promote equality in employment—between women with children and those without and, ultimately, between women and men.

This chapter explores these issues by analyzing variation, across thirteen industrialized countries, in government policies that might improve economic outcomes for families with children while promoting employment continuity for women. To isolate the role of government policy from the considerable effect of single parenthood on these outcomes, we concentrate our analysis on two-parent families. We consider three outcomes: (a) economic security, or the reduction in the risk of poverty for families with children; (b) economic equality, or the extent to which government policies reduce poverty for families with children relative to families without children; and (c) employment equality between mothers and nonmothers. Poverty-related outcomes are analyzed using two measures: income transfers and employment supports. Although all industrialized countries currently provide some level of assistance in both policy areas, the form and the generosity of benefits vary substantially. We use this naturally occurring variation to explore the association between government policies and economic outcomes and to consider the role of family policy in gendered welfare state outcomes.

Background

Families with children may be economically disadvantaged in several respects. As an economic unit, families with dependent children incur costs associated with their care. Some of these costs are externalized, for example, through provision of education at public schools. The majority of costs, however, remain private and have increased throughout the century as children have ceased to contribute income to the household (Folbre 1994). Although most costs remain private in all societies, some countries "socialize the costs of children" largely through more redistributive social policies.

The care of children also increases economic risk for families indirectly by creating barriers to employment, especially for women. Although women's employment rates in developed countries have increased dramatically in the last fifty years, their employment rates, employment continuity, hours worked, and earnings continue to lag those of men (OECD 1994). The causes of these continuing disparities are multiple and interactive. The evidence is unambiguous, however, that care for young children reduces both the probability that women will be employed and, among those who are employed, their hours of paid work (Mallier and Rosser 1986; Connelly 1991; Leibowitz, Klerman, and Waite 1992; Phipps 1993; Gornick 1994; Knudsen and Peters 1994). These labor market reductions increase the risk that families with children will be poor, particularly during the years when children are young and caregiving demands on women are high.

The extra costs that families incur caring for children affect income security and income equality. Neoclassical economics treats the decision to have children as a private choice and the economic consequences for the household as a private concern. The income gap between families with and without children may be a matter of public concern, however, when issues of equality are at stake. If families with dependent children are, on average, much poorer than other families in their country, this is an outcome quite at odds with the profamily rhetoric of most modern societies. It may also be at odds with principles of equality in assuring income security both across and within households. That children are so expensive penalizes families with children relative to those without.[1]

Because this elevated poverty risk flows from reductions and interruptions in maternal employment, it reflects another equality issue. Many mothers respond to the competing demands of employment and child rearing by loosening their attachment to paid work, for example, by engaging in intermittent employment and/or in various forms of reduced-hour and contingent work. Because these accommodations are concentrated among women, they have implications for gender equality. In the short run, women's opportunities and earnings may be more constrained than those of men. In the longer term, women may be disadvantaged by accumulating less work experience and other forms of human capital that raise earning potential (Callaghan and Hartmann 1991; Dex 1992; Rosenfeld 1993 Gornick and Jacobs 1996).

Family Policies: Cash Transfers and Employment Supports

Recognizing the heightened poverty risk for families with children, all industrialized countries provide some form of assistance directed toward parents (Ergas 1990; Kamerman 1991a, 1991b; Kamerman and Kahn 1991a, 1991b; OECD 1990b). Two components of the family policy package that are particularly relevant to economic outcomes are those that provide cash transfers to families and those that facilitate maternal employment.

Cash transfers have received the most scrutiny by researchers studying family policy. Most cash transfers have been designed to protect families from the primary earner's loss of market-based income, due to disability, labor market conditions, old age, and other life events. Cash transfers also have an income-equalizing effect, transferring income, for example, from younger to older workers (through old-age insurance) and from families with high income to those with lower income (through progressive taxation and social assistance).

As part of a country's family policy package, income transfers may also reduce economic risks associated with the care of dependent children (Smeeding and Torrey 1988; Wong, Garfinkel, and McLanahan 1993). Their main effect is to directly increase disposable income and thereby reduce the probability that a family with children will fall into poverty. Universal income transfers that target families with children—child or family allowances—directly offset a portion of the extra expenses incurred by families rearing children. Social insurance and means-tested income transfers also reduce the poverty risk for families by providing a floor under household income. In addition to their poverty reduction effects, transfers can have important income equalizing effects by reducing the extent to which families with children are more at risk for poverty than other groups in the same country (Smeeding and Torrey 1988; Coder, Rainwater, and Smeeding 1989; Smeeding 1996). Income transfers that raise the income of families with children reduce the share of the poverty burden these families bear (Casper, McLanahan, and Garfinkel 1994).[2]

Maternal earnings are an increasingly important factor in the economic security of families, but policies that support maternal employment have received little attention as an antipoverty component of family policy packages. Chief among these policies are those that provide protections for working women at the time of childbirth, including legislated job protections and wage replacements for as long as twelve or eighteen months following a child's birth and public childcare, in the form of public centers or public subsidies for private care arrangements.

Generous maternity leave provisions are generally believed to increase women's attachment to paid work, at least in the short term. In addition to offering income support, many maternity policies are explicitly designed to discourage women from exiting employment following childbirth (Trzcinski 1991). A small empirical literature suggests that the availability and generosity of maternity leaves are associated with earlier returns to work after childbirth and positive employment outcomes in the short term (O'Connell 1990; Winegarten and Bracy 1995; Waldfogel 1999; Joesch 1997; Glass and Riley 1998; Ruhm 1998).

Government support for childcare is expected to facilitate maternal employment and earnings by increasing the supply, and reducing the cost, of alternatives to full-time parental care. Economic theory predicts that women who face higher costs or less desirable options for substitute care will reduce their hours of work and their use of these arrangements (Ribar 1991; Michalopoulos, Robins, and Garfinkel 1992; Blau and Ferber 1992; Connelly 1992).[3] Policies that lower the cost or increase the quality of care, through direct public provision or subsidization of private provision, are predicted to offset some of these effects. Considerable empirical research supports the prediction that lower costs for childcare are associated with higher labor force participation among mothers who have young children (Blau and Robins 1988; Leibowitz, Waite, and Witsberger 1988; Connelly 1990, 1991, 1992; Leibowitz, Klerman, and Waite 1992; Kimmel 1995; Michalopoulos, Robins, and Garfinkel 1992; Ribar 1992; Stolzenberg and Waite 1994; U.S. General Accounting Office 1994).

Family Policy Packages in Cross-national Perspective

Although all industrialized countries have some form of family policy, the elements, generosity, and mix of policies vary widely. In particular, the levels and relative balance between cash transfers and employment supports appear to vary substantially. Some countries are notable for the generosity of their support to families; families in Sweden, for example, typically receive generous income supports along with access to employment supports such as paid maternity leave and public childcare. Others are notable for the paucity of their policies; the United States stands out both for the stinginess of its cash transfers and, until quite recently, the lack of any form of maternity leave. Still others exemplify middle levels of provision with an unknown balance between the two policy types (Gornick, Meyers, and Ross 1997).

This variation in policy suggests the value of cross-national comparative study of policy packages and the outcomes for families and for women. There is a rich literature describing cross-national variation in a range of family policies (see e.g., Kamerman and Kahn 1978, 1994; Olmsted and Weikart 1989; Ergas 1990; Gauthier 1991; Woodill, Bernhard, and Prochner 1992; Cochran 1993; Leira 1993a; Gustafsson 1994; Baker 1996). Other scholars have examined cross-national variation in families' economic well-being, in both absolute and relative terms (Smeeding and Torrey 1988; Coder, Rainwater, and Smeeding 1989; Wong, Garfinkel, and McLanahan 1993; Danziger, Smeeding, and Rainwater 1995). Most of this scholarship has viewed the role of the welfare state in terms of the economic security of households and the employment of men. In recent years, feminist scholars have challenged this conception by identifying the often quite different implications of welfare state policies for women, whose roles are more diversified than those of men and whose work is often unpaid (O'Connor 1993b, 1996; Orloff 1993, 1996; Sainsbury 1994b). A number of feminist scholars now suggest that public policies that promote women's employment and support gender equality in the labor market form the core of the "woman-friendly" welfare state (Pateman 1988a; Lister 1990). Until quite recently, this scholarship has been primarily theoretical. Current research is now empirical and explicitly comparative, stressing variation across countries in the extent to which welfare states ameliorate market-based gender inequalities and shape women's economic outcomes (Wong, Garfinkel, and McLanahan 1993; Siaroff 1994; Gornick, Meyers, Ross 1997, 1998).

While comparative scholars have considered family policies, antipoverty policies, and woman-friendly policies in isolation, they have yet to fully specify the association among combinations of policies and economic outcomes for families and for women across a large number of countries. Substantial research links income transfers to poverty reductions; other research links employment support policies to women's employment outcomes. But if, as argued above, cash transfers and employment supports have both direct consequences for economic security and equality (by increasing families' disposable income) and indirect consequences (by influencing maternal employment), the *net* effect on families' economic well-being will depend on both the generosity of these policies and the way in which they are combined into a "package" of family policies at the national level. Likewise, if some family policies discourage maternal employment (by providing high levels of transfer income) while others facilitate it (by providing alternatives to full time maternal care), the *net* effect on women's employment outcomes will depend on the entire package of family policies.

Research Questions

The research for this chapter uses cross-national comparisons of social policy and economic outcomes for two-parent families with children to address four questions. First, to what extent do western industrialized countries vary in the generosity of income transfers for families with children and in public policies that support maternal employment? Second, how are variations in the generosity of these policies associated with relevant economic outcomes? More specifically, to what extent does cross-national variation in the generosity of income transfers explain variation in levels of family poverty? And to what extent does variation in the adequacy of childcare and maternity leave explain variation in patterns of maternal employment? Third, how are these policies balanced or packaged in different countries? Do the two approaches represent tradeoffs or do they vary together in generosity? Finally, how are family policy packages associated with economic outcomes? We are particularly interested in two questions with immediate policy relevance: the extent to which employment support policies increase the anti-poverty effectiveness of cash transfers and the conditions under which generous income transfers are compatible with maternal employment. We conclude by considering the implication of policy variations for assuring the economic security of families and for the development of a woman-friendly welfare state.

Methods

This research used cross-national variation in government policies and in rates of family poverty and maternal employment to link the generosity of national family policy packages to economic outcomes. Microlevel (family and individual level) and macrolevel (institutional) data from the Luxembourg Income Study (LIS) are used to develop policy and economic outcome measures for thirteen industrialized countries. The following sections describe the data source, the sample selection procedures, the construction of measures, and the analytic approach.

Sample and Data Sources

Data were obtained from the Luxembourg Income Study, an archive of datasets gathered from a large number of industrialized countries.[4] Microdatasets available for each country contain demographic, labor market, and detailed income data at the household and individual level. LIS also provides an Institutional Database that contains country-level (macrolevel) information on major social welfare policies. Thirteen countries are measured in this study: Australia, Belgium, Canada, Denmark, Finland, France, Germany, Luxembourg, the Netherlands, Norway, Sweden, the United Kingdom, and the United States. The years for which LIS microdata are available for each country dictated the selection of the analysis period, ranging from 1984 to 1987.

LIS microdata were used to measure economic and employment outcomes at the household level. Because these analyses concern government benefits and economic outcomes for two-parent families with children, microdata samples from each country are restricted to married families in which adults were in the childrearing years. Families are defined for this purpose as those with two resident adults between the ages of twenty and forty-five.[5] Families are further categorized as having young children (at least one resident child under age six) or no children (no resident children under age eighteen). For calculating women's employment outcomes, women in families with young children are coded as mothers; those in families without children under eighteen are coded as nonmothers.[6]

Government policies were measured using both micro- and macrodata. Household-level data were used to construct measures of income transfer generosity and coverage.[7] Macrodata on employment-supporting policies for the corresponding years were added by the authors to the LIS Institutional Database. These data include measures of national maternity leave policies (including job protections, length, coverage, and benefit levels) and public childcare provision (including legislative childcare guarantees, generosity of childcare tax credits, enrollments in publicly funded childcare places, and age of compulsory school enrollment).

Measures

Multiple components of the primary explanatory factor for the study—the generosity of national family policies—are measured with two indices: one measures the generosity of national income transfer policies; the second measures government policies that support continuity in maternal employment. The outcomes of interest are security and equality in both income and maternal employment. The economic security and equality of families with children is measured as (a) the post-tax-and-transfer poverty rate for families with young children and (b) the effectiveness of government policies in reducing poverty for families with children relative to the effectiveness of policies in reducing poverty for similar households without children (calculated as a ratio). To measure equality in employment women's outcomes, we calculate (a) maternal employment rates and (b) an indicator of employment equality between mothers and nonmothers—the ratio of the employment rates of mothers with young children to those of nonmothers in the same country. The following sections briefly describe the data and measurement of each of these variables; additional detail is provided in the Methods Appendix.

Policy Indices: Income Transfers and Employment Supports. The generosity of national income transfers is compared by developing an *Income Transfer Policy (ITP) Index.* LIS microdata are used to measure three types of government transfers that potentially benefit two-parent families with children under the age of six: (a) "family allowances" (universal cash transfers for families with children), (b) "means-tested transfers" (cash and near-cash transfers that were distributed to families with incomes below some cutoff point), and (c) "other social transfers" (public transfers paid in the event of retirement, unemployment, sickness, accidents, disability, war benefits, and other cash or near-cash payments).[8] (Parental and maternity leave cash benefits are included in a second index, described below.)

The ITP Index is the weighted sum of the average benefit levels in each country. We first measure average transfer amounts, by category, that were reported by families in each country, controlling for household type. Because the relative generosity of transfer programs in each country also depends on the proportion of families who receive benefits, the average transfer amounts are then weighted by coverage (the percent of each household type that reported any income in each of the three transfer categories). The ITP Index is the weighted sum of average benefits for each of the three forms of transfer; scores are calculated separately for families with children under age six and those with no children under eighteen.

The *Employment-Supporting Policy (ESP) Index* measures the adequacy of national policies that facilitate employment for parents with children under the age of six. Although many of these policies are available to both men and women, they are most relevant to the employment of mothers because mothers are the primary caregivers for young children.

Women's labor force participation decisions are hypothesized to respond to the form and intensity of a number of different policies that function as complements and/or substitutes. Because these policies also differ for families with children of varying ages, two composite indices of national policy effort are constructed from the LIS Institutional Database, one for families with children under age three and a second for those with children aged three to six. The two indices are then combined into a single index of policies affecting families with children under six.

The first index is the weighted sum of eight indicators of policies affecting mothers with children under three ("infants"): five measures of the coverage, length, and generosity of short-term parental leaves; two measures of support for childcare through tax relief and national guarantees of access to public childcare; and one measure of the availability of public childcare for children under three based on enrollments in publicly subsidized childcare. The second index is the weighted sum of four indicators of government policies affecting mothers with children from age three until school enrollment ("preschoolers"): two measures of public support for childcare through tax relief for private childcare and guaranteed access to public childcare; one measure of the supply of public childcare based on the enrollment of children between three and five in publicly subsidized care; and one measure of the influence of the age of compulsory public school based on the enrollment of children aged five in public childcare, preprimary or primary school.[9]

Although final results for the ITP and ESP indices are presented in comparable units, numeric scores are very sensitive to the selection, coding, and standardization of individual items in the index. Therefore, numeric scores are not comparable *across indices*. Cross-national rankings facilitate comparisons of national performance between the two policy categories.

Poverty, Poverty Reduction, and the Parent/Non-Parent Poverty Reduction Ratio. Poverty-related outcomes are analyzed using two measures calculated from the LIS microdata. Household poverty rates are based on a poverty line set at 50 percent of the country-specific median household income, adjusted for household size. They are calculated as the rate of poverty after adjusting for government cash or near-cash transfers and taxes. By capturing the level of household income relative to a country-specific standard, after accounting for government tax and transfer policies, this measure controls for cross-national variation in other aspects of national economic performance and provides a comparable measure of household well-being across countries. Poverty levels do not, however, reflect government efforts to reduce market-generated economic inequalities between families with children and those without. We capture the contribution of government policy to the reduction of economic inequality by measuring the parent/non-parent poverty reduction ratio. This is the ratio of the percent reduction in the poverty rate for two-parent families with children, once government tax and transfers are considered, to the percent reduction in the poverty rate for two-adult families without children. This captures the effectiveness of government policies that reduce poverty for families with children relative to the effectiveness of policies that reduce poverty for otherwise similar families, without children, in the same country.

These measures of economic outcomes have some important strengths and some limitations. The use of a relative measure of poverty, keyed to the median income of all households in the country, controls for a number of economic and demographic factors that influence the standard of living for all households in that country. The use of equivalence scales, which adjust household income by family size, further controls for factors relating to family composition. Finally, by comparing the effectiveness of government tax and transfer policies for otherwise similar two-adult families with and without young children, the analysis highlights government policies that help offset economic inequality across households that differ primarily in the presence of dependent children, controlling for parents' ages, marital status, and country of residence.

This comparison assumes that pre-tax-and-transfer inequality between these households is primarily due to the presence of children. It cannot correct for the selection bias that might be introduced by the failure to measure other individual, human capital, and household characteristics that are associated with both the likelihood of childbearing and of poverty. To the extent that families with young children are systematically different from other families within the same country, for example, in their levels of education and work experience, these unmeasured differences may be responsible for a portion of the variation in pre-tax-and-transfer poverty that is not offset by government policy. Our measure of the ratio of the extent to which government tax and transfer policies offset market-generated poverty rates for the two groups will also fail to capture the effect of government policies that influence the level of market-generated poverty.

Maternal Employment. Two measures of maternal employment are calculated from the LIS microdata. The first is simply the employment rate of mothers (aged twenty to forty-five). Although maternal employment rates continue to rise across the industrialized countries, there is no consensus across these countries—and sometimes little agreement within national borders—as to whether higher levels of maternal employment are a desirable outcome per se. For this reason, we concentrate our analysis on a second measure that captures equality in employment between women with and without their childrearing responsibilities: the ratio of the employment rates between mothers of young children and nonmothers in the same age group.

There are at least two analytic benefits associated with using the employment ratio as our central indicator. One, by focusing on the ratio of employment rates between women with and without young children, we isolate an employment outcome that might be specifically tied to childrearing responsibilities. Second, by first estimating the influence of having young children on employment outcomes for women within the same country and then comparing these estimates across countries, the ratio captures cross-national variation in employment outcomes that are largely independent of intercountry differences in labor market conditions.

It is also important to note some limitations in this measure. Although the use of within-country ratios controls for some intercountry differences that are expected to influence employment, such as labor market conditions and cultural norms about gender roles, it does not control for individual-level differences between women who have young children and those who do not. It is likely that women without children differ from those with children in a number of ways: for example, better educated and more professionally oriented women are likely to delay childbirth and have fewer children than their less-educated counterparts. This may confound measures of association between policy and employment outcomes.

Analytic Approach

The first stage of analysis is descriptive. Policy and economic outcomes are compared, across countries, for two-parent families. The separate effect of each type of policy is then examined using linear regression (OLS) analysis to test the association, first between the ITP Index and the family poverty rate and the parent/nonparent poverty reduction ratio and second, between the ESP Index and equality in maternal/nonmaternal employment (the employment rate ratio). Finally, the two types of policies are examined jointly as a "family policy package." The joint contribution of income transfer and employment supporting policies is analyzed by comparing the simple association of each package with measures of economic security and equality.

Findings

Income Transfer Policy

Countries fell into three tiers on the ITP Index of the generosity of income transfers that benefit families (figure 1; see appendix table 10.1 for full data). The United States and Australia were the least generous countries, providing the lowest benefit levels and most limited coverage for families with young children. The United States, with no child allowance, minimal social assistance provisions,

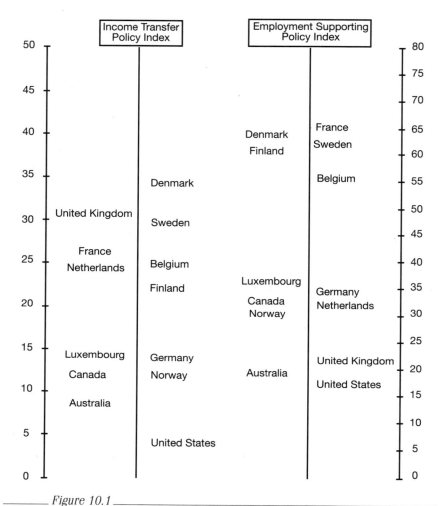

_____ *Figure 10.1* _____

Index comparison, married families with a child under 6 years of age.

and low levels of other social transfers, ranked last. Australia, with a small universal child allowance and low benefit levels in the other transfer categories, ranked only slightly higher.[10]

Canada, Germany, Luxembourg, and Norway formed a middle tier with respect to the generosity of income transfers. Although all four had both universal family allowances and means-tested programs, the family allowances were generally low—ranging from $301 per year in Canada to $685 in Luxembourg (1987 U.S. dollars), and their means-tested programs either had low benefit levels ($464 in Canada), were provided to few families (12% of German families), or were low in both benefit levels and coverage (in Luxembourg and Norway).

The remaining countries of Belgium, Denmark, Finland, France, the Netherlands, Sweden, and the United Kingdom were the most generous in their provision of income assistance. Some relied most heavily on universal family allowances that were received by nearly all families: for example, families in Belgium received an average benefit of $863 and those in France received $1,340. Other countries provided more generous means-tested assistance (e.g., 24% of families in the United Kingdom received means-tested assistance averaging $2,449). Finland and Sweden provided both generous universal family allowances and relatively high means-tested benefits to nearly one-quarter of all families; the Netherlands had a similar, but less generous package that mixed family allowances with means-tested assistance.

Employment-Supporting Policy

Three tiers of relative generosity are also evident on the Employment-Supporting Policy Index (figure 1). Australia and the United States once again formed a cluster of low policy performers, joined by the United Kingdom. In all three countries, space in publicly supported childcare was extremely limited and only a small percentage of women had access to paid maternity leaves.[11] Five countries—Canada, Germany, Luxembourg, the Netherlands, and Norway—formed a middle cluster. These countries typically provided moderate to very generous maternity leave to nearly all employed women but had limited publicly supported childcare, especially for children under age three. None of these countries had legislation guaranteeing access to childcare.

Belgium, Denmark, Finland, France, and Sweden formed an upper tier of countries with extensive policy provision. These countries generally provided universal maternity leaves with full, or nearly full, wage replacement, lasting for several months up to a year. In addition, space was available in publicly supported childcare for one-third to one-half of all infants and nearly all preschool-aged children. Several of these countries had also adopted national legislation that guaranteed parents access to childcare.

Income Transfers and Poverty Reduction

Poverty rates among families with young children varied enormously across these countries (Figure 2; see Appendix Table 10.2 for data). Once government taxes and transfers are considered, poverty rates for families with children under six ranged from a low of 3 percent in Norway to a high of 17.7 percent in the United States. In most countries, tax-and-transfer policies reduced poverty rates among families with children from a few to several percentage points. In some countries with high levels of pre-tax-and-transfer poverty, government

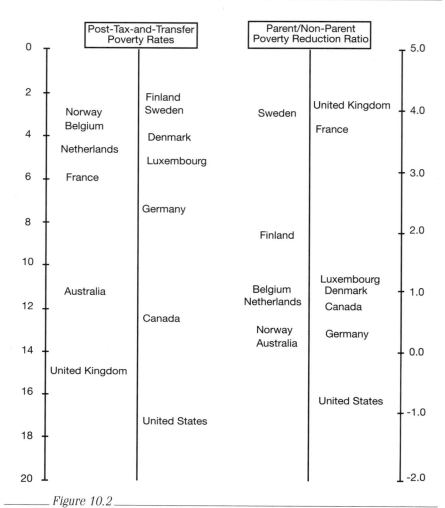

_____ *Figure 10.2* _____
Poverty outcome comparison, married families with a child under 6 years of age.

policies reduced poverty for families very dramatically: from 22.5 to 6 percent in France, for example, and from 15.4 to 3.6 percent in Belgium. The extraordinarily high post-tax-and-transfer poverty rate in the United States reflects both high rates of market-generated poverty (pre-tax-and-transfer) and the fact that the United States stands out as the only country in which government taxes and transfers actually made families with young children poorer, increasing poverty by nearly two percentage points.

Differences in the extent to which government policies reduced economic inequality associated with raising children were also dramatic. The parent/

nonparent poverty reduction ratio—measuring the extent to which taxes and transfers reduced poverty among two-parent families with children in comparison with two-adult couples without children—was very high in three countries: the United Kingdom, France, and Sweden. Although poverty rates varied across these countries (from a high of 15.2% in the United Kingdom to a low of 3.1% in Sweden), high poverty reduction ratios in all three countries indicate that government tax and transfer policies had a more dramatic effect in reducing poverty for families with children than they did for reducing the poverty of adult couples without children within the same country.

The story was different in countries with low parent/nonparent poverty reduction ratios. Three of the lowest ranking countries on this measure—Norway, Australia, and Germany—also had varying poverty rates (from 3 in Norway to 11.5 in Australia) but similar ratios (close to zero). In these countries, the low ratios suggest that government tax-and-transfer policies had about the same poverty-reduction effect for families with children as they did for two-adult couples without children. Once again, the United States stands out as an exceptional case. Along with very high poverty rates, the United States had a negative parent/nonparent poverty reduction ratio. This suggests that, in terms of the net effect of government tax-and-transfer policies on income, families with children under six actually fared worse than two-adult families without children.

The effect of government transfers for families with children on income security and equality is tested by regressing poverty rates and poverty reduction ratios on country scores on the ITP Index. Ordinary least squares regression (OLS) results confirm a negative association between the ITP Index and post-tax-and-transfer poverty, reflecting lower poverty rates among families with young children in countries with more generous income transfer policies. Policy variation is found to explain a modest amount of the variation in post-tax-and-transfer poverty rates ($R^2 = 0.20$). Although the inverse relationship between generosity and poverty rates is clear, it is weaker than might be expected. Some countries have lower poverty rates than would be predicted from their policy generosity. This is most notable in Norway, where, despite relative low benefits, pre-tax-and-transfer poverty levels are low. The United Kingdom represents an opposite case, in which post-tax-and-transfer poverty rates were very high, despite generous government benefits.

The association is stronger between the generosity of government transfers that benefit families with children and our measure of the reduction in income inequality for families with children. When scores on the parent/non-parent poverty reduction ratio are regressed on the ITP Index, the association is positive and the explanatory power is substantial ($R^2 = 0.51$). This suggests that countries that adopted more generous income transfer policies were more effective in reducing the poverty of families with children relative to that of two-adult

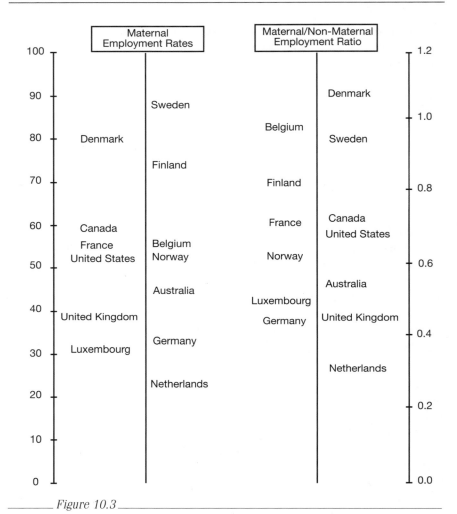

_____ *Figure 10.3* _____

Employment outcome comparison, married families with a child under 6 years of age.

couples without children. Countries that were stingy in the structure or generosity of benefits, particularly the United States, were less effective than others in reducing market-generated inequality between parents and nonparents.

Employment Supports and Maternal Employment

Maternal employment rates varied across the thirteen countries, from a low of 23 percent in the Netherlands to a high of 87 percent in Sweden (Figure 3). Of more specific interest to this analysis, there was a substantial variation in the ratio of employment among mothers to that of nonmothers. In three countries—Belgium, Finland and Sweden—the ratio was .82 or higher; in Denmark, remarkably, married mothers of young children were more likely to be employed than were their counterparts without children. Although these countries varied in their underlying maternal employment *rates* (from 54.8 to 86.8 percent), the data suggest that in each of these countries mothers with young children were not substantially less likely to be attached to employment than were women without children. This is in sharp contrast to the very low maternal employment ratios in other countries, in which the ratio of employment for mothers to nonmothers was as low as .44 in Germany and .45 in the United Kingdom.

The association between employment-supporting policies and maternal employment patterns was tested by regressing the measure of employment equality between mothers and women without children—the employment ratios—on the generosity of the ESP Index. Maternal employment ratios and the generosity of government employment supports had the predicted positive association, and the explanatory power was high ($R^2 = 0.52$). In other words, the countries with the highest ESP Index scores also had the highest maternal employment ratios, regardless of their underlying maternal employment rates. At the low end, the countries with the least generous employment-supporting policies generally had lower mother/nonmother employment ratios.

Some exceptions to this pattern are notable. Three continental European countries (Luxembourg, Germany, and especially the Netherlands) had maternal employment ratios that were lower than would be predicted by their middle tier level of employment supports. This suggests that other factors not captured by the ESP Index may have had an "employment-depressing" effect on mothers in these countries. Nonpolicy factors, including culturally based attitudes toward maternal employment, may explain part of the relatively low employment ratios. Other policy factors may also be important. Chief among these are discontinuities in the school day, including part-day schedules and unsupervised lunch breaks that may have depressed employment among mothers who also had older children.[12] Extremely low levels of maternal employment in the Netherlands and higher than predicted levels in the United States are also striking. In the Netherlands, relatively generous income transfers may have had a depressing effect on maternal employment; very low levels of income support in the United States, in contrast, may have been employment forcing for women.

Family Policy Packages

The possibility that policies interact to produce economic outcomes underscores the importance of analyzing income transfers and employment supports jointly as a package of family policies. Figure 4 illustrates this interaction by comparing the generosity of employment-supporting policy (ESP Index) with that of cash transfers (ITP Index). With two exceptions, income transfers and

INCOME TRANSFER INDEX	← EMPLOYMENT SUPPORT INDEX →		
	LOW	MEDIUM	HIGH
HIGH	United Kingdom pov: 15.2% (4.0) emp: 37.8% (0.5)	Netherlands pov: 4.8% (0.7) emp: 22.5% (0.3)	Belgium pov: 3.6% (0.9) emp: 54.8% (0.9)　　Denmark pov: 4.1% (0.8) emp: 78.5% (1.1) Finland pov: 2.7% (1.9) emp: 72.8% (0.8)　　Sweden pov: 3.1% (0.7) emp: 89.9% (0.3) France pov: 6.0% (3.7) emp: 54.4% (0.7)
MEDIUM		Luxembourg pov: 5.5% (0.9) emp: 30.9% (0.5)　　Germany pov: 7.6% (0.4) emp: 32.4% (0.4) Canada pov: 12.7% (0.7) emp: 57.7% (0.7)　　Norway pov: 3.0% (0.4) emp: 52.0% (0.6)	
LOW	Australia pov: 11.5% (0.4) emp: 44.1% (0.5) United States pov: 17.7% (-0.8) emp: 51.8% (0.7)		

_____ Figure 10.4 _____

Family policy packages, poverty and maternal employment outcome

Note: pov refers to post-tax and transfer poverty rate (parent/non-parent poverty reduction ratio); emp refers to maternal employment rate (maternal/non-maternal employment ratio).

employment supports varied together, suggesting that these benefits were provided as complements rather than substitutes in most countries.

Within this overall pattern, clusters of countries with distinct family policy packages are evident. At one extreme are the countries with low income transfers and low levels of employment support: Australia and the United States. These countries provided limited universal, means-tested, and other cash assistance to families. Public policies to support maternal employment were also limited, forcing families to rely on private resources to replace wages lost at the time of childbirth and to arrange and pay for private childcare. At the opposite extreme are the countries with high income transfers and generous employment support. Belgium, Denmark, Finland, France, and Sweden all provided continuous support for maternal employment through paid maternity leaves at childbirth and public childcare for preschool-aged children, as well as generous cash transfers through a combination of means-tested benefits and family allowances. The middle tier countries of Canada, Germany, Luxembourg, and Norway were characterized by moderate levels of income transfers and moderate levels of employment support, which was concentrated in maternity leaves for employed women at the time of childbirth.

Two countries are exceptions to this pattern and suggest alternative packaging strategies. The most striking anomaly is the United Kingdom, which is the sole exemplar of a country combining high income transfers with low levels of employment support. Although income transfers for families were generous, support for maternal employment was limited. The Netherlands provides a second, less dramatic example of a country in which the generosity of transfers exceeded that of employment supports. Dutch family policy combined moderate levels of employment support with a combination of universal, means-tested, and other transfers that were similar to the most generous countries.

Family Policy Packages, Poverty, and Equality

Figure 4 also considers the outcomes of policy interactions by linking family policy packages to family poverty rates (post-tax-and-transfer), the parent/nonparent poverty reduction ratio, maternal employment rates, and the ratio of maternal/nonmaternal employment. Three findings stand out.

First, the policy packages were strongly associated with the degree of economic security and equality. The countries with the most generous package of transfers and employment supports had the lowest rates of absolute poverty among families with young children (2.7 to 6%). In three of the five countries, the family/nonfamily poverty reduction ratio is also high, suggesting that government policies were also effective in reducing market-generated economic inequalities between families with children and those without. A high ratio of maternal to nonmaternal employment is also observed in these countries, suggesting that the combination of generous transfers and income supports also supported mothers' attachment to the labor market. It is possible that maternal earnings made an important contribution to poverty reduction.

Poverty rates increased and the parent/nonparent poverty reduction ratio generally decreased as the generosity of the family policy package decreased. In the countries that are middle ranked on both policy indices, poverty rates and ratios generally fell between those of countries with stronger and weaker social policies. The maternal employment ratios for these countries were also low, closer in fact to countries with the least generous package of childcare and maternal leave protections. This implies that there may be a threshold in the generosity of employment supports below which mothers find it difficult to remain attached to employment while their children are young. When women find it necessary to withdraw from employment to care for young children, this may compromise both women's longer-term employment prospects and the immediate economic welfare of their families.

The least favorable outcomes for families were evident in the United States and Australia, the countries with the weakest performance on both policy dimensions. Poverty rates for families with children were two to three times those of the most generous countries. While Australia had a parent/nonparent poverty reduction ratio close to zero, suggesting that government policies were about equally effective in reducing the poverty of both, the negative ratio in the United States suggests that government policies actually advantaged families with children less than they helped families without children. In contrast, these countries had maternal employment rates and ratios that were similar to countries in the middle tiers of benefit generosity. The paucity of income supports in these countries does appear to have acted as an "employment-forcing" factor for all women, including those with young children. Higher levels of maternal employment were not sufficient, however, to protect many families from poverty.

Second, income transfers combined with generous employment supports were more effective than transfers alone in producing low poverty rates among families with children. Though generous income transfers were associated with poverty reduction, high transfers alone were not the most effective strategy for reducing family poverty or inequality. Among countries that provided similar levels of employment support, neither the poverty rate nor the parent/nonparent poverty reduction ratio consistently improved as the level of transfer generosity increased. This is evident in the United Kingdom. Despite the provision of generous and apparently targeted transfers for families with children, rates of poverty among these families were nearly as high as they were in the United States. Likewise, among the middle-ranked countries on employment support, the Netherlands provided much more generous transfers but made little further progress against poverty.

The outcomes for the United Kingdom and Netherlands suggest the limitations of an income strategy, alone, as antipoverty policy. Neither country provided extensive assistance to help women reconcile the demands of employment with the care of young children; both also had very low maternal employment ratios, evidence of substantial inequality in employment between mothers and nonmothers. It is possible that in these countries, high transfer payments did have an employment-depressing effect by providing mothers with alternatives to market earnings. Without public policies that helped women continue in paid employment when their children were young, the employment-depressing effects of high transfers may have substantially offset their antipoverty effectiveness.

Third, high income transfers are compatible with high maternal employment, if employment supports are generous. The countries that combined generous income transfers with extensive support for maternal employment also had some of the highest levels of maternal employment and equality among these countries. The ratio of maternal to nonmaternal employment ranged from .82 to more than 1, indicating that, in countries with both high- and middle-ranking rates of maternal employment, women who cared for young children were not significantly less likely to be employed than their childless counterparts. This indicates that when provisions for childcare and maternity leave are sufficiently generous, direct transfers to families with children can help reduce poverty without discouraging maternal employment. The net effect on economic security and equality was even more encouraging. All five countries that combined the most generous income transfers with the most extensive provisions for childcare and maternity leave had achieved low levels of poverty; most were also notable for the extent to which they reduced economic inequality between families with and families without children.

Summary

This study suggests that both the generosity and the structure of family policies matter in promoting economic security and equality, for families with children and for women who assume the primary burden of care for young children. Across thirteen industrialized countries, several distinct packages of family policies were found to be associated with different poverty and employment outcomes. The most generous packages, with high income transfers and well-developed maternity and childcare provisions, might be thought of as "high security/employment-supporting" family policies. Countries with these policies had the most successful outcomes, including the lowest rates of poverty and the highest ratios of employment between mothers and nonmothers.

The least generous package, with low transfers and minimal employment supports, might be described as "low security/employment-forcing" family policy. The low benefits and limited coverage of the income transfer programs left families with few alternatives to labor market earnings. Government policies did not, however, support maternal employment by providing extensive maternity leaves or public childcare to reduce the costs of employment or help women resolve the conflicting demands of caregiving and waged work. Relatively high levels of maternal employment in these countries suggest that these policies may have helped propel women into the labor market. Low employment ratios, however, revealed substantially less employment among mothers with young children than among other women. Not only did mothers appear to be disadvantaged relative to nonmothers in their employment options, families with children in these employment-forcing policy regimes were also much more likely to be poor than were those in other countries.

A third package, observed in the United Kingdom and possibly the Netherlands, might be described as "high security/employment-depressing" family policy. These countries provided generous income transfers but were moderate to low in their provision of maternity leave and, especially, childcare. This approach might be expected to achieve substantial poverty reductions, which were observed in the Netherlands. In the United Kingdom, however, poverty rates were not far from the other English-speaking countries that provided far less generous direct assistance. This may be due in part to very low levels of maternal employment. These countries were less successful than others were in either reducing poverty among families with children or in achieving greater equality in employment opportunities between mothers and nonmothers.

Discussion

By associating packages of family policies with economic outcomes, this analysis demonstrates the importance of examining the joint or combined effect of multiple policies on economic outcomes. A number of researchers have documented the positive association between income transfers and income poverty reductions. Other scholars have shown that policies such as maternity leave and childcare are associated with higher levels and more continuity in maternal employment. The positive correlation between income transfers and employment-supporting policies, evident in this study of thirteen countries, suggests that analyzing policies in isolation may have failed to account for important policy interactions. It is possible, for example, that in countries that we have described as having "high security/employment-supporting" family policies, high levels of income security—traditionally credited to generous transfers—may also result from policies that have supported employment during women's childrearing years. It is also possible that comparative studies of employment-supporting policies have conflated the contribution of childcare and maternity leave with the contribution of direct income transfers.

A substantial body of comparative welfare state research has categorized countries on dimensions relating to economic outcomes at the household level or to labor market outcomes at the individual level. By framing issues primarily in terms of class, rather than gender, these schemes have missed important subtleties in the implications of welfare state policies for women, who bear more of the costs of child rearing in terms of both expenditures and labor supply reductions. When multiple policies are considered along with multiple outcomes, the standard clusterings of countries proposed by welfare state scholars are challenged in several respects. Most prominent among these studies is Esping-Andersen's (1990) theory of welfare state regimes. His empirically based model identifies three variants of the capitalist welfare state: the social democratic (primarily the Nordic countries), the conservative-corporatist (dominated by the European continental countries) and the liberal (primarily the English-speaking countries). Each regime type has a characteristic configuration of social policies that differ in the extent to which they decommodify workers by providing alternatives to dependence on private markets. Each regime type is also seen to have a distinctive pattern of socioeconomic and labor market outcomes.

The results of this study partially confirm and partially challenge this model. In terms of the generosity of their income transfers for families with children, most countries perform as would be predicted, with high benefit levels in the social democratic countries, moderate levels in the conservative continental countries, and meager benefits in most of the liberal, English-speaking countries. Some countries diverge from this pattern, however, most prominently Norway (in the provision of medium levels of benefits) and the United Kingdom (in the provision of very generous transfers). Divergence from these regime types is even more evident in the provision of employment-supporting family policies. Among the social democratic countries, Norway provides much less generous support for maternal employment than the other Nordic countries, particularly in the areas of public childcare and early school enrollments. The conservative countries reveal little commonality: France is among the most generous countries in its provision of maternity leaves and childcare, whereas Germany is among the least generous. Among the liberal countries, Canada pulls away from the other English-speaking countries in providing more adequate maternity leave and somewhat better childcare coverage. Employment outcomes—particularly the equality of employment between mothers and nonmothers—are seen to correspond closely to this alternative clustering of countries.

This comparative analysis of the relative generosity and the interaction of benefits that constitute the core "family policy package" in most modern welfare states indicates that these policies have consequences for families and for women that do not correspond neatly to dominant theories of welfare regime types. In this, it provides empirical support for the observation of many feminist scholars that women have a more complex and multidimensional relationship to the state. It also raises complex questions about how welfare states balance interests across and within households.

There is substantial convergence across the industrialized countries about what constitutes the core of modern welfare state protections for the aged, the disabled, and involuntarily unemployed workers. There is remarkably little consensus across these same countries about the role of the state in offsetting the private costs of rearing children, in part, because these costs are differentially distributed across households and over time. At one extreme are the liberal democratic countries, such as the United States, that "privatize" the costs of child-rearing by providing minimum levels of public support through income transfers or health, social, or early education and care programs for children. At the other extreme are the Nordic countries such as Sweden and Denmark that choose to "socialize the costs of children" through extensive and redistributional social policies that partially offset private costs to families. This analysis demonstrates that the balance between private and state responsibility, in the form of the generosity of transfers and employment supports, is consequential for families' economic security when children are young. It also has consequences for the degree of economic equality across different families in the same society and for the extent to which women are able to participate fully in the market sphere.

Policies that attempt to balance the interests of individuals within the family are even more contested. Our analysis demonstrates that both transfers and employment supports are important for women and for families with children. But these policies interact in ways that may have different implications for households, for women and, potentially, for children. We begin to measure differences in the extent to which various welfare state regimes are woman friendly in supporting both economic security for families and women's integration into the labor market. We do not finally answer the more difficult question of what constitutes the optimal balance of nurturing and market activities, for men and for women, or the most equitable package of government assistance.

Policies that facilitate employment among mothers with young children have been identified as one component of the woman-friendly welfare state. Equal opportunities for women to participate in market work and to achieve parity with men may be a critical first step toward full social citizenship for women. Employment also contributes to women's capacity to form and maintain autonomous households, thereby lessening dependence on men. But as Fraser (1994) has argued, policies that increase labor market opportunities for women, without affecting the gender bias in responsibility for unpaid work in the home, will yield, at best, a partial form of gender equality. In the longer term, the contribution of employment-supporting policies to the achievement of full economic and social participation for women will depend on the extent to which they influence the organization of both paid work in the market and unpaid caregiving work in the home. A woman-friendly welfare state may well be one that is parent-friendly in supporting the efforts of both men and women to combine caregiving and waged work without undue—and gender-biased—sacrifices in either family or employment opportunities.

Appendix A: Index Construction
Income Transfer Policy Index

To construct the ITP Index, we sum the mean benefit levels (expressed in 1987 United States dollars) weighted by coverage. We calculate benefit levels separately for each family type as the average amount of transfers received by all families who reported each of the three transfers in each country-specific microdataset. Means are calculated first in national currency (nominal amount) and then converted to 1987 U.S. dollars, adjusting for purchasing power parity, for cross-country comparisons. Because we are primarily interested in those policies directed at families with dependent children, we reduce the contribution of other social transfer programs by one-half, by multiplying their value (level by coverage) by .5. The final formula for the ITP Index is:

Income Transfer Policy Index =
[(family allowance coverage) x (mean family allowance received)]
+ [(means-tested coverage) x (mean means-tested transfers received)]
+ [(.50) x (other social transfer coverage) x (mean other social
transfers received)]

Finally, the level of benefits, weighted by coverage, is scaled from zero to 100, as a percentage of one-half of the median adjusted disposable income for all families in the country.

Employment Supporting Policies Index. The ESP Index is constructed from eight measures of policies affecting families with children under the age of three and five measures of policies affecting families with children between the ages of three and the start of public school enrollment. Data on policy indicators are standardized as proportions of variable-specific maximum values. The two age-specific indices were first constructed as weighted sums of the standardized measures. A second standardization converts index scores to a percentage of the theoretical maximum per index, so that scores ranged from zero to 100. Finally, the two indices were combined into a single index of policy generosity for families with children under age six, weighting each of the two component indices equally.

Index scores were calculated using weighted combinations of the relevant indicators as follows:

Policies for mothers with children under age three:
[0.50 * [Legislated job protection + (Coverage)*(Paid maternity leave)
+ Wage replacement rate + Maternity leave coverage + (0.50 * paternity
benefits)]]
+ [Tax relief for childcare + Guaranteed childcare coverage (0–2 years)
+ Percent children (0–2) in publicly funded childcare]

Policies for mothers with children age three to six:
Tax relief for childcare + Guaranteed childcare coverage (3–5 years) +
Percent children (3 to 5) in publicly funded childcare +
(0.33 * percent children (5 years) in preprimary or public school)

Policies for mothers with children under age six:
[0.50 * Index score for Policies for mothers with children under age three] +
[0.50 * Index score for Policies for mothers with children age three to six]

Poverty Measures

Poverty rates for each country are calculated using a relative poverty line derived from country-specific household income distributions. The poverty line is set at one-half of the adjusted median disposable income for all households within the country. Disposable income includes all household income after payroll and income taxes and after public transfers. Our poverty line definition follows the convention of many cross-national scholars and organizations, such as the European Commission and the OECD (Forster 1993; Smeeding, 1997). Poverty rates are the percentage of families whose incomes fall below this line.

The parent/nonparent poverty reduction ratio is a measure of the relative effect of government tax and transfer policies on poverty reduction for two-parent families with children and two-adult families without children. We use LIS microdata to first calculate the percent of each group that had pre-tax-and-transfer income below the poverty line for two groups: married couples with children under age six and young married couples with no children under age eighteen. Pre-tax-and-transfer income includes all forms of earnings, capital and property income, private transfer income (e.g., child support), and occupational pensions, both public and private; it does not include taxes or public transfers. We then compare the pre-tax-and-transfer poverty level to a post-tax-and-transfer poverty level for each of the two groups. Post-tax-and-transfer income includes taxes and all public cash and near cash transfers. Poverty reduction then indicates the percentage of families that were poor before, but not after, taxes and transfers. We calculate the ratio between the groups by dividing the percent reduction in the poverty rate for two-parent families with children by the percent reduction in the poverty rate for two-adult families without children.

Employment Measures

Maternal employment rates are calculated, first, for women aged twenty to forty-five who had children under age six ("mothers") and, second, for women of the same age who had no children under age eighteen ("nonmothers"). To capture the extent to which having young children exerted downward pressure on maternal employment, LIS microdata are then used to calculate an *employment ratio* in each country: the employment rate for women with children under six over the rate for women with no children.

Table 10.1
Income Transfer Policy Index

Country	Year	Family Allowance			Means-Tested Social Assistance			Other Social Transfers			Income Transfer Policy Index[a]	
		Coverage Rate	Nominal	US 1987$	Coverage Rate	Nominal	US 1987$	Coverage Rate	Nominal	US 1987$	Score	Rank
Australia	1985	96.4	342	322	0.0	0	0	17.3	2,176	2,050	8.2	12
Belgium	1985	100.0	34,792	863	1.7	18,514	459	22.3	94,271	2,337	24.5	5
Canada	1987	95.0	364	301	56.4	561	464	57.4	1,523	1,259	11.7	10
Denmark	1987	97.1	4,630	494	13.2	52,752	5,624	63.8	21,830	2,327	33.7	1
Finland	1987	100.0	4,617	802	23.6	5,048	877	42.4	5,264	914	21.8	7
France	1984	90.3	8,420	1,340	0.9	7,184	1,143	27.7	3,065	488	26.0	4
Germany	1984	97.5	925	419	11.5	2,606	1,181	19.1	2,923	1,325	13.6	9
Luxembourg	1985	98.2	27,515	685	0.9	19,452	484	7.3	184,420	4,589	14.0	8
Netherlands	1987	100.0	1,165	498	12.9	5,215	2,229	8.0	10,900	4,659	24.1	6
Norway	1986	94.4	5,086	586	14.0	3,826	441	9.4	17,496	2,017	11.6	11
Sweden	1987	100.0	5,711	717	22.7	6,893	865	89.1	8,609	1,080	29.2	3
UK	1986	98.0	366	669	24.0	1,338	2,449	23.4	1,101	2,017	30.7	2
US	1986	0.0	0	0	10.9	1,385	1,435	17.8	1,393	1,444	3.8	13

[a] See Appendix A for index formula

Table 10.2
Poverty Outcomes

Country	Year	Pre-Tax-and-Transfer Poverty		Post-Tax-and-Transfer Proverty		Parent/Nonparent Poverty Reduction Ratio	
		Rate	Rank	Rate	Rank	Ratio	Rank
Australia	1985	13.1	8	11.5	10	0.38	2
Belgium	1985	15.4	10	3.6	4	0.88	8
Canada	1987	15.3	9	12.7	11	0.69	5
Denmark	1987	8.6	5	4.1	5	0.83	7
Finland	1987	9.4	6	2.7	1	1.93	10
France	1984	22.5	12	6.0	8	3.67	11
Germany	1984	8.5	3	7.6	9	0.39	3
Luxembourg	1985	7.7	2	5.3	7	0.89	9
Netherlands	1987	9.4	6	4.8	6	0.74	6
Norway	1986	3.8	1	3.0	2	0.42	4
Sweden	1987	8.5	3	3.1	3	3.92	12
UK	1986	25.2	13	15.2	12	4.03	13
US	1986	15.9	11	17.7	13	−0.82	1

Notes

1. Folbre (1994) also argues that the costs of children are disproportionately borne by mothers, who spend a higher percentage of what they earn on children.

2. The effect of cash transfers on maternal employment and the potential for maternal earnings to increase the economic security of families with children is more uncertain. Economic theory unambiguously predicts that an increase in a family's unearned income will discourage employment. Actual employment effects will vary, however, with the form, eligibility structure, and level of transfers (see review by Moffitt 1992). The consensus in the literature, both in the United States and cross-nationally, is that the magnitude of these effects is relatively small for men, who tend to remain attached to employment regardless. The effects are greater for women, particularly for married women and for mothers, who may have much greater demands and/or incentives to spend time at home. Estimates of the actual magnitude of women's responses to nonearned income vary widely. Most analysts find, however, that women's employment reductions are modest in absolute terms (although they may be large as a percentage of total market time, given low base levels of employment).

3. The conventional labor supply model suggests at least two ways in which childcare affects women's employment. The first depicts childcare conditions as affecting the value that a woman places on her time at home, with more attractive childcare options decreasing the value of women's "home time" relative to market time. Alternately, childcare can be seen to affect women's budget constraints. The cost of childcare may be viewed as a tax levied on mothers' hourly wages so that higher-priced care would have the same effect as lower net wages—a decrease in both employment and hours of paid work.

4. For further information on the Luxembourg Income Study (LIS), see the LIS Web site (http://lissy.ceps.lu).

5. In general, women who were cohabiting were coded as married. In the datasets from Italy and the United States, women who are cohabiting but not legally married could not be coded as married. This may introduce a selection bias if the characteristics of cohabiting women are distinctive.

6. This coding scheme treated families as "not having children" and women as "nonmothers" under three different conditions: they had not yet had children, they had never had children, or all their children were over age eighteen. Limiting the sample to adults between the ages of twenty and forty-five reduces some of this heterogeneity by excluding older adults who might have been parents of adult children.

7. The term "coverage" is typically used to describe the population designated for assistance under government programs. As such, it does not reflect behavioral responses that might affect the take-up rate among covered (or eligible) populations. In this analysis, we are interested in the final effect of government benefits on the disposable income of households. We are therefore interested in the combined influence of rules governing coverage (and eligibility) and the participation decisions of covered populations. We use the term "coverage" in this broader sense to mean the rate of participation within the population.

8. These income transfer categories correspond to the following LIS variables: child/ family allowance (V20); means-tested transfers, both cash (V25) and near-cash (V26); other social transfers, including sick pay (V16), accident pay (V17), disability pay (V18), retirement benefits (V19), unemployment benefits (V21), military benefits (V23), and other social insurance (V24).

9. This study uses enrollments as a proxy for childcare supply. Although this utilization measure is arguably responsive to female employment and demand for care, spaces in public programs at a point in time will depend on past government decisions rather than current demand and can therefore be considered exogenous to individual employment decisions. OECD (1990b) also notes that enrollments are a reliable proxy for available spaces because utilization rates are approximately 100 percent.

10. In the LIS dataset, the Australian data do not allow a breakout of means-tested benefits (see appendix table 10.1). However, income transfers received by low-income families are included in the other two categories of transfers that make up the Income Transfer Policy index, that is, family allowances and "other social transfers." Thus, total income transfers received would be comparable with the other countries, although the .5 weighting of the "other social transfers" in the index may cause some incomparability. It is not clear whether the inability to isolate means-tested benefits has the effect of increasing or decreasing Australia's score on the ITP index.

11. The United States lacked (and continues to lack) any national policies for paid maternity leave, although an estimated 25 percent women were covered under state-mandated, private disability policies in 1986. In Australia, paid leaves were guaranteed only for public employees, approximately 10 percent of women workers. Provisions for paid leave had been adopted in the United Kingdom, but with such stringent restrictions on tenure and other job characteristics that only an estimated 60 percent of working women were eligible (Gornick, Meyers, Ross 1997).

12. In this analysis, families with children under age six may also have included older, school-age children. For a more complete discussion of cross-national variation in school schedules, see Gornick, Meyers and Ross 1997.

Eleven

Susan Christopherson

Women in the Restructuring of Care Work

Crossnational Variations and Trends in Ten OECD Countries

Critics of welfare state "modernization" in advanced economies commonly attribute what they see as deteriorating protections from market risks to a loss of power among the political parties and labor coalitions that constructed social and labor market policies in the post-World War II era. The loss of left political power, however, tells us very little that can explain the kinds of policies being adopted across a wide range of advanced economies: (a) decentralized local provision, (b) privatized services, and (c) emphasis on contribution-based benefits over citizenship-based entitlements. Why are decentralization and localization of responsibility for social welfare favored as methods to modernize the welfare state? Why is it that wage work and status as a "stakeholder" are replacing other forms of social inclusion and entitlements? Why are social welfare services the target of reform while contribution-based entitlements remain relatively untouched?

The answers to these questions reside not only in the rise and fall of left political power but also in the history of the postwar welfare state. To fully understand the strategies being undertaken to restructure the welfare state, we also need to examine how the expectations and treatment of women within the welfare state created conditions enabling the policies that are being adopted now.

As many feminist analysts of the welfare state have elucidated, postwar social welfare policy constructed a form of equality that was limited and shaped by presumptions about the family, its ideal form, and its role in society (McDowell 1991). In the dominant model, women provide services critical to social reproduction, particularly caring for children and the elderly, but for the male breadwinner, too. Postwar welfare policy assumed female responsibility for these functions although, in some instances, shifting them to female wageworkers in the public sector (Esping-Andersen 1990). Women were defined as dependents with responsibility for the care of other dependents and the male breadwinner. Social norms, the concept of a family wage, and limited female labor force participation outside family enterprises reinforced this gender division of labor. Even in the socialist economies of Central and Eastern Europe, where the majority of women became wage workers and families depended on two incomes to make ends meet, women maintained ultimate responsibility for domestic order and care work.

In Anglo-American economies, a sea change began in the early 1970s as demand for service and clerical workers pulled increasing numbers of women into the workforce. This "pull" was paralleled by a "push" stimulated by declining male wages and the need for women to do wage work to maintain household income standards. Policies across industrialized countries intended to increase educational attainment affected both push and pull. A much larger proportion of women entering the workforce in the 1970s expected to work for the majority of their adult lives, if only part-time. Western European countries have followed this trend, albeit slowly in some cases, and increasing female labor force participation is acknowledged as one of the central changes in advanced economies during the last half of the twentieth century into the twenty-first century.

The dramatic transformation in women's wage work patterns only marginally altered their responsibility for family care, however. They continued to provide care, whether paid or unpaid, and when they were not providing care directly, to assume responsibility for care management and financing. Surveys of household expenditures throughout the period regularly demonstrate that women's wages go to pay for care on the assumption that the paid carer directly replaces the services of the woman wage earner.

The separate and subsidiary role accorded to women in the postwar welfare state was marked by their unequal position with respect to protection from labor market risks. They were largely excluded, by practice if not by law, from access to protections accorded the breadwinner, including unemployment insurance and pensions. The limited unionization of service occupations employing women contributed to their lack of bargaining power. If she worked for a wage, a woman typically was perceived as a subsidiary contributor to family income rather than as a "worker."

Because of policies that defined women as dependent carers and limited the protections they received as workers and, at the same time, created conditions that tacitly encouraged women to enter the workforce, a contradictory dynamic was established. According to some observers (Sarceno 1996), this dynamic has resulted in declining fertility rates and contributed to the looming crisis in social welfare provision—in the costly dependency ratios and caring gap for children and the elderly that hovers over the twenty-first century.

Ironically, perhaps, the contradictions of postwar social welfare policy are also providing a short-term solution to the quandary that policymakers confronted with dramatically rising social costs associated with an aging, dependent population face. The still-weak position of many women with respect to labor market protections and, now, the compelling need to work for a wage have created a space where changes in how and under what conditions social services are provided can take place. In what follows, evidence from a multicountry study of how the reorganization of social services is affecting women's employment in caring activities in OECD countries sheds light on this hidden face of welfare state restructuring. The results of this research add another dimension to the debate over the future of the welfare state, demonstrating how the gendered character of welfare state policies is producing "feedbacks" in contemporary reforms. It also raises questions about the sustainability of efforts to reduce welfare expenditures by relying on a division of labor in which women carry virtually an exclusive burden for the management and provision of care.

The Debate over the Future of the Welfare State

Ostensibly, policymakers are rushing to reform the welfare state because of a perceived crisis. There are those who perceive this crisis as manufactured, emerging from essentially political decisions to reduce the scale of welfare expenditures. These political decisions may emanate from an ideological bias against government regulation or intervention or a preference for what appear to be lower cost private family or market solutions. The view that short-term political opportunism is at the root of a drive to fundamentally alter social protections is, perhaps unexpectedly, the more optimistic of two takes on welfare reform. In this scenario, one political rationale could be overturned by another, potentially leading to a reestablishment of generous benefits.

The other, more ominous, and ultimately more convincing, argument behind the drive to alter welfare policies ties the need for altering social welfare policies to long-term changes in labor demand and basic demographic patterns. Within this explanatory framework, the growing demand for a more flexible work force to respond to rapid changes in global market demand requires nothing less than a reworking of the social contract. Flexibility, in this case, refers not to task or skill flexibility, but to wage and numerical flexibility—the ability to match worktime and total wages to demand fluctuations. The argument here is that benefits such as unemployment insurance will limit peoples' willingness to enter the labor market under less than ideal conditions and, together with the cost of other benefits, such as health insurance, will produce labor market rigidities. Employers will not be able to easily adjust the number of workers and their worktime in response to change in the demand for a product or service. So, a flexible workforce requires the development of a flexible social welfare system, one that ties benefits more closely to productivity and, ideally, allows for rapid workforce turnover. For example, the recent OECD Jobs Study makes the following policy recommendation:

> Non-wage labour costs—employers' social security contributions, pay for time not worked etc.—drive a wedge between what employers must pay to hire a worker and the value of his/her product . . . there is a need in both the public and private sectors for policies to encourage greater wage flexibility and, in countries where the scope for increasing such flexibility is limited, to reduce non-wage labour costs. Actions on these fronts would involve changes in taxation, *social policy*, competition policy and collective bargaining. (1994b: 45)

Dramatic shifts in demographic patterns drive the other component of this argument. A number of analysts (compare, Esping-Andersen 1996a; Saraceno 1996) have detailed changing marriage patterns, childbearing, and dependency ratios (i.e., the number of nonworkers that every working member of a society support). For example, OECD projections indicate that if current benefit standards are maintained, aging alone will cause expenditures on pensions and health to triple by 2040 (OECD 1994a). In most advanced industrialized countries, the fertility rate is well below the substitution level, meaning that age-dependency ratios will increase significantly in the next twenty years. And, the average duration of marriages that end in divorce has been declining, while the proportion of marriages that dissolve remains significant. These tendencies, together, are contributing to more diverse family and living arrangements over the life cycle. The consequence is that traditional norms with respect to responsibility for care are being questioned and overturned.

Demographic trends and the need to increase labor flexibility could be addressed in a variety of ways. For example, new institutions could be encouraged to provide workers with social welfare protections while, at the same time, introducing flexibility into the labor market. Legal opportunities for collective bargaining could be provided to temporary workers and independent contractors so they could acquire social protections within the context of their flexible work status (Christopherson forthcoming). Loosening immigration restrictions and providing realistic family benefits to those rearing children might avert difficulties created by a high-dependency ratio.

These alternatives and others, however, are not on the policy agenda except, to a limited extent, in Scandinavian countries. Instead, the policies of preference emphasize the link between wage work and social security while excluding many flexible workers from access to those social securities. And, with respect to the provision of social welfare, national governments are finding ways to reduce their role as an equalizer and ameliorator of conditions facing families with different economic capacities. The state is, instead, emphasizing private, community, and family solutions to dependent care responsibilities, with little regard for the ability of families and communities to meet these obligations and without regard for how the costs of care are distributed within families.

To fathom why these are the policies of choice, we need to understand their roots in prior policies as well as in current political pressures, what is referred to as "policy feedback effects." Thus far, the concept of policy feedback has been used to explain the continuity of support for entitlements across industrialized countries. These explanations suggest that the very success of social welfare policies spawned consumption-based interest groups that support continued entitlements. Paul Pierson, for example, finds little evidence that welfare states have undergone dramatic cutbacks (1994, 1996). Instead, he argues that the politics of welfare state development are unlike the politics of welfare state retrenchment. The "new politics" mitigating against welfare state retrenchment relies on a wider range of nonunion, non-Left interest groups (such as the American Association for Retired Persons in the U.S.) and the "taken for granted" status of established entitlements. To buttress his empirical argument supporting welfare state stability, he uses statistics on government outlays as percent of GNP and government employment as percent of total employment. His analysis indicates continued support for "entitlement" programs that provide income to households.

Pierson does note, however, that "when a government can obscure the consequences of reform—or better yet, turn reform into a source of tangible benefits—the welfare state may be vulnerable" (1994, 163). It is in this realm that other researchers have focused their attention, arguing that surface stability can mask myriad changes in the protections afforded by the welfare state and, important for this analysis, in the allocation of the costs of providing for necessary social needs.

A critique of Pierson's analysis (Clayton and Pontusson 1998) disputes his argument for welfare state resilience, pointing to changes in the overall configuration of welfare spending and to changes in state-produced services as key to understanding a restructured welfare state. It suggests that the pressure for retrenchment or restructuring might be coming from a cross-class coalition of employers and workers who fear that increasing public expenditures may drive up the cost of production in export sectors. While this is a plausible explanation, it does not tell us how politicians have been able to restructure the welfare state without incurring opposition from workers or the recipients of services. Why has the ideology of "reform" been successful and achieved so quietly and without protest?

What gives weight to this question is that someone has to do the work. The complete absence of childcare or elderly care, for example, would not be socially acceptable or tolerated. As Esping-Andersen describes:

The welfare state may be lean or generous, residual or comprehensive, yet the underlying quest for social protection hardly differs. Modest public welfare commitments imply that responsibilities are reallocated to either employers or families. And vice versa. Hence, it is unlikely that any effort at cost-shifting between state, market, and families will affect aggregate national social protection costs. But it will affect societies' capacity to adapt to family and labor market change. Therefore, the public-private mix has profound implications. (1996a, 16)

For answers to how changes in the public/private mix have been achieved, we need to look at some additional policy feedbacks of the postwar welfare state. As was already suggested, the postwar consensus was based on a package of relations, institutions, and arrangements that linked a logic of economic development with a complementary set of norms (Brodie 1996). Inherent in this package were contradictory elements that produced social and economic outcomes that the gender ideology of the postwar welfare state did not anticipate.

An Alternative Interpretation of Postwar Welfare State Policies

Since the 1970s, feminist analysis of the social welfare state has pointed to the ways in which the ideology of the male breadwinner and dependent mother/wife was central to construction of the postwar welfare state. While political economists analyzing women's position in the immediate post-World War II period (from 1945 to approximately 1970) frequently described women as choosing between wage work and household work, feminist analysts of women's economic situation recognized that, in reality, there was no choice. Women retained responsibility for domestic work and caring activities whatever their position in the workforce (Orloff 1993). This ongoing responsibility frequently translated into labor force marginalization as they took on work, especially part-time work, which allowed them to juggle their competing responsibilities.

The narrow realm within which women were able to influence the politics of social welfare policy, a realm largely defined in terms of their moral role as guardians of the family, reinforced their marginalization (Lewis, 1992, 1994; Fraser 1997). For example, despite the impression that family allowances created a comparable "wage" for women's unpaid work, the political support for these allowances was based not on equality principles, but on beliefs that they would reduce wage demands and encourage childbearing. As women have entered the workforce, these rationales have weakened and allowances have been one of the areas of welfare state support to be undermined during the current reforms.

In contrast, with the analysis of differences among welfare states rooted in the power resources of labor coalitions and parties, feminist scholars have differentiated among welfare states based on their gender ideologies and treatment of work by women with children. Typologies based on strong-versus-weak male breadwinner systems have produced a somewhat different arrangement of countries than those based in the strength of governing political coalitions. Notable cases include France, whose weak unions but strong labor parties have placed it somewhere right of center in the analyses of political coalition models. French social policies, however, have supported female employment (e.g., via universal childcare) because of a tradition of women working in agriculture and family business. In the United Kingdom, liberal economic policies have combined with historically strong unions and a powerful labor party to produce contradictory results as described in coalition models. The United Kingdom has a much clearer position in the feminist typology because of United Kingdom adherence to a strong male breadwinner system. Low rates of full-time female labor force participation place the United Kingdom closer to Germany than to its liberal economy counterparts with their high female labor force participation rates.

Thus, as Orloff (1999) suggests, the social organization of welfare—the ways countries organize the provision of cash and care through families, states, voluntary organizations and market—reflects not only ideologies about the role of the state but also cultural assumptions about gender difference, most important, women's responsibility for caring work (see also Orloff, this volume).

While policies that emphasized and idealized their family role limited the protections afforded to women as workers, the social welfare state also supported increased educational attainment for women. In addition, labor-based political coalitions advanced conceptions of equity in the workplace and educational institutions, eventually leading to more diverse wage work opportunities for women. These developments would not have had the influence they did were it not for the dramatic shifts in labor demand in areas such as clerical work that had come to be considered women's jobs.

As women's work credentials and the demand for their skills changed dramatically, other features of the postwar social contract remained virtually unchanged. With the exception of France, postwar welfare states did not encourage full-time female labor force participation by providing childcare. Instead part-time work for women developed as the preferred way of providing for care, even in social democratic states (Jensen and Kantrow 1990). And, apart from the solidaristic labor policies of the Scandinavian countries and their consequences for wages and working conditions in the public sector (where the majority of women were employed), women's jobs were not incorporated into the wage-bargaining agreements that protected large segments of the male workforce in the postwar era.

As women moved into the workforce in ever larger numbers from the 1970s to the 1990s, the male breadwinner model gave way to the dual earner model of family income. This new model retained two significant attributes of the postwar welfare state: women's continuing responsibility for care, either as direct carers or as care managers; and an absence of decommodification protections (in the form of social security, pensions, and unemployment benefits) in part-time jobs held by women. These two conditions: (a) the highly limited entitlement protections for women workers and (b) the continuing ideology of female care combined to create opportunities for policy entrepreneurs to quietly restructure care within contemporary welfare reforms.

Paths to Retrenchment

As policy makers attempt to devise politically safe ways to restructure the welfare state and reduce expenditures, the care question looms as a particularly difficult one (see Kittay, Tronto, and Fineman, this volume). On the one hand, policymakers can and do use the ideology of family responsibility to shift the cost of care to family members and to make it appear that that is the preferable solution. On the other hand, the increasing reliance on female employees creates an interest among employers to reduce the cost (disruptions, absences) associated with a dual responsibility for caring and full-time wage work. Flexible time schedules have been the preferable solution, but they do nothing to alleviate the total burden. They do make it easier to juggle multiple responsibilities with less cost to the employer. Consequently, women are still stuck with the "double shift" as Arlie Hochschild dubbed it.

A third factor entering the equation is the predominance of women in paid caring occupations, more than 95 percent across OECD countries. Women's employment is intertwined with the provision of caring services in complex ways. The loss of informal family care givers as women enter the workforce affects both child and elderly care sectors (Acker and Gottely 1996; Meifort 1997). At the same time, the demand for waged carers, jobs that women primarily hold, increases.

Despite the expansion in demand for caring workers, the labor force is relatively invisible because carers are rarely represented by collective bargaining organizations and their work is frequently done in individual households. A recent set of national case studies focused on women's employment patterns in childcare and elderly care work provides perspective on how the responsibility for caring is being redistributed even as the need for it increases. The case study countries include the Netherlands, Canada, the United States, the United Kingdom, Germany, Belgium, France, Finland, Norway, and Spain (Christopherson 1997) and provide evidence that demonstrates how the increasing demand for female labor and the drive to decrease state responsibility for a basic need is being resolved.[1]

These case studies take us beyond national figures describing the total amounts spent on care services (which have been rising in industrialized countries because of the increasing employment of mothers of young children and a growing elderly population). They tell us about changes in how services are pro-vided and by whom, as well as about alterations in entitlement policies related to care of children and particularly, of the elderly. Together, they demonstrate the inextricable connection between social policy and employment policy. Women's disadvantaged position in one sphere—labor market protections—trans-lates into disadvantage in the other—social policy.

Cross-national Trends

The findings from these case studies indicate some common trends in the restructuring of care provision, interesting in themselves given the range of political economic regimes represented in the case study countries.

Separation of Care Financing from Care Provision

Among the prominent cross-national trends is increasing separation of care financing from care provision. For example, while care for the elderly and children may still be financed via national taxes, the actual service is provided by local government, private providers, or subsidized family members. In one politically popular variant of this trend, the public resources to provide for car-ing are redistributed in the form of a cash benefit to families. This strategy shifts the burden of providing for or managing care (and accountability) directly to fam-ily members and those whom they employ. It creates competition in the caring labor market, potentially driving down the wages of those carers still employed in the public sector. In some cases, the benefit is needed to supplement family income, creating pressure on family members to supply care rather than employ a carer.

Decentralization and Devolution of the Provision of Care

A second, closely related, trend is the decentralization and devolution of responsibility for the provision of caring services to the local government, com-munity, and family. The welfare state has historically been conceived of as a na-tional set of institutions, one purpose of which was to ameliorate differences in access to basic social needs (adequate food, education, health care, security in old age) across regions and places within the country. Decentralization, which has been carried out under the banner of efficiency and public choice theory, has undermined this evening out function, constructing ever greater differences in the cost and quality of basic needs provision from place to place. Decentrali-zation and the differentiation that accompanies it also makes it difficult, if not impossible, to replicate effective training practices, credentialling, or "best prac-tice" across a national or even subnational regional terrain.

The country studies indicate that these two trends—separation of financing from care provision and devolution of responsibility for provision are operationalized through: (a) commercialization of care services; (b) requirements for compulsory insurance programs; and (c) individualization of service contracting through individual households, whether from private funds or government household subsidies; and (d) decentralized and, in many cases, individualized bargaining to determine wages and working conditions.

In the area of childcare, decentralization of financing and provision is reflected in increasing differentiation in wages and working conditions across localities and among public, commercial, and nonprofit service providers. This differentiation is most characteristic of countries such as Canada, where a significant portion of care services are provided via the market. It is also occurring in countries such as France, with nationally financed and organized childcare systems. In the French case, however, increasing differentiation among types of care providers is largely confined to the portion of the sector concerned with the care of infants via home care.

With respect to elderly care, many of the case study countries have moved from institutional care for the "young" elderly to home care services. In conjunction with the move toward more home-based care, a general decentralization of service provision and employment from the national to the local level is occurring. In some cases, the need to cut costs has driven the move to home health care. In other cases, home care is one dimension of a widening range of services to the elderly that respond to an increasing variability in services needed as the elderly population grows. The appearance of a widening range of services within market driven systems provides a political screen that draws attention away from the basic processes—withdrawal from and lowering of standards for basic services across population groups.

As a consequence of policies to restructure health and social service provision, localized, community care in some countries has evolved into a system in which care in the community is, in reality, care by female relatives (Waerness 1990a) The use of relatives or self-employed workers to carry out caring functions is a very different concept than that of community care, which emphasizes coordinated care that brings the recipient of care as well as the providers into a community of care.

As community care has become the preferable policy in OECD countries, a critical literature has developed, particularly in Scandinavia, which recommends that policymakers recognize the extent to which community care means care by female family members and orient policy to support these informal carers (Waerness 1990a). In countries with already high levels of community care, such as Denmark, there is pressure for more support because of the expectation that such care substitutes for both family-member-provided care and institutional care. In other countries, increasing support for informal carers is intended to dampen demand for institutional care, which is much more expensive. It is important to note that support for home-based "community carers" is more extensive in those countries with social welfare state commitments to provide for people in their old age. Where care for the elderly has remained unchanged as a family (i.e., a female) responsibility, for example, in Southern Europe, family members who care for elderly relatives have fewer community resources to assist them. This may possibly help account for the dramatic fall in birthrates in countries such as Spain and Italy, where the demands of caring work fall even more heavily on women than they do in the European countries of the north.

Market-oriented approaches to care provision are, of course, neither new nor original. Decentralized financing and wage bargaining have been the norm for the provision of caring activities in some countries, most notably Canada and the United States. In Canada, provincial government regulation and financing of so-cial services has created a complex of different systems within the Canadian na-tional polity. In the United States, where caring services are almost exclusively provided by individuals and commercial or nonprofit organizations, a plethora of subnational state regulations dramatically affect and differentiate the working conditions and wages of caring workers. This evolving regulatory role is argu-ably more significant as a political tool than a vehicle through which to positively affect clients or caregivers.

From Macro to Micro Social Regulation

Despite the implementation of policies that limit the role of the state in the financing and provision of caring services, the nation state continues to play an active role in social policy provision—in the guise of regulator. There is still an important influence on the structure of employment in caring occupations ema-nating from national and local regulation. This regulation may determine:(a) the number and skills of workers in caring institutions (staffing norms); (b) stan-dards of care for individual and institutional care; and (c) occupational qualifica-tions. In many cases, these regulatory frameworks have been reworked to respond to the increasing demand for care. Either directly or indirectly, changes in regulation, especially the move to local or microlevel regulation (in the firm or family) have served to increase the private provision of care, to weaken gov-ernmental controls over the qualifications of some workers (particularly in home care), and to weaken the influence of collective bargaining on the conditions of work. Changes in staffing patterns, increasing the ratio of unqualified to quali-fied staff in childcare centers, for example, are one result. Another is the increase in the use of unqualified homecare workers in elderly care. An example of the significance of regulation is the law passed in 1991 in France creating the family employee (aide a domicile). This law resulted in dramatic growth in private em-ployees serving the needs of the aged and caring for young children in French households (Acker and Gottelier 1996). Another is a change in staffing requirements in the United States that allows childcare centers to employ a larger number of less-skilled carers as a proportion of total staffing (Whitebook, Howes, and Phillips 1990).

As caring activities become increasingly individualized and devolved to family and community, however, the ability to enforce this expanding regulatory regime comes into question. There is little enforcement capacity accompanying the new regulatory welfare state. Regulation becomes a micro matter—of families, neighborhoods, and local "whistle-blowers." Standards are honored only nominally. Why then, the regulation? One answer is that it serves a political purpose—to protect the state from accusations of being "uncaring" and to allow blame shifting when abuses come to light. Regulation is a cheap way out of responsibility and accountability.

Changes in the Organization of Caring Work
The Expansion of Part-time Work

In conjunction with changes in the provision and financing of care, cost savings are also being realized by restructuring how the actual work is done. Possibly, the most significant work-restructuring trend is the increasing use of a part-time workforce to provide care for children and the elderly. Although there is a paucity of information on part-time work in the public sector, there is sufficient aggregate data to demonstrate a general trend toward the use of part-time work to provide social services. Much of this increase is in response to a drive to provide more flexible care services.

Even in the corporatist economies of Northern Europe, such as Germany and the Netherlands, part-time workers receive fewer benefits than their fully employed counterparts. In West Germany, for example, the growth of women's public sector employment in the 1980s was almost entirely in part-time work. In the governmental sector, women's full-time employment increased only marginally while part-time employment increased by 47 percent. This is especially significant given the fact that part-time work has historically been more prevalent in the private sector in Germany. In the United Kingdom, the share of women part-time workers in the public sector rose from 4.8 percent to 11.5 percent in the 1980s. In both Germany and the United Kingdom, the available evidence indicates that women part-time workers are concentrated at the bottom of the public service hierarchy (OECD 1991). Although scanty, the information on hours of work indicates that the trend toward part-time employment of women was widespread in European countries by the beginning of the 1990s.

While part-time work is affecting the income and opportunity structure for caring workers in the European states, part-time work across Europe differs significantly from the volatile and high turnover character of part-time work in the Anglo-American economies. The market driven and parent-centered childcare system in the United States, for example, has produced an unstable and highly flexible childcare sector (Whitebook, Howes, and Phillips 1993). A workforce rarely committed to permanent work in the sector carries out childcare. The sector is, however, very labor absorptive, allowing less-qualified workers to enter the sector easily and gain experience. A sector that is child oriented and publicly funded and organized in such a way as to offer child care that can be used consistently over time (as is the case in France) can offer the expectation of more permanent employment. The availability of stable permanent work in the sector is associated with high entry requirements for childhood educators. It also provides a rationale for further on-the-job training for the permanent workforce. On the other hand, the highly organized childcare system is limited in its ability to absorb potential workers who may have obtained relevant experience in another context.

Growing Barriers to Career Mobility

Across countries, the changing organization of caring work is making it more difficult to compose a career in caring work, whether in child care or elderly care. As in other sectors employing large numbers of women (such as banking), it is difficult to find a route to advancement in an extremely decentralized hierarchy. Where hierarchies do exist, such as in institutional childcare systems, job ladders are being eliminated. So, for example, in the United States the tendency has been to increase productivity by increasing the ratio of unskilled to skilled personnel. The average number of assistant teachers in U.S. childcare centers rose from 5.8 in 1988 to 7.7 in 1992 (Whitebook, Howes, and Phillips 1993).

A Canadian study on wages and working conditions in childcare centers across the country found that one-fifth of childcare center staff had advanced in their center from their starting position. In the Canadian case, the auspice of the center (municipal, nonprofit, or commercial) had little effect on advancement potential though it had a significant effect on other employment variables such as wages and turnover rates (Canadian Child Care Federation 1992). And in the United Kingdom, only nursery nurses that the local authority social services departments employ have the possibility of promotion to more senior posts such as nursery or center manager. There are no possible promotion paths for playgroup workers or parental assistants (nannies or child minders), and whatever skills they have acquired are not recognized should they move into childcare center situations (DFEE 1996).

There are several definable types of barriers to career mobility. One is tracking, which places entrants into career training and workplace situations that, although related, are difficult to cross without enormous effort. An example is the separation of daycare training and école maternelle, or preschool training, in

France. A second barrier is the dependence on formal educational credentials for placement in the career path. This is not as critical if there are intermediate training opportunities, but these are rarely available to the work force entering the field, particularly in Canada, the United States, and the United Kingdom.

A third barrier is the absence of training and employment linkages between childcare skills and those in other social and educational services. In this regard, it is notable that more integrated approaches to service provision are related to more integrated approaches to training (Moss and Melhuish 1990); for example, in situations where common institutions serve the care needs of young children and those of other segments of the community such as the elderly or physically handicapped. Multipurpose institutions are being experimented with in Denmark and Sweden (Oberhuemer 1995). This model is also intended to be labor saving but, nevertheless, provides a wider range of opportunities for workers employed in social services.

In the elderly care sector, attempts to rationalize provision in response to increasing demand have led providers to create separate occupational categories for more skilled and expensive work (e.g., diagnostic medical care) and less skilled work (e.g., assistance with personal care or domestic work). These pressures, however, have produced different responses. In some countries, such as Finland, because personal care and domestic help activities continue to be provided predominantly by one employer—the public sector— work organization is more coordinated, and there are a limited number of venues, allowing control over working conditions. In countries, such as France, where responsibility for the entire range of less-skilled caring work has shifted to the client, the division of labor among less-skilled jobs (domestic assistance and personal care) has become more ill defined. Working conditions in these occupations have diversified and are more likely to be defined by negotiations with the individual employer rather than, as formerly, by state regulation.

From Vertical to Horizontal Care Management

As countries represented in these case studies respond to pressures to reorganize work, there has been a generalized tendency to replace vertical hierarchies of care with horizontal care management groups or teams. The purpose of teams is to better manage and coordinate care for efficiency and quality. These care teams or groups can be organized in different ways. In one case, care providers employed by the public sector work together to provide the elderly person with the types of assistance needed. This is generally the character of the Scandinavian model and is illustrated in this study by the Finnish elderly care system. The other model, one that is developing in many countries, is that in which medical care is provided through tax-based or social insurance systems, while personal care and domestic assistance are the responsibility of the family of the elderly person or of self-employed workers. These two approaches have different implications for caring workers, the first drawing on a team of skilled and less-skilled workers and the second, emphasizing the managerial skills of the social worker or family member who organizes and monitors less-skilled workers performing the care work.

In summary, the employment of personal care or domestic assistance workers may be the unsubsidized responsibility of the individual, as it is in the United States, or subsidized through tax deductions and exemption from social security contributions, as it is in France. The trend toward more individualized employment, however, has combined with the differentiation of work sites to fragment already quite limited career paths and increase the tendency toward bifurcated employment structures. These organizational changes are reflected in working hours and earnings patterns and in other human resources management issues.

Major Sources of Divergence in Restructuring Strategies

Together with recent work on women and the restructuring of the welfare state (Saraceno, 1996; Gornick and Jacobs 1997; Gonas 1998), evidence from these case studies suggests some significant differences among countries in resolving the question of how to provide care more inexpensively and efficiently.

Two broad factors emanating from the history of social and employment policy in each country are important in differentiating contemporary policy strategies: the existing structure of provision and the extent to which there is the capacity to transfer service provision to lower cost alternatives such as profit or not-for-profit providers or family members. This capacity is affected by, for example, the female labor force participation rate, particularly in full-time work, and the wage differential between public sector and other types of service providers (the family, not-for-profit, and for-profit). To the extent that this differential is greater, there is an incentive to provide services outside the public sector. So, for example, in Scandinavian countries, where the differential between public sector and private sector wages is narrow, the incentive to transfer service provision to the private sector is relatively weak. In contrast, in countries such as the United States, where the public/private sector differential is significant because of stronger equity regulation and opportunities for collective bargaining in the public sector, expansion of caring work is taking place almost exclusively in the private market.

With respect to capacity, the tendency to expand service provision via the market is most pronounced in those countries with a history of private provision and characterized by means-tested and earner-contributory social welfare systems—in the case study countries, the United States, and Canada.

The trend toward nonpublic sector social service provision is also increasingly characteristic of the social welfare systems of continental Europe. These societies, exemplified by the Netherlands and France, are arguably undergoing the most significant changes in how social services, including childcare and elderly care, are provided. Finally, in the Scandinavian states with a history of public sector provision and universal coverage, restructuring is occurring through downsizing the public sector, by job combination, and by the decentralization of wage bargaining to the local level. In all cases, women's changing employment patterns within the broader labor market are at the heart of the incentives and capacities reshaping caring services.

Conclusion

The evidence from these country case studies is not definitive, but it does give an "on the ground" feel for how the provision of social services in the welfare state is being restructured and raises some provocative questions. First, it suggests that as social service work is becoming more decentralized and employment more fragmented both geographically and with respect to work site, class differences among women are likely to increase. Those women with educational credentials and in favorable local labor markets situations are likely to be able to use their potential mobility to advantage. Women without credentials and in noncompetitive labor markets are likely to lose even the small amount of economic power that employment in public sector social services once conveyed.

Second, the evidence suggesting that more caring responsibilities are being transferred from the public sector to family members, particularly women, raises questions about care-based (as opposed to citizenship-based) rationales for public assistance. The assumption that women hold primary, if not exclusive, responsibility for care has made it easier to engage that responsibility to reduce public costs. This strategy has been less feasible in those societies in which a large portion of women work full time.

Finally, the similar trends across countries—bifurcation of caring work, decentralization, and fragmentation of job hierarchies—raise questions about how the tendencies we see in caring occupations might be reflected in other occupations employing a predominantly female labor force. For example, recent evidence indicating that the wage gap between men and women is widening in the United States may be an artifact of increasing differences in women's employment and income opportunities as a consequence of the kinds of changes that are occurring in social service provision.

Across countries, the restructuring of care has been rooted in a contradiction between enhanced public expectations for higher quality care and a drive to reduce the costs of care. The case studies suggest that the primary strategy used to meet these contradictory political pressures has been to depend on a smaller more-skilled set of managerial and technical workers and an expanding low-waged, low-skilled workforce that, in many countries, works outside the boundaries of the protected public sector.

The evidence also contributes to the broader question of how welfare reform is taking place and why changes in citizen-based services are not evoking a political response. The case studies demonstrate how countries are pursuing different paths to welfare "reform," based on bureaucratic capacity and the ability to decentralize service provision through changing regulation, privatization, and the transfer of responsibility for provision to the local level. Within this process, "reformers" are using women's historically marginal labor market position to great advantage. The position of women, their concentration in full-time or part-time work, and especially, the intersectoral wage differential between public and private sectors construct an incentive system affecting what options are available to policymakers who want to reduce costs while appearing to meet the demands of the public for more choices in caring services.

That women remain an unorganized and incoherent interest group when it comes to their rights as citizen-workers is a too often neglected legacy of the postwar welfare state. Welfare state reformers have used that historical weakness and a traditional family ideology to justify and implement changes in welfare services. The increased emphasis on family (or community) responsibility for care is almost exclusively defined as a female responsibility, including economic responsibility for paying for care; responsibility for managing care given by others; and working as a caregiver, formally or informally. It is the strength of this ideology that has allowed for the surreptitious and politically noncontroversial shift of the costs of socially necessary care to women both in families and as workers.

Note

1. The studies, organized by the Working Party on Women's role in the Economy of the Organization for Economic Cooperation and Development, vary considerably in the extent of information provided. Because of significant differences in publicly available information and definitional problems, it is difficult to make direct cross-national comparisons. But because the researchers were responding to the same questions, however, the case studies are able to broadly illuminate changing patterns in financing and provision of care and in the situation of the caring worker.

Twelve

Ulrike Liebert

Degendering Care and Engendering Freedom

Social Welfare in the European Union

Compared with the liberal welfare state of the United States, European systems of social provision are often seen as being considerably more "woman friendly" (Bergmann 1997). A frequently held assumption is that with higher levels of public expenditure for social policy, the support of welfare states for families will be more pronounced (Siaroff 1994, 92). Among European welfare states, in particular, the Swedish, Finnish, Norwegian, and Danish regimes are recognized as being most generous in providing welfare for women, families, and children (compare, Lewis 1993; Fraser 1994; Sainsbury 1994a, 1996, 1999a). This view corresponds to Helga Hernes's original notion of a woman-friendly state that enhances a "gender-just" society through the effective participation of women within the state (Hernes 1987b). In fact, while Sweden, Norway, Finland, and Denmark are worldwide the most advanced with respect to women's parliamentary representation, they also lead in economic gender equality: though women's share in national income per capita may be higher in the United States than in the Scandinavian countries, disparities between female and male income per capita are considerably smaller in Sweden, Norway, and Denmark (UN 1999).[1] Nevertheless, the idea and practices of a woman-friendly welfare state over the past decade have become controversial among feminists in view of womens always more differing interests and perspectives (Leira 1993b; Borchorst 1994). The Nordic social democratic path to social and economic gender equality based on a woman-friendly state appears to be just one of several roads to an egalitarian gender order and, as one that is, compared with the Anglo-American formula of strong markets and weak social policy, particularly costly (Schmidt 1998). Overall, it has become for feminists more difficult to sustain claims of a woman-friendly state modeled after the Nordic pattern. The restructuring of welfare states in European countries during the 1990s has put this vision to a serious and, maybe, final test. What appears to be at stake is the viability of, not to mention further advancements toward, this ideal of a woman-friendly social welfare state conducive to a gender-just society.

Seen from this perspective, the multilevel polity of the European Union has become a continental social laboratory where, in the context of markedly different gender relations and regimes, a diversity of strategies for adapting national social welfare states to pressures of the global economy, to requirements of the Economic and Monetary Union, and to domestic changes in demographic and family structures are being experimented with (Pierson 1994; Esping-Andersen 1996c, 1999; Ruggie 1996; Rhodes 1997; Rhodes and Mény 1998; Bussemaker 1999). On one hand, one can study the influences that various reform policies have had on different groups of women—policies following the neoliberal, market-driven type of retrenchment strategy compared with policies of the type of conservative labor reduction strategy reinforcing familialism, or reform policies that followed a social investment approach to social welfare reforms (Esping-Andersen 1996c). On the other hand, domestic social welfare reform debates can be studied comparatively to explain why ideas of woman-friendly reform strategies had relatively little influence on them. As Diane Sainsbury noted in her 1996 book on gender, equality, and welfare states, the recent literature on welfare reforms in the United States and the United Kingdom as well as in the Netherlands and Sweden gave scant attention to the idea of restructuring welfare systems from the perspective of gender equality (1996, 173). The same can be said of Germany, the pioneer in social security systems, and laggard in retrenchment policies within the OECD world (compare, Pierson 1996; Clayton and Pontusson 1998; but compare Mushaben, this volume). Here, despite the steep increase in women's political representation since unification, between 1990 and 1998, and although party political controversy about the issue of restructuring the German social welfare state was rising,[2] women's strange silences in this public policy debate were striking. Although feminist analysts depicted women as running the risk of becoming the losers in the current struggles on the transformation of the social welfare state, they deplored the fact that in these debates "visions of a viable social welfare regime that builds on gender justice are lacking" (Braun and Jung 1997, 16, 7)[3]. Has the vision of a woman-friendly welfare regime become obsolete, given the new quality of supranational retrenchment pressures? Or can this idea be rescued as a critical standard for assessing current processes and designing future strategies of welfare state transformation?

In the United States, the idea of woman-friendly welfare reforms was certainly not publicly touted as a rationale for adopting the welfare-to-work reform act of 1996. Yet, a number of feminist critiques have used the idea to demonstrate the antiwomen ethos of this provision that sharply limited the entitlement of single mothers to receive public welfare benefits. Other analysts, in contrast, pointed to the ambiguous character of the new welfare-to-work policies and its mass public appeal, especially from the point of view of the rising number of women with children having to work (see Orloff, this volume). This ambiguity among feminist assessments revealed that the vision of a woman-friendly welfare regime and what it should mean with respect to retrenchment policies obviously lacked clarity. Because of the dilemmas arising from the attempt to evaluate the welfare reform act of 1996, a new debate among feminist theorists emerged. As the chapters included in the theory section of this volume exemplify, the central issue of this debate is the attempt to clarify the notion of a woman-friendly welfare state by submitting its conceptual and normative premises to critical revision.

In this chapter, I argue that the idea of the woman-friendly welfare state has to be substantially revised: to be reshuffled as a discursive strategy for countering neoliberal, political-economic discourses on welfare retrenchment on one hand, and to be used as a critical standard for assessing current and future processes of welfare state transformation on the other. In particular, I show, first, that the two most important propositions emerging from the feminist welfare debate suggest revising the original idea of a "woman-friendly" welfare state, by substantially revaluating the two complementary notions of freedom and of care. With the principle of *engendering freedom rights by degendering care* at the heart of this revision, I follow Nancy Hirschmann and Joan Tronto (this volume). Second, the revaluation of both principles has implications for how to reconceptualize a gender equal welfare regime, more precisely, how to reconstruct it in terms of a triangular model of state-market-family relations. Third, I give a few empirical illustrations from comparative welfare state research in Europe to demonstrate that this revised model can be effectively used as a normative standard for assessing the evolving practice of welfare states. In the summary, I discuss some of the implications of European integration as opportunities for and constraints to the viability of this model.

Engendering Freedom by Degendering Care: The Idea of the "Woman-Friendly" Welfare State under Revision

Norwegian sociologist Helga Hernes first coined the term "woman-friendly welfare state" to describe how states could create "gender-just" societies through the effective participation of women in all stages of policy development (Hernes 1987b)[4]. Subsequently, other scholars helped develop this vision from a variety of perspectives. The evolution of this concept closely reflects the evolution of feminist thinking but has not yet been matched with appropriate indicators used in current empirical approaches to comparative welfare research. Drude Dahlerup (1989), in contrast to Hernes, conceived woman-friendliness in terms of "the differential impact of public policies on men and women," emphasizing unintended consequences of sex neutral policies as well as of sex specific policies. Anette Borchorst (1994b), in her interpretation of the idea of woman friendliness, focused on the degree to which welfare regimes questioned existing patriarchal patterns of power (compare, Borchorst and Siim 1987; Borchorst 1994a). A broader definition of woman-friendly states encompassing all "options available to European governments to improve the status of women" was put forward by Gardiner and Leijenaar. This notion includes policies that enhance women's roles as "policy takers" or as "policy makers;" policies that are based on feminist concerns such as sex or gender equality or women's policy; or that are not explicitly feminist, for instance, sex-neutral policies (Gardiner and Leijenaar 1997, 61, cit. after Mazur 1999). If state policies that enhance women's status and advance gender equality constitute the core of a woman-friendly welfare state, then this notion will privilege either a gender-equality or a gender-recognition approach to social policy and discard other options: policies that are framed in gender-neutral terms, policies conducive to gender reinforcement, and even policy strategies aiming at gender reconstruction (Sainsbury 1996) will not be included.[5] This notion, therefore, appears to be too reductionist.

A second limitation is that this idea of a woman-friendly welfare regime focuses on women's interests, conceiving women as a homogeneous group and, as such, stands in the way of a more inclusive conception. So far, Nancy Fraser (1994) has put forward the most inclusive conception of a gender-friendly welfare regime. Framed as an ideally humane and just welfare system, this regime is based on five negatives: fighting poverty; fighting exploitation; fighting inequalities in income, time, and status; fighting political marginalization; and, fighting the androcentrism of state institutions and policies. Fraser uses this conception to assess the two rival ideal models that dominate the feminist welfare debate—in the United States the universal breadwinner and in Europe, the caregiver parity model. She finds neither would satisfy all five requirements of her model sufficiently and, therefore, suggests a third alternative—the model of integration. This model would change the lives of men and women by discouraging freeriding of individuals on behalf of others regarding care work and domestic labor (Fraser 1994). Without developing this vision of a possible synthesis further, however, she leaves the question open as to how one conceptualizes a gender-friendly welfare regime so that the two contrasting interpretations of the principle of equality—universal breadwinner versus caregiver parity—instead of complementing, will conflict with one another.

Controversial Issues

In recent welfare debates in the United States, feminist scholars found themselves caught in normative dilemmas they could not easily resolve. Because they were committed to the norm of gender equality, they were not able to argue against the neoliberal onslaught on those maternalist welfare policies that in their view reinforced gender hierarchies: "Because women have been for so long described and confined to the boundaries of the private sphere of care and by maternal and related images of women as selfless carer, meeting neoliberal arguments with demands for greater support for domestic care seems to be reactionary at best" (Tronto, this volume). Meanwhile, in Europe, feminist welfare analysts and theorists have been divided on the fundamental norms constituting a woman-friendly welfare regime. Here, a number of complexities have rendered feminist debates on how to recast the welfare state in woman friendly terms contentious, as well.

First, the extremely heterogeneous gender orders and cultures that contribute to the territorial fragmentation of the European Union complicate the question of the normative presumptions of such a regime (Ostner and Lewis 1995; Garcia-Ramon 1996; Pfau-Effinger 1996; Sackmann 1998). In view of this plurality of gender roles and norms, it thus appears arguable as to whether a woman-friendly welfare regime could be defined for the European Union in any coherent way.

Second, given the strong social democratic and state tradition in some societies and the liberal, civil society traditions in others, there is the unresolved question among feminists as to how far public responsibilities should go and where the private sphere would begin. The question of the appropriate mixes between state, market, and private responsibilities is, therefore, an extremely hot issue pervading feminist discussions about the welfare state.

Third, welfare analysts in Europe query whether the nation state should be defended as a framework for developing a women- or gender-friendly vision of a welfare regime, not only vis-à-vis individual citizens or markets, but contrasting it with new options of redesigning a multilevel welfare regime in the framework of the European Union. The notion of a woman-friendly welfare state, in this situation, has hardly been useful to overcome these divisions.

In view of these contrasting interpretations of the principle of gender equality at the heart of particular notions of a woman-friendly regime on one hand, and of more universal conceptions of a gender-friendly welfare regime on the other, the crucial question is how to recast a normatively more coherent conception. As long as issues such as how to define gender equality remain controversial among feminist welfare analysts, a diversity of different approaches and heterogeneous empirical standards for comparatively assessing welfare state regimes and policies will continue to fragment the field.

The state of the art in feminist theory and comparative research on social welfare suggests a further step to sketch a normatively more coherent and empirically grounded conception. This should make it possible to synthesize the different ideas and meanings hidden under the label of a woman-friendly welfare state. For this reconceptualization, I draw on Nancy Hirschmann and Joan Tronto's (this volume) work that suggests recasting the two fundamental concepts of freedom and care.

Theoretical Assumptions Concerning the Household

While economic theory and policy alike focus on productive and paid work and tend to ignore reproductive work and the unpaid or domestic work of child rearing and caregiving, the feminist approach emphasizes the interrelationships between both in the reproductive economy. At best, mainstream approaches understand public and private organizations of reproduction as investments in economic infrastructures and in human capital. As Martha MacDonald argues, with the transfer of reproductive work to the domestic sphere, the economic costs of off-loading social security provisions—health, education, welfare—onto the community or household by no means "disappear . . . when caregiving is relegated to the family or community through cutbacks in social expenditures, it is mainly women who assume that workload" (1998, 8). And while most welfare state researchers concentrate on the relationship between the labor market and the state, with a key interest in the modification of market inequities while largely ignoring the interrelationships of both within the sphere of households, feminist approaches suggest inverting this perspective. They turn the focus from the labor market and paid work as a basis of entitlements to the domestic or private sphere, care activities, and nonpaid work.

The assumption that the household is central combines with two further premises common to feminist welfare analyses: first, that the patriarchal family is eroding, giving way to newly emerging varied forms of households;[6] and second, that where patriarchal families persist, intrahousehold inequalities represent important dimensions with external influences. Feminist welfare theorists see both conditions as requirements for reconstructing the normative foundations on which social security and welfare policies are built.[7] Two proposals for such normative foundations of social welfare are included in this volume: Nancy Hirschmann reclaims the concept of freedom from the Right as she recasts it in gendered and in positive terms and Joan Tronto reconceptualizes the state as a caring state built on inclusive citizenship and a revaluation—and degendering—of care. Both approaches are gender sensitive and universal in different ways: while the first engenders the conception of freedom, the second seeks to degender the notion of care. Moreover, they are universal, because they require rethinking the foundations of social security and welfare systems in a way that would not exclude or marginalize half or more of the population not engaged in paid work.

Engendering Freedom

In her chapter, "A Question of Freedom, a Question of Rights? Women and Welfare" (this volume), Nancy Hirschmann reclaims the concept of freedom from neoliberals and from the Right who both have appropriated it in dominant discourses on dismantling the welfare state as a notion of individual negative liberty from state dependency, intrusion as well as tax burden. She argues that to reconceptualize freedom in a more complex and positive way, it is necessary to revise formal and substantial rights by considering women's freedom and, more specifically, by focusing on women's traditional responsibilities—the activities of care work. A necessary condition for enhancing women's "positive freedom" is to extend the range of choices available to them by institutionalizing rights that reward and support care activities, while at the same time "degendering" the way care is done. Therefore, recognizing citizenship rights derived from activities of care represents the core device by which Nancy Hirschmann liberates the welfare state discourse from conservative and neoliberal hegemony. The fact that the Right has constructed women predominantly as "dependent welfare subjects" should not, as she argues, keep us from understanding the power of the welfare state in constructing selfhood and subjectivity. In this, "freedom is one such core concept . . . that feminist attempts to reconstruct the welfare state in more woman-friendly terms need to consider" (Hirschmann, this volume).

Degendering Care

Joan Tronto, in her chapter entitled "Who Cares? Public and Private Caring and the Rethinking of Citizenship" (this volume), further develops the notion of citizenship rights derived from care. Private care and its relationship to the state are seen in the context of social transformations marked by changing family structures, women's unequal double shift, and the erosion of the myth of home as haven in a heartless world. Departing from established frameworks of citizenship and the state, Tronto suggests a modest paradigm shift, namely the consideration of care responsibilities as collective public responsibilities and no longer as individual and private ones. This requires reconceiving the welfare state, on one hand, as a caring state, helping citizens, for instance, reconcile their care responsibilities with their work. On the other hand, this paradigm shift requires replacing dominant conceptions of citizens, too. In the past modeled on property owners or soldiers, at present primarily on workers, breadwinners, and independent individuals, these models tend to be exclusive, discriminating, and unrealistic. In contrast, Tronto's notion of inclusive citizenship is modeled on a citizen who derives his or her rights and entitlements principally from his or her care work—hence activities in the domestic sphere that are presently undervalued.[8]

This rethinking of state, citizenship, and individual rights allows one to revise substantially the original idea of the woman-friendly welfare state by including two features: (a) a caring state, enhancing women's positive freedom, and (b) inclusive citizenship rights, deriving from individuals' records in providing and receiving care. To further sharpen this concept of a gendered welfare regime and reconstruct the model, I turn to gender-neutral comparative welfare state research and borrow some of its distinctions that appear useful for empirical and comparative research.

Engendering The Social Welfare Triangle

Mainstream welfare research provides conceptual definitions and distinctions that can be used for constructing an empirical model of a welfare state conducive to engendering freedom and degendering care: the distinction between state-regime-policy, between types of policies, and the notion of different configuration of the triangle state-market-household. By integrating both gender-sensitive notions and mainstream models of welfare regimes, the vision and idea of a woman-friendly welfare regime can be developed into an analytic model.

Definitions of the Welfare State

There is not any single definition for "welfare state" on which social welfare scholars would agree. Three terms—welfare state, policies, and regime—are sometimes used as synonyms, and often in incoherent and inconsistent ways. Various empirical disciplines tend to interpret these terms differently, emphasizing more structures, norms, or agency/interests depending on their conceptual and analytic frameworks.

From a gender perspective, however, welfare analysts might agree on three general features of a concept of a gender-sensitive welfare state regime. First, such a concept should include a large range of state activities relevant to issues of gender welfare. Second, it should put particular emphasis on women's and gender policies. Third, it should be embedded within an analytic framework encompassing power structures and relations between public and private activities, with a particular focus on relations between state and family. First, while the concept of welfare state can be described as a form of the state (public patriarchy, maternalist welfare state), empirical welfare analysts usually attach the term to one or several sectors of state activities. Gender analysts typically do not follow the minimalist version of the term, which reduces welfare to social assistance programs (e.g., AFDC in the United States).

Most analysts certainly favor more inclusive concepts of the social welfare state: Ann Shola Orloff (1993), for instance, claims that a feminist concept of social welfare state should include policies such as daycare, education, housing, healthcare, care for dependent citizens, and even measures against male predominance. In her analysis of the distribution of child costs, Kirsten Scheiwe (1999) scrutinizes large subsystems of public and private law, such as tax law, social and labor law, public law, and school law. And in order to correct the bias of mainstream welfare research privileging paid labour market activity,[9] gender approaches deliberately focusing on intrafamily divisions of labour between reproductive, unpaid work, and paid labour market activity when constructing welfare regime typologies (Ostner and Lewis 1995).

Redistributive or Regulatory Policies?

Helga Hernes made the distinction between women's and gender policies that is useful for the purpose of defining a gender welfare regime (Julia O'Connor 1993a): while women's policies aim at improving the situation of women and children, gender policies are primarily concerned with gendered status hierarchies and social power differentials. While the former are concerned with issues of material redistribution between women and men, the latter are a type of regulatory policy. Oriented toward inclusion in the labor market or toward decreasing gender hierarchies in decision making, they (re-)regulate the standards and conditions of inclusion and participation. Such state activities aiming at regulating gender equality need not necessarily be conceived as a separate policy sector. As Martha MacDonald (1998) argues, all social security programs typically provide employment-related benefits and work to the disadvantage of those who are engaged primarily in caregiving, predominantly women. Given that the labor-market experiences of women and men differ, with more women being concentrated in nonstandard, informal, and lower-wage employment, the use of male work norms to establish eligibility and calculate social security provision will inevitably penalize women. To avoid mirroring women's labor-market inequality in social security benefits, regulatory policies "must be based on an understanding of the distinct labour market experience of women and men" (12), which entails different labor-market opportunities, constraints, returns, and life-cycle work patterns.[10] Regulatory policies need to scrutinize social security provisions with women's practical needs for support in the traditional context in mind, without undermining their strategic interest in changing unfair gender relations: "This is a difficult road to walk" (14).

The Welfare Triangle: State-Market-Household

Finally, the notion of the welfare regime—in contrast to that of the welfare state—captures the primary concern with different triangular configurations of state-market-family in the provision of welfare policies, as well as interest in exploring the interactions and mutual influences between these three spheres. While feminists always have been sensitive to questions about the relationship between the public and the private sphere, in the domain of welfare regime research, it is more precisely the household that constitutes the center of research interest. On the one hand, the concept of welfare regime allows one to capture the patterned relations between state and the domestic sphere that the power structures, class, and political alliances across classes shape. On the other hand, however, such a regime approach is necessary, but hardly sufficient, to account for welfare state origin, change, and decline if it is not "enculturated" in a social constructivist, interpretative approach.[11]

These distinctions help us to provide a more elaborate definition of a gender-sensitive social welfare regime that is capable of engendering freedom while degendering care:

> A "gender-sensitive" social welfare regime is a specific configuration of state-market-household relations that does not privilege rights derived from paid labor-market activity, but rather revaluates private and public care work. On the one hand, by institutionalizing a public care sector as well as supporting and rewarding private care, the state in relation to private households will develop incentives to degender reproductive work and the domestic division of labor. On the other hand, in relation to labor markets, the state will provide a legal framework for reconciling market activities with family responsibilities, thus engendering freedom, and enhancing women's economic citizenship.[12]

To enhance collective and individual welfare, such a gender-sensitive welfare regime does not necessarily have to feature a strong interventionist state but could be based on various forms of a state-market mix. States, as well as markets, need to be involved in the provision of inclusive citizenship that recognizes and rewards, supports and facilitates private care activities and that allows them to reconcile paid work and family responsibilities. A regulatory caring state supports individuals and groups in providing and receiving care. The market economy equally needs to develop and sustain human resources by supporting individuals in their capacities to reconcile paid productive and unpaid care or reproductive responsibilities.[13] To the degree that such welfare policies successfully contribute to revaluing currently undervalued activities of reproductive work, they will contribute to the degendering of care. On the other hand, a gender-sensitive welfare regime will engender political and civil freedom rights as a necessary prerequisite for effectively enhancing freedom rights and promoting equality of opportunity in the contexts of gender imbalances and hierarchies.

In the following review of comparative research on social welfare systems, I discuss the question of standards for assessing welfare regimes and their gender sensitivity and provide some empirical illustrations. Will the Nordic welfare regime that originally served as the cradle of the woman-friendly welfare state qualify as a model of gender-sensitive welfare regimes, too?

The Question of Empirical Standards: Assessing the Gender Sensitivity of Welfare Regimes

After having recast the idea of a "woman-friendly welfare regime" in terms of a more systematized model of a gender-sensitive social welfare triangle, it is now time to relate this discussion to empirical evidence. To what extent do existing welfare regimes enhance gender-sensitive public policies in the real worlds of welfare capitalism, and how can we measure it? Examinations of the "three worlds of welfare capitalism" from the perspective of gender have revealed a great deal of variation in how welfare regimes are gendered (Lewis 1992; Pfau-Effinger 1994; Ostner and Lewis 1995; Sainsbury 1996). The question is now which of the standards developed in these analyses can be used for identifying those policies and achievements oriented toward the degendering of care and the engendering of freedom.

Feminist comparativists have developed a variety of approaches and methods of analysis that range from feminist economics, over macrostructural analyses based on quantitative data, to comparative discourse, institutional and regional analysis (Garcia-Ramon and Monk 1996; Bussemaker 1999). From the perspective of feminist economics, Martha MacDonald (1998) has suggested reframing the conventional evaluation standards used in comparative welfare research accordingly, incorporating gender analyses into the assessment of the equity, efficiency, sustainability, and affordability of welfare programs.[14] The approach adopted in this chapter here addresses questions of measurement based on quantitative data but when doing so, it draws on feminist academic discussions about norms underlying such gender-based assessments of social welfare systems, emphasizing the degendering of care and the engendering of freedom.[15]

My assessment of EU-member states and how their social welfare regimes are gender sensitive will be based on the three-sided triangle constituted by state, market, and private households. With respect to each of the three dimensions, the comparative literature on gender and the welfare state suggests a variety of variables. Among these, the following three sets of variables shall be emphasized:

1. *State-household dimension*: the degree to which caring states contribute to the degendering of care activities by means of public policies and services: (a) institutionalize social citizenship rights and provide for income transfers that recognize care work and care needs; (b) decouple social welfare entitlements from marital and family status;[16] (c) take positive action to induce men to equally share care responsibilities as fathers, sons, or partners until a gender-just distribution of the costs of caring for children, the frail, and elderly is achieved. This requires directing financial transfers for families, the elderly, and children to those effectively in charge of care responsibilities and also imposing financial costs on those able-bodied persons not taking part in or freeriding on other people's care activities;

2. *Market-household dimension*: the degree to which economic citizenship is engendered, with women's freedom to seek employment in the labor market being enhanced, especially for mothers engaged in care for dependent family members: (a) effective regulations providing for equal pay, equal treatment, and equal opportunities of promotion, enhancing the desegregation of private labor-market sectors; (b) supports for the employment of parents and, in particular, of mothers by private childcare facilities close to the workplace; (c) the offer of part-time work schedules by the private sector that avoid gendered differentials in wages and job security;

3. *State-market dimension*: the degree to which state-market mixes relieve individuals from the burdens and risks of caring for dependants: (a) by sharing the costs for child care and parental leave between the public and the private sector; (b) by regulating parental leave in the public and private sector to allow parents to reconcile productive work and care responsibilities; and (c) by adopting measures consisting of positive action coupled with income supports to promote women's capacity to form autonomous households.

In the following, I will draw on empirical indicators to assess social welfare policies, although due to rapid changes in this domain of comparative research, some of the reported findings may be outdated. Selection criteria are the following: (a) assessments are included that construct rank-orders of European welfare states and the United States; (b) the empirical standards on which these assessments are based represent possibilities to operationalize some aspect of the three sides of the gender-sensitive welfare triangle outlined earlier. The limitations of these rank-orders are several: first, they differ with respect to the range of welfare regimes covered—ideally all of the current fifteen EU-member states and the United States; second, the data on which they are based derive from different sources and relate to different years/time points; third, not for all of the three sets of indicators outlined above are there data and rank-orderings available.

Assessing Caring States: Defamilizing Child Costs and Degendering Care

The issues at stake here are three: how the costs of raising children are distributed among public and private households; how single-parent families (lone mothers) are treated in comparison to two-parent families; and which legal provisions redistribute care responsibilities between men and women.

Meyers, Gornick and Ross (this volume) argue that "given that the rearing of children imposes costs on families, mothers who care for dependent children are more likely than other women to live in poor families." Three factors determine that risk: (a) the barriers to employment that women who have young children face, (b) government policies that transfer income to families with dependent children that increase their economic security and reduce economic inequality between women who care for children and those who do not, (c) the availability of government policies such as maternity leave and childcare that allow continuous employment for women during their childbearing years.

As a result of their thirteen-country comparison, based on a dataset from 1984 to 1987, Meyers et al. find that "although employment has increased among women in all industrialized countries in recent years, levels of family poverty, and the added likelihood of poverty associated with having children, also vary enormously across the industrialized welfare states". While they find a "substantial convergence across the industrialized countries about what constitutes the core of modern welfare state protections for the aged, the disabled, and involuntarily unemployed workers," they see "remarkably little consensus . . . about the role of the state in offsetting the private costs of rearing children" (Meyers et al., this volume). As a result of these substantially distinct family policy packages—of forms and generosity of benefits provided to families and working mothers—in the United States, one out of five two-parent families with a child under age six lives in poverty, while in Sweden, it is fewer than one in thirty families with children. In general, welfare regimes with the most generous packages—high income transfer policy scores (Denmark, UK, Sweden) and well-developed maternal employment supports (France, Denmark, Sweden)—generally turned out to be the most successful in reducing parental/nonparental poverty ratios (UK, Sweden, France). Germany, with its family policies ranked ninth and seventh and with its parent/nonparent poverty reduction score after the United States and Australia, reached only the third to last place.

Kirsten Scheiwe (1999a, 1999b), in a four-country comparison, drew on more recent data from the 1990s to plot the distribution of direct child costs and the provision of care work and services along an axis between the two poles of private households and public/state agencies. Focusing on legal models of caring and paying for children, she showed that in the United Kingdom most of these costs were privatized, followed by Germany, while in Belgium and even more in Sweden, these costs were assumed predominantly by the state, which also provides the most generous services. Time rights of parents and social security rights derived from care work were also most developed in Sweden, followed by Germany, while they were weakest in the United Kingdom, with Belgium in between.

Bradshaw et al. (1993) based their ranking of seventeen countries on thirty-six scores measuring different income-support programs for families with children, including child and housing allowances, medical costs, and so forth (compare Saraceno 1999, 7ff). As a result, they found that France, Luxembourg, and Belgium cluster with the Scandinavian countries in providing the most generous supports, while Spain, Ireland, Japan, Greece, and the United States are found in the opposed group of countries with lowest levels of public family supports. Germany, together with the Netherlands and Australia, are located in between these two extremes (see Table 12.1).

These approaches toward comparatively assessing caring states providing for children, however, largely focus on two-parent families. To cope with the increased fragility of marriages,[17] with the changing nature of family relations, and the emergence of new types of households, it is necessary to include the concept of the "defamilization" of welfare state policies. This has been conceived as indicating "the terms and conditions under which people engage in families, and the extent to which they can uphold an acceptable standard of living independently of the (patriarchal) family (McLaughlin and Glendinning 1994, 65; cit. after Saraceno 1999, 18). Three indicators are included here: A first, general indicator would measure defamilization by the extent to which social provisions are based on individual entitlements, independently granted from family status. A second, more specific indicator, measures state policies and transfers directed toward single parents and, especially, lone mothers (Hobson 1994; Bradshaw et al.1996; Duncan and Edwards 1996). Finally, a third indicator measures subjective orientations: crossnational survey studies on how individuals evaluate the family and its role for individual well-being have provided empirical evidence "that social welfare systems, to the extent that they constitute strong institutional supports for individuals outside of marriage, may make marriage less important for general-life satisfaction" (Ryan, Hughes, and Hawdon 1998).[18] In particular, general life satisfaction of individuals has been found to depend to varying degrees on marital status and gender. While for the United States a positive correlation between marital status and reported individual happiness has been established, studies on Sweden or Finland do not confirm this finding (Ryan, Hughes, and Hawdon 1998).

Engendering Freedom: Assessing Women's Economic Citizenship

Engendering freedom requires, among other things, to enable women to choose to be a mother and, at the same time, to opt for paid employment in the labor market without becoming economically dependent on their male partners or the state. While many scholars assume there is emerging a changed and probably increasingly pluralist model of the division of labor between the sexes, which will gradually replace the male breadwinner model, Catherine Hakim (1995) argues that this assumption is one of several myths about women's employment. In her analysis of female full-time work rates in Great Britain and Western Europe, she finds that the perception of a narrowing gap in labor-market participation between women and men is mistaken: First, she notes that the rate of female employment since WWII, particularly with regard to full employment and to married women, did not increase, but that female labor force participation and full-time work rates have remained rather steady from the mid-1900s until the present. Second, female job commitment and dedication to careers remain significantly weaker than those of men. Third, the assumption of a childcare barrier to working women and the belief in both the exploitation of part-time workers and in female working instability further the myth of women as victims of the employment market

Barbara Hobson has calculated, based on the Luxembourg Income Study, that the share of economically independent women across Western industrialized countries is still a minority. If economic independence is measured by women in egalitarian marriages with earnings differences of less than 10 percent (in the mid-1980s), only in Sweden did more than 10 percent of women fall into that category, followed by the United States with 9.6 percent.Only 6.2 percent of German women achieved an income no less than 10 percent below that of their husbands. Women's economic dependence can be supposed to be always less the result of female inactivity in paid employment and, instead, more related to the increasing share of women opting for part-time employment: according to data provided by the E.C. Childcare Network from 1993, the employment rate of mothers aged twenty to thirty-nine, with at least one child under eleven, was highest in Denmark (74 percent) and Portugal (70 percent) and lowest in Ireland (34 percent) and Spain (35 percent), with Germany (West 46 percent, East 69 percent) being in between (Rubery, Smith, and Fagan 1998). EUROSTAT reported that in 1997, in the EU-13 (except Denmark and Sweden), 24 percent of women with at least one child under fifteen years of age were employed part time, compared with 32 percent in full-time work, with 36 percent being economically inactive, and 8 percent unemployed. Hence, to the degree to which wage differentials between full- and part-time work are significant and sex-related patterns of labor-market segregation are in place, both explain the economic dependency of women with dependent children.

In contrast, Rosemary Crompton, in her comparative study of women's employment patterns in Norway, France, the Czech Republic, and the United Kingdom, found that variations in male-female wage differentials were largely unrelated to the proportion of female part-time work (compare, Crompton 1998, 175). While at the beginning of the 1990s, the share of female part-time work in Norway (47 percent) and in the United Kingdom (45 percent) were similar,[19] male-female wage differentials did not only vary significantly between both countries,[20] but they even increased in the period from 1975 to 1991/1992.

These wage differentials also affect female and male employment distribution across the public and the private sector. Janet Gornick and Jerry A. Jacobs, in a seven-country comparison, have explored the influence of government employment on the gender gap in earnings. Although, they did not study part-time work but only full-time labor and, although not including Norway, but Sweden and the

United Kingdom, their findings shed some light on public/private earnings differentials and their variations across liberal and social democratic welfare regimes. In particular, they found that public employment provided relatively few but high-paying jobs for women in liberal welfare states, in the United Kingdom with 21 percent of the women (14 percent of the men) working in the public, and 79 percent of the women (86 percent of the men) being employed in the private sector. In social democratic welfare states, government positions were much more numerous compared with private jobs, and it was especially women who held them: in Sweden, 60 percent of working women were in the public sector (23 percent men), while only 40 percent of the women (77 percent of the men) worked in the private sector. On the other hand, the public sector in Sweden paid relatively less than public jobs in the United Kingdom (Gornick and Jacobs 1997).

While Swedish government statistics show that nearly all Swedish fathers take "daddy days" and that about one-half take paid parental leave, studies on the private sector demonstrated that here fathers were less likely to take family leave than men working in the public sector (Haas and Hwang 1995). The major obstacles for this gap are in the gendered nature of work organization in the private sector. A 1992 law required that by 1993, one-fourth of all private companies and half of all companies with more than 200 employees submit an annual plan to promote gender equality in the workplace and to induce fathers to take parental leave.

It is to be assumed, hence, that women's economic independence—particularly if they have dependent children—is a function of a combination of at least three developments: (a) wage politics targeted at reducing gender bias in pay equity; (b) working time regimes, in particular with parental leave regulations and part-time schedules for parents with dependent children; and (c) company provisions supporting equal parenthood and, in particular, men's usage of family leave benefits in the private sector. All of these developments can hardly be expected to be the result of the "free play of the market forces". Rather, they require state regulations and legal frameworks.

Legal Frameworks for Reconciling Employment and Carework

Evaluating the family policies of twelve European EC countries "from a female perspective . . . to better understand women's life chances, integrity and autonomy" Ulla Bjornberg took a closer look at the interaction of taxation schemes with other regulatory policies (1993, 3ff). In general, women in the EC, she admitted, were granted formal rights to employment and to keep their job when they had children, and men were granted leave when they became fathers. In reality, however, she found that women's economic dependence on men was rather reinforced as a result of the joint effects of taxation schemes, allowance regulations, and legal rights that allow women to reconcile the responsibilities of employment and family, and chronic shortages of available child care (Bjornberg 1993). Which are then the legal frameworks conducive to reconcile paid work in the economy and care responsibilities in the private sphere?

Diane Sainsbury, in her comparative analysis of gender, equality, and welfare states in Sweden, the United States, the United Kingdom, and the Netherlands, identified social rights and entitlements as policy mechanisms responsible for excluding women from or granting them access to welfare resources. She found that social rights based on citizenship or residence showed fewest stratifying effects, while welfare entitlements do have stratifying influences on women depending on whether women's access to benefits is granted to them primarily as wives, as mothers, or as workers with a given labor-market status (Sainsbury 1996).

For measuring the extent to which the welfare regimes with their state/market mixes support the reconciliation of paid and care work, Janet Gornick, Marcia Meyers, and Katherin Ross have constructed a score measuring social policies that support the employment of mothers with preschool children. This scheme is based on sixteen indicators, including parental leave regulation, the existence of childcare facilities, and the scheduling of public education (Gornick et al. 1997; see table 12.1, column 5). In their ranking—based on data from the mid-1980s by the Luxembourg Income Study—France and Italy outperform all of the Scandinavian countries, with the United States, Norway, the United Kingdom, and the Netherlands ranking last.

The Dutch case, where during the 1990s public childcare facilities have been considerably developed, illustrates "that a positive relation between women's autonomy and public childcare should not be taken as self-evident" (Bussemaker 1998, 91). Bussemaker argues that the perception that childcare was both undesirable and generally unnecessary in a well-developed welfare state like the Netherlands, while still prevalent in the 1960s, had been transformed by the 1990s with the notion that public daycare was immoral, being "now replaced by a notion of day care as an instrument of socioeconomic political policy and a means to combat the waste of women's human capital and investments in education" (89). The dominant rationale was now one of efficiency, with a hidden assumption that care and labor constituted a zero-sum relation, so that the less women were compelled to care for their children at home, the more the female labor-market supply will increase. From a normative position, feminists criticized this rationale of economic efficiency for not providing public space to discuss moral and ethical dimensions of care (Sevenhuijsen 1993). The role of fathers, they argued, was not taken up as an issue of discussion, rather childcare provisions were exclusively seen as instrumental to women's labor-market participation.

Table 12.1 summarizes some of the measures and data reported in the preceding comparative assessments.

_____ Table 12.1_____

	Public spending for families & children[1] %	Family support 36 policies/ aver. score[2]	Parent/ Non-parent poverty reduction[3] rank	Women's economic dependency[4] %	Supporting the employment of mothers[5]
Austria	11, 0 (3, 3)				6
Belgium	7, 7 (2, 3)	5.1	6		3
Denmark	12, 0 (4, 1)	7.0	7		5
Finland	12, 9 (4, 2)		4		1
France	8, 5 (2, 6)	3.7	3		8
Germany	7, 2 (2, 1)	8.0	9	49, 3 (1984)	
Greece		14.3			
Ireland	11, 2 (2, 2)	13.1			2
Italy	3, 4 (0, 8)	10.3			7
Luxemb.	12, 8 (3, 2)	3.8	5		9
Netherl.	4, 4 (1, 4)	9.4	8	68, 2 (1984)	11
Norway		4.8		25, 0 (1979)	
Portugal	5, 1 (1, 1)	11.3			
Spain	1, 8 (0, 4)	12.8			4
Sweden	11, 2 (4, 0)	5.3	2	11, 2 (1981)	10
UK	8, 7 (2, 4)	7.6	1	32, 6 (1979)	12
USA		14.9	10	29, 5 (1986)	

_____

[1] Public transfers 1995 for families and children, in % of total social expenditure (as % of GDP); Source: Eurostat 1998a

[2] Average score, calculated on the basis of 36 different family policy programs, including housing subsidies; scores ranging from 1 (most generous) to 17 (least generous); Source: Bradshaw et al. 1993

[3] Rank order according to parent/nonparent poverty reduction rate, based on Luxembourg Income Study 1984–1987, from 1 (highest reduction) to 10 (lowest reduction) (Meyers, Gornick, and Ross, this volume);

[4] Economic dependency of married women from husbands, measured as intrahousehold income inequality between women and men; source: Luxembourg Income Study (Hobson 1993: 173)

[5] Rank order of strength of public policies supporting the employment for mothers with pre-school children, based on parental leave regulation, the existence of child care facilities, and the scheduling of public education; from 1 (strongest) to 12 (weakest) (Gornick et al. 1997).

Models for Gender-Sensitive Social Welfare Policy

These empirical assessments of crossnational patterns of distributing child costs, of supporting family policy packages, of reducing family and maternal poverty rates, of enhancing women's economic independence, and of supporting the employment of mothers are by no means exhaustive. A number of criteria have been formulated that cannot be matched with available empirical and comparative data. Table 12.1 reveals, however, two things:

First, the empirical patterns point to the fact that indicators that are conventionally used in comparative social welfare research such as social security spending in percent of Gross National Product (GNP) are not sufficient for capturing the picture of gender inequalities that are a consequence of labor-market dynamics, as well as of public policymaking.

The second finding is that the empirical patterns described in table 12.1 do not neatly correspond to the established welfare regime typologies. On one hand, they do not fit with the distinction that Gösta Esping-Andersen (1999) made between the conservative/corporatist, liberal and social-democratic regime types that is based on the principle of decommodification. The United Kingdom, as a case of a liberal welfare regime, for instance, performs better than Finland and Sweden with regard to its parental/nonparental poverty reduction rate (table 12.1, column 3), while France, as a case of a conservative-corporatist welfare regime, outperforms Denmark, Norway, and Sweden with respect to its score in thirty-six family support policies (table 12.1, column 2). On the other hand, although gender-based typologies of breadwinner regimes have included the United Kingdom together with Germany and the Netherlands into the category of the strong breadwinner model (Ostner 1995; Ostner and Lewis 1995), women's economic dependency appears to be much less pronounced in the United Kingdom than in Germany and above all in Holland. Regarding France (classified as a moderate-breadwinner model), it appears contradictory that French public supports for the employment of mothers rank first, followed second by Italy, ahead of Denmark and the other Scandinavian countries (table 12.1, column 5).

This misfit between both, the power resources typologies of welfare regimes, and the feminist breadwinner models can be attributed to the fact that policy incentives to enhance a two breadwinner model and to increase maternal employment by no means appear to be restricted to social-democratic, moderate-breadwinner models of welfare regimes such as Sweden, Norway, Finland, or Denmark. Instead, public policymakers have effectively adopted them elsewhere, for instance, in France, Italy, and the United Kingdom. Such policies have, instead, remained so far marginal or absent in Belgium and Germany—both relying still primarily on the male breadwinner model with mothers expected to be carers (Scheiwe 1999).

Feminist critiques of Scandinavian welfare states—such as Anette Borchorst's—have brought woman-friendliness into question and—such as Yvonne Hirdman's—make use of the term "public patriarchy." Deborah Figart argues that although family leave policy in Sweden is the most progressive in the world, women there use part-time jobs to balance work and family responsibilities and, as a result, frequently must accept dead-end jobs that reinforce their occupational segregation (Figart 1998). On the other hand, Ulla Bjornberg emphasizes that women's dependence on men is reinforced in the other EU-member states much more than in Denmark, Sweden, Finland, or Norway, due to the combined effects of tax systems, allowance regulations, and lack of childcare facilities that constitute barriers to women's employment when they have children (Bjornberg 1993).

As the comparative assessments included in table 12.1 show, other countries have also made relative progress toward a more gender-sensitive social welfare policy mix. For instance, in Italy and France, where policies are based on constructions of gender differences rather than abstract notions of equality interpreted as sameness, during the 1980s and 1990s, socialist and social democratic policy makers have developed welfare policy mixes that have enhanced the employment opportunities and protections of mothers. While Mediterranean welfare states have been misinterpreted in the past as backward and defective, it has been overlooked that, for instance in Italy, certain categories of workers and broader categories of the population have achieved a relatively high level of protection, among them certain categories of single or divorced mothers (Trifiletti 1999).

Mechthild Veil (1997), in her comparison of social and family policy in France, Sweden, and Germany, concludes that the construction of women's social rights in the European Union could benefit from the experiences of such culturally different regimes. It should build on France, she argues, because here the best arrangement for reconciling work and family has been developed; on Sweden where the public sector is important for women's employment; and on Germany with its tradition of an autonomous women's movement. After the adoption of the Maastricht Treaty on Political and Monetary Union in 1993, however, the question arises and is placed in the center of feminist debates in Europe, whether the model of a gender-sensitive social welfare regime will have a future under the joint pressures of global economic competition, European integration, and the denationalization of governance. Only within this complex web of social, economic, and political challenges that the international context poses to national welfare systems can one understand their current crises and better assess their ambivalent impacts.

Degendering Care and Engendering Freedom in the Context of the European Union? New Constraints and Opportunities for Social Welfare Reforms

The necessity for welfare state transformation has intensified in the European Union, given that structural changes generally characteristic of postindustrial societies—ageing populations, women's entrance in the labor force, and changing functions of families—have combined with problems that are more specific to European countries, such as extremely low fertility rates, a slowdown of economic productivity in the 1990s, and high structural unemployment. Ultimately, pressures on national welfare systems have further increased in Europe after the Maastricht Treaty, with the preparation of member states for the Economic and Monetary Union and the adoption of a fiscal stability pact. These new constraints that derive from governance in the multilevel process of joint decision making in the European Union entail also new issues for the feminist welfare debate: Do strategies of degendering care and engendering economic freedom have a future thanks to the corporatist problem-solving capacity of multilevel governance in the European Union within the domain of social policy (Falkner 1998) or, more particular, thanks to mainstreaming as a recent innovative approach of EU equal opportunity policy development (Schunter-Kleemann 1999)? Or are such visions doomed to fail due to requirements for convergence between the more generous and the more minimal social welfare regimes in EU-member states?

The transformation of national systems of social welfare that became visible during the 1990s has triggered some of the most controversial debates that European integration has provoked so far among political parties in general, and feminists in particular. Traditionally, the Left typically advocated the protection of the welfare state and the expansion of social services in the midst of market failures, while the Right proposed to free the market of welfare state failures and reinforce the family. In the European Union, neither alternative seems viable. Conservative governments—despite their rhetoric—frequently failed with their retrenchment strategies aimed at reducing the size and reach of the welfare state because of the resistance of domestic groups that defended the status quo. Ironically, social democratic leaders in Sweden, Italy, the United Kingdom, and Germany have performed more successfully in restricting public expenditure and cutting down social expenses (compare, Mahon 1998).

Ultimately, the European Central Bank acts as a watchdog guarding domestic household discipline and monetary stability, thus restricting the domestic maneuvre spaces for expansive social welfare reform policies. In this context, the realignment of social welfare states remains the crucial strategy for adapting EU-member states to new environmental pressures. As Mary Ruggie puts it, policymakers who adopt strategies of realignment remain actively involved in social provisions, acting less as providers and more as overseers of broader-based social provisions, experimenting with alternative forms of social regulation, with new roles for both the state and for social actors (Ruggie 1996). Feminist analysts of the European Union debate whether EU-social policies and, in particular, gender-equality policies provide a framework that might effectively enhance gender equality in domestic welfare regimes.

The principal actors who formed the European Communities in the 1950s were Christian democrats from the conservative-welfare regime type (France, Germany, Italy), with the only Scandinavian member state with a social democratic welfare regime between 1973 and 1995 being Denmark. Thus, EC social policy regulations were heavily biased toward the social doctrine, with strong emphasis on the family and the principle of subsidiarity (Borchorst 1993). It was notable, however, that the Community did not embrace such conservative welfare policies. Instead, the Community as well as the European Union supported the integration of women into the labor market. Treaties and social policies included equal pay and equal treatment in social insurance schemes, childcare, fourteen weeks of paid maternity leave (following Art. 119 of the Treaty of Rome; compare, directives issued on gender equality and women's working rights from 1975 to 1986). The Amsterdam Treaty that was adopted in 1997 reinforced gender-equality regulations by formalizing principles of nondiscrimination and gender equality (Liebert 1999).

Feminists see national social welfare regimes to be under pressure from European integration across several main frontiers (Schunter-Kleemann 1990).[21] The most visible one is where EU-social policies directly affect national social welfare and labor-market regimes. The second, less visible frontier, is where the unintended consequences of European Union policies conducive to the Single Market and to Economic and Monetary Union indirectly influence national welfare regimes. However, welfare retrenchment, for instance in Great Britain, appears to have been less a consequence of European integration, but rather of changes in social security policies that the conservative governments adopted, along with growth in social exclusion and poverty in the 1980s and 1990s.[22]

More recently, feminists have started to explore a third frontier relevant to gender welfare, namely the sexual politics involved in the Single European Market, where sexual trafficking and the trading of pornography alter the boundaries of national policy making (Elman 1996). The controversial issue among feminists is how to evaluate these new trends in European integration that threaten to erode and subvert national welfare policy regimes with unpredictable consequences from the perspective of gender equality.

As a consequence of European Union equal opportunity policies, the Danish European Union critic Anette Borchorst expects an increase in differences among women. EC equal opportunity regulations will magnify inequalities, enabling women with higher education to compete directly with men, while further marginalizing and disadvantaging those employed part time—either in the public sector under the threat of retrenchment or locked within lower and badly paid segments of the private labor market. With public services being cut, these women might also be those expected to carry a heavier burden of unpaid work in the family. As an overall effect of European integration, Borchorst argues, the dualism between workers with secure full-time jobs and workers outside or only partly attached to the labor market will be enhanced, a dualism she sees as heavily structured along gender lines (Borchorst 1993). Despite the difficulties to construct a common position "as women," in Denmark more than in most other EU-member states, such critical feminist perspectives have found space in the public debate (Bertone 1998).

Other feminist European Union analysts from a British, Italian, or Spanish perspective arrive at more ambiguous and even at some optimistic assessments (Rossilli 1997; Mazey 1998; Valiente 1999; Walby 1999a, 1999b). Sylvia Walby, for instance, claims that feminist analyses of European integration often underestimate the significance of EU gender-equality norms for domestic policies. In her view, the social powers of the European Union derive from its nature as "a new regulatory state" that has made significant changes to the governance of gender relations by developing equal opportunity policies (Walby 1999a; 1999b). The impact of European Union equal opportunities directives and jurisdiction were underestimated for three reasons: (a) the traditional focus on dimensions of the social welfare state rather than on social regulation, (b) the theorization of gender relations through the lens of the family and welfare rather than in relation to employment, and (c) the underestimation of the power of law: "Employment is likely to become more rather than less important in shaping women's opportunities. Hence policies which address inequalities in employment are of fundamental and increasing significance for gender relations," representing "an increasingly significant response to continuing demands for gender justice" (Walby 1999b, 76–77).

Assuming as basic norms for a gender-sensitive welfare regime the two principles that this chapter (and book) has outlined—the "degendering of care" and the "en-gendering of freedom"—the crucial question is what type of new perspectives and challenges the European Union offers for a redefinition of citizenship that is based on both these norms. Does the European Union present rather a set of constraints or of opportunities with respect to such gender-sensitive welfare reform options? On one hand, because recent European Union legislation and jurisdiction have definitely crossed the threshold between the sphere of paid productive employment and the reproductive sphere (namely with the two directives on maternal protection and on parental leave), it will only be a matter of time for gendered patterns of reproduction to be brought into question. On the other hand, the European Union treaties that are based on the four freedoms— freedom of workers, freedom of movement, freedom of capital, and freedom of services—constitute a fundamental framework of legal opportunity structures within which structural constraints still hamper the development of women's positive economic freedom.

Summary

If gender equality is relatively advanced in parts of the European Union, if social welfare reforms are in fact women's and gender issues—affecting entrenched interests and values held by women and being shaped by women's distinct economic behaviours—and if female constituencies make a difference in national and European politics, why is it then that perspectives based on gender equality are strikingly missing in public debates as much as in political agendas for welfare reforms? Where are the women, and what are their needs regarding ongoing transformations of national welfare regimes and the emergence of a postnational world of welfare capitalism in the European Union?

These gender gaps that characterized public and academic welfare reform debates in EU-member states during the 1990s appear paradoxical. A number of scholars have given compelling reasons why policymakers or advisers should not dismiss gender-sensitive assessments of alternative welfare reform strategies. First, following Paul Pierson's (1996) proposition that welfare retrenchment policies are constrained by their path-dependency in European, and especially in Scandinavian, countries—ranked worldwide as the most woman-friendly regimes, with top positions in the scales of gender development and "gender empowerment" (U.N. 1999)—reformers of the welfare state should be warned to find their efforts limited by those institutions and organized groups that try to protect past achievements in gender development and empowerment. Second, there is the research on social welfare regimes in Europe from women's, gender, or feminist perspectives that provides evidence why studies of social welfare reforms should also assess impacts on women and gender hierarchies, given the changing norms and behaviours that women bring into the welfare reform politics game, be it as political decision makers, in the labor market, vis-à-vis the state, or in the divisions of domestic labor. Finally, public support to the European Union declined in member states during the 1990s, with Euroskeptic attitudes especially entrenched in Scandinavian mass publics but also in other EU-member states (Liebert 1999). In these contexts, feminist critiques of European integration have pointed to the double democratic deficit of European Union politics and to the controversial merits and real deficiencies of a Social Europe, with negative impacts being expected for national systems of social security and welfare and on the status that women have attained in them (Mushaben 1994; Ostner and Lewis 1995).

As plausible explanations for this paradox of academic and mass public silences on gender and women's issues in social welfare reform debates during the 1990s in Europe, two alternative hypotheses come to mind: On one hand, it could be argued that "state feminism" (McBride Stetson and Mazur 1995), the increase in social welfare expenditure and the expansion of female labor-market participation had already achieved such a high level of an egalitarian gender order that claims for more woman-friendly or gender-sensitive welfare reforms would seem pointless and the gender-equality rhetoric might have become simply obsolete.[23] On the other hand, it has to be objected that empirical assessments of the gender sensitivity of welfare regimes still show large gaps and deficiencies along several dimensions, even in Scandinavian and, above all, in Anglo-American countries. In this perspective, claims of a more woman-friendly welfare state necessarily to clash with the dominant discourses of welfare regime reform.

Certainly, the normative premises underlying the conceptions of degendering care and engendering freedom in a gender-just welfare state are too distinct as not to collide with the norms that are enshrined in established welfare state institutions. On the normative grounds of gender equity, they reject any variety of social welfare policy conducive to reinforcing women's dependencies and gender hierarchies. Furthermore, freedom rights constituted not from the perspective of the male working citizen but from that of women's choice, such as Nancy Hirschmann (this volume) formulates them; or notions of citizenship and of a state based on the recognition of caring, such as Joan Tronto (this volume) conceptualizes them, obviously do not fit easily into the frameworks of public discourses on welfare state realignment and retrenchment.

First, policy proposals derived from this model of a gender-just welfare regime involve claims for strengthening public responsibilities for regulating and changing gender relations, especially regarding the reconciliation of individual care responsibilities with paid employment in the private sector. Second, the expansion of welfare state services or transfers would obviously clash with neoliberal calls for privatization and budget cuts. On the other hand, arguments for cost efficiency can be developed to demonstrate that although new types of expenditures might be involved, gender welfare reform devices will be more efficient, sustainable, and equitable (MacDonald 1998). On these normative grounds and because of conflicts of interest that are more intense the more fiscal pressures increase, and to the degree that these normative and interest conflicts between gender-sensitive and gender-neutral welfare reform discourses cannot be accommodated, it appears plausible that the former become silenced.

In this chapter I have aimed, first, at reconceptualizing the vision and idea of a woman-friendly social welfare regime by drawing on the notions of freedom and care. Second, I have used the revised concept of a gender-sensitive welfare regime to reconstruct the welfare-regime triangle, based on a mix of state-market-household interactions. Third, I have illustrated this model empirically, by drawing on feminist comparative assessments of welfare regimes in the European Union and the United States, from the double perspective of engendering freedom and degendering care. Fourth, I have formulated some conclusions concerning the viability of the model of a gender-sensitive welfare state under the constraints and in the context of the new opportunities that derive from processes of European governance. The question whether a gender-just welfare state could be redesigned in the context of EMU (Economic and Monetary Union) such that care and freedom could be revalued in this framework was answered with reservations, but within the search, some positive trends and new opportunities arose. After all, the European Union offers the framework of a regulatory supranational state, with novel sets of incentives, instruments, and institutions—such as the European Court of Justice—that enhance or even require the transformation of national welfare state. Feminist European Union analysts remain divided on the significance and full range of implications of these changes. But it is arguable the case that any model of a gender-sensitive welfare regime in Europe will have to take into account the new mode of governing gender relations emerging in the multilevel system of the European Union.

Notes

1. The UN *Human Development Report* (1999) provides two yearly ranking lists, calculated for about 130 countries. First, a "gender development index" based on differences in female and male share of earned income, life expectancy, adult literacy rates, and combined primary, secondary, and tertiary gross enrolment ratios. Second, a "gender empowerment measure," based on percent of positions held by women in parliament, as administrators and managers, as professional and technical workers, and including the earned income share.

2. Major alternatives range from the strategy of market-oriented destatalization, the option of a tax-financed basic income, to demands for a further expansion of the social state and proposals for incremental reform.

3. For such a gender-blind assessment of welfare reform policy alternatives discussed in Germany that neither considers gender-based welfare reform strategies nor does it include any gender related criteria for assessing the alternative devices, compare. ZeS (Centre for Social Policy Research) 1998.

4. In her state of the art account of feminist comparative policy analysis, Amy Mazur (1999) draws on what she calls the path-breaking concept of the woman-friendly welfare state as a contrast to define her own key concept feminist policies. While her concept presupposes that policymakers follow explicitly a feminist agenda, this is not necessarily the case with woman-friendly state policies.

5. Gender legislation differences: (a) gender neutral legislative reforms consist of reformulating laws in gender neutral terms; (b) gender recognition legislation assumes that equality can be achieved only by taking certain differences between women and men into account; (c) gender reinforcement legislation is based on an ideology of separate gender roles and the principle of care, upgrading wifely and motherly labor, and making unpaid domestic work the basis of entitlement to standard social security benefits; (d) gender reconstruction legislation "strives for equality through transforming the strict division of labor between the sexes so that the tasks of earning and caring are commonly shared by women and men" (Sainsbury 1996, 173–174).

6. Under the pressures of modernization, and due to the increased status of women, the social institutions of marriage and family have changed significantly. This trend is indicated by lower marriage rates, higher rates of nonmarital cohabitation, of marital dissolution, of single households, and of female-headed or single-parent households (compare, Ryan, Hughes, and Hawdon 1998, 225).

7. Family wages and family-based welfare programs, however, continue to be biased against unattached individuals or unmarried couples, with tax systems allowing income-splitting between spouses; social policies institutionalizing a male family wage, or by differentiating between male and female survivors, etc.

8. Defining care as "a species activity that includes everything that we do to maintain, continue, and repair our 'world' so that we can live in it as well as possible" (Tronto, this volume), this notion would suggest to include also paid work. Although Tronto

does not consider this possibility explicitly, such a strategy would allow her to revalue not only (certainly undervalued) unpaid care activities but also to reassess (possibly overvalued) paid work, both not from the perspective of profitability, but from their perspective of caring for a liveable world.

9. Jane Lewis argued in her critique of "The three worlds of welfare capitalism" that women could only enter Gösta Esping-Andersen's analysis, in so far as they entered the paid labor market (Lewis 1993, 14).

10. Joint taxation of spouses prevails in Germany and the United States, while Sweden, Canada, the Netherlands, Italy, and Australia have individual taxation; but in the latter, many deductions and credit provisions are based on total spousal income, presuming a support relationship and encouraging dependency (MacDonald 1998).

11. Feminist economists, feminist philosophers, and sociologists continue to disagree on whether to focus on dynamics derived from global economic changes or on domestic social demographic transformations, whether to choose a cultural or social constructivism or societal stratification approach. Feminist constructivists, in particular, consider issues such as the formation of identities at the intersections of gender, class, race, and sexual orientation and gender-differentiated influences of institutional arrangements and power structures as central to the heart of welfare state analysis.

12. Engendering economic citizenship, hence, means not only having opportunities for paid work for both genders, but presupposes working conditions and social rights and protections that enable women, in particular mothers and parents, and in general all individuals with family obligations, to reconcile full and equal labor-market participation and family life.

13. Feminist economists have argued that the costs of reproductive labor still have to be dealt with and that the resources used and produced in the reproductive sphere need to be incorporated into any efficiency analysis, for instance, Nilufer Cagatay, Diane Elson, Caren Grown, Isabella Bakker, Ingrid Palmer, Martha MacDonald, and Lourdes Beneria have contributed to measuring unpaid work, to developing extended national accounts, and to including reproduction in macroeconomic models. These models can be used as a basis for answering the question how to "reward" these activities in terms of social welfare benefits.

14. Martha MacDonald, accordingly, claims that the criteria of "equity" must include gender equity, with redistribution effects being not only broken down by gender, but also including intrahousehold inequalities; that the standard of "efficiency" must take also the unpaid resources used in reproductive work into account; and that an analysis of work incentives has to take women's labor-market opportunities and childcare responsibilities into account (1998, 20).

15. Assessments of social welfare systems from a gender perspective frequently adopt "benefit parity" between both genders as the measurement standard. Accordingly, women's public pension quality, for instance, is measured in terms of the parity produced by pension benefits, with earnings related pension systems generally faring worse for women—such as the United States, Austria, Belgium, and Germany; with universal systems producing full parity, such as Australia, Denmark, Finland, Iceland, Ireland, and the Netherlands; and with combined systems in between (Davis, Hill, and Tigges 1995).

16. Defamilization of welfare policies has been defined as a device for granting institutional and financial supports to individuals independently from family status and, in particular, to women and mothers independently from the male breadwinner family

(Shaver and Bradshaw 1995). A number of authors have emphasized this necessity of women's autonomy and social security independent from their family status (Sainsbury 1996; Bussemaker 1997; Lister 1998). Martha MacDonald (1998) claims that policies should not be biased in favour of particular family arrangements or assume a particular family arrangement. Jane Lewis and Ilona Ostner (1992) focus on the strength with which states adhere to the traditional idea of a gendered division of labor, by means of tax and social security schemes, public provisions of social services regarding childcare and the pattern of married women's participation in labor markets.

17. While the number of marriages has decreased during the past twenty-five years in the EU-15, from 7.6 per 1,000 inhabitants in 1970 to 5.1 in 1995, in the same period the divorce rate has nearly doubled, from 1.0 to 1.8 per 1,000 inhabitants (Eurostat 1998b).

18. In this eight-nation study, based on data from 1973–1976, except for Finland, marital status was found to be a significant predictor of general-life satisfaction in Britain, Germany, Netherlands, Austria, the United States, Italy, and Switzerland; gender appeared to be significant only in the Netherlands, Italy, and Switzerland (Ryan, Hughes, and Hawdon 1998).

19. Only 24 percent of the women in France and 9.5 percent in the Czech Republic did part-time work.

20. Male/female wage differentials were measured by percentage of female-to-male hourly rates among manual workers and manufacturing: while in Norway, this rate raised from 78 percent in 1975 to 87 percent in 1991–1992; in the United Kingdom, it was at 68 percent, remaining nearly stable throughout the whole period. Gender wage gaps in France and the Czech Republic ranged between 79 percent and 75 percent (Crompton 1998).

21. To my knowledge, Susanne Schunter-Kleemann was the first to distinguish between direct and indirect effects of European integration with respect to the dynamics of national welfare regimes. Focusing on the indirect ones, she predicted that the overall effects of the integration process on the balance between market, state, family would affect gender relations and women's control of their options (Schunter-Kleemann 1990).

22. These policy changes included growth in means-testing; radical cutbacks in National Insurance schemes, pensions, family and child tax allowances, unemployment benefits; and changes in taxation (Walker and Walker 1997).

23. M.G. Schmidt claims that even under conditions of stagnating or declining public expenditures on social welfare, gender differences in social welfare benefits would diminish, simply as a function of the narrowing gap of male/female labor-market participation (Schmidt 1998). However, considering the combined effects of gender-related wage differentials and distribution of part-time work, as well as the typically more discontinuous patterns of female labor-market participation due to the unequal division of care work within the family, this claim appears highly unrealistic, even in Scandinavian countries.

References

Abrahamson, Peter E. 1991. Welfare and poverty in the Europe of the 1990s. *International Journal of Health Service* 21, 2:237–264.

Abramowitz, Mimi. 1988. *Regulating the lives of women: Social welfare policy from colonial times to the present.* Boston: South End Press.

Abramowitz, M. 1996. *Regulating the lives of women.* Boston: South End Press.

Acker, F., and J. Gotteley. 1996. *Draft report.* Paris: Ministère des Affaires Sociales (SESI).

Acs, Gregory, Norma Coe, Keith Watson, and Robert Lerman. 1998. *Does work pay? An analysis of the work incentives under TANF.* Washington, D.C.: Urban Institute.

Adams, C. T., and K. T. Winston. 1980. *Mothers at work: Public policies in the United States, Sweden, and China.* New York: Longman Inc.

Adler, M. 1993. *Disability among women on AFDC: An issue revisited.* Washington, D.C.: HHS Office of Community and Long-Term Health Policy.

Albiston, Catherine R., and Laura Beth Nielsen. 1995. Welfare queens and other fairy tales: Welfare reform and unconstitutional reproductive controls. *Howard Law Journal* 38, no. 3:473–519.

Alestalo, Matti, Sven Bislev, and Bengt Furaker. 1991. Welfare state employment in Scandinavia. In *The welfare state as employer,* J. Kolberg, ed. London: Armonk.

Amott, Teresa L. 1990. Black women and AFDC: Making entitlement out of necessity. In *Women, the state and welfare,* Linda Gordon, ed. Madison: University of Wisconsin Press.

Aronow, I. 1993. Doulas step in when mothers need a hand. *New York Times,* Westchester Weekly, 1 August.

As welfare rolls drop, request to charities rise. *New York Times,* 18 August 1998.

Austin, Jan, ed. 1996. *Congressional Quarterly Almanac 1995.* Washington, D.C.: Congressional Quarterly, Inc.

Austin, Jan, ed. 1997. *Congressional Quarterly Almanac 1996.* Washington, D.C.: Congressional Quarterly, Inc.

Bachu, A. 1993. *Fertility of American women.* Pub. No. P20–470. U.S. Bureau of the Census. Washington, D.C.: GPO.

Baier, A. 1987. The need for more than justice. In *Science, morality, and feminist theory*, Marsha Hanen and Kai Nielson, eds. Calgary: University of Calgary Press.

Baker, M. 1996. *Canadian family policies: Cross-national comparisons.* Toronto: University of Toronto Press.

Bane, Mary Jo, and David Ellwood, eds. 1994. *Welfare realities: From rhetoric to reform.* Cambridge, Mass.: Harvard University Press.

Bartky, Sandra Lee. 1990. *Femininity and domination: Studies in the phenomenology of oppression.* New York: Routledge.

Bell, D. 1976. *The cultural contradictions of capitalism.* New York: Basic Books.

Bell, Winifred. 1965. *Aid to dependent children.* New York: Columbia University Press.

Bergmann, Barbara R. 1986. *The economic emergence of women.* New York: Basic Books.

Bergmann, Barbara R. 1997. Government Support for families with children in the United States and France. *Feminist Economics* 3, 1:85–94.

Bergmann, Barbara R., and Heidi Hartmann. 1995. A welfare reform based on help for working parents. *Feminist economics* 1:85–89.

Berke, Richard. The 1994 elections: The voters. *New York Times*, 11 November 1994.

Berlin, Isaiah. 1971. Two concepts of liberty. In *Four essays on liberty.* New York: Oxford University Press.

Bickford, Susan. 1996. *The dissonance of democracy: Listening, conflict, and citizenship.* Ithaca, N.Y.: Cornell University Press.

Bjornberg, Ulla. 1993. Family policies in the EC countries from a female perspective. *Sociologisk Forskning* 30, 3:3–29.

Blackburn, Sheila. 1995. How useful are feminist theories of the welfare state? *Women's History Review* 4, 3: 369–394.

Blackstone, W. 1799. *Commentaries.* Oxford: Clarendon Press.

Blair, Diane D., and Jeanie R. Stanley. Forthcoming. What helps and what hurts: The effectiveness of women in adverse legislative environments. In *The impact of women in public office*, Susan J. Carroll, ed. Bloomington: Indiana University Press.

Blank, Rebecca. 1997. *It takes a nation: A new agenda for fighting poverty.* New York: Russell Sage Publisher.

Blau, D. M., and P. K. Robins. 1988. Childcare costs and family labor supply. *The Review of Economics and Statistics* 70, 3:374–381.

Blau, F., and M. A. Ferber. 1992. *The economics of women, men, and work.* Englewood Cliffs, N.J.: Prentice-Hall.

Bobo, Lawrence. 1998. Comments at panel on Du Bois's century: African-American political participation. Social Science History Association annual meeting, Chicago.

Boling, Patricia. 1996. *Privacy and the politics of intimate life.* Ithaca, N.Y.: Cornell University Press.

Bonner Koalition setzt Gesundheitsreform mit Kanzlermehrheit durch. *Der Tagesspiegel*, 13 June 1994.

Boo, Katherine. Braving welfare's new world. *Washington Post Weekly*, 23 December 1997.

Borchert, Jens. 1995. *Die konservative Transformation des Wohlfahrtstaates: Großbritannien, Kanada, die USA, und Deutschland im Vergleich.* Frankfurt: Campus Verlag.

Borchorst, Anette. 1994a. Welfare state regimes, women's interests and the EC. In *Gendering welfare states,* Diane Sainsbury, ed. Thousand Oaks, Calif.: Sage.

Borchorst, Anette. 1994b. The Scandinavian welfare state: Patriarchal, gender neutral, or woman-friendly? *International Journal of Contemporary Sociology* 31, 1:45–68.

Borchorst, Anette. 1998. Feminist thinking about the welfare state. In *Revisioning gender,* Beth Hess, et al., eds. Thousand Oaks, Calif.: Sage.

Borchorst, Anette, and Birte Siim. 1987. Women and the advanced welfare state: A new kind of patriarchal power? In *Women and the state: The shifting boundaries of public and private*, Anne Showstack Sassoon, ed. London: Hutchinson.

Boris, Eileen. 1995. The racialized gendered state: Constructions of citizenship in the United States. *Social Politics* 2,160–180.

Bradshaw, Jonathan, John Ditch, Hilary Holmes, and Peter Whiteford. 1993. A comparative study of child support in fifteen countries. *Journal of European Social Policy* 3, 4:255–271.

Brasher, Keith. Widest gap in incomes? Research Points to U.S. *New York Times*, 27 October 1995.

Braun, Helga, and Dörthe Jung. 1997. *Globale Gerechtigkeit? Feministische Debatte zur Krise des Sozialstaats*. Hamburg: Konkret Literatur Verlag.

Briscoe, D. "All work and no pay" world. *Times London*, 8 September 1992. Available from LEXIS-NEXIS/Times database.

Bubeck, Diemut. 1995. *Care, justice, and gender*. New York: Oxford University Press.

Bussemaker, Jet. 1998. Rationales of care in contemporary welfare states: The case of childcare in the Netherlands. *Social Politics* (spring): 70–96

Bussemaker, Jet, ed. 1999. *Citizenship and welfare state reform in Europe*. London: Routledge.

Bussemaker, Jet, and Kees van Kersbergen. 1994. Gender and welfare states: Some theoretical reflections. In *Gendering Welfare States*, Diane Sainsbury, ed. London: Sage.

Bussiere, Elizabeth. 1997. *(Dis)Entitling the poor: The Warren court, welfare rights, and the American political tradition*. State College: Pennsylvania State University Press.

Callaghan, P., and H. Hartmann. 1991. *Contingent work: A chart book on part-time and temporary employment*. Washington, D.C.: The Economic Policy Institute.

Canadian Childcare Federation. 1992. *Caring for a living: A study on wages and working conditions in Canadian Child Care*. Ottawa: Canadian Childcare Federation.

Casey, Kathleen, and Susan J. Carroll. 1998. Wyoming wolves and deadbeat dads: The impact of women members of Congress and welfare reform. Paper read at the annual meeting of the American Political Science Association, 3–6 September, Boston.

Casper, L. M., S. S. McLanahan, and I. Garfinkel. 1994. The gender-poverty gap: What we can learn from other countries. *American Sociological Review* 59:594–605.

Catanzarite, Lisa, and Vilma Ortiz. 1995. Racial/ethnic differences in the impact of work and family on women's poverty. *Research in Politics and Society* 5:217–237.

Center on Hunger, Poverty, and Nutrition Policy. 1995. *Statement on key welfare reform issues: The empirical evidence*. Boston, Mass.: Center on Hunger, Poverty and Nutrition Policy, Tufts University.

Chodorow, Nancy. 1978. *The reproduction of mothering: Psychoanalysis and the sociology of gender*. Berkeley: University of California Press.

Christopherson, Susan. Why do national labor market practices continue to diverge in a global economy? *Economic Geography* (forthcoming).

Christopherson, Susan. 1997. *Child care and elderly care: What occupational opportunities for women?* Labor Market and Social Policy Occasional Paper no. 27. Paris: OECD

Clayton, Richard, and Jonas Pontusson. 1998. Welfare-state retrenchment revisited: Entitlement cuts, public sector restructuring, and inegalitarian trends in advanced capitalist societies. *World Politics* 51:67–98.

Clemmitt, Marcia, Leslie Primmer, and Marjorie Sims. 1997. *The record: Gains and losses for women and families in the 104th Congress (1995–1996)*. Washington, D.C.: Women's Policy, Inc.

Clymer, Adam. White House and the G.O.P. announce deal to balance budget and trim taxes. *New York Times*, 29 July 1997.

Cochran, M., ed. 1993. *International handbook of child care policies and programs*. Westport, Conn.: Greenwood Press.

Cochrane, Allan, and Kevin Doogan. 1993. Welfare Policy: The dynamics of European Integration. *Politics and Policy* 21, 2:85–95.

Code, Lorraine. 1995. *Rhetorical spaces*. New York: Routledge.

Coder, J., L. Rainwater, and T. Smeeding 1989. Inequality among children and elderly in ten modern nations: The United States in an international context. *The American Economic Review* 79:320–324.

Colen, Shelee. 1985. "With respect and feelings": Voices of West Indian child care and domestic workers. In *All American women: Lines that divide, ties that bind*. New York: The Free Press.

Collins, Patricia Hill. 1990. *Black feminist thought: Knowledge, consciousness, and the politics of empowerment*. New York: Routledge.

Collins, Patricia Hill. 1994. Shifting the center: Race, class, and feminist theorizing about motherhood. In *Representations of motherhood*, Donna Bassin and Margaret Honey, eds. New Haven, Conn.: Yale University Press.

Commission of the European Communities. 1993. *Green Paper: European social policy: Options for the Union*. Brussels: Commission of the European Communities.

Congressional Caucus for Women's Issues. *Letter to conference committee on HR 4*, 11 October 1995.

Congressional Quarterly Weekly Report. 7 January 1997. Washington, D.C.: Congressional Quarterly, Inc.

Congressional Quarterly Weekly Report. 23 March 1997. Washington, D.C.: Congressional Quarterly, Inc.

Congressional Quarterly Weekly Report. 27 May 1995. Washington, D.C.: Congressional Quarterly, Inc.

Congressional Quarterly Weekly Report. 24 June 1995. Washington, D.C.: Congressional Quarterly, Inc.

Congressional Quarterly Weekly Report. 16 September 1995. Washington, D.C.: Congressional Quarterly, Inc.

Congressional Quarterly Weekly Report. 21 September 1996. Washington, D.C.: Congressional Quarterly, Inc.

Congressional Record. 104th Cong., 1st sess., 1995. Vol. 141 pt. 50.

Connelly, R. 1990. *The effects of child care costs on the labor force participation and AFDC recipiency of single mothers*. Discussion Paper No.920–90. Madison, Wis.: Institute of Research on Poverty.

Connelly, R. 1991. The importance of childcare costs to women's decision making. In *The economics of child care*, David M. Blau, ed. New York: Russell Sage Foundation.

Connelly, R. 1992. The effect of childcare costs on married women's labor force participation. *Review of Economics and Statistics* 74, 1:83–90.

Cruikshank, Barbara. 1994. The will to power: Technologies of citizenship and the war on poverty. *Socialist Review* 23, 4:29–35.

Culpitt, Ian. 1992. Citizenship and "moral generosity": Social needs, privatization, and social service contracting. In *Welfare and citizenship: Beyond the crisis of the welfare state?* London: Sage.

Dahlerup, Drude. 1987. Confusing concepts–confusing reality: A theoretical discussion of the patriarchal state. In *Women and the state: The shifting boundaries of public and private*, Anne Showstack Sassoon, ed. London: Hutchinson.

Dahn, Daniela. 1994. *Wir bleiben hier oder wem gehört der Osten*. Reinbek: Rowohlt.

Daly, Mary. 1994. Comparing welfare states: Towards a gender-friendly approach. In *Gendering welfare states*. Thousand Oaks, Calif.: Sage.

Danziger, S., T. Smeeding, and L. Rainwater. 1995. *The Western welfare state in the 1980s: Toward a new model of anti-poverty policy for families with children*. LIS Working Paper #128. Walferdange, Luxembourg: The Luxembourg Income Study.

Darling, R. B. 1983. Parent-professional interaction: The roots of misunderstanding. In *The family with a handicapped child: Understanding and treatment*. M. Seligman, ed. New York: Grune and Stratton.

Davidson, Joe. Welfare mothers stress importance of building self-esteem if aid system is to be restructured. *Wall Street Journal*, 12 May 1995.

Davis Hill, Dana, and Leann M. Tigges. 1995. Gendering welfare state theory: A cross-national study of women's public pension quality. *Gender and Society* 9, 1:99–119.

Davis, J. 1996. Enhanced earning capacity/human capital: The reluctance to call it property. *Women's Rights Law Reporter* 17:109.

Dawson, Michael. 1994. *Behind the mule: Race and class in African-American politics*. Princeton, N.J.: Princeton University Press.

Day, Jennifer Cheeseman. 1996. *Projections of the number of households and families in the United States: 1995 to 2010*. Washington, D.C.: U.S. Bureau of the Census, Current Population Reports.

DeParle, Jason. Despising welfare, Pitying its young. *New York Times*, 18 December 1994.

DeParle, Jason. Getting Opal Caples to work. *New York Times Magazine*, 24 August 1997.

DeParle, Jason. Shrinking welfare rolls leave record high share of minorities. *New York Times* electronic edition, 27 July 1998. [On-line] Available http://www.nytimes.com.

Deutscher Bundestag Protokol. Vol 13, 105, Bonn, 10 May 1996.

Department for Education and Employment. 1996. *United Kingdom contribution to OECD study on caring occupations*. London: DFEE.

Dex, S. 1992. Women's part-time work in Britain and the United States. In *Working part-time: Risks and opportunities*. B. Warme, K. Lundy, L. Lundy, eds. New York: Praeger.

Dietz, Mary. 1985. Citizenship with a feminist face: The problem with maternal thinking. *Political Theory* 13, 1:19–37.

Dionne, E. J. Up from the bottom. *Washington Post* electronic edition, 21 July 1998. [On-line] Available: http://www.washingtonpost.com/wp-adv/archives.

Dodson, Debra L., and Susan J. Carroll. 1991. *Reshaping the agenda: Women in state legislature*. New Brunswick, N.J.: Center for the American Women and Politics.

Dodson, Lisa. 1998. *Don't call us out of name: The untold lives of women and girls in poor America*. Boston: Beacon Press.

Dodson, Lisa, Pam Joshi, and Davida McDonald. 1998. *Welfare in transition: Consequences for women, families, and communities*. A report from the Radcliffe Public Policy Institute, Harvard University, Cambridge, Mass. October. [On-line] Available: http://www.radcliffe.edu/pubpol/wit.html.

Donahue, James P. The corporate welfare kings. *Washington Post Weekly*, 21–27 March 1994.

Drakich, J. 1989. In search of the better parent: The social construction of ideologies of fatherhood. *Canadian Journal of Women and Law* 3:83–87.

Dujon, Diane. 1996. Out of the frying pan: Reflections of a former welfare recipient. In *For crying out loud: Women's poverty in the United States*. Diane Dujon and Ann Withorn, eds. Boston: South End Press.

Duncan, Simon, and Ros Edwards. 1996. Lone mothers and paid work: Neighborhoods, local labor markets, and welfare state regimes. *Social Politics* (summer/fall): 195–221.

Dworkin, Ronald. 1977. *Taking rights seriously.* Cambridge: Harvard University Press.

Eardley, Tony, Johnathan Bradshaw, John Ditch, Ian Grough, and Peter Whiteford. 1996. *Social assistance in OECD countries: Country reports.* U.K. Department of Social Security Research Report nos. 46 and 47. London: HMSO.

Eardley, Tony, and Merrin Thompson. 1997. Does case mangement help unemployed job seekers? SPRC reports and Proceedings no 132. Sydney: Social Research Centre, University of New South Wales.

Eckardt, Thomas. 1997. *Arm in Deutschland: Eine sozialpolitische Bestandsaufnahme.* Munich: Guenter Olzog Verlag.

Edin, Kathryn J. 1991. Surviving the welfare system: How AFDC recipients make ends meet in Chicago. *Social Problems* 38, 4:462–474.

Edin, Kathryn J., and Laura Lein. 1997. *Making ends meet: How single mothers survive welfare and low-wage work.* New York: Russell Sage Foundation.

Edsall, Thomas Byrne, and Mary Edsall. 1991. *Chain reaction: The impact of race, rights, and taxes on American politics.* New York: W. W. Norton.

Eisenstein, Hester. 1996. *Inside agitators: Australian Femocrats and the State.* Philadelphia: Temple University Press.

Elliott, Marta. 1996. Impact of work, family, and welfare receipt on women's self-esteem in young adulthood. *Social Psychology Quarterly* 59, 1:80–95.

Ellwood. David. 1988. *Poor support.* New York: Basic Books.

Ellwood. David. 1996. Welfare reform as I knew it: When bad things happen to good policies. *The American Prospect* 26: 22–29. [On-line] Available: http://epn.org/prospect/26/26ellw.html.

Elman, Amy, ed. 1996. *Sexual politics in the European Union. The new feminist challenge.* Providence, Oxford: Berghahn Books

Elshtain, Jean Bethke. 1982. Feminism, family, and community. *Dissent* 29, 4:442–449.

Ergas, Y. 1990. Child-care policies in comparative perspective. In *Lone-parent families: The economic challenge,* OECD, ed. Paris: OECD.

Esping-Anderson, Gösta. 1990. *The three worlds of welfare capitalism.* Princeton, N.J.: Princeton University Press.

Esping-Andersen, Gösta. 1996a. *Welfare states at the end of the century: The impact of labour market, family and demographic change.* Working Paper, Working Party on Social Policy, 11–12 July. Paris: OECD.

Esping-Andersen, Gösta, ed. 1996b. *Welfare states in transition. National adaptations in global economies.* London: Sage.

Esping-Andersen, Gösta. 1996c. Welfare states without work: The impasse of labour shedding and familialism in continental European social policy. In *Welfare states in transition. National adaptations in global economies.* Gösta Esping-Anderson, ed. London: Sage.

Esping-Andersen, Gosta. 1999. *Social foundations of postindustrial economies.* New York: Oxford University Press.

Estin, A. L. 1993. Maintenance, alimony, and the rehabilitation of family care. *North Carolina Law Review* 71:776, 780.

Etzione, Amitai. 1998. The responsive communitarian platform. In *The essential communitarian reader.* A. Etzioni, ed. Lanham, Md.: Rowman and Littlefield.

Eurostat. 1995. *Les femmes et les hommes de l'Union Européenne: Un portrait statistique.* Luxembourg: Statistical Office of the European Communities.

Eurostat. 1998a. *Social protection expenditure and receipts 1980–1995*. Luxembourg: Statistical Office of the European Communities.

Eurostat. 1998b. *Living conditions in Europe: Selected social indicators*. Luxembourg: Statistical Office of the European Communities.

Falkner, Gerda. 1998. *EU social policy in the 1990s: Towards a corporatist policy community*. London: Routledge.

Figart, Deborah. 1998. It's about time: Will Europe solve the work/family dilemma? *Dollars and Sense* 215:27–31.

Finch, Janet. 1996. Family responsibilities and rights. In *Citizenship today: The contemporary relevance of T. H. Marshall*. London: UCL Press.

Finch, Janet, and Dulcie Groves. 1983. *A labour of love: Women, work, and caring*. London: Routledge.

Fineman, Martha A. 1991. Images of mothers in poverty discourses. *Duke Law Journal* 1991, no. 2:274–295.

Fineman, Martha A. 1995. *The neutered mother: The sexual family and other twentieth-century tragedies*. New York: Routledge.

Fisher, Berenice, and Joan C. Tronto. 1990. Toward a feminist theory of care. In *Circles of care: Work and identity in women's lives*. Emily Abel and Margaret Nelson, eds. Albany, N.Y.: SUNY Press

Flanders, Laura. 1996. Media lies: Media, public opinion, and welfare. In *For crying out loud: Women's poverty in the United States*. Boston: South End Press.

Flathman, Richard. 1987. *The philosophy and politics of freedom*. Chicago: University of Chicago Press.

Folbre, Nancy. 1994. *Who pays for the kids? Gender and the structures of constraint*. New York: Routledge.

Forster, M. 1993. Comparing poverty in 13 OECD countries: Traditional and synthetic approaches. In *Studies in Social Policy #10*. Paris: OECD.

Foucault, Michel. 1986. *The care of the self*. New York: Pantheon.

Fraser, Nancy, ed. 1989a. *Unruly practices: Power, discourse, and gender in contemporary social theory*. Minneapolis: University of Minnesota Press.

Fraser, Nancy. 1989b. Women, welfare and the politics of need. In *Unruly practices: Power, discourse, and gender in contemporary social theory*. Nancy Fraser, ed. Minneapolis: University of Minnesota Press.

Fraser, N. 1990. Struggle over needs: Outline of a socialist-feminist critical theory of late-capitalist political culture. In *Women, the state, and welfare*. Linda Gordon, ed. Madison: University of Wisconsin Press.

Fraser, Nancy. 1994. After the family wage: Gender equality and the welfare state. *Political Theory*, 22, 4:591–618.

Fraser, Nancy. 1997. *Justice interruptus, critical reflections on the "postsocialist" condition*. New York: Routledge.

Fraser, N. 1997. After the family wage: A postindustrial thought experiment. In *Justice interruptus: Critical reflections on the "postsocialist" condition*. New York: Routledge.

Fraser, Nancy, and Linda Gordon. 1992. Contract versus charity: Why is there no social citizenship in the United States? *Socialist Review* 22, 3:45–67.

Fraser, Nancy, and Linda Gordon. 1994a. "Dependency" demystified: Inscriptions of power in a keyword of the Welfare State. *Social Politics* (spring): 4–31.

Fraser, Nancy, and Linda Gordon. 1994b. A genealogy of dependency: Tracing a keyword of the U.S. welfare state. *Signs* 19:309–336.

Friedman, M. 1987. Beyond caring: The demoralization of gender. In *Science, Morality, and Feminist Theory.* Marsha Hanen and Kai Nielson, eds. Calgary, Canada: University of Calgary Press.

Friedman, T. L. Clinton concedes he erred on Baird nomination. *New York Times,* 23 January 1993.

Galston, W. 1998. A liberal-democratic case for the two parent family. In *The essential communitarian reader.* A. Etzioni, ed. Lanham, Md.: Rowman and Littlefield.

Garcia-Ramon, Maria Dolores, and Janice Monk, eds. 1996. *Women of the European Union: The politics of work and daily life.* London: Routledge.

Gardiner, Frances, and Monique Leijenaar. 1997. The timid and the bold: Analysis of the "woman-friendly state" in Ireland and the Netherlands. In *Sex equality policy in Western Europe.* F. Gardiner, ed. London: Routledge.

Gauthier, A. 1991. *Family policies in comparative perspective.* Discussion Paper No. 5. Oxford: Nuffield College, Centre for European Studies.

Gilens, Martin. 1996. "Race coding" and white opposition to welfare. *American Political Science Review* 90:593–604.

Gilens, Martin. 1999. *Why Americans hate welfare.* Chicago: University of Chicago Press.

Gilligan, Carol, and Grant Wiggins. 1984. The origins of morality in early childhood relationships. In *Mapping the Moral Domain.* Carol Gilligan, et al., eds. Cambridge: Harvard University Press.

Glass, Jennifer L., and Lisa Riley. 1998. Family responsive policies and employee retention following childbirth. *Social Forces* 76, 4: 1401–1435.

Glenn, Evelyn Nakano. 1992. From servitude to service work: Historical continuities in the racial division of paid reproductive labor. *Signs* 18:1–43.

Golay, Michael. 1997. *Where America stands 1997.* New York: John Wiley and Sons.

Goldberg, Carey. Most get work after welfare, studies suggest. *New York Times* electronic edition, 17 April 1999. [On-line] Available: http://www.nytimes.com.

Gonas, L. 1998. Has equality gone too far? On changing labour market regimes and new employment patterns in Sweden. *European Urban and Regional Studies* 5, 1:41–53.

Goodin, R. 1985. *Protecting the vulnerable.* Chicago: Chicago University Press.

Goodin, R. 1988. *Reasons for welfare.* Princeton, N. J.: Princeton University Press.

Gordon, Linda. 1988. What does welfare regulate? *Social Research* 55:609–630.

Gordon, Linda. 1990a. Introduction to *Women, the state, and welfare.* Madison: The University of Wisconsin Press.

Gordon, Linda, ed. 1990b. *Women, the state, and welfare.* Madison: University of Wisconsin Press.

Gordon, Linda. 1994. *Pitied but not entitled: Single mothers and the history of welfare.* New York: Free Press.

Gordon, L. 1995. Thoughts on the help for working parents plan. *Feminist Economics* 1, 2:91–94.

Gornick, J.C. 1994. Women, employment, and part-time work: A comparative study of the United States, the United Kingdom, Canada, and Australia. Ph.D. diss., Harvard University.

Gornick, J. C., and J. A. Jacobs. 1996. A crossnational analysis of the wages of part-time workers: Evidence from the United States, the United Kingdom, Canada, and Australia. *Work, Employment and Society* 10, 1:1–27.

Gornick, J. C., M. K. Meyers, and K. E. Ross. 1997. Supporting the employment of mothers: Policy variation across fourteen welfare states. *Journal of European Social Policy* 7, 1:45–70.

Gornick, J., and J. Jacobs. 1997. Gender, the welfare state, and public employment: A comparative study of seven industrialized countries. Luxembourg Income Study Working Paper, no. 168. Luxembourg: The Luxembourg Income Study.

Gornick, J. C., M. K. Meyers and K. E. Ross. 1998. Public policies and the employment of mothers: A crossnational study. *Social Science Quarterly* 75, 1:35–54.

Green, Kenneth, J. Jaros, Lisa Paine, and Mary Story. *Health and welfare for families in the 21st century*. Sudbury Mass.: Jones and Bartlett Publishers.

Greene, J. P. 1976. *All men are created equal: Some reflections on the character of the American Revolution*. Oxford: Clarendon Press.

Greenstein, Robert, and Isaac Shapiro. 1998. *New research findings on the effects of the earned income tax credit*. Washington, D.C.: Center on Budget and Policy Priorities.

Gregson, Nicky, and Michelle Lowe. 1994. *Servicing the middle classes: Class, gender and waged domestic labour in contemporary Britain*. New York: Routledge.

Gullette, Margaret M. 1997. *Declining to decline: Cultural combat and the politics of the midlife*. Charlottesville: University of Virginia Press.

Gustafsson, S. S. 1994. Childcare and types of welfare states. In *Gendering welfare states*, Diane Sainsbury, ed. Thousand Oaks, Calif.: Sage.

Haas, Linda, and Philip Hwang. 1995. Company culture and men's usage of family leave benefits in Sweden. *Family Relations* 44, 1: 28–36.

Hacker, Jacob S. 1996. National healthcare reform: An idea whose time came and went. *Journal of Health Politics, Policy and Law* 21, 4:647–695.

Hakim, Catherine. 1995. Five feminist myths about women's employment. *The British Journal of Sociology* 46, 3:429–455

Halper, Evan. 2000. Critics: Pa. tethers poor to welfare. *Philadelphia Inquirer*, 29 May.

Handler, J. 1987. *Dependent people, the state, and the modern/postmodern search for the dialogic community*. Special Publications. The Institute for Legal Studies. Madison: University of Wisconsin-Madison, Law School.

Handler, J. 1995. *The poverty of welfare reform*. New Haven, Conn.: Yale University Press.

Hartman, H. I., and D. Pearce. 1989. *High skill and low pay*. Report prepared for Child Care Action Campaign. Washington, D.C.: Institute for Women's Policy Research.

Hauser, Richard. 1997. Armut in Deutschland. In *Sozialpolitik: Aktuelle Fragen und Probleme*. Hof: Westdeutscher Verlag.

Hekman, Susan J. 1995. *Moral voices moral selves: Carol Gilligan and feminist moral theory*. State College: Pennsylvania State University Press.

Held, V. 1987. Non-contractual society: A feminist view. *Canadian Journal of Philosophy* 13:111–137.

Held, Virginia. 1993. *Feminist morality: Transforming culture, society, and politics*. Chicago: University of Chicago Press.

Held, Virgina, ed. 1995. *Justice and care: Essential readings in feminist ethics*. Boulder, Colo.: Westview Press.

Hernandez, Donald J. 1997. Poverty trends. In *Consequences of growing up poor*. G. Duncan and J. Brooks-Gunn, eds. New York: Russell Sage Foundation.

Hernes, Helga Maria, ed. 1987a. The transition from private to public dependence. In *Welfare state and woman power: Essays on state feminism*. Oslo: Norwegian University Press.

Hernes, Helga Maria. 1987b. *Welfare state and women power: Essays in state feminism*. Oslo: Norwegian University Press,

Hershey, Alan M., and LaDonna A. Pavetti. 1997. Turning job finders into job keepers. *The Future of Children* 7, 1:74–86.

Hinrichs, Karl. 1995. The impact of German health insurance reforms on redistribution and the culture of solidarity. *Journal of Health Politics, Policy and Law*. 20, 3: 653–686.

Hirschmann, Nancy J. 1992. *Rethinking obligation: A feminist method for political theory.* Ithaca, N.Y.: Cornell University Press.

Hirschmann, Nancy J. 1995. Domestic violence and the theoretical discourse of freedom. *Frontiers: Journal of Women Studies* 16, 1:126–151.

Hirschmann, Nancy J. 1996a. Rethinking obligation for feminism. In *Revisioning the political: Feminist reconstructions of traditional concepts in western political theory*. Nancy Hirschmann and Christine DiStefano, eds. Boulder, Colo.: Westview Press.

Hirschmann, Nancy J. 1996b. Toward a feminist theory of freedom. *Political Theory* 24, 1:46–67.

Hirschmann, Nancy J. 1999. Difference as an occasion for rights: A feminist rethinking of rights, liberalism, and difference. *Critical Review of International Social and Political Philosophy* 2, 1:27–55.

Hobson, Barbara. 1994. Solo mothers, state policy regimes, and the logics of gender. In *Gendering welfare states*. Diane Sainsbury, ed. London: Sage Publications.

Hobson, Barbara. 1998. Recognition and redistribution: The interplay between identities and institutions in Swedish women's mobilization. Paper presented at annual meeting of the American Sociological Association.

Hochschild, Arlie. 1989. *The second shift: Working parents and the revolution at home.* New York: Viking.

Hochschild, Arlie. 1997. *The time bind.* New York: Henry Holt.

Hoge, Warren. First test for Britain's Camelot: Welfare reform. *New York Times*, 4 January 1998.

Horn, W., and A. Bush. 1997. *Fathers, marriage, and welfare reform.* Washington, D.C.: Hudson Institute.

Huber, Evelyne, and John Stephens. 1999. *Welfare state and production regimes in the era of retrenchment.* Occasional Paper Number 1. Institute for Advanced Study, School of Social Science, Feb. [On-line] Available: http://www2.admin.ias.edu/ss/home/papers.html

Hudman Julie, and Barbara Starfield. 1999. Children and welfare reform: What are the effects of this landmark policy change? In *Health and welfare for families in the 21st century*, Helen M. Wallace, et al., eds. Jones and Bartlett Publishers, Sudbury Mass.

Ignatieff, Michael. 1985. *The needs of strangers.* New York: Viking.

Im Osten die Hälfte der Jobs befristet. *Leipziger Volkszeitung*, 11 February 1997.

Institute for Women's Policy Research.(IWPR). Domestic violence and welfare receipt. *Welfare Reform Network News* 4, April 11, 1997.

Institute for Women's Policy Research (IWPR). Forthcoming. *An IWPR report on low-income families: Survival strategies and well-being.* Washington, D.C.: Institute for Women's Policy Research.

Interagency Forum on Families and Children Statistics. 1998. *America's children: Key national indicators of well-being.* Washington, D.C.: Government Printing Office.

Isbister, John. 1996. *The immigration debate. Remaking America.* West Hartford, Conn.: Kumarin.

Isin, Engin F. 1997. Who is the new citizen? Towards a genealogy. *Citizenship Studies* 1, 1:115–132.

The IRP Evaluation of the Wisconsin Works Child Support Waiver Demonstration. 1998. *Focus* (newsletter of the University of Wisconsin Institute for Research on Poverty) 19, 2:61–62.

Jaggar, Alison. 1995. Caring as a feminist practice of moral reason. In *Justice and care: Essential readings in feminist ethics,* V. Held, ed. Boulder, Colo.: Westview Press.

Jencks, C. 1992. *Rethinking social policy.* Cambridge: Harvard University Press.

Jensen, Jane. 1996. Introduction: Some consequences of economic and political restructuring and readjustment. *Social Politics* 3:1–29.

Jensen, Jane. 1997. Who cares? Gender and welfare regimes. *Social Politics* 4, 2:181–187.

Jensen, Jane, and R. Kantrow. 1990. Labor market and family policy in France: An intersecting complex for dealing with poverty. In *The feminization of poverty. Only in America?,* G. Schaffner Goldberg and Eleanor Kremen, eds. New York: Greenwood Press

Jensen, Jane, and Rianne Mahon. 1993. Representing solidarity: Class, gender, and crisis in social-democratic Sweden. *New Left Review* 201:76–100.

Joesch, J. M. 1995. Paid leave and the timing of women's employment surrounding birth. *Journal of Marriage and the Family* 59 (November): 1,008–1,021.

Jones, J. 1985. *Labor of love, labor of sorrow: Black women, work, and the family, from slavery to the present.* New York: Vintage Books.

Jones, Kathy B. 1993. *Compassionate authority.* New York: Routledge.

Kamerman, S. B. 1991a. Parental leave and infant care: United States and international trends and issues, 1978–1988. In *Parental leave and child care: Setting a research and policy agenda,* J.S. Hyde and M.J. Essex, eds. Philadelphia: Temple University Press.

Kamerman, S. B. 1991. Child care policies and programs: An international overview. *Journal of Social Issues* 42, 2:179–196.

Kamerman, S. B., and A. J. Kahn. 1978. *Family policy, government, and families in fourteen countries.* New York: Columbia University Press.

Kamerman, S. B., and A. J. Kahn. 1991a. *Child care, parental leave, and the under 3s: Policy innovation in Europe.* New York: Auburn House.

Kamerman, S. B., and A. J. Kahn. 1991b. *Government expenditures for children and their families in advanced industrialized countries, 1960–85.* UNICEF Innocenti Occasional Papers, Economic Policy Series, Number 20. Florence, Italy: UNICEF.

Kamerman, S. B., and A. J. Kahn. 1994. *A welcome for every child: Care, education, and family support for infants and toddlers in Europe.* Arlington, Va.: Zero to Three/National Center for Clinical Infant Programs.

Kane, Thomas J., and Mary Jo Bane. 1994. The Context for Welfare Reform. In *Welfare realities: From rhetoric to reform,* Mary Jo Bane and David Ellwood, eds. Cambridge: Harvard University Press.

Kelly, Brian. The pork that just won't slice: Everything gets cut-but not corporate welfare. *Washington Post,* 10 December 1996.

Kennedy, David M. 1993. California welfare reform. In *Gender and public policy: Cases and comments,* Kenneth Winston and Mary Jo Bane, eds. Boulder, Colo.: Westview.

Kessler-Harris, Alice. 1996. Designing women and old fools: The construction of the Social Security amendments of 1939. In *U.S. history as women's history: New feminist essays,* Linda Kerber, et al., eds. Chapel Hill: University of North Carolina Press.

Kimmel, J. 1995. The effectiveness of child care subsidies in encouraging the welfare to work transitions of low-income single mothers. *The American Economics Review* 85:271–275.

Kittay, E. F. 1995. Taking dependency seriously: The family and medical leave act considered in light of the social organization of dependency work and gender equality. *Hypatia* 10, 1: 8–29.

Kittay, E. F. 1996. Human dependency and Rawlsian equality. In *Feminists rethink the self,* Diana Tietjens Meyers, ed. Boulder, Colo.: Westview Press.

Kittay, E. F. 1999. *Love's labor: Essays on women, equality and dependency.* New York: Routledge.

Knappe, Eckhard, and Hans-Joachim Jobelius. 1997. Millionen Arbeitsloser: Muß die Arbeit umverteilt werden? In *Sozialpolitik. Aktuelle Fragen und Probleme.* Hof: Westdeutscher Verlag.

Knijn, Trudie. 1994. Fish without bikes: Revision of the Dutch welfare state and its consequences for the (in)dependence of single mothers. *Social Politics* 1:83–105.

Knijn, Trudie, and Monique Kremer. 1997a. Gender and the caring dimension of welfare states toward inclusive citizenship. *Social Politics* 4, 3:328–361.

Knijn, Trudie, and Clare Ungerson. 1997b. Introduction: Care work and gender in welfare regimes. *Social Politics* 4, 3: 323–327.

Knudsen, C., and H. E. Peters. 1994. *An international comparison of married women's labor supply.* Luxembourg Income Study Working Paper No. 106. Luxembourg: Luxembourg Income Study.

Kornbluh, Felicia A. 1996. Review essay: The new literature on gender and the welfare state: The U.S. case. *Feminist Studies* 22 (spring): 171–197.

Kornbluh, Felicia. 1998. The goals of the National Welfare Rights Movement: Why we need them thirty years later. *Feminist Studies* 24 1:65–78.

Kramer Fredrica D. 1998. *Job retention and career advancement for welfare recipients.* The Welfare Information Network. [On-line] Available:http://www.welfareinfo.org/issueretention.htm.

Lambert Susan. 1999. Lower-wage workers and the new realities of work and family. *Annals of the American Academy of Political and Social Science,* vol. 562. Thousand Oaks: Sage Publications.

Leibfried, Stephan, and Paul Pierson. 1995. Semisovereign welfare states: Social policy in a multitiered Europe. In *European social policy: Between fragmentation and integration,* S. Leibfried and P. Pierson, eds. Washington, D.C.: Brookings.

Leibowitz, A., J. A. Klerman, and L. J. Waite. 1992. Employment of new mothers and child care choice: Difference by children's age. *Journal of Human Resources* 22, 1:223–233.

Leibowitz, A., L. J. Waite, and C. Witsberger. 1988. Child care for preschoolers: Differences by child's age. *Demography* 25, 2:205–221.

Leira, Arnaug. 1992. *Welfare states and working mothers.* Cambridge, U.K.: Cambridge University Press.

Leira, Arnaug. 1993a. *Combining work and family: Working mothers in Scandinavia and in the European community.* Paper presented at the ISA Conference on Comparative Welfare States in Transition, Oxford.

Leira, Arnaug. 1993b. The "woman-friendly" welfare state? The case of Norway and Sweden. In *Women and social policies in Europe: Work, family, and the state,* Jane Lewis, ed. Brookfield, Vt.: Edward Elgar

Lewis, Jane. 1992. Gender and the development of welfare regimes. *Journal of European Social Policy* 2, 3:159–173.

Lewis, Jane, ed. 1993. *Women and social policies in Europe: Work, family, and the state.* Brookfield, Vt.: Edward Elgar.

Lewis, Jane. ed. 1994. *Women and social politics in Europe.* London: Edward Elgar.

Lewis, Jane. 1997. Gender and welfare regimes: Further thoughts. *Social Politics* 4, 2: 160–177.

Lewis, Jane, ed. 1999. *Gender, social care and welfare state restructuring in Europe.* Ashgate, U.K.: Aldershot.

Lieberman, Robert C. 1998. *Shifting the color line: Race and the American welfare state.* Cambridge: Harvard University Press.

Liebert, Ulrike. 1999. Gender politics in the European Union: The return of the public. *European Societies* 1, 2:191–232.

Lister, R. 1990. Women, economic dependency, and citizenship. *Journal of Social Policy* 19, 4:445–467.

Lister, Ruth. 1995. Dilemmas in engendering citizenship. *Economy and Society* 24, 1:1–40.

Lister, Ruth. 1997. *Citizenship: Feminist perspectives.* London: Macmillan.

Lugaila, T. 1992. Households, families, and children: A 30–year perspective. Publication Number P23–181, U.S. Bureau of the Census. Washington, D.C.: GPO.

Lyall, Sarah. Blair scolds British "workless class" in outline of welfare plan. *New York Times*, 3 June 1997.

MacDonald, Martha 1998: Gender and Social Security Policy: Pitfalls and Possibilities. *Feminist Economics* 4, 1:1–25

MacIntyre, A. 1999. *Dependent rational animals : Why human beings need the virtues.* Paul Carus Lectures, 20th Ser. LaSalle, Ill.: Open Court Publishing Company.

Magyar, Mark. 1998. Welfare and the politics of abortion. *New Jersey Reporter* 28:22–23.

Mahon, Rianne 1998. Death of a model? Swedish social democracy at the close of the twentieth century. Paper presented at the 1998 APSA Annual Meeting, Boston.

Mallier, A. T., and M. J. Rosser. 1986. *Women and the economy: A comparative study of Britain and the US.* London: Macmillan.

Mancoske Robert J., Alice Abel Kemp, and Taryn Kindlhorst. 1998. *Exiting welfare: The experiences of families in metro New Orleans, LA.* Report from the Welfare Reform Research Project. New Orleans, La.: Southern University of New Orleans.

Manschot, Henk, and Marian Verkerk, eds. 1994. *Ethiek van de Zorg: Een discussie.* Amsterdam: Boom.

Manza, Jeff, and Clem Brooks. 1998. The gender gap in U.S. elections: When? why? implications? *American Journal of Sociology* 103:1235–1266.

Marcus, R. Baby-sitter problems sink second Clinton prospect: Wood withdraws from consideration as attorney general. *Washington Post*, 6 February 1993.

Marcuse, Herbert. 1971. Industrialism and capitalism. In *Max Weber and sociology today.* New York: Harper and Row.

Marmor, T. R., J. L. Mashaw, and P. L. Harvey. 1990. *America's misunderstood welfare state: Persistent myths, enduring realities.* New York: Basic Books.

Marshall. T. H. 1981. [1969]. Reflections on power. In *The right to welfare and other essays*, T.H. Marshall, ed. New York: The Free Press.

Marshall. T. H. 1992 [1950]. *Citizenship and social class.* Concord, Mass.: Pluto Press.

Mazey, Sonia. 1998. The European Union and women's rights: From the Europeanization of national agendas to the nationalization of a European Agenda? *Journal of European Public Policy* 1:131–152

Mazur, Amy. 1999. *Gender, policy, and comparative theory: Intersections in feminist analysis and political science.* Oxford: Oxford University Press.

McDowell, L. 1991. Life without father and Ford: The new gender order of post-Fordism. *Transactions, Institute of British Geographers* 16:400–419

McGeever, Patrick J. 1997. The prospects for welfare reform. Paper presented at the Midwest Political Science Association Meeting, 10–12 April, Chicago.

McLanahan, Sara, and Gary Sandefur. 1994. *Growing up with a single parent: What hurts, what helps.* Cambridge: Harvard University Press.

McLaughlin E., and C. Glendinning 1994. Paying for care in Europe: Is there a feminist approach? In *Family policy and the welfare of women*, L. Hantrais and S. Mangen, eds. Loughborough, Cross-National Research Papers.

Merkl, Peter. 1995. An impossible dream? Privatizing collective property in Eastern Germany. In *The Federal Republic of Germany at forty-five*, P. Merkl, ed. New York: New York University Press.

Meyer, Bruce D., and Dan T. Rosenbaum. 1998. Welfare, the earned income tax credit, and the employment of single mothers. *Joint Center for Poverty Research Working Paper, #2*. [On-line]. Available: http://www.jcpr.org/labormothers.html.

Meyer, Madonna Harrington. 1996. Making claims as workers or wives: The distribution of social security benefits. *American Sociological Review* 61:449–465.

Meyer, Traute. 1994. The German and British welfare states as employers: Patriarchal or emancipatory? In *Gendering welfare states,* Diane Sainsbury, ed. London: Sage Publications.

Michalopoulos, C., P. K. Robins, and I. Garfinkel. 1992. A structural model of labor supply and child care demand. *Journal of Human Resources* 27, 1:166–203.

Michel, Sonya. 1997. Response to Jane Lewis. *Social Politics* (summer): 203–207.

Millar, Jane. 1996. Poor mothers and absent fathers: Support for lone parents in comparative perspective. In *The politics of the family*, Helen Jones and Jane Millar, eds. Aldershot, U.K.: Avebury.

Mills, Charles. 1997. *The racial contract*. Ithaca, N.Y.: Cornell University Press.

Mink, Gwendolyn. 1990. Lady and the tramp: Gender, race and the origins of the welfare state. In *Women, the state, and welfare*, Linda Gordon, ed. Madison: University of Wisconsin Press.

Mink, Gwendolyn. 1994. *Women and welfare reform: Women's poverty, women's opportunities, and women's welfare*. Conference Proceedings. Washington, D.C.: Institute for Women's Policy Research.

Mink, Gwendolyn. 1995. *The wages of motherhood: Inequality in the welfare state, 1917–1942*. Ithaca, N.Y.: Cornell University Press.

Mink, Gwendolyn. 1998. *Welfare's end*. Ithaca, N.Y.: Cornell University Press.

Mitchell, Deborah, and Geoffrey Garrett. 1996. Women and the welfare state in the era of global markets. *Social Politics* (summer/fall): 185–193.

Moffitt, R. 1992. Incentive effects of the U.S. welfare system: A review. *Journal of Economic Literature* 30:1–61.

Moody-Adams, M. 1997. The social construction and reconstruction of care. In *Sex, preference, and family: Essays on law and nature*, D. Estlund and M. Nussbaum, eds. New York: Oxford University Press.

Moon, D. J. 1988. The moral basis of the democratic welfare state. In *Democracy and the welfare state*, Amy Gutman. Princeton, N.J.: Princeton University Press.

Moon, Marilyn, and Thomas Juster. 1995. Economic status measures in the health and retirement study. *Journal of Human Resources* 30 (special supplement).

Moss, P., and E. Melhuish. 1990. *Current issues in daycare for young children*. London: HMSO.

Mushaben, Joyce Marie. 1994. The other "democratic deficit": Women in the European community before and after Maastricht. In *Europe after Maastricht. American and European Perspectives,* M. Luetzeler, ed. Oxford: Providence Press.

Mushaben, Joyce Marie. 1998. The politics of critical acts: Women, leadership, and Democratic deficits in the European Union. *European Studies Journal* 15, 2:51–91.

Myles, John, and Paul Pierson. 1997. Friedman's revenge: The reform of "liberal" welfare states in Canada and the United States. *Politics and Society* 25:443–472.

Naegele, Gerhard. 1997. Örtliche Altenpolitik auf der Suche nach Visionen. In *Sozialpolitik. Aktuelle Fragen und Probleme.* Hof: Westdeutscher Verlag.

Naples, Nancy A. 1992. Activist mothering: Cross-generational continuity in community work of women from low-income urban neighborhoods. *Gender and Society* 6, 3:217–236.

Naples, Nancy. 1997. The "new consensus" on the gendered "social contract": The 1987–88 U.S. Congressional Hearings on Welfare Reform. *Signs* 22:907–945.

Nelson, H. L., and J. L. Nelson. 1992. Frail parents, robust duties. *University of Utah Law Review* 1992:747.

Nelson, Barbara. 1984. Women's poverty and women's citizenship: Some political consequences of economic marginality. *Signs* 10:209–232.

Nelson, Barbara. 1990. The origins of the two-channel welfare state: Workmen's compensation and mothers' aid. In *Women, the state, and welfare.* Linda Gordon, ed. Madison: University of Wisconsin Press.

Newman, K. S. 1999. *No shame in my game: The working poor in the inner city.* New York: Knopf.

Nichols, Laura, and Barbara Gault. 1999. The effects of welfare reform on housing stability and homelessness: Current research findings, legislation, and programs. *Welfare Reform Network News* 2, no. 2. [On-line] Available: http://www.iwpr.org/.

Niemi, A. W., Jr. Education: Women's ticket to pay equality. *Georgia Trend,* 1 May 1994.

Oberhuemer, P. 1995. Who works with young children? Concepts and issues of staffing and professionalization in European countries. Paper presented at the Fifth European conference on the Quality of Early Childhood Education, September, Paris.

O'Connell, M. 1990. Maternity leave arrangements: 1961–1985. In *Work and Family Patterns of American Women.* Current Population Reports, Special Studies Series P-23, No. 165, 11–27.

O'Connor, Julia S. 1993a. Gender, class and citizenship in the comparative analysis of welfare state regimes: Theoretical and methodological issues. *British Journal of Sociology* 44, 3: 501–518

O'Connor, Julia. S. 1993b. Labour market participation in liberal welfare states regimes: Issues of quantity and quality. Paper prepared for International Sociological Association Conference on Comparative Research on Welfare States in Transition, University of Oxford.

O'Connor, Julia S. 1996. From women in the welfare state to gendering welfare state regimes. *Current Sociology* 44, 2:1–124.

O'Connor, Julia S., Ann Shola Orloff, and Sheila Shaver. 1999. *States, markets, families: Gender, liberalism, and social policy in Australia, Canada, Great Britain, and the United States.* New York: Cambridge University Press.

OECD. 1990a. *Employment outlook.* Paris: OECD.

OECD. 1990b. Child care in OECD countries. In *Employment Outlook.* Paris: OECD.

OECD. 1994a. *Caring for frail elderly people.* Social Policy Studies no 14. Paris: OECD.

OECD. 1994b. *The OECD jobs study, facts, analysis, strategies.* Paris: OECD.

OECD. 1994c. *Women and structural change: New perspectives.* Paris: OECD.

O'Hare, William. 1996. A new look at poverty in America, *Population Bulletin* 51, no. 2.

Okin, S. 1989. Reason and feeling in thinking about justice. *Ethics* 99, 2: 229–249.

Olmsted, P. P., and D. P. Weikart. 1989. *How nations serve young children: Profiles of child care and education in 14 countries.* Ypsilanti, Mich.: The High Scope Press.

Olson, Lynn M., and LaDonna Pavetti. 1996. *Personal and family challenges to successful transition from welfare to work.* Washington D.C.: The Urban Institute.

Omolade, Barbara. 1994. *The rising song of African American women.* New York: Routledge.

O'Neill, James M. New rules alter course of students on welfare. *Philadelphia Inquirer,* 25 April 1999.

Orloff, Ann Shola. 1993a. Gender and the social rights of citizenship: The comparative analysis of gender relations and welfare states. *American Sociological Review* 58:303–328.

Orloff, Ann Shola. 1993b. *The politics of pensions: A comparative analysis of Britain, Canada, and the United States, 1880–1940.* Madison: University of Wisconsin Press.

Orloff, Ann Shola. 1996. Gender in the welfare state. *Annual Review Sociology* 22:51–78.

Orloff, Ann Shola. 1999. Gender and the politics of welfare reform in the United States, Britain, Canada, and Australia. In *States, Markets, Families: Gender, Liberalism, and Social Policy in Australia, Canada, Great Britain and the United States.* J. O'Connor, et al., eds. New York: Cambridge University Press.

Ostner, Ilona.1994. Back to the Fifties: Gender and welfare in unified Germany. *Social Politics* 1, 1: 32–59.

Ostner, Ilona. 1997. Lone mothers in Germany before and after unification. In *Lone mothers in European welfare regimes: Shifting policy logics,* Jane Lewis, ed.. London: Jessica Kingsley.

Ostner, Ilona, and Jane Lewis. 1995. Gender and the evolution of European social policies. In *European Social Policy.* Washington, D.C.: Brookings Institute.

Painter, Nell Irvin. 1992. Hill, Thomas, and the use of racial stereotype. In *Race-ing justice, en-gendering power: Essays on Anita Hill, Clarence Thomas, and the construction of social reality,* Toni Morrison, ed. New York: Pantheon Books.

Pateman, Carole. 1988a. The patriarchal welfare state. In *Democracy and the welfare state,* Amy Gutmann, ed. Princeton, N.J.: Princeton University Press.

Pateman, Carole. 1988b. *The sexual contract.* Palo Alto, Calif.: Stanford University Press.

Pateman, C. 1989. The patriarchal welfare state. In *The disorder of women.* C. Pateman, ed. Cambridge, Mass.: Polity.

Patterson, Martha Priddy. 1996. Women's employment patterns, pension coverage, and retirement planning. In *The American Woman, 1996–97: Where we stand.* New York: W. W. Norton and Co., Women's Research and Education Institute.

Pavetti, LaDonna. 1993. The dynamics of welfare and work: Exploring the process by which women work their way off welfare. Ph.D. diss., Harvard University.

Pavetti, LaDonna. 1997. *How much more can they work? Setting realistic expectations for welfare mothers.* The Urban Institute. [On-line]. Available: http://www.urban.org/welfare/howmuch.htm.

Pear, Robert. House backs bill undoing decades of welfare policy. *New York Times,* 25 March 1995.

Pear, Robert. 1999. States declining to draw billions in welfare money. *New York Times* electronic edition, 8 February. [On-line] Available: http://www.nytimes.com Archives

Pearce, Diana. 1986. Toil and trouble: Women workers and unemployment compensation. In *Women and poverty.* Chicago: University of Chicago Press.

Pedersen, Susan. 1993. *Family, dependence, and the origins of the welfare state: Britain and France, 1914–1945.* New York: Cambridge University Press.

Pennsylvania Department of Public Welfare. 1999a. *Temporary assistance for needy families: State plan.* [On-line]. Available: http://www.dpw.state.pa.us/oim/pdf/TANFstateplan.pdf.

Pennsylvania Department of Public Welfare. 1999b. *1999–2000 budget highlights*, 2 February.

Pfau-Effinger, Birgit 1996. Erwerbspartnerin oder berufstätige Ehefrau: Soziokulturelle Arrangements der Erwerbstätigkeit von Frauen im Vergleich. *Soziale Welt* 3:322–337.

Phillips, Kevin. 1991. *The politics of rich and poor: Wealth and the American electorate in the Reagan aftermath*. New York: Harper Perennial.

Phipps, S. A. 1993. *Determinants of women's labor force participation: An econometric analysis for five countries*. Luxembourg Income Study Working Paper No. 99. Luxembourg: Luxembourg Income Study.

Pierson, Paul. 1994. *Dismantling the welfare state? Reagan, Thatcher and the politics of retrenchment*. Cambridge, U.K.: Cambridge University Press.

Pierson, Paul. 1996. The new politics of the welfare state. *World Politics* 48 (January): 143–179.

Pierson, Paul. 1998. The deficit and the politics of domestic reform. In *The social divide: Political parties and the future of activist government*, Margaret Weir, ed. Washington, D.C.: Brookings.

Piven, Francis Fox. 1984. Women and the state: Ideology, power, and the welfare state. *Socialist Review* 74 (March/April): 13–19.

Piven, Frances Fox 1985. Women and the welfare state. In *Gender and the life course*, A. Rossi, ed. New York: Aldine.

Piven, Frances Fox. 1996. Women and the state: Ideology, power, and welfare. In *For crying out loud: Women's poverty in the United States*, Diane Dujon and Ann Withorn, eds. Boston: South End Press.

Piven, Frances Fox, and Richard Cloward. 1977. *Poor people's movements*. New York: Pantheon.

Piven, Frances Fox, and Richard Cloward. 1988. Welfare doesn't shore up traditional family roles: A reply to Linda Gordon. *Social Research* 55:631–647.

Piven, Frances Fox, and Richard Cloward. 1997. We should have made a plan! *Politics and Society* 25:525–532

Plumwood, Valerie. 1993. *Feminism and the mastery of nature*. New York: Routledge

Popenoe, D. 1996. Family values: A communitarian perspective. In *Macro socio-economics: From theory to activism*, D. Sciulli, ed. N.Y.: M. E. Sharpe.

Quadagno, Jill. 1988. *The transformation of old age security*. Chicago: University of Chicago Press.

Quadagno, Jill. 1994. *The color of welfare: How racism undermined the war on poverty*. New York: Oxford University Press.

Quindlen, A. Abhors a vacuum. *New York Times*, 9 September 1992.

Rainwater, L, and Smeeding, T. M. 1995. Doing poorly: The real income of American children in a comparative perspective. Manuscript in preparation, on file with author and at Maxwell School of Citizenship and Public Affairs, Syracuse, New York-Luxembourg

Rank, Mark R. 1989. Fertility among women on welfare. *American Sociological Review* 54, 2:296–304

Raphael, Jody. 1996. *Prisoners of abuse: Domestic violence and welfare recipient*. A second report of the Women, Welfare and Abuse Project. Chicago: Taylor Institute.

Rawls, John. 1971. *A theory of justice*. Cambridge: Harvard University Press.

Rawls, John. 1980. Kantian Constructivism in *Moral Theory: The Dewey Lectures 1980. The Journal of Philosophy* 77, 9:515–572.

Reich, Robert. Clinton's leap in the dark. *Times Literary Supplement*, 22 January 1999.

Reskin, Barbara, and Irene Padavic. 1994. *Women and men at work.* Thousand Oaks, Calif.: Pine Forge Press.

Revkin, A.C. Welfare policies alter the face of food lines. *New York Times*, 26 February 1999.

Rhodes, Martin, ed. 1997. *Southern European welfare states. Between crisis and reform.* London: Frank Cass

Rhodes, Martin. 1996. Globalization and West European welfare states: A critical review of recent debates. *Journal of European Social Policy* 6:305–327.

Rhodes, Martin, and Yves Mény, eds. 1998. *The future of European welfare: A new social contract?* New York: St. Martin's Press.

Ribar, D. C. 1991. Child care and the labor supply of married women: Reduced form evidence. *The Journal of Human Resources* 27, 1:134–165.

Roberts, Dorothy. 1995. Race, gender and the value of mothers' work. *Social Politics* 2:195–207.

Rogers-Dillon, Robin. 1995. The dynamics of welfare stigma. *Qualitative Sociology* 18, 4, 439–456.

Rosenfeld, R. A. 1993. Women's part-time employment: Individual and country-level variation. Paper presented at the 1993 Meeting of Research Committee #28, the International Sociological Association, Durham, N.C.

Rossilli, Mariagrazia. 1997. The European Community's policy on the equality of women: From the Treaty of Rome to the present. *The European Journal of Women's Studies* 4:63–82.

Rousseau, Jean Jacques. 1973. *The social contract and discourse.* Translated by G.D.H. Cole. London: J. M. Dent and Sons, Ltd.

Ruddick, Sara. 1990. *Maternal thinking: Towards a politics of peace.* Boston: Beacon Press.

Ruggie, Mary. 1996. *Realignments in the welfare state: Health policy in the United States, Britain, and Canada.* New York: Columbia University Press.

Ruhm, Chrisotpher J. 1998. The economic consequences of paternal leave mandates: Lessons from Europe. *The Quarterly Journal of Economics* 113, 1: 285–317.

Ryan, John, Michael Hughes, James Hawdon 1998. Marital status, general-life satisfaction, and the welfare state. A cross-national comparison. *International Journal of Comparative Sociology* 39, 2:224–236

Sackmann, Rosemarie. 1998. European gender roles: Public discourses and regional practices. *Innovation* 11, 2:167–190

Sainsbury, Diane, ed. 1994a. *Gendering welfare states.* London: Sage Publications.

Sainsbury, Diane. 1994b. Women's rights and men's social rights: Gendering dimensions of welfare states. In *Gendering welfare states,* Diane Sainsbury, ed. Thousand Oaks, Calif.: Sage.

Sainsbury, Diane. 1996. *Gender, equality, and welfare states.* New York: Cambridge University Press.

Sainsbury, Diane. 1999a. Gender inequality and the Social Democratic welfare state regime. In *Gender and welfare state regimes.* Oxford: Oxford University Press.

Sainsbury, Diane, ed. 1999b. *Gender and welfare state regimes.* Oxford: Oxford University Press.

Sapiro, V. 1990. The gender basis of American social policy. In *Women, the state, and welfare,* Linda Gordon, ed. Madison, Wis.: University of Wisconsin.

Saraceno, Chiara. 1994. The ambivalent familism of the Italian welfare state. *Social Politics* 1, 1:60–82.

Saraceno, Chiara. 1996. *Family change, family policies, and the restructuring of welfare.* Working paper, Working Party on Social Policy, 11–12 July. Paris: OECD.

Saraceno, Chiara. 1999. *Gendered policies: Family obligations and social policies in Europe.* San Giacomo Charitable Foundation Working Paper 99.3. Ithaca, N.Y.: The Institute for European Studies, Cornell University.

Sarvasy, Wendy. 1992. Beyond the difference versus equally policy debate: Postsuffrage feminism, citizenship, and the quest for a feminist welfare state. *Signs* 17, 2:329–362.

Sassoon, A. S., ed. 1987. *Women and the state.* London: Hutchinson.

Scheiwe, Kirsten 1994. German pension insurance: Gendered times and stratification. In *Gendering welfare states,* Diane Sainsbury, ed. Thousand Oaks, Calif.: Sage.

Scheiwe, Kirsten 1999a. Legal model of caring and paying for children and gender inequalities in comparative perspective. Paper presented at Gender and Markets in the Reconstruction of European Welfare States Conference, Centre for Feminist and Gender Studies, 8–10 July, Bremen University.

Scheiwe, Kirsten 1999b. *Kinderkosten und Sorgearbeit im Recht: Eine rechtsvergleichende Studie.* Frankfurt a.M.: Klostermann Verlag

Schmidt, Manfred G. 1998. *Sozialpolitik in Deutschland. Historische Entwicklung und internationaler Vergleich.* 2nd ed. Opladen: Leske+Budrich.

Schmidtz, D., and R. E. Goodin. 1997. Social welfare as an individual responsibility: For and against. New York: Cambridge University Press.

Schunter-Kleemann, Susanne, ed. 1990. *EG-Binnenmarkt: Europatriarchat oder Aufbruch der Frauen?* Bremen: Hochschule, Bremen.

Schunter-Kleemann, Susanne. 1999. Mainstreaming as an innovative approach of the EU policy of equal opportunities? Hochschule, Bremen, Discussion Papers, March.

Schwarzenbach, Sibyl. 1986. Rawls and ownership: The forgotten category of reproductive labor. In *Science, morality and feminist theory,* Marsha Hanen and Kai Nielson, eds. Calgary: University of Calgary Press.

Schwarzenbach, Sibyl. 1996. On civic friendship. *Ethics* 107 (October): 97–128.

Seccombe, Karen. 1999. *So you think I drive a Cadillac? Welfare recipients' perspectives on the system and its reform.* Boston: Allyn and Bacon.

Seelye, Katharine Q. Future U.S.: Grayer and More Hispanic. *New York Times,* 27 March 1997.

Sen, A. 1989. Gender and cooperative conflict. In *Persistent inequalities: Women and world development,* Irene Tinker, ed. New York: Oxford University Press.

Sevenhuijsen, Selma. 1993. Paradoxes of gender, ethical and epistemological perspectives on care in feminist political theory. *Acta Politica* 28, 2:131–149

Sevenhuijsen, Selma. 1996. Feminist ethics and public health care policies. In *Feminist ethics and social policy,* P. DiQuinzio and I.M. Young, eds. Bloomington: Indiana University Press.

Sevenhuijsen, Selma. 1998. *Citizenship and the ethics of care: Feminist considerations of justice, morality, and politics.* London: Routledge.

Siaroff, A. 1994. Work, welfare, and gender equality. In *Gendering welfare states.* Thousand Oaks, Calif.: Sage.

Siegel, R.B. 1994. Home as work: The first women's rights claims concerning wives' household labor, 1850–1880. *Yale Law Journal* 103,1:214.

Siim, B. 1988. Toward a feminist rethinking of the welfare state. In *The political interests of gender,* K. Jones and A. Jonasdottir, eds. Newbury Park, Calif.: Sage.

Simon, W. H. 1983. Legality, bureaucracy, and class in the welfare system. *Yale Law Journal* 92, 1:198.

Singer, Rena. Welfare cutoffs need adjustments, committee told. *Philadelphia Inquirer*, 17 February 1999.

Sklar, Kathryn Kish. 1995. Two political cultures in the Progressive Era: The National Consumer's League and the American Association for Labor Legislation. In *U.S. history as women's history: New feminist essays*, Linda Kerber et al., eds. Chapel Hill: The University of North Carolina Press.

Skocpol, Theda. 1988. The limits of the new deal system and the roots of contemporary welfare dilemmas. In *The politics of social policy in the United States*, Margaret Weir, ed. Princeton, N.J.: Princeton University Press.

Skocpol, Theda. 1992. *Protecting soldiers and mothers: The political origins of social policy in the United States*. Cambridge: Harvard University Press.

Skocpol, Theda. 1995. *Social policy in the United States: Future possibilities in historical perspective*. Princeton, N.J.: Princeton University Press.

Skocpol, Theda. 1997a. *Boomerang: Clinton's health security effort and the turn against government in U.S. politics*. New York: W.W. Norton and Co.

Skocpol, Theda. 1997b. A partnership with American families. In *Toward a popular progressive politics*, Stanley Greenberg and Theda Skocpol, eds. New Haven, Conn.: Yale University Press.

Smeeding, T. M. 1996. America's income inequality: Where do we stand? *Challenge* 39:45–53.

Smeeding, T. M. 1997. *Financial poverty in developed countries: The evidence from LIS*. Final report to the UN. New York: United Nations.

Smeeding, T. M., and B. T. Torrey. 1988. Poor children in rich countries. *Science* 242:873–877.

Solow, R. M. 1998. Who likes workfare? In *Work and welfare*, Amy Gutmann, ed. Princeton, N.J.: Princeton University Press.

Sorenson, Annemette. 1994. Women's economic risk and the economic position of single mothers. *European Sociological Review* 10, 2:173–188.

Spalter-Roth, R. 1995. Welfare that works: Increasing AFDC mothers' employment and income. Testimony before the Subcommittee on Human Resources. Washington, D.C. 20036: Institute for Women's Policy Research.

Spalter-Roth, Roberta M., and Heidi I. Hartmann. 1994. AFDC recipients as care-givers and workers: A feminist approach to income security policy for American women. *Social Politics: International Studies in Gender, State, and Society* 1:190–210.

Spalter-Roth, Roberta, Beverly Burr, Heidi Hartmann, and Lois Shaw. 1995. *Welfare that works: The working lives of AFDC recipients*. A Report to the Ford Foundation. Washington, D.C.: Institute for Women's Policy Research.

Spillers, H. J. 1987. Mama's baby, papa's maybe: An American grammar book. *Diacritics* (summer) :65–81.

Stack, Carol. 1974. *All our kin: Strategies for survival in a black community*. New York: Harper and Row.

Stevens, Beth. Blurring the boundaries: How the federal government has influenced welfare benefits in the private sector. In *The politics of social policy in the United States*, Margaret Weir, et al., eds.. Princeton, N.J.: Princeton University Press.

Stiehm, Judith. 1984. Our Aristotelian hangover. In *Discovering reality*, M. Hintikka and S. Harding, eds. Amsterdam: Elsevier.

Stolzenberg, R. M., and L. J. Waite. 1994. Local labor markets, children, and labor force participation of wives. *Demography* 21:157–170.

Taylor-Gooby, P. 1991. Welfare state regimes and welfare citizenship. *Journal of European Social Policy* 1:93–105.

Textor, Martin, ed. 1997. *Sozialpolitik: Aktuelle Fragen und Probleme.* Hof: Westdeutscher Verlag.

Thomas, D. Q., and M. E. Beasley 1995. Domestic violence as a human rights issue. *Albany Law Review* 58:1128.

Thomas, Sue. 1994. *How women legislate.* New York: Oxford University Press.

Tillmon, J. 1976. Welfare is a woman's issue. In *America's working women: A documentary history—1600 to the present,* R. Baxandall, L. Gordon, and S. Reverby, eds. New York: Vintage Books.

Tragardh, Lars. 1990. Swedish model or Swedish culture. *Critical Review* 4, 4:569.

Tronto, Joan C. 1993. *Moral boundaries: A political argument for an ethic of care.* New York: Routledge.

Tronto, Joan C. 1996. Care as a political concept. In *Revisioning the political: Feminist reconstructions of traditional concepts in Western political theory,* Nancy Hirschmann and Christine DiStefano, eds. Boulder, Colo.: Westview Press.

Trzcinski, E. 1991. Employers' parental leave policies: Does the labor market provide parental leave? In *Parental leave and child care: Setting a research and policy agenda,* J.S. Hyde and M.J. Essex, eds. Philadelphia: Temple University Press.

Turner, Bryan S. 1997. Citizenship studies: A general theory. *Citizenship Studies* 1, 1: 5–18.

Tweedie, Jack, and Dana Reichert. 1998. *Tracking recipients after they leave: Summaries of state follow-up studies.* Report from National Governor's Association, National Conference of State Legislatures and the American Public Welfare Association.

Ungerson, Clare. 1990. The language of care: Crossing the boundaries. In *Gender and caring: Work and welfare in Britain and Scandinavia,* C. Ungerson, ed. London: Harvester, Wheatsheaf.

Ungerson, Clare. 1997. Social politics and the commodification of Care. *Social Politics* 4, 3: 362–381.

U.N. Development Programme. 1995. *Human development report.* C. Underson, ed. New York: Oxford University Press.

U.N. Development Programme. 1999. Progress in Gender Equality. In *Human Development Report.* New York: Oxford University Press.

U.S. Bureau of the Census. 1996. Income, poverty, and valuation of noncash benefits: 1994. *Current Population Reports,* Series P60–189. Washington, D.C.:GPO.

U.S. Committee on Ways and Means, House of Representatives. 1996. Background material and data on programs within the jurisdiction of the committee on ways and means. *1996 Green Book.* Washington, D.C.: GPO.

U.S. Committee on Ways and Means, House of Representatives. 1998. Background material and data on programs within the jurisdiction of the committee on ways and means. *1998 Green Book.* Washington, D.C.: GPO.

U.S. Department of Commerce, Bureau of the Census. 1995. *Voting and registration in the election of 1994.* Washington, D.C.: GPO.

U.S. Department of Health and Human Services. 1995. *Clinton administration makes awards to change the culture of welfare* (press release), 6 November.

U.S. General Accounting Office. 1994. *Child care subsidies increase likelihood that low-income mothers will work* (GAO/HEHS-94-87). Washington, D.C.: GAO.

U.S. General Accounting Office. 1998. *Welfare reform impact on public housing program: A preliminary forecast.* Washington D.C.: Office of Policy Development and Research, March.

U.S. House Subcommittee on Public Assistance and Unemployment Compensation, of Ways and Means Committee. *Family Welfare Reform Act: Hearing on H.R. 1720.* 100th Congress, 1st sess., 1987.

U.S. Social Security Administration. 1993. *Statistical supplement to the social security bulletin, 1992.* Washington, D.C.: U.S. Department of Health and Human Services.

Van Parijs, P. 1995. *Real freedom for all. What (if anything) can justify.* Oxford, U.K.: Oxford University Press.

Veil, Mechthild. 1996. Debatten zur Zukunft des bundesdeutschen Sozialstaats: Feministische Einwände. *Feministische Studien* 2:61–74

Veil, Mechthild. 1997. Zwischen Wunsch und Wirklichkeit: Frauen im Sozialstaat: Ein Ländervergleich zwischen Frankreich, Schweden und Deutschland. *Aus Politik und Zeitgeschichte* B52:29–38.

Venner, Sandra H., and J. Larry Brown. 1999. *State investments in income and asset development for poor families.* Report from the Center on Hunger and Poverty. Medford, Mass.: Tufts University, January.

Vogel, Ursula. 1994. Marriage and the boundaries of citizenship. In *The condition of citizenship*, Bart Van Steenbergen, ed. London: Sage.

Voges, Wolfgang. 1996. Konsequenzen neuer Familienformen und heterogener Armutslagen. In *Sozialstaat wohin? Umbau, Abbau oder Ausbau der sozialen Sicherung*, Werner-Schönig and Raphael L'Hoest, eds. Darmstadt: Wissenschaftliche Buchgesellschaft.

Waerness, K. 1987. On the rationality of caring. In *Women and the State*, Ann Showstack Sassoon, ed. London: Hutchinson.

Waerness, Kari. 1989. A more symmetrical family: A greater demand for public care? *Marriage and Family Review* 14, 1–2: 41–67.

Waerness, Kari. 1990a. Berufsbildung, Beschäftigung, und Karrieremöglichkeiten von Frauen in der Alterpflege in der Bundesrepublik Deutschland. Bundesministerium für Familie, Senioren, Frauen, und Jugend. *Materialien zur Frauenpolitik,* no 60, Bonn.

Waerness, Kari. 1990b. Informal and formal care in old age: What is wrong with the new ideology in Scandinavia today? In *Gender and caring: Work and welfare in Britain and Scandinavia*, C. Ungerson, ed. London: Harvester, Wheatsheaf.

Walby, Sylvia. 1999a. The new regulatory state: The social powers of the European Union. *British Journal of Sociology* 50, 1:118–140

Walby, Sylvia. 1999b. The European Union and equal opportunity policies. *European Societies* 1, 1:59–80.

Waldfogel, Jane. 1999. The impact of the Family and Medical Leave Act on coverage. *Journal of Policy Analysis and Management* 18, 2: 281–302.

Walker, Alan, and Carol Walker, eds. 1997. *Britain divided: The growth of social exclusion in the 1980s and 1990s.* London: Child Poverty Action Group.

Walker, Laura. 1996. If we could, we would be someplace else. In *For crying out loud: Women's poverty in the United States,* Diane Dujon and Ann Withorn, eds. Boston: South End Press.

Walker, Margaret Urban. 1997. *Moral understandings: A feminist study in ethics.* New York: Routledge.

Walker, Margaret Urban. 1999. Getting out of line: Alternatives to life as a career. In *Mother time: Women, aging and ethics,* M. Walker, ed. Boulder, Colo.: Rowman and Littlefield.

Walwei, Ulrich 1996. Mehr Beschäftigung durch Umbau des Sozialstaats? In *Sozialstaat wohin? Umbau, Abbau, oder Ausbau der sozialen Sicherung.* Darmstadt: Wissenschaftliche Buchgesellschaft.

Weaver, Kent. 1998. Ending welfare as we know it: Policymaking for low-income families in the Clinton/Gingrich era. In *The social divide: Political parties and the future of activist government*, Margaret Weir, ed. Washington, D.C.: Brookings.

Weinbaum, Batya, and Amy Bridges. 1979. The other side of the paycheck: Monopoly capital and the structure of consumption. In *Capitalist patriarchy and the case for socialist feminism*, Zillah Eisenstein, ed.. New York: Monthly Review Press.

Weir, Margaret. 1992. *The politics of jobs*. Princeton, N.J.: Princeton University Press.

Weir, Margaret. 1995. Poverty, social rights, and the politics of place in the United States. In *European social policy: between fragmentation and integration*, S. Leibfried and P. Pierson, eds. Washington, D.C.: Brookings.

Weir, Margaret, ed. 1998. *The social divide: Political parties and the future of activist government*. Washington, D.C.: Brookings.

Weir, Margaret, Ann Shola Orloff, and Theda Skocpol, eds. 1988. *The politics of social policy in the United States*. Princeton, N.J.: Princeton University Press.

Weiss, Benjamin L. 1997. Single mothers' equal right to parent: A Fourteenth Amendment defense against forced-labor welfare "reform." *Law and Inequality* 15, 1: 215–274.

Wennemo, Irene. 1994. *Sharing the costs of children: studies on the development of family support in the OECD countries*. Stockholm: Swedish Institute for Social Research Dissertation Series No.25.

White House Conference on Aging. *Washington Post Weekly*, supplement, 1–7, May 1995.

White, Lucie E. 1993. No exit: Rethinking "welfare dependency" from a different ground. *The Georgetown Law Journal* 81, 1:961–2,002.

Whitebook, Marcy, Carollee Howes, and Deborah Phillips. 1990. *Who cares? Child care teachers and quality of childcare in America*. Washington, D.C.: National Center for the Early Childhood Workforce.

Whitebook, Marcy, Carollee Howes, and Deborah Phillips. 1993. *National childcare staffing study revisited*. Washington, D.C.: National Center for the Early Childhood Workforce.

Wilensky, H. L. 1990. Common problems, divergent policies: An 18–nation study of family policy. *Public Affairs Reports* 3, 31. Berkeley, Calif.: Institute of Government Studies.

Williams, Fiona. 1995. Race/ethnicity, gender, and class in welfare states: A framework for comparative analysis. *Social Politics* (summer): 127–159.

Williams, Linda Faye. 1998. Race and the politics of social politics. In *The social divide: Political parties and the future of activist government*, Margaret Weir, ed. Washington, D.C.: Brookings

Williams, Lucy A. 1992. The ideology of division: Behavior modification welfare reform proposals. *The Yale Law Journal* 102, 3:719–746.

Williams, Patricia. 1995. Scarlet, the sequel. In *The rooster's egg*, P. Williams, ed. Cambridge: Harvard University Press.

Wilson, William J. 1997. *When work disappears: The world of the new urban poor.* New York: Knopf.

Winegarten, C. R., and Paula Bracey. 1995. Demographic consequences of maternal-leave programs in industrial countries: Evidence from fixed effects models. *Southern Economic Journal* 61, 4:1,025–1,035.

Withorn, Ann, and Pamela Jons. 1999. *Worrying about welfare reform: Community-based agencies respond*. Report for the Academics Working Group on Poverty, Boston.

Women's Policy, Inc. 1997. *The record: Gains and losses for women and families in the 104th Congress*. Washington, D.C.: Women's Policy, Inc.

Wong, Y. L., I. Garfinkel, and S. McLanahan. 1993. Single-mother families in eight countries: Economic status and social policy. *Social Service Review* 67:177–197.

Woodill, Gary A., Judith Bernhard, and Lawrence Prochner, eds. 1992. *International handbook of early childhood education*. New York: Garland Publishing.

Xinhau News Agency. 1992. *Women work harder but paid less*, 6 September. Retrieved from LEXIS-NEXIS, XINHAU database.

Yak, Bernard. 1993. *The problems of a political animal*. Berkeley: University of California Press.

Yant, Monica. Imagining her life, no longer on welfare. *Philadelphia Inquirer*. 16 February 1999.

Young, C. 1997. Public taxes, privatizing effects and gender inequality. Paper read at the Feminism and Legal Theory Workshop, March 15, New York.

Young, I. 1995. Mothers, citizenship, and independence. *Ethics* 105, 3:535–557.

Zack, N. 1995. Mixed black and white race and public policy. *Hypatia* 10, 1:120–132.

Zentrum für Sozialpolitik Forschung (Centre for Social Policy Research). 1998. Thesen zur Sozialpolitik in Deutschland. Arbeitspapier no. 5, University of Bremen.

Zwicker-Pelzer, Renate. 1997. Den Kindern eine Chance: Lebenswelten für Kindergestalten. In *Sozialpolitik: Aktuelle Fragen und Probleme*, Martin R. Textor, ed. Hof: Westdeutscher Verlag.

About the Contributors

SUSAN J. CARROLL is professor of political science at Rutgers University and senior research associate at the Center for American Women and Politics (CAWP) of the Eagleton Institute of Politics. She has conducted research on women candidates, voters, elected officials, and political appointees and is the author of numerous works on women's political participation, including *Women as Candidates in American Politics*. Her current research focuses on the influence of women in Congress and on media coverage of women voters and the gender gap.

KATHLEEN J. CASEY is Roberta S. Sigel Doctoral Fellow of the Center for American Women and Politics (CAWP) at Rutgers University where she is a Ph.D. candidate in women and politics in the department of political science. She has been a research associate with the center since 1992, working on the center's research about abortion and politics and studies on the influence of women in the U.S. Congress. She is currently working on the center's research about women in the 104th Congress (1995–1997) while completing her dissertation on gender and welfare policy.

SUSAN CHRISTOPHERSON is a professor in the City and Regional Planning Department at Cornell University where she teaches courses on social policy and the economic development impacts of industry restructuring. Her policy-oriented research has focused on the sources of industry restructuring in different national contexts, women's employment, labor flexibility, and the contemporary service industries, particularly media industries. She has served as a consultant to the OECD Working Party on the Role of Women in the Economy for two key projects. In 1992, she prepared a policy study on women's employment in the service sector. In 1997, she coordinated a ten-country study of how changes in public sector policies are affecting women's employment, particularly in childcare and elderly care occupations. She has also served as a consultant to the United Nations Conference on Trade and Development on the privatization of media services. Christopherson's work on labor flexibility is internationally recognized. In 1997, she completed a study for the International Bureau of Labor Affairs of the U.S. Department of Labor on the reasons for the persistence of different types of labor flexibility patterns across industrialized countries. She recently completed a study of New Media industry workers in the city of New York that will be published by the Economic Policy Institute.

LISA DODSON is a fellow at the Radcliffe Institute for Advanced Study at Harvard University. She teaches on women, girls, and poverty in the faculty of arts and sciences, Harvard University, and is the author of *Don't Call Us Out of Name: The Untold Lives of Women and Girls in Poor America*. She is also the lead researcher on a multicity study exploring the strategies and insights of women as they juggle jobs and familykeeping in low-wage America.

MARTHA A. FINEMAN holds the Dorothea S. Clarke Chair in Feminism Jurisprudence at Cornell Law School. Previously, she was the Maurice T. Moore Professor at Columbia University, and a professor at the University of Wisconsin Law School. She has numerous publications to her credit, including: *The Illusion of Equality: The Rhetoric and Reality of Divorce Reform, The Neutered Mother, The Sexual Family, and Other Twentieth Century Tragedies*, and is coeditor with Ann Mykitiuk of *The Public Nature of Private Violence*. Fineman is director of the Feminism and Legal Theory Conference, and serves on the editorial board of *Yale Journal of Law*; the *Columbia Law Journal of Gender and Law;* and *Law & Society Review*.

JANET C. GORNICK is associate professor of political science at Baruch College, City University of New York. Her research is primarily crossnational and focuses on the effects of social and labor market policies on women's economic outcomes. Recent articles have appeared in *American Sociological Review, Journal of European Social Policy, Social Science Quarterly*, and *Journal of Policy History*.

HEIDI HARTMANN is the director of the Institute for Women's Policy Research in Washington, D.C. She was the recipient of a MacArthur fellowship award in 1994, in recognition of her pioneering work in the field of women and economics. Hartmann has authored or coauthored several IWPR reports as well as numerous journal articles on issues such as welfare reform, pay equity, and women's wages. She has served as the director of the women's studies program at Rutgers University, on the graduate faculty at the New School for Social Research, and is currently a research professor of women's studies at George Washington University. She has also delivered congressional testimony on a variety of issues of concern to women and families, and is currently the chair of the National Council of Women's Organizations' Task Force on Women and Social Security. She holds an honorary doctor of laws degree from Swarthmore College as well as the Wilbur Cross Medal for distinguished alumni of the graduate school of Yale University.

NANCY J. HIRSCHMANN is associate professor of government at Cornell University. She is the author of *Rethinking Obligation: A Feminist Method for Political Theory*, and articles that explore theoretical aspects of women's lived experiences such as domestic violence and veiling. She is also coeditor with Christine Di Stefano of *Revisioning the Political: Feminist Reconstructions of Traditional Concepts in Western Political Theory*. She has been a fellow at the Bunting Institute of Radcliffe College, a NEH fellow at the Institute for Advanced Study in Princeton, New Jersey, and a recipient of an ACLS fellowship. Hirschmann is currently finishing a book on the concept of freedom from a feminist perspective.

EVA FEDER KITTAY is professor of philosophy at SUNY, Stony Brook. She has written numerous articles on issues pertaining to women, ethics, and social and political philosophy and is an expert on metaphor and the philosophy of language. She has most recently begun to publish on issues of disability and welfare. Her most recent book is *Love's Labor: Essays on Women, Equality, and Dependency* . Among her other books are *Women and Moral Theory* (edited with Diana Meyers); *Metaphor: Its Cognitive Force and Linguistic Structure*; *Fields, Frames, and Contrasts* (edited with Adrienne Lehrer). While the federal welfare reform was pending, she helped organize feminist opposition to punitive welfare legislation by founding the Women's Committee of One Hundred that lobbied Congress, initiated an ad campaign, and promoted education concerning women and welfare. She is currently the chair of the APA Committee on the status of women.

ULRIKE LIEBERT is professor of comparative politics at the University of Bremen, Germany, where she is also engaged at the Center for Feminist and Gender Studies. She received her Ph.D. at the European University Institute in Florence in 1983 and has taught as a German Academic Exchange Foundation (DAAD) visiting professor in the government department at Cornell University 1995–1997. Liebert has published several books on comparative democratization and the institutionalization of parliamentary and lobby-regimes. Currently, she is directing an international research project and network on Gender Politics in Governing the European Union and writing a book, *Gender and Europeanization: Transformations of Public Spheres.* She also codirects the interdisciplinary research project Social Constructions of Body and Gender, based at Bremen University.

MARCIA K. MEYERS is associate professor of social work and public affairs at Columbia University and associate director of the New York City Social Indicators Survey Center. Meyers's research focuses on public policies and programs for vulnerable populations, including public welfare services, child welfare programs, and child care services She has published in the *Journal of Public Policy and Management*, the *European Journal of Social Policy, Social Services Review,* and *Social Science Quarterly.*

JOYCE MARIE MUSHABEN is professor of comparative politics and women's studies and a research fellow at the Center for International Studies at the University of Missouri-St. Louis. She has lived and researched for more than ten years in Germany, East and West, among others at the Universität Hamburg (1971–1973) and the Freie Universität Berlin (1977–1979), the Universität Stuttgart and the Johann Wolfgang von Goethe Universität in Frankfurt. She was also Senior Fulbright Lecturer in Erfurt, Germany, in 1996. Her publications include studies of German national identity, peace and ecology movements, youth protest, rightwing violence, abortion politics, women's movements in East and West Germany, gender politics/leadership in the European Union, "collective memory" in East/West Germany, and welfare reform in the United States and the Federal Republic of Germany. She is the author of *From Post-war to Post-wall Generations: Changing Attitudes Towards the National Question and NATO in the Federal Republic of Germany, 1949–1995.* She is currently at work on a book titled *What Remains? The Dialectical Identity of Eastern Germans, Before and After Unity* as well as on an edited volume (with Gabriele Abels and Stefani Stift) *Geschlechterverhältnisse im europäischen Integrationsprozess; Neue Ansätze in der feministischen Europaforschung.*

ANN SCHOLA ORLOFF is professor of sociology at Northwestern University. She is author of *The Politics of Pensions: A Comparative Analysis of Britain, Canada and the United States, 1880–1940* and coauthor with Julia S. O'Connor and Sheila Shaver of *States, Markets, Families: Gender, Liberalism and Social Policy in Australia, Canada, Great Britain, and the United States.*

JOAN TRONTO is professor of political science and women's studies at Hunter College and the Graduate School, City University of New York. She is the author of *Moral Boundaries: A Political Argument for an Ethic of Care* and many articles on the political and moral dimensions of the concept of care.

HSIAO-YE YI holds a Ph.D. in sociology. She is a former study director at the Institute for Women's Policy Research. Her research focused on poverty, work, and welfare among women and parents in low-income families. She has also conducted studies on issues concerning the minimum wage, unemployment insurance, and the economic security of elderly women. She is currently a senior associate with CSR, Incorporated, working on health-related research projects.

Index

abortion, access to, 39
abortion rights, 145
Abramowitz, Mimi, 84
abusive relationships, 31, 57
activist mothers, 184–189
AFDC, 57, 98, 118; abusive relationships
  and, 57, 84; elimination of, 136, 143,
  153–156; single mothers and, 149;
  temporary nature of, 203–204; work
  incentives and, 151. *See also* TANF
age-dependency ratios, projected
  increase in, 247
Agriculture Committee (U.S.), and
  welfare reform, 116, 117
Aid to Dependent Children, 43–44
Aid to Families with Dependent
  Children. *See* AFDC
aliens, welfare benefits and, 118
American family, 40
Amsterdam Treaty, 282
antipoverty policy, 234
Australia. *See* crossnational comparisons
  of social policy (study)

Baby-Year Pensions (Germany), 205,
  207
Baird, Zoé, 31
Basic Law (Germany), 195, 204–205, 206
Belgium. *See* crossnational comparisons

of social policy (study)
Berlin, Isaiah, 86, 87, 88
birth rate: decline in, 31; for never-
  married mothers, 32. *See also* fertility
Bjornberg, Ulla, 276, 279
Blackstone, William, 31
Blair, Tony, 106n4, 148
block grants, 111. *See also* Childcare and
  Development Block Grant; TANF
Bobo, Larry, 147
Boling, Patricia, 83
Borchorst, Anette, 264, 279, 281, 282
Boxer, Barbara, 112
Bradshaw, Jonathan, 273
Braun, Carol Moseley, 112
breadwinner model, (male) 6, 68, 204–
  206, 250–251, 264
Bush, George, 209
business tax deductions, as form of
  welfare, 90
Bussiere, Elizabeth, 99–100, 103

Canada, 258; caring work career
  barriers in, 256, 257; childcare
  centers in, 256; childcare in, 253, 254;
  racialization and welfare politics in,
  147; tax system, 27. *See also*
  crossnational comparisons of social
  policy (study)